Can We Price Carbon?

American and Comparative Environmental Policy
Sheldon Kamieniecki and Michael E. Kraft, series editors

For a complete list of books in the series, please see the back of the book.

Can We Price Carbon?

Barry G. Rabe

The MIT Press
Cambridge, Massachusetts
London, England

This book was set in ITC Stone Serif Std by Westchester Publishing Services. Printed and bound in the United States of America.

Library of Congress Cataloging-in-Publication Data

Names: Rabe, Barry George, 1957– author.
Title: Can we price carbon? / Barry G. Rabe.
Description: Cambridge, MA : MIT Press, [2018] | Series: American and comparative
   environmental policy | Includes bibliographical references and index.
Identifiers: LCCN 2017040421 | ISBN 9780262037952 (hardcover : alk. paper) |
   ISBN 9780262535366 (pbk. : alk. paper)
Subjects: LCSH: Carbon taxes. | Environmental impact charges. | Climatic changes—
   Government policy.
Classification: LCC HJ5316 .R33 2018 | DDC 363.738/747—dc23
   LC record available at https://lccn.loc.gov/2017040421

10   9   8   7   6   5   4   3   2   1

To Dana, Matthew, and Andrew

Contents

Series Foreword

Climate change presents a daunting array of scientific and political challenges that very few other environmental and energy problems can rival. It is complex technically and requires elaborate data collection and sophisticated modeling and forecasting to clarify the environmental, economic, and health risks that we face over time, both nationally and globally. The political barriers to action are equally formidable because most of the impacts of climate change are long term, intangible, distributed unequally, and somewhat uncertain, while the costs are short term, concrete, and quite visible. Moreover, nations at different stages of development must cooperate in an unprecedented manner in the face of continuing disagreement about which policy approaches will work best. They also struggle to build public support sufficient to compete with entrenched economic interests, particularly the fossil fuel industry, that often benefit from inaction.

In the United States and many other developed nations, the policy debate has turned on the relative effectiveness and political appeal of government regulation, such as fuel economy standards and renewable energy mandates, versus market incentives such as carbon taxes and cap-and-trade. The ideological fault lines are similar to what we see for other public problems, but in this case political conservatives who normally would embrace market approaches have exhibited considerable skepticism, although they can be even more critical of regulatory approaches. No doubt this reflects the enormous political pressure being placed on them by the fossil fuel industry and other interests. Moreover, many policymakers, particularly Republican lawmakers and Trump administration appointees, continue to question the very existence of anthropogenic climate change and seek to curtail scientific research and public education on the subject that are essential to the advancement of feasible solutions. What would help to move this debate forward is careful and comprehensive analysis of actions taken to date to put a price on carbon emissions. This is the contribution that Barry Rabe makes in this important volume.

The idea of pricing carbon, and of developing suitable mechanisms for governments to use such a price to decrease our collective reliance on carbon-based fuels, is an intriguing solution. But as Rabe tells us, there is no shortage of questions about how a carbon tax or cap-and-trade might be developed and applied even if the proposal itself is widely endorsed by economists as the best way to address climate change. In particular, how might one persuade the US Congress, state legislatures, and other governing bodies around the world to endorse the idea, and then to develop appropriate policies?

This book offers an exceptionally valuable and insightful analysis of the political barriers to adopting and implementing carbon pricing. It does so through an in-depth examination of diverse cases, primarily in the United States and Canada but also drawing from Europe and Asia, over an extended period of time. In this way, it helps to fill major gaps in our understanding of how carbon pricing is seen by policymakers and others, as well as both the barriers to action and the forces that produce viable policies. Rabe's study offers a sobering rejoinder to the prevailing view among economists that carbon pricing is both simple and a sensible solution to climate change, while also noting that formidable political hurdles can be cleared in at least some instances.

This book offers the most complete picture to date of the political realities that surround the concept of carbon pricing, a major focus in the debate over possible solutions to controlling greenhouse gas emissions, and the adoption and implementation of such policies through what Rabe calls the carbon pricing policy life-cycle. In the end, he notes, adoption of carbon pricing policies is not sufficient. Analysts also must delve into the conditions that promote policy effectiveness and durability over time. That end requires the small-N case studies which he relies upon because such an approach permits in-depth exploration of the multiple factors that make a difference in which policies governments choose to adopt, why they adopt them, how they implement them, and what most determines success over time. No one is better suited to address these core questions than Barry Rabe, who has been a participant in and keen observer of these processes for over two decades.

The book illustrates well our purpose in the MIT Press series in American and Comparative Environmental Policy. We encourage work that examines a broad range of environmental policy issues. We are particularly interested in volumes that incorporate interdisciplinary research and focus on the linkages between public policy and environmental problems and issues, both within the United States and in cross-national settings. We welcome contributions that analyze the policy dimensions of relationships between humans and the environment from either a theoretical or empirical perspective.

At a time when environmental policies are increasingly seen as controversial and new and alternative approaches are being implemented widely, we especially encourage studies that assess policy successes and failures, evaluate new institutional arrangements and policy tools, and clarify new directions for environmental politics and policy. The books in this series are written for a wide audience that includes academics, policymakers, environmental scientists and professionals, business and labor leaders, environmental activists, and students concerned with environmental issues. We hope they contribute to public understanding of environmental problems, issues, and policies of concern today and also suggest promising actions for the future.

Sheldon Kamieniecki, University of California–Santa Cruz
Michael Kraft, University of Wisconsin–Green Bay
Coeditors, American and Comparative Environment

Preface

One of the greatest rewards in teaching at a university is seeing former students assume roles of leadership in society. One such reward was offered in 2015, in a University of Michigan conference room just before I left Ann Arbor for a year to write this book during a leave in Washington, DC. The room was packed with university faculty, administrators, and students. We had been charged by our university president to review the greenhouse gas emissions reduction record of our campus and how to accelerate those reductions in future decades. So we began to review a wide range of policies and technologies that might enable the University of Michigan to reduce its carbon footprint.

In many respects, there can be no political venue in America that is likely more receptive to bold steps to address climate change than its colleges and universities. In recent decades, campuses both large and small, public and private, have launched major sustainability campaigns. They routinely place carbon dioxide and methane emission reductions at the center of these efforts. New offices have been created, staff employed, and funds raised to support greening initiatives. This is reflected in campus construction and renovation, active promotion of behavioral change in energy use and environmental stewardship, investment in alternative energy technologies, exploration of divestment from fossil fuel stocks, curricular and research expansion, and much more. In some ways, the modern American academy appears to be engaged in an active competition to determine which colleges or universities have the boldest green credentials, one comparable in many ways to their quest for high marks in national rankings of academic excellence or athletic prowess.

Our committee produced a long and impressive list of options. Expanded development of wind turbines and solar arrays. Increased planting of trees to promote carbon sequestration. Installation of a new natural gas turbine at the central campus power plant. Expanded collaboration with other public universities in Michigan. Pursuit of the highest levels of energy efficiency in new campus construction. The list went on and on, with few objections.

But then a former student of mine who was serving on the committee raised a provocative alternative. He had recently graduated from the College of Engineering but had taken my upper-division course in environmental politics and policy in his final semester of studies. "Why don't we use a carbon price and adopt a carbon tax across campus to drive down fossil fuel use?" he asked. And then, with a smile, he looked over at me and added, "Just like they did in British Columbia."

We had indeed discussed the issue of carbon taxation and the British Columbia model in class, much as we will in this book. There has been a massive body of analysis across many decades from the discipline of economics that has argued relentlessly that some form of a carbon price, such as a tax on carbon emissions, represents the superior way to achieve a cost-effective reduction in greenhouse gas emissions. This was not an easy political lift, however, given the direct and visible imposition of an added cost in the use of a familiar and essential commodity. Future benefits, measured in climate protection impacts, could be extremely difficult to calculate. So this often tends to be the last thing political systems do in responding to climate change, as we will discuss in subsequent chapters.

But there are occasions when political systems embrace good policy ideas, demonstrate political courage, and ultimately achieve policy goals. So the placement of a carbon tax on the agenda of this committee represented just such an opportunity. Some of the members were clearly intrigued and we discussed at length various models for both collecting and reallocating any revenue from such an effort to increase the cost of energy on our campus, thereby driving down consumption. As a former interim dean of a professional school, I was aware that each of our schools and colleges in Ann Arbor receives a regular energy bill from central campus authorities. It would not be difficult to adjust these, adding a levy reflecting carbon content. The greater the energy use, the greater the environmental damage, hence the greater the cost imposed on that action. Funds generated by such a tax could be used for a range of purposes, from underwriting costs of next-generation energy research and development to student tuition reduction.

All of this could be highly transparent, with disclosure of respective emission trends triggering races to the top in energy efficiency among various schools, colleges, and departments. As a scholar examining recent decades of experience with these policies, I knew that there were a few governments in North America and Europe that had taken such steps and had proved fairly successful environmentally, economically, and politically.

But while this committee was steadfast in its commitment to reduce campus emissions, the carbon tax proposal was clearly divisive among a number of members, particularly faculty. Would such a tax be discriminatory toward the natural and physical sciences because their research laboratories require much more energy than colleagues in the social sciences or the humanities use in their offices? Would a carbon price cause problems in securing federal grants, as these added energy prices might make our applications less competitive with peers from institutions that lacked a carbon price? Would such a pricing mechanism constrain our mobility, including air travel for field work, conferences, and professional meetings? Would it impose a particular hardship on service units that use prodigious amounts of power, whether the university hospital system or the massive scoreboards that run almost constantly in and around our iconic football field?

No one really challenged the idea of the carbon tax in principle or on a state, national, or global scale. The concern was the kinds of challenges and inconveniences that it might impose on our academic community or some of its members. Ultimately, the committee settled on a long and diverse set of firm recommendations. The carbon tax proposal was inserted into two paragraphs with encouragement for further consideration but received no formal endorsement for immediate action. Most of the committee recommendations were embraced several months later when President Mark Schlissel announced the university's far-reaching plans to address climate change through university actions. His decision not to pursue disinvestment in fossil fuels perhaps received the most campus and media controversy. But there was no reference to a carbon tax or price, and this option seemingly disappeared from the campus agenda. And there was no groundswell of campus support calling for such a tax to drive down emissions, even among students who were lobbying the university to sign a petition calling for a national carbon tax.

The University of Michigan story on carbon taxation is played out across hundreds of other college and university campuses. These institutions want to address climate change and are prepared to take bold steps and spend significant funds to achieve their goals. A few occasionally talk about some kind of a tax on carbon use. But hardly any move beyond this stage to serious policy development, much less adoption and implementation over time. If soft targets like colleges and universities cannot take this step, what is the prospect of political systems such as Congress, state legislatures, and governing bodies around the world moving in these directions given the likely political backlash? According to most economists, a carbon tax or price would absolutely be the best way to address one of the most vexing policy challenges of our time. It is not a new idea and it actually has a track record in a number of places, including British Columbia. But it appears to be one of the hardest political lifts imaginable. Even a university campus—where faculty, students, and staff show far more concern about climate change than just about any other political system in the world—does not provide an exception to this political reality.

Plan of the Book and Case Selection

This book considers the political stumbling blocks to the adoption and implementation of carbon pricing through the examination of a wide range of cases over an extended time period. It intends to help fill significant gaps in our understanding of a topic dominated to date by an active and affirming army of economists. The body of existing scholarly work has persuasively made the case that carbon pricing could play a pivotal role in addressing climate change. However, any policy tool examined almost exclusively through the lens of a single discipline, even one with the analytical heft of economics, may face significant limitations. In this instance, carbon pricing looks far less compelling when weighed against political realities that are not easily surmounted.

These attempts to price carbon have played out in the United States and many other national and subnational contexts over the past two decades. The breadth and ferocity of political opposition to them thwarted many proposed policies. This suggests considerable risk in either ignoring political factors when designing policy or assuming that they will somehow be resolved simply because the policy idea behind carbon pricing is so compelling to proponents. In some instances, initial political support later faded,

whether through a shift of political currents and leadership or due to failures in effective management of emerging carbon pricing programs.

This book goes well beyond the more commonplace question from economists of whether carbon pricing policies would be a good policy idea if one
could assume a world free of politics. Instead, it begins by asking whether
the adoption of such policies is politically feasible. But it also considers their
ability, if adopted, to endure inevitable political and managerial challenges
and transitions over time. There have been, as we shall see, significant
struggles at every stage of what we will call the carbon pricing policy life-cycle
in multiple nations and continents, even when the initial adoption hurdle is
cleared.

This experience serves as an important reminder that compelling policy
ideas do not automatically or necessarily translate into politically feasible
or sustainable policies. Our policy life-cycle begins with adoption and the
question of whether there is a sufficient political foundation in government
to adopt a carbon pricing policy. But it also explores cases where adoption
occurred and asks whether that political foundation was sufficient to complete an initial and successful launch of the policy. It then assesses cases
navigating that hurdle to determine whether the policy survived politically
through subsequent elections and changes of leadership or partisan control
of government.

This life-cycle analysis calls for more than resilience through that key
transition point, however. It further asks whether political supporters of
a policy could establish management systems capable of achieving effective implementation. This would include capacity to make adjustments or
modifications necessary to allow the policy to operate effectively over time,
thereby enduring politically and building constituency support for the
longer haul. Only then would it be possible to pose one final question in the
policy life-cycle. This requires that the policy surmount all of these previous hurdles. But it also asks whether there is empirical evidence that the
policy produces the tangible benefits that its proponents promised initially.
In the case of carbon pricing, that would entail a significant reduction of
greenhouse gas emissions in a cost-effective manner over a decade or more
of operation.

Much scholarly and popular writing in favor of carbon pricing has
implicitly assumed that all of these things would occur seamlessly if only

governmental leaders could muster the political courage to adopt it in the first place. But the policy life-cycle has imposed a tall order, beginning with governments taking that first step but ultimately finding that carbon pricing policies do not necessarily self-implement and flourish. Serious political and managerial attention is necessary if a policy is to navigate each stage of the policy life-cycle. Its absence is evident in a number of flawed or incomplete cases that we will examine, a telling reminder that policy adoption represents only the beginning of constructive policy development.

This life-cycle analysis of a compelling policy idea places carbon pricing into a growing body of political science analysis of policy durability. Much of this work has been applied to social welfare programs rather than those at the intersection of energy development and environmental protection.[1] But we will find numerous points of overlap with this scholarship, both in asking whether a carbon pricing policy can realistically clear each life-cycle hurdle and whether it can demonstrate hard evidence on performance over a reasonable time period. Consistent with that literature, this analysis finds many cases of failure or incomplete outcomes; these receive substantial attention in chapter 3.

This book, however, provides considerably more than a compendium of carbon pricing failures and travails. There are significant cases, albeit relatively few in number, that have run the political and management gauntlet over a half-decade or more and survived. They have, in essence, successfully delivered carbon pricing and offer important insights on when it is most likely to work. Each of these successes overcame significant challenges and demonstrated ways to sustain and build on an initial political foundation while expanding political and public support. Chapter 4 examines these more effective cases using carbon taxation and chapter 5 examines comparable cases employing cap-and-trade. Chapter 6 offers a close look at a prominent case that has received substantial global attention and demonstrates considerable promise. But it remains in early stages of operation and faces significant challenges as it moves beyond initial stages of the policy life-cycle.

This sets the stage for chapters 7 and 8, which summarize key findings but also consider the future of carbon pricing. They attempt to draw larger lessons from recent experience, incorporating them into a discussion of the evolving political context for climate change. This analysis guards against attempts to provide quick fixes to the political challenges that carbon pricing faces but also offers reflections on what might be plausible politically in concert with other policy instruments. In so doing, this book rules out no policy options. But it tries to put carbon pricing and its political feasibility into a perspective commensurate with political realities rather than into an ideal world that is not likely to be realized anytime soon. It also explores possible options that include alternative forms and applications of carbon pricing that might be more viable politically in adoption and across stages of the policy life-cycle.

The design of this project was influenced by prior research on the development of a wide range of climate policies at the state level, presented initially in a 2004 book entitled *Statehouse and Greenhouse*.[2] In that case, I tracked policy adoption patterns across all fifty states over approximately one decade but ultimately focused most intensively on a dozen cases selected to maximize case diversity across criteria of partisan control, geography, and policy capacity and commitment. This persuaded me of the merits of such medium-N studies that allow for in-depth tracing of policy processes across multiple cases.[3] The factors to be considered might indeed be unique to an individual jurisdiction, are unlikely to be replicated elsewhere, and can easily be overlooked in large-N studies using quantitative techniques.[4] Studying a midrange set of comparative cases is an intensive process, especially over an extended period and across successive stages of the policy process.[5] However, it offers the potential to move beyond some of the limitations common in research with a small-N case design.

This project sought to understand a broad set of cases while preserving the ability to pursue in-depth process tracing. I also wanted to examine an extended and more complex period including enactment and operational stages. Consequently, I examined all cases between 2000 and 2015 involving governmental consideration of either a carbon tax or cap-and-trade, or a hybrid version of the two, including cases that were rejected at the proposal stage, reversed after initial adoption, or sustained implementation after adoption.

Not all cases are treated equally, with deepest coverage and analysis provided for those from two neighboring federations with somewhat comparable climate policy records: the United States and Canada. Both nations have sustained high rates of per capita carbon emissions, provided early endorsements of carbon pricing in international contexts,[6] ratified the 1992 Rio Declaration but struggled mightily with the Kyoto Protocol,[7] and gave substantial legal and political latitude to respective states and provinces to design their own independent or regional carbon pricing policies. There are, of course, significant differences between the American and Canadian political systems, including divergent paths taken (at different times) in considering carbon taxation and cap-and-trade.

The United States and Canada are thus treated as the *primary* and *linked* cases in these chapters, respectively. The American experience at the federal level and its fifty states is the primary focal point, reflecting the global significance of this case and my own research emphasis. At the same time, the Canadian experience at its federal level and ten provinces also receives intensive analysis. These national cases are not only comparative in the sense of allowing for examination of two independent federations but are also linked through substantial integration of their electricity, manufacturing, and transportation sectors and a long-standing history of cross-border policy engagement. This includes considerable exploration of possible areas of carbon pricing collaboration, ranging from formal partnership on cap-and-trade to the borrowing of policy ideas on carbon taxation and severance taxes.

I have closely observed carbon pricing proposals during this period and, in a number of instances, adoption and early implementation. This work included multiple field visits to relevant state and provincial capitals, regional offices representing multijurisdictional bodies, and federal capitals of Washington, DC, and Ottawa. I participated in more than four dozen climate policy briefings and workshops between 2005 and 2015, including a number of instances where I was invited to testify, give a formal presentation, or take questions. Venues include either public or invitation-only meetings of the Regional Greenhouse Gas Initiative, the Western Climate Initiative, the National Conference of State Legislatures, the Environmental Council of the States, the National Governors' Association, the US Environmental Protection Agency, the American Embassy in Ottawa, the Canadian Embassy in Washington, DC, and the National Round Table on the Environment and the Economy, as well as workshops and conferences convened by federal agencies, universities, and foundations. Nearly two-thirds of these events occurred in the United States, with the remainder in Canada or the European Union. In a great many of these events outside the United States, I was the lone American participant. At other events in both countries, I was the lone noneconomist among participating social scientists. I draw on observations from all of these experiences, supplemented in many instances by in-person interviews. However, I only provide direct attribution to individual remarks where preestablished ground rules allow.

In short, I have spent substantial time in virtually every American state or Canadian province that has given serious consideration to either carbon taxation or cap-and-trade since the beginning of the twenty-first century. This has been supplemented with analysis and field work on state severance taxes and royalties on fossil fuel extraction. This area of carbon pricing warrants expanded political science consideration as the United States and other nations navigate the shale era, whereby natural gas and oil production expand while coal production declines. Combined with extensive and ongoing examination of academic publications drawn heavily from political science, law, and economics, government documents, and media coverage of such policies in these energy-producing jurisdictions, I have an extended body of evidence exploring the key questions of this book. This is reflected in the case analyses presented in portions of chapters 3 through 8.

The primary and linked cases are then supplemented with observations from two other sets of cases from outside North America. I define as *shadow* cases those from other nations during this period, particularly those in which policy enactment occurred between the beginning of 2000 and the end of 2010. This allows for consideration of not only adoption but also early stages of implementation, assuming the policy survived through 2015. This facilitated inclusion of some additional case material from nations (or their states) from Europe and Asia. However, I was not able to conduct site visits in the shadow cases and generally lack the depth of understanding possessed in the primary and linked ones.

One other kind of case is discussed, primarily in the final chapter. Between 2011 and 2015, a number of governments in Asia, Africa, and Latin America began to explore the possibility of adopting their own version of carbon pricing. This process began to accelerate in 2014–2015, culminating in numerous endorsements of carbon pricing by national leaders at the December 2015 international climate change meetings in Paris. These cases are referenced in the final chapter, but with the caveat that they are new and best characterized as *emerging* cases. A diverse and growing set of nations, including China, South Korea, Mexico, South Africa, Japan, and Chile, among many others, have begun to explore carbon pricing.

To date, however, many of these emerging policy developments appear largely aspirational and symbolic, albeit presenting possibilities of evolving into more substantial initiatives over time. It is much too soon to undertake any evaluation of these new efforts across the stages of the policy life-cycle. As with their predecessors, these potential carbon pricing converts have frequently declared intent or preference to pursue some form of carbon pricing. But many then approach their respective political processes with trepidation, aside from modest and largely experimental programs that allow leaders to claim credit on an international stage but move very gingerly into any consequential pricing of carbon. These emerging cases further suggest that carbon pricing may have a promising future. However, hopes for such a future underscore the need to be mindful that the political realities of attempting to launch such policies, manage them effectively, and sustain them over time are best addressed in early stages rather than after political rejection, upheaval, reversal, or failure.

Acknowledgments

It is possible that work on this book began in the 1970s. My dad, George Rabe, would often agonize at his home desk in trying to come to terms with pressures from his employers to engage in the political process. Dad sold tobacco products in Chicagoland, although he stopped smoking for good in the 1960s immediately after the first surgeon general's reports were released about smoking health risks.

Dad's struggles reflected pressures from his employer to contribute money to campaigns to confront political challenges to tobacco use, including proposals to increase excise taxes. He was frequently asked to send checks for the opposition campaign and also write letters to federal and state legislators about the threat these proposals would pose to his livelihood. This was excruciating for Dad, both because he was tight with his money but also because he struggled with a serious reading disability that was never diagnosed. He was an exceptionally intelligent and capable person, but reading and writing were extremely difficult for him. So, he would routinely enlist me during my teenage years in writing and editing much of his correspondence. Jeremiads against tobacco regulation and taxation were my first writing assignments beyond the classroom.

Dad did not live long enough to receive this book, as he passed away in 2014, after more than nine decades of a robust life. And he would be the first to say he really would not be able to read it, even though he would have obtained copies (if I could get a discount) and displayed them prominently (even if it annoyed friends who dismissed climate change). He also would have continued his lifelong practice of sending me newspaper clippings on topics relevant to my research, some of which influenced my thinking about this book.

So I have thought about him often in conceptualizing and then writing this book. And I am deeply grateful to Ken Warner, a good friend and colleague who was instrumental in recruiting me to the University of Michigan. Ken invited me a few years ago to be one of four outside examiners of a fascinating workshop on tobacco control policy. Unlike climate policy, tobacco control policy has been robust in many nations and achieved substantial reductions in smoking in past decades. This has included extensive use of the very excise taxes Dad was pressured to oppose. This project considered how tobacco use might build on prior success and achieve an "endgame" that would eventually eliminate smoking. That led to a vigorous workshop of tobacco control experts and their proposals, helping me to realize that there were important distinctions between our hugely successful use of "tobacco pricing" to combat smoking and largely (thus far) unsuccessful use of carbon pricing to confront climate change.

So tobacco loomed large in my thinking, even though it only surfaces in limited ways in this book. My much deeper exploration into climate policy and carbon pricing was actively supported by a series of generous colleagues and friends over these past years. At the Gerald Ford School of Public Policy, Dean Susan Collins helped me navigate a path toward completing this book while also continuing to serve as the director of the Center for Local, State, and Urban Policy (CLOSUP). At the Program in the Environment, directors Paul Webb and Gregg Crane have respected my commitment to this topic and supported all of my efforts to share my research with exceptional undergraduate students. At CLOSUP, Tom Ivacko, Sarah Mills, and Bonnie Roberts have been patient and supportive.

The Arthur F. Thurnau Professorship and the J. Ira and Nicki Harris Chair have provided regular sources of funding to cover all of my professional travel and also hired a sensational platoon of student research assistants for this project. I particularly want to thank Erica Brown, Lindsay DeCarolis, Kristine Hartman, Heather Kirkpatrick, Michael Lerner, Kerri Metz, Kyle O'Meara, Andrea Paine, Carolyn Rice, Paul Sherman, Hannah Smith, Nina Tannenbaum, Emily Upton, and Thomas Van Heeke for the many insights they have provided and their passion for this scholarly work.

Most of the initial writing took place in Washington, DC, during an academic leave and an appointment as a Public Policy Scholar at the Canada Institute of the Woodrow Wilson International Center for Scholars. David Biette, the founding director of the Canada Institute, believed in this project and actively encouraged me to come to Wilson during key stages. His successor, Laura Dawson, and other members of the Wilson community, including Lawrence Allman, Ruth Greenspan Bell, Savannah Boylan, Arlyn Charles, Lindsay Collins, Kim Connor, Andrew Finn, Michelle Kamalich, Steve Lagerfeld, Robert Litwak, John Milewski, Kate Salimi, Andrew Selee, Janet Spikes, and Katherine Wahler routinely confirmed that the Wilson Center is one of the truly great places in the world to have a serious conversation about public policy.

My time in Washington was further enriched by colleagues at the Brookings Institution, the School of Public Affairs at American University, and the Michigan in Washington Program. I remain deeply grateful to Tim Boersma, William Finan, Christopher Foreman, John Hudak, Mark Muro, the late Pietro Nivola, Devashree Saha, Philip Wallach, and Kent Weaver at Brookings; David Baratta, Daniel Fiorino, Riordan Frost, Bradley Hardy, Alison Jacknowicz, Jocelyn Johnston, Daniel Puskin, and Sonja Walti at American; and Edie Goldenberg, Margaret Howard, Donald Kinder, and Nathaline Smith at Michigan in Washington, for being such supportive colleagues. I also appreciate insights provided by Jim Adams, Daniel Abele, Jenna Bednar, Brendan Boyd, Brendan Burke, Josh Busby, Sanya Carley, Brian Cook, Paul Courant, Robert Cox, Monica Gattinger, Kathryn Harrison, Anne Khademian, Bill Lowry, the late Elinor Ostrom, Alastair Roberts, Susan Tierney, and Janet Weiss during various seminars, conferences, and presentations during this period.

I have also had the great fortune to collaborate formally with other scholars on papers and book chapters on topics that helped sharpen my thinking about the issues raised in this book. In particular, I want to thank the late David Amdur, Christopher Borick, Christopher Gore, Rachel Hampton, David Houle, Erick Lachapelle, and Sarah Mills for their many insights as we explored some of the finer points of carbon pricing together. Engagement on the energy policy durability project at the American Academy of Arts and Sciences was an invaluable opportunity to think about these issues in the context of the Clean Air Act while invariably applying those lessons to carbon pricing in this project. My thanks to Joseph Aldy, William Boyd, Dallas Burtraw, Ann Carlson, the late Robert Fri, Eric Patashnik, Hannah Wiseman, John Randall, and Elizabeth Wilson. Presentation of key findings through invited talks and seminars at Virginia Tech, the University of Ottawa, the University of Vermont, the University of Pittsburgh,

Washington University, the Levine Lecture at American University, the National Research Council, and annual meetings of the American, Canadian, and Midwest Political Science Associations led to many suggestions that were enormously beneficial in the completion of this work.

Work with MIT Press has been a privilege and a joy. I had been involved in other MIT projects as a reviewer or contributor of a book chapter to an edited volume. But I am profoundly grateful to have been able to work with such an able and dedicated team, headed by Beth Clevenger as acquisitions editor, Anthony Zannino as acquisitions assistant, and Sheldon Kamieniecki and Michael Kraft as editors of the American and Comparative Environmental Politics series. Erin Davis and Roxanne Balmas were splendid manuscript editors who made many invaluable suggestions, with Roxanne also preparing the index. Three anonymous reviewers offered exceptionally thorough and thoughtful reviews in this process. And I must thank colleagues who read some version of the entire manuscript and offered helpful comments, including Larry Abbott, Rachel Hampton, David Konisky, Andrea Paine, Leigh Raymond, and Hannah Smith.

I have customarily concluded acknowledgments in prior books with reference to members of my immediate family. This will be no exception. I have learned so much from my wife, Dana Runestad, and our sons, Matthew and Andrew Rabe. They ask profoundly good questions, demonstrate remarkable perseverance in the face of life challenges, have phenomenal senses of humor, strive to conduct all of their affairs with humility and integrity, and never stop exploring how they can play a constructive role in whatever situation they encounter. They make this world a better place, as they do in my life. It is an honor to dedicate this book to them.

1 Why Carbon Pricing Is Appealing

Imagine a commodity considered an integral part of American culture for many generations. This commodity could be found in many corners of the world and yet was uniquely abundant within American boundaries. It offered significant employment opportunities in production, refinement, and distribution. The commodity was actively promoted through multimedia advertising as an essential component of American life. Both the US Capitol and many statehouses heralded this commodity in their architecture and artwork and it has been prominently featured in film and literature.

A broad base of manufacturers and distributors expanded over multiple generations to protect and promote commodity use through public policy. This included production subsidies and protection against cyclical losses, fueled in part by generous donations to political candidates and parties. Scholars characterized this political support base as an "iron triangle" of sorts, reflecting a steadfast coalition between industry, legislators, and executive agencies.[1] Vast numbers of Americans used one or more refined versions of this product on a daily basis, a formidable constituency that expected this commodity to be made widely available and provided at the lowest possible price. American firms also saw potentially vast international demand and sought government support to expand all aspects of their operations internationally.

But there was a problem. A diverse and growing body of scientific evidence warned that continued use of this commodity posed significant risks to societal well-being. This was reflected in an avalanche of scholarly papers and government reports issued by national, state, and global agencies. The overwhelming consensus of this scientific work highlighted these risks and projected future consequences to the public. They triggered calls for new policy steps to curb demand for the commodity, although an enduring minority of Americans continued to doubt the veracity of these findings.[2]

Opponents of tobacco use launched a multifaceted assault to elevate public concerns over risks from continued use. They championed a range of regulatory strategies to discourage use and vilify industry leaders as corrupt and disingenuous in their efforts to refute or downplay scientific evidence. These opponents further characterized Americans as mired in a web of addiction in using tobacco and urged governments to confront this challenge. But their efforts never seriously attempted to ban tobacco cultivation or make its use illegal, mindful that public opinion surveys demonstrated no support for such extreme measures.

Instead, these opponents frequently endorsed a public policy silver bullet. This built on an example that Adam Smith had introduced hundreds of years earlier—namely, increasing the cost of tobacco use through taxation.[3] All states and the federal government had previously established modest excise taxes on tobacco products, providing a foundation for expansion. Numerous economists and policy advocates argued for taxes with the goal of raising consumption costs to reverse growing tobacco use.

This strategy seemed highly suspect, given the enduring American aversion to taxation. The revolutionary response to British taxation of whiskey in the eighteenth century is routinely revisited when virtually any new taxes are proposed, woven into the American political fabric long before the advent of the Tea Party movement. In the instance of tobacco, the well-funded and organized iron triangle confronted the taxation campaign at all levels of government.[4] And there was no evidence that the American public was clamoring for steadily higher prices on this commodity via taxation in order to promote the public well-being.

Against all odds, the taxation campaign exceeded expectations. Coastal states set the pace with major tax increases, triggering responses from neighboring states and the federal government. These coastal states followed the lead of Nordic and northern European countries that were early adopters of unusually steep rates.[5] Consequently, tax rates (and commodity purchase prices) soared and consumption plunged, as reflected in figure 1.1, in ways that were politically unthinkable as recently as the 1980s or 1990s. The federal excise tax on tobacco increased 321 percent between 1995 and 2015, while individual states adopted a total of 126 separate excise tax increases during this period to collectively increase the mean state tax rate by nearly

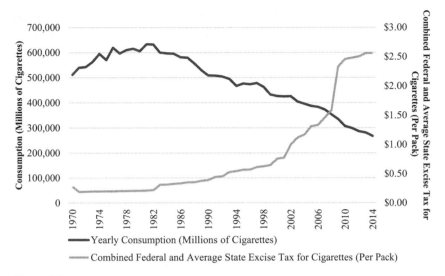

Figure 1.1
US cigarette tax and consumption rates from 1970–2014.
Sources: For smoking rates, see American Lung Association, *Trends in Tobacco Use* (Washington, DC: American Lung Association, 2011), http://www.lung.org/assets /documents/research/tobacco-trend-report.pdf; and Ahmed Jamal et al., "Current Cigarette Smoking among Adults—United States, 2005–2014," *Morbidity and Mortality Weekly Report* 64, no. 44 (2015): 1233–1240, http://www.cdc.gov/mmwr/preview /mmwrhtml/mm6444a2.htm?s_cid=mm6444a2_w. For taxes and consumption, see Orzechowski and Walker, *The Tax Burden on Tobacco*, Historical Compilation Volume 49 (Arlington, VA: Federation of Tax Administrators, 2014), 7, 110–195, http://www .taxadmin.org/assets/docs/Tobacco/papers/tax_burden_2014.pdf; and Centers for Disease Control (CDC), "Federal and State Cigarette Excise Taxes: United States, 1995–2009," *Morbidity and Mortality Weekly Report* 58, no. 19 (2009): 524–527.

300 percent. Other policies and factors contributed to this historic shift, but the sustained elevation of the commodity price remains widely viewed as the most consequential driver of use reduction.[6] Taxation offers a double dividend of sorts in this case, setting not only a price signal to deter use but also generating pools of funds that can be used to support other strategies to further discourage use.

This transformation ranks among the great American public policy achievements of the past half-decade. Tobacco use rates for adults exceeded 40 percent in the 1980s but have steadily plunged below 20 percent in less than two generations. Health gains from reduced tobacco use have been measured and are expected to continue in future decades.[7] The American tobacco industry has been thoroughly discredited and faces relentless political pressure to downsize operations domestically, though it has increasingly sought friendlier international markets. Industry opponents continue to explore steps toward an international "endgame" of tobacco use.[8] This story is not confined to the United States, given comparable policy developments in many other developed nations in recent decades.[9]

Why Economists Want to Price Carbon

Was tobacco a fluke case, or could its story be replicated in other risk-creating commodities? Fossil fuels, such as coal, oil, and natural gas, present some significant parallels ever since the initial surge in their extraction and refinement for use began in the mid-nineteenth century. Fossil fuels have long been widely used and promoted across the United States, with no serious questions surrounding their popularity or legality. They face some modest forms of federal and state taxation but also enjoy generous policy support from governments through production subsidies and infrastructure to maximize output and distribution. Their benefits in terms of providing low-cost, accessible, and reliable energy and transportation are well known. Fossil fuels have underpinned substantial employment and economic growth around the nation, but they also create significant risks. These range from injuries during extraction to exposure to air contamination following use.

The carbon content of fossil fuels, albeit greater for coal than oil or natural gas,[10] elevates concerns about negative externalities from combustion to an entirely new level. Climate change poses less of a direct link between individual commodity use and health consequences than does tobacco. Instead, it opens up a staggering set of environmental and public health risks for current and particularly future generations. As in the tobacco case, not all Americans accept the thrust of the vast preponderance of climate science. Many citizens have misgivings about policies that would limit access to or use of the commodity. The fossil fuel industry is a formidable political player, making challenges to its traditional operations politically daunting.

These points have not been lost on those who oppose sustained fossil fuel use due to its role in expanding climate risks. For many, the answer is a version of the same silver bullet that transformed tobacco: a tax on the use of fossil fuels. The tobacco case is routinely framed as having similar features, reflected in economist William Nordhaus's lament that "allowing people to emit CO_2 into the atmosphere for free is similar to allowing people to smoke in a crowded room."[11] Legal scholar Michael Graetz noted in the prologue of his political history of American energy policy that decades of legislation have routinely evaded imposing a price on fossil fuels that accurately reflects the damage. Graetz concluded that nothing America "did or might have done has had as much potential to be as efficacious as paying the true price. The contrast with tobacco, for example, where taxes have been used over time both to reduce its consumption and to help finance some of the costs it imposes on public budgets and society at large can hardly be more stark."[12]

Comparisons between tobacco and fossil fuels have emboldened an ever-growing chorus of economists to embrace carbon pricing as the linchpin to address climate risks. The establishment of such a price, argue supporters, is the most efficient and plausible way to launch and sustain a major shift away from fossil fuels. It would send clear and compelling signals to consumers to conserve fuel, to major carbon emitters to find cleaner alternatives, and to alternative energy developers to expand operations.

Nordhaus has emerged as a particularly visible champion of this cause. In 2015, he explained that "the real point of the [carbon] pricing is not to gouge people, not to extract resources from people. It's to tilt the playing field in such a way that people, firms, government—everybody—moves toward carbon-free or low-carbon activities."[13] As he later warned, "If we don't have carbon pricing, we will never solve this problem."[14]

Ideologically diverse economists in both the United States and beyond have converged around these ideas in recent decades. This is reflected in the remarkable volume of academic publications on this topic as well as the frequency with which their authors' views on carbon pricing have dominated discussion of various climate policy options in scores of congressional hearings since the 1970s.[15] Surveys also routinely conclude that dominant majorities of economists deem carbon pricing as vastly superior to such alternatives as procurement mandates or performance standards.[16] Supporters range from Gary Becker, Martin Feldstein, and Arthur Laffer on the right to Paul Krugman, Joseph Stiglitz, and Lawrence Summers on the left.[17] Economic and policy advisers to every president since the late 1960s have endorsed this idea during their careers (including George Shultz and Marina Whitman for Richard Nixon, Frank Zarb for Gerald Ford, Paul Courant for Jimmy Carter, Murray Weidenbaum and James Baker for Ronald Reagan,

Michael Boskin for George H. W. Bush, Robert Reich for Bill Clinton, Gregory Mankiw for George W. Bush, Peter Orszag and Lawrence Summers for Barack Obama, and Kevin Hassett for Donald Trump).

The embrace of carbon pricing is not confined to card-carrying members of a single social science discipline. A staggering array of public and private institutions and thought leaders embrace this idea, including the World Bank, the International Monetary Fund, and the Organization of Economic Co-operation and Development. American opinion-leaders Charles Krauthammer, David Brooks, Thomas Friedman, and many anonymous writers for *The Economist* routinely throw bouquets toward carbon pricing. Scholars from such diverse think tanks as the American Enterprise Institute, the Brookings Institution, the Niskanen Center, the Hudson Institute, the Rand Corporation, Resources for the Future, and the Wilson Center further expand the carbon pricing chorus, although scholars at such think tanks as the Heritage Foundation and Competitive Enterprise Institute would likely lose their jobs if they even hinted at such support. The idea of global carbon pricing has animated nearly all major international conclaves seeking long-term climate strategies, including the 1992 Rio Declaration and 1997 Kyoto Protocol. The 2015 adoption of the Paris climate accord featured numerous and impassioned endorsements of the need for carbon pricing strategies both nationally and internationally.

Carbon Pricing Options

One point of contention is what form carbon pricing should take. Nearly all carbon pricing adherents pay homage to Arthur Pigou, an early twentieth-century British economist who championed the idea of using taxes to mitigate the damages caused by externalities.[18] This tax provides signals to those causing harm that they should modify their behavior. For Pigou, this logically led toward a set of potential pollution taxes to mitigate environmental damages inflicted upon air, land, or water, and public health. When applied to carbon emissions via fossil fuel consumption, such policies are known as carbon taxes.

There is, however, one prominent alternative that reflects similar sensitivity to market forces but operates quite differently. It builds on economist Ronald Coase's famous article that indicated that taxation might not be as efficient as an approach in which participants would be allowed to negotiate their own optimal solution.[19] In this case, government would not impose a uniform compliance plan through exacting regulation but instead structure the terms of negotiation among parties. This provides stakeholders latitude in achieving an outcome superior to anything regulation could impose as long as their outcome was satisfactory to government.

In the 1960s, the work of economists Thomas Crocker and John Dales built on Coase's finding and ultimately took the pricing movement in a novel direction.[20] Under this reinterpretation, governments could assign transferable rights to environmental damages, allowing the market to set a price and determine the most cost-effective mitigation strategy. Governments could allocate these rights for free or auction them to polluters. Both methods would establish a "price to pollute" while simultaneously generating governmental revenue through the auction of pollution permits. When applied to carbon emissions, such policies are known as carbon cap-and-trade.

Economist Dallas Burtraw notes that "a persistent parlor question in economic thinking is the relative advantage of cap-and-trade versus an emissions tax."[21] Most economists endorse either option before anything else, although there appears to be significant leaning toward carbon taxation as the preferred approach from a purely economic standpoint. But there remain significant doctrinal divides on the respective merits of each option. This line is replicated in subsequent rounds of policy adoption in the United States and beyond.

The Case for Cap-and-Trade

Cap-and-trade ascended from academic drawing board to policy pantheon through Section IV of the 1990 Clean Air Act Amendments. This policy tool helped shatter a decade-long deadlock in the legislation's reauthorization for reducing sulfur dioxide emissions and their accompanying acid deposition, as will be discussed further in chapter 5.[22] The extensive and near-euphoric scholarly response to the early performance of this pioneering cap-and-trade system heralded its ability to produce greater reductions than anticipated at lower cost. The timing of this experiment made cap-and-trade ripe for adoption as a carbon reduction option; it was aggressively pushed by both Republican and Democratic administrations during the 1990s as a centerpiece for international climate policy during the Rio and Kyoto negotiations.

Cap-and-trade proponents contend that it promotes far greater flexibility in emissions reduction than conventional command-and-control approaches and delivers cost-effective reductions. Applied to carbon emissions, cap-and-trade establishes an overall allocation, or budget, for carbon releases (the "cap") that is reduced over time. Once emission allowances, or permits, are allocated to individual emission sources or jurisdictions, they are then free to negotiate transactions for the most inexpensive possible reductions (the "trade"). Reductions may be achieved through so-called offsets, such as carbon sequestration for newly planted trees, subterranean storage, or other emission reduction strategies.[23]

Advocates note that cap-and-trade delivers the exact established level of emission reductions by enforcing noncompliance penalties. This allows not only considerable predictability in achieving emission reduction goals but also informs emitters of the short-term expectations and the long-term adjustments that they need to make. Ideally, this stimulates creative exploration of new and, in turn, more climate-friendly technologies alongside expeditious consideration of the most cost-effective route to compliance.

Assuming successful compliance, cap-and-trade facilitates a steady path toward de-carbonization. If the United States, for example, decided to reduce its carbon emissions by 26 to 28 percent by 2025 from 2005 levels, as it pledged for the Paris accord, cap-and-trade could make the expectations imposed by each stage in such a transition abundantly clear. If designed effectively, legislation drafted once might largely self-implement without further revision, leaving oversight and compliance with executive agencies and, if needed, the courts, rather than relying on periodic legislative fixes. In contrast, carbon taxes could establish specific price increases but it would not be possible to accurately estimate their impact on emissions. This could lead to sustained failure to achieve emission reduction goals and the possible need for ongoing tax adjustments or supplemental policies.

Cap-and-trade also has considerable appeal since it does not require government officials to select and impose a direct price. Unlike taxes, any price increase related to the emissions trading system reflects the compliance options chosen by firms and their bids for allowances rather than the response to an explicit price command. Under cap-and-trade, prices for energy and related products may well increase, but the fingerprints will likely be harder to link to political officials than under a tax. Nordhaus has acknowledged that environmental taxes have only rarely been used to date, in large part because "tax is almost a four-letter word."[24] In contrast, auctioning allowances produces revenue for governments without having to confront public opposition to taxation.

Cap-and-trade offers a happy compromise, whereby cost-effectiveness is advanced alongside political feasibility by shielding responsibility for (and perhaps awareness of) cost imposition. Moreover, it produces a political constituency of sorts that includes lawyers, insurers, auditors, traders, and offset providers, all of whom flourish in such a reformed market and can provide sustained support. These features may explain the bandwagon effect, whereby cap-and-trade ascended from relative obscurity in the 1990s, according to Jonas Meckling, to emerge "as the central pillar of climate policies. In this process, it outcompeted carbon taxes, regulatory standards, and voluntary climate policy."[25] Political scientists Robert Keohane and David Victor confirmed that cap-and-trade "has become the policy instrument of choice for nearly all governments."[26] Other scholars noted a rapid diffusion process for cap-and-trade by federal, sub-federal, and local governments and even nonprofits in the United States and beyond through 2010.[27] This seemed to position cap-and-trade for a dominant role in climate governance, while nudging carbon taxes to the backrooms of academic theory and think tank speculation.

The Case for Carbon Taxes

Carbon taxes, however, have hardly evaporated as an alternative to cap-and-trade, maintaining a large and loyal set of aficionados in economics that likely exceed cap-and-trade supporters in pure numbers. "Economists would generally prefer carbon taxes, with cap-and-trade a close second," said economist Ted Gayer in 2010.[28] They lacked a dramatic environmental counter-example to the American sulfur dioxide case to anchor their advocacy for a tax. Yet they could point to several carbon tax experiments in northern Europe nations from the early 1990s that delivered significant emission reductions and encouraged expanded use of alternative technologies without imposing any economic trauma.[29] This suggests that carbon taxes have a broader and more established track record than cap-and-trade, which might augur well for their adoption across the numerous sources of carbon emissions. There is also, of course, the precedent with tobacco taxes.

Carbon tax proponents are particularly adamant that one of the greatest virtues of their approach is the ability to transmit clear price signals about future energy use. Cap-and-trade is unable to specify actual costs of compliance and runs some risks of significant price volatility while carbon taxes make costs transparent. This provides entities facing new tax burdens with incentives to reduce emissions and save money, including an impetus to pursue renewable or low-carbon energy sources.

These price signals can be directly linked to the environmental and social damage caused by fossil fuel consumption, consistent with Pigouvian principles. National governments and international authorities have intensified efforts to systematically determine the social cost of carbon, including American federal efforts that established a $37 per ton rate in 2015, measured in 2007 dollars.[30] By pegging a tax rate to this social cost, a carbon tax would directly reflect the marginal damages caused by a specific amount of carbon emitted into the atmosphere. Cap-and-trade or regulation would produce compliance costs, but both would be less likely to provide this direct link between cost and actual environmental damage.

A tax-based policy also holds out promise of relatively simple design and straightforward implementation. Many governments already have experience with energy taxation, such as excise taxes for gasoline or taxes applied to monthly electricity bills. The United States has more than 400 separate environment-related taxes or fees in place at the federal and state levels.[31] These range from taxes on extraction of fossil fuels through drilling and mining to those on tire purchases to cover eventual recycling costs. Therefore, it is eminently possible to build on this base of experience in fashioning carbon taxes rather than beginning from scratch as with cap-and-trade.

Carbon taxes could either build on these established policies or create parallel ones. Implementation would not require hiring large numbers of new governmental staff or creating new administrative units. In turn, the time from enactment to operation is quite brief, particularly in comparison to regulatory or trading programs with far greater complexity. As economist Shi-Ling Hsu notes, "greenhouse gas reduction opportunities are diverse, disparate, and beyond the comprehension of any single agency, a group of agencies, or even any network of governmental entities."[32] Carbon tax compliance would provide a direct and immediate reward for any emission reductions by compelling consumers to simply avoid a higher cost. In contrast, command-and-control policies and some forms of cap-and-trade would require substantial bureaucratic definition and verification of approved reduction methods, among many other provisions. This could invalidate some plausible emission reduction methods for administrative reasons or provoke interagency or legal conflicts.

Carbon taxes also afford relative ease in coordinating across subnational or national borders. Neighboring jurisdictions in the United States and beyond routinely work to harmonize many tax rates, including tobacco and gasoline excise taxes, in order to minimize incentives for smuggling or luring customers over borders for cheaper purchases.[33] International forms of this coordination exist through either bilateral negotiations or border-adjustment taxes that apply to imported goods from nations without such taxes.[34]

Carbon taxes expeditiously collect revenues that governments can use in a number of ways to either mitigate adverse impacts or further the goals of emission reductions.[35] Consumption taxes have long triggered concerns about disproportionate impacts on lower-income groups. However, there are established precedents to mitigate these effects by allocating at least some of the revenues for tax credits or energy bill rebates. In turn, many governments also have prior experience in targeting revenue use in order to further ameliorate the problem that provides the impetus for the tax. In the case of tobacco, substantial portions of federal excise tax revenues have been allocated to smoking cessation and related public health programs as well as covering some costs of health services delivery linked to smoking. One could easily envision a range of possible investments related to expanded use of renewable energy or pursuit of energy efficiency made possible by carbon tax proceeds.

Absence of Constitutional Constraints

Constitutional constraints can at times impede or even preclude the development of new policies, however appealing they might be in theory. But none of these strictures apply to the case of carbon pricing in the United States. The US Supreme Court first declared excise taxes constitutionally legitimate in 1796, in a case that addressed taxation of carriages;[36] it has never reversed this position on the myriad excise taxes that have followed, ranging from tobacco and gasoline to luxury goods such as yachts and jewelry. Subsequent Supreme Courts deemed state taxation of fossil fuel extraction through drilling and mining legally legitimate in a set of cases from the 1980s.[37]

All fifty states hold authority from their respective constitutions to follow similar policy paths; they have long used a combination of sales and excise taxes for gasoline, and some apply taxes to electricity usage. Earlier cap-and-trade programs, including the one for sulfur dioxide, have faced no significant constitutional challenges. In turn, the constitutional receptivity to carbon pricing in the United States also appears applicable to a great many other nations, including federations such as Canada and Australia and multilevel systems such as the European Union. Many of these governments blend centralized and decentralized constitutional controls over taxes, with particularly strong delegation to states and provinces in North America.[38] There is no record of serious court challenges to the legitimacy of carbon tax or cap-and-trade policies from a constitutional perspective in these governments.

This constitutional latitude creates considerable opportunity for carbon pricing by an individual government. It also opens wide a door to substantial diffusion of innovative policies across jurisdictions that face no constitutional barriers to emulation. In the United States, the absence of a federal carbon price allows for policy experimentation by a single state or region. Assuming a track record of successful adoption and implementation, this might ultimately lead to diffusion across multiple states and regions. It might even provide a tipping point for vertical diffusion, whereby the federal government draws from best state practices and bases a nationwide program on these lessons.

Precedents for this pattern include federal tobacco and gasoline excise taxes, which began as single-state experiments.[39] Cap-and-trade also diffused in this manner, as reflected in the pioneering sulfur dioxide mitigation programs in New York and Wisconsin that ultimately influenced national air quality legislation. Tobacco, energy, and environmental policy have seen numerous instances of policy diffusion from the state (and, in some instances, local level) to the national level.[40] With these precedents and no consequential constitutional impediments, scholars contemplated alternative paths toward rapid diffusion of carbon pricing in the United States and beyond.[41] As recently as 2010, the future of carbon pricing seemed boundless, particularly if a handful of governments could muster the political courage to adopt carbon pricing policies, successfully put those policies into operation, and launch a bandwagon effect that could sweep nations and perhaps the globe.

2 Why Politicians Are Reluctant to Price Carbon

Economists excel at evaluating alternative policy options and designing optimal ones. However, in practice, the world is full of political constraints, managerial limitations, and public doubts, requiring optimal policy ideas to be tempered against these realities.[1] This does not preclude the development of policy that reflects the aspirations of economics. But it greatly complicates the transition of carbon pricing policies from the seminar room to the legislative chamber.

These complex realities were downplayed by economists and carbon pricing advocates amid expectations that a few prior experiences (tobacco taxes from around the world, American sulfur dioxide emissions trading, and northern Europe carbon taxes) could be easily replicated. But these hopeful policy ideas would repeatedly deflate upon colliding with political reality. In turn, carbon pricing developed a shaky life-cycle record of political adoption, management, resilience, and performance. As we will see in subsequent chapters, carbon pricing may well have theoretical promise and political potential. But it also faces significant and enduring political hurdles that were originally dismissed as a mere distraction and were widely expected to yield in due season to the power of the carbon pricing idea.

Oil Is Politically Thicker than Tobacco

Even the hope of mounting an effective campaign to phase out fossil fuels that follows the playbook of the tobacco control case seems naïve on closer review. Decades of active promotion of tobacco use through aggressive advertising and subsidized production still failed to lure more than one-half of adult Americans to smoke. Its addictive qualities were potent and yet tens of millions of citizens found effective paths toward use reduction or elimination. Tobacco consumption was hardly necessary to meet fundamental daily needs or sustain the national economy. It is, in many respects, more of an optional or even luxury good than an essential one, albeit one that can create a chemical dependency that compels ongoing use. There has been an ever-growing set of products and programs that facilitate transition away from significant use, including the controversial alternative of e-cigarettes that avoid direct tobacco combustion while sustaining tobacco use.

The fight against tobacco has routinely emphasized its consequential, direct, and highly measurable threats to its users and society. This could be measured in sophisticated assessments of direct health risks, including the incidence of lung cancer, related cancers, and heart disease. A broad body of scientific analyses cutting across multiple disciplines has demonstrated linkages between usage and various life-threatening maladies, and has charted anticipated average shortening of life span through product consumption. The initial focus on health impacts for smokers has yielded growing evidence that consumption has broader societal consequences. Family members or fellow workers could face their own harms through repeated exposure to tobacco smoke.

The economic base for cultivating and refining tobacco has remained substantial and yet regionally concentrated. Tobacco cultivation long has been dominated by just a handful of US states, with 90 percent of total American production in the 2010s concentrated in North Carolina and Virginia. Additional output from four neighboring southern states (Kentucky, Tennessee, Georgia, and South Carolina) brought the regional total to more than 98 percent of national output. This indicates a concentrated base of political support but one with a limited capacity to fend off political challenges to product use through taxation.

Tobacco thus features a far less formidable political base than fossil fuels. Fossil fuel usage in the United States is nearly universal, addressing essential needs such as electricity, heating, cooling, and transportation. Usage fosters a number of environmental problems, including climate change, but it is far more difficult to link fossil fuel use to personal health risks than in the tobacco case. Fossil fuel extraction, refinement, and distribution have a substantially greater economic footprint than tobacco processing, involving far more regions, states, and legislative districts in an active way, thereby creating a much bigger base of constituency support.[2]

The highly divergent paths of the well-established state and federal excise taxes for cigarettes and gasoline reflect the differences between these two cases. The diffusion of these policies across states and ultimately the federal government means that their rates could be adjusted upward to raise prices, drive down consumption, and produce added government revenue. This would not require political debate over pricing mechanisms and legislation but simply altering the price imposed in the existing tax instrument.

Transportation infrastructure funding has long been dependent on revenue from gasoline taxes. But, as demonstrated in figure 2.1, gasoline tax

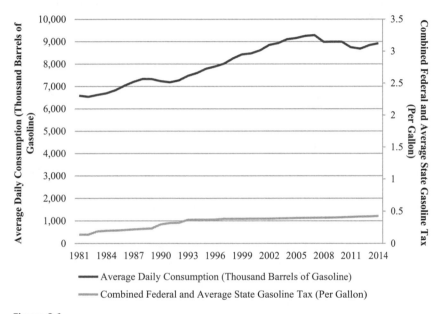

Figure 2.1

US gasoline tax and consumption rates from 1981–2014.

Sources: For taxes, see US Department of Transportation Federal Highway Administration (US DOT FHWA), "Highway History," November 18, 2015, accessed April 28, 2016, www.fhwa.dot.gov/infrastructure/gastax.cfm; US Energy Information Administration (US EIA), "Petroleum Marketing Monthly Archives," accessed April 28, 2016, www.eia .gov/petroleum/marketing/monthly/archive; US DOT FHWA, "Highway Statistic Summary to 1995" (Washington, DC: FHWA, 1997), table MF-205; US DOT FHWA, "State Motor-Fuel Tax Trends in the 1990s: Why Has the Pace of Rate Increases Declined?" (Washington, DC: FHWA, 1998), 22. For average daily consumption in the United States, see US EIA, "International Energy Statistics," accessed April 28, 2016, www.eia.gov /cfapps/ipdbproject/iedindex3.cfm?tid=5&pid=62&aid=2&cid=US,&syid=1980&eyid =2013&unit=TBPD.

rates have changed only modestly in past decades, quite contrary to the cig-arette tax patterns noted in figure 1.1. Gasoline consumption has steadily climbed throughout recent decades, aside from occasional interruptions where prices soared temporarily due to supply restrictions, most commonly linked to disruptions in the Middle East.

Alongside the frequent and significant increases in state and federal tobacco excise taxes, gasoline taxes remain stable. As of 2015, nearly two-thirds of state fuel taxes failed to keep pace with two decades of inflation, and nearly one-half of them had not been adjusted at all in the prior decade.[3] Most rate increases over the past quarter-century were moderate, commonly confined to one or two cents per gallon and only occasionally reaching five cents or more. There is no evidence that any state increased its gas taxes in order to deter consumption and reduce emissions, contrary to the mission of carbon taxes. Instead, producing revenue that was most commonly used for highway and bridge construction or repair has remained the driver behind increases.[4]

Politicians from both parties at both the federal and state levels have long approached gasoline taxation with enormous trepidation. From Rich-ard Nixon's 1970s vow to keep a gallon of gas below one dollar to Al Gore's 2000 election push to release strategic petroleum reserves to suppress prices,[5] cheap oil and gas prices are core concerns of American political leaders. Most exercise extreme caution when making any upward adjustments in gasoline excise taxes for fear of adverse electoral consequences. Even growing con-cerns about dependency on imported oil and gas or environmental dam-ages associated with use failed to budge this enduring political hesitancy to increase taxes. Presidents who backed some form of modest federal tax rate increase (a nickel per gallon under George H. W. Bush in 1990 and 4.3 cents under Bill Clinton in 1993) faced fierce political backlash in subsequent elections, chilling any serious consideration of tax increases on oil and gas by their successors. In turn, many Republican and Democratic governors also experienced political repercussions after state gasoline tax increases, even in instances where funding was directly tied to urgent infrastructure repairs.

Super-Wicked Problem

The political aversion to gasoline tax increases offers a glimpse into the steep political climb facing any carbon pricing strategy. The political com-plexity of such a step only mounts when expanding the focus beyond a single commodity, such as gasoline at the pump, to include coal and natural gas, with prices elevated across fuels. This reflects the significant political sensitivity inherent in a "super-wicked" policy problem such as climate change. Such problems are generally defined as featuring enormous scientific and political complexity and requiring communities whose behavior creates a problem to make significant adjustments in that behavior. In particular, wicked problems require near-term changes on a large scale with the expectation—or hope—that any immediate adversities will be offset by long-term benefits.[6]

Carbon pricing may constitute the most cost-effective plausible policy to reduce risks from climate change. But it proposes to do so by offering the near-certainty of political pain through increased prices on gasoline, oil, coal, and natural gas. Prices for fossil fuel use are highly visible, perhaps best illustrated by the massive signs for gasoline prices at service stations scattered across the nation. In many communities, it is difficult to travel very far without being confronted with these price declarations. While electricity price information is not as prominent, consumers still are aware of the costs. Electricity bills are delivered monthly and many states require that they include detailed information about cost trends in comparison to prior months and years. For many Americans, it is difficult *not* to know how much energy costs; any increase in regular expenditures for power, heat, and transport are likely to trigger attention and consternation. As Stephen Ansolabehere and David Konisky have noted, "Americans are acutely aware of energy prices."[7]

Imposing higher costs through taxation represents a powerful form of political pain.[8] This pain can be particularly intense when applied to a popular commodity and a price increase becomes readily apparent. Citizens tend to feel economic pain imposed by political action far more than the balm of any attending benefits.[9] It is, however, possible to make related benefits sufficiently compelling and visible to create and maintain political support for sustained cost imposition through careful crafting of the benefits and direct linkage to the costs. Social Security, for example, has endured across multiple generations, retaining steadfast political support by coupling the promise of long-term income protection in advanced age with ongoing payroll taxation during working-age years.[10]

Even energy taxes are not immune from this calculus. President Dwight Eisenhower broke a long-term logjam in the development of an interstate highway system that was commonly perceived as a national necessity but routinely thwarted by lack of political consensus on how to generate funds to cover construction costs. In this case, he drew from prior American experience with gasoline excise taxes to champion a federal version that generated funds to facilitate interstate highway development.[11] All fifty states had adopted such taxes between 1919 and 1929 and a federal tax was created in 1932, providing a base for direct expansion as opposed to other financing options such as tolls and bonds.

Programs like Social Security and the initial gas tax can acknowledge costs while linking them to direct and demonstrable benefits. Carbon pricing is rather different. It is likely that any carbon tax or cap-and-trade system would increase energy prices and thereby trigger backlash. But what exactly is the benefit from reducing carbon emissions, particularly if calculated on a personal scale?

By 2015, total American carbon emissions returned unexpectedly to 1995 levels despite considerable population and economic growth. This had little if anything to do with carbon pricing and instead reflected a combination of effects from the Great Recession, rapid transition from coal to (less carbon-intensive) natural gas through hydraulic fracturing, and a mixture of state and local policies to promote greater energy efficiency and renewable energy use. Most Americans likely had no idea that this emission reduction occurred. Even if they did, how would they begin to calculate any direct societal or personal benefit from this? Would they, in some tangible way, be better off because of this step? Would their children or grandchildren be better off as a result?

In all likelihood, it is impossible to calculate such benefits. There are simply too many sources of carbon emissions, most emanating from beyond American borders, for any singular reduction to have a demonstrable effect. So any carbon reduction benefit is elusive at best to measure. This is fundamentally different from seeing tangible outcomes connected to other policies, whether it be the reliance on Social Security checks across generations, the establishment of an interstate transportation system, or even the air quality improvements that have followed the sulfur dioxide cap-and-trade program of the 1990s. Any carbon pricing proposal faces a more perilous political footing, quite likely to be perceived as heavy on the imposition of front-loaded costs while uncertain at best on delivery of long-term benefits.

Formidable Base of Political Opposition

The sheer scope and geographic range of American fossil fuel production, distribution, and use creates a substantial constituency that is likely to be more sensitive than the general public to any political imposition of greater costs on their core products. The fossil fuel industry dwarfs the tobacco industry in overall economic size, with its interests spread across far more regions, states, and congressional districts. Twenty-four different US states rank among the top ten domestic producers of coal, oil, or natural gas. This includes states such as Texas, California, Pennsylvania, Illinois, and Colorado, all of which have substantial clout in the House of Representatives. Thirty-six states generate some amount of one of more fossil fuels. This translates into 72 of 100 Senate seats with some degree of fossil fuel industry representation. Such a political base may well prove difficult to move on the issue of carbon pricing, particularly given the considerable challenge of specifying near-term climate benefits that might accompany any costs.

Beyond sheer size, the fossil fuel industry has also proved extremely effective in building a coalition of industries that routinely rely on its products, including auto and truck manufacturers and distributors. This alliance also extends to industries that transport fossil fuels, such as rail and truck transport firms and small armies of supplemental service providers. This coalition could face considerable loss of economic viability if carbon pricing triggered development of non-fossil fuel energy sources and fostered less-carbonized transportation options. In response, it loudly and aggressively provides political opposition, predicting dire economic consequences and severe job losses if carbon pricing policies were adopted.

These threats further serve to bolster a coalition opposed to carbon pricing. Industry partners include unions, such as those representing coal miners, fearful of potential salary, benefit, and job cuts.[12] Organizations and political parties philosophically opposed to any form of increased taxation, such as the Tea Party movement, might also join forces. This broad and diverse base is particularly influential in legislative contexts where carbon pricing proposals require super-majority approval for adoption due to constitutional provisions or legislative rules.[13]

Such organized opposition could take numerous forms, including direct assaults on carbon pricing proposals through lobbying and advertising. These might accentuate public fears about steep costs and their potential economic consequences. They might also challenge the issue of anticipated benefits and question whether or not any benefits will be generated. Many industry groups have challenged the very existence of evidence that climate change is occurring, or in a more nuanced version, contend that use of fossil fuels is not a driving factor behind any observed climatic changes. This includes direct attacks against the veracity of established climate science as well as support for alternative research designed to dismiss or downplay any burgeoning threat from carbon-induced climate change.[14]

Partisan Divides Sharpen amid Recession

This oppositional base assumed an increasingly partisan quality in the late 2000s and beyond. It was widely thought in earlier periods that climate change and carbon pricing might foster bipartisan collaboration as issue saliency rose, galvanizing broad political support to take constructive steps to reduce emissions. In theory, carbon pricing might secure support from center-right parties interested in cost-effective strategies in response to their growing concerns about climate risks that included threats to national security. This might be integrated with support from parties on the center-left where concerns about threats to public health from climate change were paramount. Many carbon pricing bills introduced into Congress during this period had some level of bipartisan support, including legislation sponsored by such Republican senators as John McCain (Arizona), John Warner (Virginia), and Norm Coleman (Minnesota). Even such strident partisan opponents as House speakers Newt Gingrich and Nancy Pelosi shared a love seat in a 2007 television commercial, articulating their concerns about climate change and the need for a robust American response.

But this kind of partisan comity proved impossible to sustain in the United States and was also reflected in ever-sharper partisan differences on carbon pricing in other nations. Republican leaders proved increasingly likely to challenge the integrity of climate science and attacked carbon taxes and cap-and-trade as assaults on American economic vitality, often operating in close alliance with organized opponents. The expansion of fracking-related oil and gas production during this period only emboldened elected political officials who represented states and districts that increasingly saw fossil fuels as part of their economic future rather than just their past.

In turn, such opponents also capitalized on the economic anxieties that accompanied the arrival of the Great Recession in the latter years of the 2000s. Soaring unemployment and concerns about the viability of financial institutions helped reduce the political saliency of climate change in comparison with economic recovery. They also amplified worries about absorbing economic costs associated with any climate mitigation policy. This combination of factors was evident in American federal and state politics but also in other recession-battered nations such as Australia and Canada.

The growing chorus of opposing views from the political right was nurtured by well-funded political and quasi-research organizations with the mission of casting doubt about the existence of climate change. These groups also tended to oppose any conceivable governmental strategy to reduce greenhouse gas emissions, often with a particular vehemence toward carbon pricing. This included a range of industrial interests but also a more diverse array of wealthy citizens, conservative activists, and related think tanks and advocacy groups such as the Heartland Institute, the Competitive Enterprise Institute, and the American Legislative Exchange Council. Such organizations sought to discredit key tenets of climate science and oppose any policy intended to reduce fossil fuel use. They demonized any political leader embracing these issues as posing an alarmist threat to American well-being.

While Democrats and Independents on the center-left of the political continuum proved far less likely to waver in their beliefs on climate change, they were not uniform in their support for carbon pricing as a preferred policy response. Even in jurisdictions that would prove relatively friendly to a carbon tax or cap-and-trade, organized opposition to launch or maintain such a policy frequently surfaced from the political left. This reflected concerns over possible concentration of carbon pricing costs or facility emissions on economically weaker communities. This led to criticisms that carbon pricing was a form of elite advocacy that might further promote inequities across class, racial, and ethnic lines. It increasingly emerged as a major concern among many environmental justice groups with links to parties on the political left, particularly in cases where the allocation of carbon pricing revenues was under debate.

Each reflection of doubt further narrowed any political base that could be relied on to embrace carbon pricing. This meant that any policy proposal would begin with a potentially significant base of opposition, most assuredly from the right but also possibly from the left. By the mid-2010s, the early expectation that carbon pricing could build broad coalitions across partisan lines appeared suspect, a phenomenon also evident outside the United States.

Soft Base of Public Concern

Carbon pricing proponents have routinely employed the logic of economic theory to advance their case. Moral suasion is also regularly used, reflecting a call for intergenerational and international well-being through emission reduction efforts. These ideational and normative approaches have considerable persuasive power, particularly if backed by influential policy entrepreneurs who know how to work political systems. But any carbon pricing proposal must inevitably confront the realities of immediate political considerations.

Any opportunity to thwart organized opposition and adopt a carbon pricing scheme would likely require a strong and resilient body of public support. If the public were persuaded that climate change is a preeminent national and global threat, it might well be prepared to focus considerably less on short-term self-interest and instead push for policies intended to preserve a more stable longer-term future. Carbon pricing might then become an integral part of this policy mix, propelled by public support not only to take action to reduce carbon emissions but also to use some form of carbon taxation or cap-and-trade to achieve those reduction goals.

There is little evidence, however, from the avalanche of work on American public opinion on climate change that these conditions hold. Numerous studies confirm that climate change consistently ranks toward the bottom of any list of domestic and international policy concerns among Americans. Among environmental issues, climate change routinely falls well behind air and water pollution as a public priority, though even these issues rarely approach the top tier of overall public concerns.[15] And climate change falls far below such issues as the economy, terrorism, immigration, and health care in ongoing surveys conducted by organizations such as Gallup and Pew.

Not only is climate change a relatively low priority, but a good number of Americans also harbor significant doubts of its existence. Biannual national surveys conducted since 2008 by the National Surveys on Energy and Environment (NSEE) regularly ask respondents whether they think there is solid evidence that global temperatures have been warming over the past four decades.[16] Although 72 percent of Americans responded affirmatively in fall 2008, these levels subsequently dropped, reaching lows in the mid-to-high 50 percent range between 2010 and 2014. The rest of respondents were divided between those who concluded solid evidence did not exist or were unsure. As figure 2.2 indicates, there was some reversal of these trends between 2015 and 2017, beginning with a return in fall 2015 to a 70 percent level affirming the existence of warming temperatures. But even this survey produced a sizable body of respondents who did not see evidence of warming.[17]

In turn, respondents who concluded that solid evidence of warming exists did not necessarily specify human causation through carbon emissions. Many characterized climatic changes as natural occurrences that have little or nothing to do with fossil fuels. These views also exist in other nations,

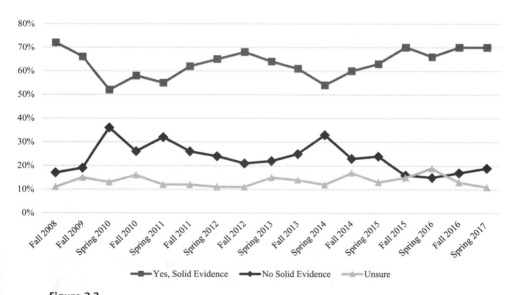

Figure 2.2
American views on the existence of global warming, 2008–2017.
Source: Christopher Borick, Barry Rabe, and Sarah Mills, "Trump's Global Warming Views Remain Elusive, but Not Those of Americans," *FIXGOV*, Brookings Institution, June 12, 2017, https://www.brookings.edu/blog/fixgov/2017/06/12/trumps-global-warming-views-remain-elusive-but-not-those-of-americans/.
Question: "From what you've read and heard, is there solid evidence that the average temperature on earth has been getting warmer over the past four decades?"

including Canada, where comparable survey analysis has been conducted. However, Americans have regularly demonstrated greater likelihood to either doubt the existence of warming global temperatures or question human influence on any changes.[18]

This level of uncertainty about whether climate change is occurring undermines support for various policy proposals to try to mitigate its effects. Why make sacrifices to solve a problem that may not even exist? Carbon pricing proposals routinely fail to gain majority support among Americans when presented as a policy option in a survey. Carbon taxes in particular tend to face greater opposition than cap-and-trade, although it is difficult to examine the body of public opinion on these policies and distill any substantial base of public support for either option. This is true whether a proposed policy may be adopted by states or at the federal level.[19]

Question massaging and the very words chosen to define terms such as "cap-and-trade" can move the needle of opinion to some extent. Explicit references to successful cap-and-trade schemes or description of various options for spending revenues can also influence opinion. But even with these framing boosts, carbon pricing policies consistently have the most limited base of political support among a wide range of policy options to reduce carbon emissions. This limited political base further compounds the challenge of building public support for carbon pricing.

Politically Easier Policy Alternatives

The American political aversion to carbon pricing may be further amplified by the availability of a range of alternative policy options, including regulation, subsidies, and symbolic acts. These may lack the cost-effectiveness potential of carbon pricing, but their allure reflects the fact that any costs imposed by these policies are less explicit or transparent. The public might not even be aware that these policies were increasing some aspect of their energy costs. A claim of other, non-climate benefits to public health (such as cleaner air) or the economy (such as alternative energy jobs) seals the deal.

Politicians who want to demonstrate that they are doing something in response to climate change have an array of alternatives beyond carbon pricing at their disposal. In the United States, the federal government has never adopted a carbon tax or carbon cap-and-trade, even though legislative proposals for both have been introduced regularly into Congress for decades. States have no constitutional restrictions on adopting either policy. Yet no state came remotely close to adopting a carbon tax between 1990 and 2015. Between 2002 and 2010, twenty-three states adopted a version of carbon cap-and-trade. However, thirteen of these states abandoned their commitments by 2015 and no additional states came on board after 2010. Canada had a somewhat similar experience with these policies during this period. The Canadian federal government has never adopted either policy through legislation while provinces have only minimally used carbon taxes and significantly reversed initial adoption of carbon cap-and-trade. This has hardly been a robust pattern of policy adoption and diffusion, as will be explored more in chapter 3.

Although carbon taxes receive the greatest support from economists, our review of the federal and state climate policy experience, as discussed here, would suggest that their political feasibility is quite low, as noted in table 2.1. That, however, is not the end of the climate policy story. Several other policies have been adopted in the United States and are currently in operation in more than half of the states. In some instances, this has involved a set of adoption decisions by individual states. In others, the federal government often follows the policies of one or more states on a national basis, as is the practice for vehicle emission control.

Procurement Mandates

Governments can mandate production or purchase of commodities thought to present an environmental benefit. One prominent example of a state-centered policy alternative that requires clean energy procurement is a renewable portfolio standard, commonly known as an RPS. It constitutes the near-converse of carbon taxes in terms of economic desirability and political feasibility as a climate policy option, reflected in table 2.1. An RPS requires that all electricity providers within a state increase the amount of power obtained from renewable sources over a fixed time period. Most of these policies define what is "renewable" and then steadily increase RPS stringency, establishing financial penalties in the event of noncompliance.

More than one-half of US states enacted an RPS between 1983 and 2010, when the diffusion process peaked at twenty-nine states and the District of Columbia.[20] RPSs have been adopted by both Democratic and Republican political leaders in multiple states from every region of the nation except

Table 2.1
The political and economic efficacy of various carbon policy options.

	Political Feasibility[a]		
	Low	Medium	High
Economic Desirability			
Low			• Procurement mandates; Performance standards
Medium		• Cap & Trade	
High	• Carbon Tax		

a. In number of states in the United States with adopted policy.

the Southeast, where only North Carolina adopted one. Three states (Colorado, Missouri, and Washington) alternatively created them through ballot propositions. There was some political backlash against these policies during the 2010s, when original RPS mandates were fulfilled and a decision had to be made on whether to extend or expand the program. Nonetheless, there have been none of the far-reaching reversals witnessed in state cap-and-trade policy. As noted in table 2.2, in the fifty states, the number of RPS policies remained at twenty-nine between 2012 and 2016. Vermont added a renewable portfolio standard during this period while Kansas repealed theirs, although several other states were actively considering new or expanded policies in 2018.[21]

Since their inception, RPS policies have contributed to a significant expansion of renewable electricity generation, most notably wind, particularly when coupled with generous federal tax credits for renewable energy production.[22] However, they are generally more costly per unit of carbon emission reduction, as they mandate adoption of renewable technologies regardless of their costs or technical feasibility. It is often difficult to discern the actual impact of an RPS on carbon emissions, as it is not always clear which type of existing source (from which state) is being supplemented, given the complexities of electricity production and distribution. In turn, the policy does not reduce electricity demand unless the addition of renewables adds to costs and drives down use. RPSs have also, in some

Table 2.2
The prevalence of alternative climate policy options among the 50 states, 2000–2016.

	Year				
Policy	2000	2004	2008	2012	2016
Severance Tax	27	27	27	27	29
Carbon Tax	0	0	0	0	0
Cap-and-Trade	0	2	23	10	10
RPS	8	18	23	29	29

Sources: For severance taxes, see Jacquelyn Pless, "Oil and Gas Severance Taxes: States Work to Alleviate Fiscal Pressures amid the Natural Gas Boom," *National Conference of State Legislatures*, accessed April 28, 2016, http://www.ncsl.org /research/energy/oil-and-gas-severance-taxes.aspx. Only severance taxes on oil and natural gas are included, though other states also apply severance taxes to extraction of coal and other minerals. For cap-and-trade, see Barry G. Rabe, "The Durability of Carbon Cap-and-Trade Policy," *Governance* 29, no. 1 (2016): 103–199, doi:10.1111/gove.12151.

cases, become extremely complex, designating special status for politically favored energy alternatives through "carve-outs" that require exact purchase levels of specific renewable technologies regardless of their price or availability. Some states have also used the term "renewable" expansively and not always in concert with carbon reduction goals, including in some cases biofuels, animal waste, landfill gas, and waste coal.[23]

Economists have thus raised concerns about the cost-effectiveness of these policies, even in regions where renewable capacity is high and overall cost falls below national averages.[24] As one study of competing climate policy options concludes, "The RPS may be one of the less efficient means of achieving greenhouse gas emissions reductions. Unlike a more flexible carbon cap, it does not reward generation from non-renewable sources of low-carbon power, and rewards energy conservation only very weakly."[25] Another study refers to an RPS as an "implicit tax on fossil energy in the form of a mandate to buy green certificates, which then fund a subsidy to renewable energy through the certificate value."[26] Many economists thus view this option with concern and even disdain, characterizing it as a disappointing alternative to carbon pricing.

None of this concern has seriously dampened political enthusiasm for the RPS approach. This may well be linked in part to its function as an implicit tax. Much like other forms of regulation, it is difficult to discern any electricity price increases directly linked to RPSs. Any added costs are quietly tucked into monthly bills and thereby hidden from public view. At the same time, RPSs are regularly framed by proponents as delivering multiple benefits to the adopting state. They often emphasize anticipated economic development through promotion of these "homegrown" energy sources rather than reliance on imported fuels. States often take significant steps to maximize the likelihood that newly mandated renewables are principally or exclusively generated within their borders to capture these benefits, even if they result in ultimate costs greater than those from sources located in other jurisdictions. Preferences for locally based technologies or forms of renewable energy may serve to build political support among providers who stand to benefit directly from regulatory provisions.[27]

There are multiple potential benefits in terms of job creation for energy installation and management, including the anticipated development of technical expertise that could position a state for national or even global leadership in alternative energy development. There is also the possibility of royalties to land owners who lease property for renewable energy installation and operation, greater energy supply reliability and diversity, and environmental improvements such as better air quality. In this context, climate change mitigation may—or may not—be included in the list of anticipated benefits. In a state such as California, estimated carbon emission reductions will be publicly highlighted as an RPS benefit. Conversely, in Texas, they will not even be referenced in public circles. But in both cases, states will attempt to measure any carbon emission reductions that stem from RPS implementation and seek credit for them in any future national policy.[28]

Performance Standards

Procurement mandates have emerged as a prominent and politically feasible alternative to market-based policies. But they are hardly the lone option to carbon taxes or cap-and-trade. Governments can also require greater efficiency in energy use through performance standards linked to the efficiency with which energy is used in equipment or facilities. Twenty-four states have adopted an energy efficiency resource standard (EERS), requiring electricity distributors to achieve a percentage of energy savings relative to a baseline measure. EERS policies mandate a designated amount of added energy efficiency each year but offer numerous alternative routes toward compliance. Energy efficiency can also be promoted through other policies such as building and equipment standards.

In the transportation sector, vehicle tailpipe emission and fuel economy standards have long prevailed over fuel taxes as the politically preferred policy intended to reduce emissions, despite the broad consensus in economics that the latter would be superior. California began to develop performance standards for vehicle emissions in the 1940s, eager to alleviate profound smog problems while not discouraging driving and related economic growth. Federal engagement in this area in the 1960s included an unusual waiver whereby California alone was allowed to seek exemptions from national standards to set its own higher standards.[29] The state used this waiver process 133 times between 1967 and 2017, with the vast majority fully approved by Washington. This has frequently led to subsequent federal adoption of the policy launched in Sacramento. These waivers have maintained a broad base of bipartisan support, reflected in frequent waiver requests and approvals by governors in both parties and by the president, including Ronald Reagan in both roles during his political career.

President Barack Obama formally merged these tailpipe emission standards with federal fuel economy provisions in 2009. This launched a major effort to require reductions in new vehicle emissions and increases in fuel economy through 2025, and included the first application of this policy directly to greenhouse gas emissions, linked to pioneering California legislation adopted in 2002. This policy has proved far more politically feasible and durable than carbon pricing, in part because any price increases in new vehicle purchases do not disclose the added costs attributable to installation of new performance equipment. This added expense may actually deter some new purchases, thereby keeping older—and dirtier—vehicles in use longer. In turn, added fuel economy makes it cheaper to drive, potentially creating a "rebound effect" whereby some of the environmental gains from added efficiency are offset by greater use. These and other factors tend to limit the effectiveness of such a standard in performance and economic terms but help explain their political advantage over carbon pricing.[30] Indeed, proposals to replace these regulations with some form of tax or transportation sector cap-and-trade program have never secured measurable political support in California or federally.[31]

Each of these regulatory approaches have distinctive design features. They have regularly proven capable of garnering considerable political support, often crossing partisan lines and regional divides while successfully transitioning into advanced stages of the policy life-cycle. This support has generally been sustained over time, leading to policy durability that has not been evident with cap-and-trade. While all of these alternative policies possess limitations in terms of cost-effectiveness, they share an ability to hide or obscure any cost increases related to implementation. These disguised costs contribute to their political sustainability and also their enduring popularity in public opinion surveys. The National Surveys on Energy and Environment has regularly found that procurement mandates and performance standards receive substantially greater support than either carbon taxes or cap-and-trade when proposed at either the state or federal level.[32] Regulatory requirements to increase renewable electricity, energy efficiency, and tailpipe emissions routinely provide a far more popular option than carbon pricing to politicians who have a desire to make some response to the challenge of climate change.

Action Plans Politically Easier than Policy Action

Regulatory policies can garner considerable political support if any uncertainty about benefits is offset by their ability to shield costs from public view. Applied to carbon emissions, however, regulatory policies may face opposition from producers of more conventional energy sources or fuel-inefficient vehicles. An RPS, for example, will likely force electric utilities to take uncomfortable steps such as reducing use of fossil fuels and expanding use of renewables. Given their likely pushback against these pressures, the path to adoption can be contentious and politicians may search for additional alternatives. They also may seek subsidies such as tax incentives or other forms of preferential treatment in exchange for cooperation. In turn, one direct alternative to a mandatory RPS is a voluntary version, as has been established in several states. This allows politicians to claim credit for encouraging renewables and any related benefits. But it is purely aspirational, free of any penalties for noncompliance.

State politicians have also found political comfort in creating task forces and special committees to launch "action plan" review processes. These can allow states to assemble diverse stakeholders to review carbon emission histories and forecasts, thereby opening valuable exploration of climate threats unique to that context. This group often weighs a wide range of policy options and encourages the state to consider adoption. Nonprofit organizations have emerged to facilitate all aspects of this process, including modeling software that can readily be applied to an individual jurisdiction. Philanthropic foundations eager to support engagement on climate change are often prepared to underwrite some of the costs, including supplemental staff support.[33]

This review process often is launched with a bold announcement by a governor or convening officials. It leads over time to the development of a report known as an action plan. This plan does not commit any political officials to anything but rather tends to review a menu of options with some expression of preference for certain items on the list. There also may be suggestions for setting a statewide emission reduction goal, most commonly known as a target. Numerous states have conducted at least one such action plan review, with some beginning in the 1990s. Many have complemented this with the creation of greenhouse gas registries that measure emissions trends and often provide opportunities to register voluntary emission reduction efforts for possible future credit.

Such plans aim to foster policy dialogue and help guide a state toward a less-carbonized path and they may ultimately trigger policy adoption. However, politicians are not bound to do anything after the report is issued, even if it receives considerable media attention and public endorsements. Elected officials and their appointees who helped sponsor the planning process or served as a member of the oversight committee can claim credit for moving ahead in addressing climate change. Political risks are mitigated until a specific policy is adopted and costs are imposed, most likely down the road in a future legislative cycle.

For elected executives, such as state governors, action plans are attractive ways to demonstrate "climate concern" while deferring any tough political decisions until a later time. Given term limits and the rapid transition of elected leaders, action plans may even support broader political aspirations by being seen as doing something on climate change without doing anything that would upset anyone. In turn, state action plans have proved far less likely to endorse carbon taxes or cap-and-trade than a broad range of more politically palatable options. They might help propel consideration of policies but have generally favored ones that have a better political chance of adoption.

Initial scholarly analysis has raised significant doubts regarding the impact of these plans and registries on emissions.[34] This pattern has been confirmed in additional analysis conducted in Canada, where all of the ten provinces have pursued action plans, often on multiple occasions over the past two decades. These have often been linked with the creation of registries and the establishment of aspirational emission reduction targets, comparable in many ways to American states. A growing body of analysis from Canada notes that provincial emission reduction targets are rarely achieved and action plans tend to repackage existing policies rather than launch new ones.[35] There may be consequential exceptions to this pattern but it is possible that the greatest benefit offered by these options is political rather than environmental, allowing officials to substitute terms like "action" and "targets" while postponing serious exploration of carbon pricing options.

The Alternative of Taxing Carbon while Exporting Most of the Costs

Portfolio standards, vehicle emission standards, action plans, and their numerous policy siblings provide politicians leery of carbon pricing with accessible off-the-shelf options. This can allow them to demonstrate climate commitment while imposing little or no economic pain. But imagine if some politicians had a politically feasible option that imposed a direct tax on carbon, even though it was not necessarily intended to reduce fossil fuel extraction or use. States across the political spectrum were equally likely to adopt such a tax, with no significant differences in tax rates linked to partisan control of government.

This tax was inaugurated in Texas around the time of the Civil War and nearly three-fifths of all states have since adopted one or more versions for natural gas and oil, with additional ones in place for coal and other minerals (see table 2.2). No state has ever repealed this tax since adoption and Republican governors such as Alaska's Sarah Palin and Ohio's John Kasich actively sought major tax rate increases while in office. All but one of the states that extract some appreciable amounts of natural gas, oil, or coal has established such a tax (see table 2.2).[36] The lone major production state

Table 2.3
US carbon pricing revenues by year (in millions USD), 2010–2015.

Carbon Pricing Mechanism	2010	2011	2012	2013	2014	2015
Severance Tax[a]	11,095	15,608	17,048	17,221	17,509	11,587
Carbon Tax	0	0	0	0	0	0
Cap-and-Trade[b]	296	171	181	767	825	2,453

a. US Department of Commerce Census Bureau, "Quarterly Summary of State and Local Taxes," accessed November 15, 2016, https://www.census.gov/govs/qtax/.
b. Regional Greenhouse Gas Initiative (RGGI), "Auction Results: Allowance Prices and Volumes," accessed April 10, 2016, https://www.rggi.org/market/co2 _auctions/results#state_proceeds; California Environmental Protection Agency, Air Resources Board, "Cap-and-Trade Program," http://www.arb.ca.gov/cc/capandtrade /capandtrade.htm; California Air Resources Board (CARB), Climate Investments Branch, *Annual Report to the Legislature on Investments of Cap-and-Trade Auction Proceeds* (Sacramento, CA: CARB, 2015), http://www.arb.ca.gov/cc/capandtrade /auctionproceeds/2015ggrf-annual-report-to-legislature.pdf.

lacking such a tax, Pennsylvania, was led by a governor who was elected in 2014 on a platform to enact one.[37] Collectively, these states raised far more from these taxes annually between 2010 and 2015 than the total revenue generated by all state cap-and-trade and carbon tax programs combined during that period (see table 2.3).

Such a base of political consensus might seem far-fetched until one enters the arena of severance taxes. In these instances, governments do impose a tax on fossil fuels, but at the point of their extraction from below the surface of the earth rather than at the point of purchasing a refined product. Mine a ton of coal in Illinois or Montana (and every other state extracting coal) and you pay a severance tax on its gross value or volume. Drill and extract a barrel of oil in Michigan or Texas (and every other state producing oil) and you pay a similar tax. Drill and withdraw a cubic foot of natural gas in Colorado or North Carolina (and every other state producing natural gas except Pennsylvania) and the same tax rules apply. Most states extracting more than one type of fossil fuel have separate legislation and taxes for each fuel.

A few states have experimented with setting rates far below those of neighboring states as they try to create incentives for expanded drilling. Mississippi, Oklahoma, and even climate-conscious California have been prominent examples in the 2010s. Most states have resisted pressures to place rates at extremely low levels, even amid the mid-2010s plunge in fossil fuel prices and concerns about adverse state economic impacts from declining fossil fuel development.[38] The politics of launching and sustaining severance taxes are just too attractive to ignore given their ability to export most of the costs to citizens from other jurisdictions. That has made these tax policies both popular and stable over time, despite considerable opposition from oil and gas extraction firms that regularly threaten to move operations to states or nations with gentler tax treatment.

The federal government has deferred to states in this area of taxation on privately held land. It has long since created its own version of such a tax via royalties but only on federally held lands where fossil fuel drilling occurs.[39] The federal government has kept its rates quite modest for many decades, well below most state royalties for extraction on state lands, one of many ways it subsidizes fossil fuel production. But it places no restriction on overlapping state severance taxes. The lone point of serious consideration of federal encroachment on this area of state tax authority occurred during the 1980s. In this case, members of Congress from predominantly Democratic states with little or no fossil fuel production sponsored hearings at which they alleged state severance taxes were out of control and harming their constituents by inflating their energy costs. Their goal was federal preemption of state severance taxes to keep energy prices low for their constituents, indifferent to environmental or climate concerns.

This attempt was crushed by a vigorous counteroffensive led by a diverse coalition of tax supporters from energy-producing states. Many leaders of this response were among the most visible opponents of numerous forms of federal and state taxation, while making a noteworthy exception in this case. In a typical comment during Senate debate, Wyoming Republican Malcolm Wallop thundered, "No one can calculate the impact of oil loss, of erosion, of loss of habitat for wildlife. Who makes the judgment that it exceeds legitimate social costs? Have you been to Wyoming and seen those social costs?"[40]

Social costs and their possible remediation through tax revenues, however, were only part of the attraction of severance taxes. For most states that mine or drill for fossil fuels, most of their product, once converted into refined form, is ultimately consumed either in another American state or in another nation. States like Alaska and Wyoming consume less than 1 percent of the energy that they produce. Even leading energy production and consumption states such as Texas and California regularly export most of their oil and natural gas output.[41]

Consequently, state severance taxes offer governments the option of imposing a price on fossil fuels at the point of their extraction rather than consumption. So they offer a unique opportunity to impose a price on carbon, with the likelihood that most costs will be passed along to consumers located somewhere else. As one Republican member of the House of Representatives noted, this approach to state taxation was part of a common pattern. He noted comparable cases such as Nevada with gambling-focused taxation, Florida with special taxes related to tourism, and Delaware with special taxes linked to its attractive incorporation system.[42] These points were integrated into a vigorous defense of high state severance taxes by Richard "Dick" Cheney, then Wyoming's lone member of Congress and not generally perceived as a proponent of carbon pricing.

This helps explain why some forms of fossil fuel taxes cannot only be politically feasible but even broadly attractive. They can significantly elevate the costs of fossil fuels for national public use by making extraction more expensive, while shifting most of those costs elsewhere rather than concentrating them within their boundaries. Severance taxes produce significant revenues, especially when production and market prices are high. Some states use funds to mitigate the social costs of fossil fuel extraction but most revenue is used for other purposes such as funding the general budget or K-12 and higher education while keeping other tax rates low.

All of this serves to explain why nearly every state with fossil fuel reserves has adopted some version of a severance tax. As reflected in table 2.2, the adoption and diffusion pattern of this form of a carbon price looks fundamentally different from what we have seen to date in American states with other prominent carbon price options. While severance taxes receive far less scholarly and media attention than carbon pricing, politicians have long been aware of them and their political attractiveness.[43]

Severance taxes provide politicians with a far easier path to carbon pricing than what is offered by a carbon tax or cap-and-trade. With severance taxes, the political risks are comparatively low and potential revenue dividends quite high. These taxes could be characterized as a step toward deterring fossil fuel use because prices would likely increase, thereby discouraging consumption and reducing carbon emissions. Even if climate concerns were not a driver behind severance tax adoption, as has been the case to date, the politics would still be promising. Either way, the price remains in place over time and the revenue flows with little internal political blame, contrary to the political experience to date with other forms of carbon pricing.

3   Why Carbon Pricing Has Often Failed

Carbon pricing appeared to be riding a huge political wave in the middle years of the first decade of the twenty-first century. Any political impediments appeared destined to be swept away by a growing bandwagon of supporters. Europe launched an Emissions Trading Scheme with considerable fanfare in 2005. It claimed global leadership through the design of a continent-wide cap-and-trade system that built on the key principles of the hallowed US sulfur dioxide trading program. But that was only the beginning, according to the conventional wisdom of the period.

A growing number of American states and Canadian provinces also began to adopt their own form of carbon pricing, following small experiments in Massachusetts (2001) and New Hampshire (2002). Most of these states intended to pursue cross-jurisdictional coordination of their efforts to ensure the largest possible carbon market. These efforts further prompted the US Congress and the Canadian Parliament to explore their own carbon pricing options, quite possibly building on these sub-federal experiments. Carbon pricing discussions also accelerated on other continents, most notably Asia. Carbon pricing seemed inevitable, with early experiments commonly expected to evolve into an international carbon market.

Consequently, an idea long embraced by economists as good policy in theory also seemed to hold promise in the real world of politics. There were still questions about the exact political path to carbon pricing adoption and the final shape of such a policy. But it all seemed politically plausible if not inevitable, a potential triumph for ideational policy whereby an attractive policy idea ultimately wears down political opposition. Implicit in much of the advocacy for carbon pricing was the assumption that it would eventually be adopted and then transition through various stages of implementation, or what we are describing as the policy life-cycle. Existing governmental agencies could launch the policy, political support would endure and expand over time, viable long-term management would arise, and evidence would emerge on policy performance that demonstrated emission reductions achieved alongside modest costs. Anyone seriously questioning that presumed scenario tended to be dismissed as a cynic or disloyal to the cause. What was not to like?

Early Bids for Leadership Roles

A range of political leaders from across the political spectrum began to embrace some version of carbon pricing during this period, seeming to augur well for future political prospects. In many instances, they were responding to early evidence of the impacts of climate change on their jurisdictions. This offered the potential to get in early on a transformational moment that would offer handsome economic and political dividends, including a possible legacy of being a visionary leader. Early engagement in climate pricing might foster innovation in energy development and distribution, possibly boosting domestic energy sources. For leaders more politically ambitious, it also provided a chance of elevation to a larger national or international stage.

Republican governors like California's Arnold Schwarzenegger and New York's George Pataki quickly come to mind in this regard. Schwarzenegger championed and signed far-reaching climate legislation in California, implicitly placing cap-and-trade at its core. This bill, called the Global Warming Solutions Act, became law in 2006 after multiple signing ceremonies around the state. These events featured celebrity attendees and garnered state, national, and global media coverage. This adoption helped propel Schwarzenegger to election to a full term and stamp him as far more than a political fluke. Pataki worked quietly from Albany rather than Times Square. His efforts to build a regional version of cap-and-trade positioned him as a cross-continental rival to Schwarzenegger in carbon pricing leadership. Pataki thought this step would help propel him to the presidency, perhaps as early as 2008, much as early engagement on environmental issues had boosted the standing of another New York Republican governor, Theodore Roosevelt, nearly a century before.[1] The New York case will be explored more fully in chapter 5, followed by California in chapter 6.

The race to the top of carbon pricing policy development was hardly confined to big-name leaders of major American states. Consider Gary Doer, the premier of Manitoba in central Canada. Manitoba is a large province, though its territory is sparsely inhabited. Fewer than 1.3 million people live in the province, the majority of whom reside in or near the capital city of Winnipeg. Manitoba has long relied on bounteous supplies of hydroelectricity for more than 95 percent of its electricity, and its carbon footprint was negligible compared to provinces such as Alberta and Ontario.

Doer, however, decided to elevate climate change as a top political issue to make his province a national, continental, and global leader during his 1999–2009 premiership. The premier noted changing weather patterns and emerging threats to transportation and "traditional ways of life on the land," while placing particular emphasis on risks to Manitoba's polar bears.[2] Alongside climate championing came policy opportunity. Doer argued that Manitoba might help mitigate climate change through policies that simultaneously foster far-reaching economic development. Under this model, Manitoba hoped to discover ways to significantly expand its hydroelectric power generation, becoming a supplier to eastern provinces and north-central states. By expanding transmission systems, Manitoba could increase electricity production and maximize electricity exports. In addition, it aimed to develop its considerable wind energy capacity alongside hydro, coupled with a major energy efficiency campaign to drive down provincial carbon emissions via demand side reduction programs and grid improvements.[3]

With this emerging arena of carbon markets and trading, Manitoba leaders claimed that Winnipeg had the potential to evolve into a national or international hub for carbon trading, even utilizing downtown buildings originally used to market agricultural commodities. The province was well positioned to supplement these efforts with expanded development of "homegrown" biofuels and the creation of a fertile market for carbon offsets that might be swapped with other, more industrialized jurisdictions. Carbon pricing would be the ticket to this bold new future.

A provincial action plan led to the formation of a Task Force on Emissions Trading and the Manitoba Economy. This group produced a 2004 report that embraced an expedited development of a provincial cap-and-trade system. Backed by a diverse and prominent set of stakeholders, the report offered a vision whereby Manitoba would move promptly to launch a carbon emissions trading system by 2006, thereby seizing upon its "natural

advantage in offsets and clean electricity." The report outlined the numerous steps the provincial government could take to establish its program
before other Canadian provinces to become a national leader, including the
purchase of offsets to jumpstart operations.[4]

Doer and his provincial leadership team endorsed this vision whole-
heartedly and took a series of prominent steps that gained considerable
attention in Canada and beyond. Manitoba became a founding member
of the Chicago Climate Exchange (CCX), a heavily publicized nonprofit
organization that defined itself as "a self-regulatory exchange that admin-
isters the world's first multi-national marketplace for reducing and trading
GHG emissions."[5] It established the Manitoba Climate Trust to guide internal
carbon market system development and consolidated many climate-related
components of the provincial government into the new Department of
Energy, Science, and Technology (EST). The EST led Manitoba's preparations
for the new cap-and-trade program and for the public management challenges
of an expansive climate mitigation effort.[6]

Doer then traveled to actively recruit partners for his vision, building on
the CCX agreement with a formal embrace of California's efforts. Doer was
the only foreign head of state who spoke in person at the California bill
signing ceremony and entered into a memorandum of cooperation with
Governor Schwarzenegger on climate change. Upon being named (along
with Schwarzenegger) as a leader in the fight against climate change by a
leading international business magazine, Doer noted that "certainly both
Manitoba and California have been recognized as world leaders."[7]

Manitoba gained further visibility when it became the only province
or state to join not just one but two separate regional cap-and-trade organizations. In 2007, Doer joined forces with California to become a member of
the burgeoning Western Climate Initiative (WCI) along with six other states
and three provinces. He also turned toward the Midwest that year, becoming the lone provincial signatory to the Midwestern Greenhouse Gas Reduction Accord (MGGRA), which was formed in 2007 to build a "market-based
and multi-sector cap-and-trade mechanism to help achieve GHG reduction
targets."[8] Manitoba also became the lone province to join a cluster of upper
midwestern states in Powering the Prairies, an organization designed to
promote development of renewable energy and to link these efforts with
emerging carbon credit trading systems.

By the end of 2007, Manitoba appeared to be a rising carbon pricing power. Its premier was a notable carbon pricing policy entrepreneur, with visibility far beyond his provincial boundaries. Doer remained premier for two more years and then was succeeded by another member of his New Democratic Party after a full decade in power. The carbon pricing future appeared boundless, with few enduring political downsides.

Doer, Schwarzenegger, and Pataki were hardly alone. Illinois's dynamic young governor, Democrat Rod Blagojevich, largely followed the Manitoba playbook, including CCX membership, a leadership role in forming the MGGRA, partnerships with California, and a series of efforts to promote state-based renewables. "America's heartland is ready to lead our nation toward a smarter, cleaner energy future because Illinois and the Midwest can't—and won't—wait for federal action," said Blagojevich in celebrating his state's entry into MGGRA. "We can have economic prosperity, energy security, and a healthy environment at the same time."[9]

His Minnesota counterpart, Republican Tim Pawlenty, echoed these words and prepared for MGGRA membership by signing climate legislation just before its launch. On the day he signed the Next Generation Energy Act, setting statewide greenhouse gas (GHG) emission reduction targets and expanding energy efficiency programs, he said, "Here in Minnesota we are kick-starting the future by increasing our nation-leading per capita renewable fuel use, boosting cost-saving measures and tackling greenhouse gas emissions." Pawlenty, who would begin pursuit of his party's presidential nomination just a few years later, heralded the arrival of the MGGRA: "Today's agreement is an important milestone toward achieving a cleaner, more secure energy future. The Midwest is well positioned to help lead the energy revolution that our nation needs to stay competitive and strong."[10]

Cap-and-trade was at the heart of MGGRA, and there appeared to be virtually no political ceiling on these efforts to create and expand this form of carbon pricing. If Europe could launch a cap-and-trade system and nearly half of the US states and Canadian provinces were developing their own proposals into regional packages, large-scale policy diffusion might be inevitable. Three separate regional entities, representing jurisdictions in the West, the Midwest, and the Northeast, began to explore ways in which they might ultimately merge in what some described as a "three regions" process.[11] It was commonly thought that these regions would continue to acquire state, provincial, and even international partners and ultimately transition into a national, continental, or global system.[12]

However, more than a decade later, very little of this proposed system still exists. Virtually none of the policies that Manitoba unveiled in the 2000s were adopted by the 2010s. The CCX closed its doors in 2010 and the MGGRA ended operations in the following year. Though launched with much fanfare, the MGGRA staff coordinator acknowledged that few people noticed when even its website was dissolved.[13]

No new states adopted carbon cap-and-trade in the subsequent decade and both national governments spurned such proposals. Carbon taxes were discussed but rarely considered in either sub-federal or federal capitals. Even California's multijurisdictional and multinational cap-and-trade partnership via the WCI fizzled. All but one of its original ten partners had abandoned ship within four years. Quebec was the lone survivor, unlike Manitoba.

There is likewise no evidence to suggest that early embrace of carbon pricing paid political dividends for state and provincial political champions during this period. Doer ultimately served as the Canadian ambassador to the United States, but in an administration hostile to any form of carbon pricing. Blagojevich would be in federal prison within a few years for corruption charges, and Pawlenty would rapidly backtrack on earlier climate engagement as he made a serious presidential nomination bid in 2012. Schwarzenegger faced steady and enduring erosion in his public support after securing election to a full term in 2006; he returned to his former pursuits as a film actor, thereby ending his role in cross-jurisdictional climate diplomacy. Pataki would eventually seek the Republican presidential nomination in 2016 but withdrew after failing to curry any consequential support.

This chapter explores the challenging political path to carbon pricing adoption in these and many other jurisdictions. It considers policies across a life-cycle in which policy formation and adoption are only the beginning. This approach further explores each subsequent political and managerial stage that a policy must navigate over time before it can be declared durable and robust. We shall explore a number of cases that sputtered at various points along this continuum, before yielding in subsequent chapters to a small set of cases that have successfully navigated the policy life-cycle during their first decade and offer evidence of reaching intended performance goals.

The Limits of Engaging Policy Ideas

These rejections of carbon pricing elsewhere shattered earlier expectations that such policies would endure and proliferate to other states, provinces, and regions. They would demonstrate the danger of overestimating the power of an idea, even one as elegant and compelling as carbon pricing, to easily surmount political hurdles. Such ideas can potentially captivate the public and elected officials, particularly if they are linked to a compelling model case or precedent that might suggest prospects of emulation.[14] But the carbon pricing experience demonstrates the risks of assuming that ideational forces can melt significant bases of opposition.

Carbon pricing advocates had relentlessly referred to the storied American experience of sulfur dioxide as their model. The story was indeed compelling. In that instance, the idea of a trading system rather than command-and-control regulation ultimately helped forge a broad coalition to confront the challenge of reducing sulfur dioxide emissions and the threat of acid deposition, as is discussed further in chapter 5. This one-time coalition ultimately cut across partisan and regional lines in Congress, winning overwhelming support in 1990 at a time when relations between parties and among branches of government were strained. The quick launch of the trading system and recognition that emission reductions could be achieved in a surprisingly cost-effective way gave the program an aura that would make it politically untouchable in subsequent decades.

It was understandably appealing for advocates, including many scholars, to suggest that use of the same policy tool (cap-and-trade) to address climate change could be expected to advance down a similar political path. This offered an attractive model of path dependence, whereby a larger-than-life prior case could be replicated in a later one with some parallels. This extrapolation ignored that the sulfur dioxide case was quite unusual. This cap-and-trade program was eased by the opportunity to procure readily available coal alternatives—namely, domestic coal with lower sulfur content. One straightforward option toward compliance was expanded use of low-sulfur coal from Montana and Wyoming's vast supply. Their elected leaders were far more favorably disposed to a policy that might actually increase their local coal production than one that might marginalize their state's output. These Powder River Basin states were further aided by federal legislation passed in 1980 to deregulate freight rail transportation, easing the challenge of national coal distribution.

The advantages did not end there. Technology to "scrub" and reduce sulfur dioxide emissions was also readily available and provided an alternative compliance route. In turn, the entire sulfur cap-and-trade system was confined only to coal-burning electricity plants, which had long been scrutinized by government regulators. This led to a fairly straightforward regulatory oversight process, even when adding a trading component.

Carbon, in contrast, presents a far more complex challenge, both technically and politically. There is no credible version of "low-carbon coal," as any variation in actual carbon content across coal types is quite minor. There also is a lack of established technology to replicate the reliable cleansing capacity of sulfur dioxide scrubbers for carbon emissions. In turn, carbon emissions emanate from far more sources and sectors than just coal-fired electricity generation, creating a far more complex set of policy challenges.

As a result, carbon pricing faces a far more substantial set of political hurdles and, as we have learned, not just at the initial stage of policy adoption. Policy must pass through an extended life-cycle with distinct stages. Each of these stages may present significant political challenges to the survival of a policy, calling into question its ability to endure over time. Each of these stages will be explored more fully in subsequent sections.

The balance of this chapter will examine cases where one or more of these stages proved to be fundamental stumbling blocks, leading to policy rejection, termination, or reversal. Conversely, chapters 4 and 5 will examine a small set of cases that cleared each of these hurdles. These policies endured over time, demonstrating some capacity to deliver on expectations of policy performance.

Failing the Political Adoption Test

Bills are routinely introduced into legislative bodies with little or no chance of adoption. These may be intended to allow a legislator to showcase commitment to constituents, while not expecting any success. They may also be designed to draw attention to an issue and a possible policy response, perhaps setting the stage for future reintroduction when political support and policy saliency are greater. Dozens of carbon pricing bills, for example, were introduced into respective Congresses from the mid-1990s through the end of 2008. None secured passage by either the House or Senate, much less full congressional approval. Instead, most received an initial flurry of attention from media and select advocacy groups and then disappeared. A few would receive consideration in a legislative hearing or two but then fade away. None of these bills were adopted and their proponents likely never saw them as serious candidates for approval.

There are also moments where the introduction of a bill is politically significant. In such cases, there is a serious possibility of a vote and adoption, as well as accompanying expectations of a long operational life. This usually indicates a significant base of support, one that may cross partisan lines and respective branches of government. Presidents (and governors) and their lead advisers may take an active role by publicly endorsing legislative proposals or even working directly with legislators to draft the proposal. These proposals go beyond showcasing and symbolism toward an expectation of actual policy adoption.

The first stage of the political life-cycle thus poses the following question: *Is there a sufficient political foundation to adopt a carbon pricing policy?* Twenty-three US states and four Canadian provinces were able to construct such a political foundation for cap-and-trade between 2000 and 2008, either through legislation or actions by a governor or premier. During this period, twenty-eight member states of the European Union (EU) achieved a similar political outcome. A considerably smaller set of jurisdictions outside the United States, including one Canadian province, also established a meaningful carbon tax in these years. In contrast, the majority of US states and Canadian provinces never adopted either a cap-and-trade or carbon tax policy between 2000 and 2015. Neither Congress nor Parliament came particularly close to adopting one either.

These divided results indicate that carbon pricing can indeed surmount this challenge of initial political adoption, at least in some instances. However, these adoption cases were concentrated in a specific time period and dominated by governors and premiers using their power of persuasion and innovation. These entrepreneurial executives and their supporters also proved successful in framing the case for early political action as both a response to evidence of climate change within their boundaries and as an economic development opportunity. This may explain why there was considerable leadership from members of multiple political parties, as these steps occurred before the emergence of greater partisan divides on these issues. These leaders demonstrated considerable ability to move fairly quickly on an issue when a window of opportunity arose. Much of this squares with the classic formulation of the converging streams approach to policy formation.[15] But it only represents the first stage in a potentially long and contentious policy life-cycle. These policies will ultimately advance along this life-cycle where they will face subsequent challenges.

Getting BTU'd in the Clinton Era

Many serious policy proposals flounder at this initial stage, not just those associated with carbon pricing. This occurs even when political prospects for adoption seem strong. In 1992, for example, a dynamic young president named Bill Clinton was elected with substantial majorities of his Democratic Party in both chambers of Congress. He decided to make health care reform a centerpiece of his first term in office, calling for bold action in a special address to Congress and the nation. He placed his wife, Hillary Rodham Clinton, in a leadership role to develop a viable proposal and see it through to passage. A major health care policy appeared inevitable before the 1994 midterm elections. With this health care reform momentum, Clinton anticipated a successful bid for a second term in 1996.

Clinton would indeed win that election but only after a humiliating health care policy rejection. Existing health care providers feared reforms that might cost them income and alter the status quo. Established patients feared interruption of existing insurance programs and care delivery. The Hillary Clinton–led policy development process consumed many months of the legislative cycle and also proved controversial given its secretive style of operations. Plus, the proposal was so complicated and confusing that it failed to capture the public imagination and instead became a target for critiques.

The failure to build support within Congress and key constituencies forced President Clinton and allies into desperate attempts to continually bargain to keep some possibility of health care reform alive. It never happened. Indeed, neither the House nor Senate even took a vote on any major health care proposal during the 103rd Congress, much less passed anything. This debacle contributed directly to the stunning reversals demonstrated in the 1994 elections that restored Republican control of the House for the first time in more than four decades. This triggered a cottage industry of analysis by scholars and journalists on whether the rejection of Clinton

Care reflected merely a set of tactical blunders by an inexperienced president or rather a textbook example of how certain issues have no viable path forward.[16]

Health care reform, however, was not the only political adoption test failure of the Clinton presidency. Each of Clinton's four immediate predecessors, three Republicans and one Democrat, explored the possibility of a narrow form of carbon pricing. However, their proposals to increase federal gasoline excise taxes were driven by the need for added governmental revenue rather than environmental protection. This led Ronald Reagan to approve a five-cent-per-gallon increase in 1983 and George H. W. Bush to follow suit with an identical hike in 1990. Both were linked to broader deficit reduction goals, confined to gasoline, and without any serious consideration of environmental consequences.

Clinton altered that calculus by returning to energy taxation in a broader way. Clinton was prodded by Vice President Al Gore to support a "BTU tax," which taxes the heat content of respective fossil fuels.[17] Clinton had not campaigned on fossil fuel taxation and had, in fact, opposed further gasoline tax increases. However, the BTU tax was seen as a way to produce considerable revenue for chronic deficit concerns. It also offered a response to environmental problems, including climate change, caused by fossil fuel use. So the Clinton administration endorsed this proposal as part of an overall fiscal reform plan.

Unlike the health care proposal, a version of the BTU tax was vetted in the House and approved on a 219-to-213 vote. Every Republican member along with thirty-nine Democrats voted against it, demonstrating the considerable sensitivity to a policy that would increase energy prices.[18] The BTU tax then faced stiff political opposition in the Senate from a wide range of Republicans and Democrats. This reflected political worries about increased energy costs for consumers and manufacturers, all of whom would be sensitive to price increases and would be likely to vote unfavorably in reaction.[19] Consequently, the BTU tax died in the Senate and was later downsized into another modest gasoline tax hike. Gore exercised his vice presidential powers in breaking a 49-to-49 Senate tie, reflecting opposition from all forty-three Republicans and six Democrats. This resulted in a 4.3-cent-per-gallon tax increase that would produce revenue for transportation infrastructure.[20]

There were significant political consequences for some House Democrats who had backed the BTU tax in the 1994 midterm elections, in many cases linked to their support of the failed health care initiative. This experience had bracing effects on subsequent carbon pricing proposals in Congress, living on in the memory of politicians and the public. "Getting BTU'd" endured as a catchphrase that warned politicians against pursuing any policy that might increase energy prices and trigger public ire, even if linked with such causes as deficit reduction and infrastructure repair.

The Cap-and-Trade Moment Arrives—Then Fades

Policy ideas can have second acts (or more) after initial political failure. Health care is no exception. Nor is carbon pricing. Less than two decades after the election of Bill Clinton, another young and dynamic Democrat was elected who would revisit the question of carbon pricing. The Barack Obama era shared some significant parallels with the Clinton years. It also represented some important political features suggesting that the BTU tax rejection might be an anomaly. Thus, it appeared the United States was on the verge of a new era of carbon pricing through far-reaching legislation that would be adopted in 2009 or 2010.

As political scientists Paul Posner, Timothy Conlan, and David Beam have noted, there are multiple paths to securing adoption of major domestic legislation in the United States. A *partisan path* seeks to secure a unified majority party base and pick up other supporters where possible. A *pluralist path* engages diverse interests to build a broad coalition of stakeholders. An *expert path* draws on ideas from researchers or practitioners to provide a solid ideational foundation, explain the policy, and seek supporters. A *symbolic path* engages the broader public with appealing ideas for new policy. It is quite possible for one or two paths to be dominant in any particular policy adoption process. Yet Posner, Conlan, and Beam note that "good public policy should be the product of all four pathways. Each brings unique comparative advantages to policymaking."[21] Use of multiple paths might indicate a broader base of initial political support and suggest a more promising, long-term prospect for success.

Much like Clinton, Obama entered office with a significant *partisan* wave, not only giving him a decisive Electoral College victory but also returning significant Democratic majorities in both chambers for the first time since the early Clinton years. All four pathways appeared open to the new president in 2009. Unlike the BTU tax idea that only surfaced after the 1992 election, Obama had campaigned on the idea of carbon pricing in 2008, as had most of his rivals for the Democratic Party nomination. A number of carbon pricing bills were introduced by Democrats in both chambers in the half-decade prior to his election. Many of these had formal cosponsorship from Republicans, particularly in the Senate. These included his defeated rival, John McCain, who had cosponsored several carbon pricing bills with Democrats as a senator and further endorsed this approach during his presidential campaign. It appeared that the new president began with a solid base of support for carbon pricing from his own party but might reasonably be able to extend that across the aisle.

Obama also began with a more extensive and *pluralistic* base of supporters who offered the prospect of a broad coalition. The US Climate Action Partnership (CAP) represented a broad amalgam of twenty-six major corporations and five major environmental groups that sought to create a consensus position on carbon pricing and offer a model proposal. CAP built on an earlier series of stakeholder dialogues convened by the then–Pew Center on Global Climate Change and issued a broad statement of principles in 2007. It later released a major report, *Blueprint for Legislative Action*, just before Obama's inauguration.[22]

CAP also coalesced with a wide *expert* body of economists and policy analysts who jettisoned any idea of a carbon tax in favor of cap-and-trade. This represented a major shift from the BTU experience and its explicit reference to taxation as a tool of cost imposition. Instead, cap-and-trade proponents dominated congressional hearings on climate policy. They repeatedly invoked cap-and-trade as a proven method based on the sulfur dioxide experience, predicting that overall costs would be modest, with most deferred until well into operation. They claimed it could feature provisions, such as offsets, that would ease compliance issues. As Edward Markey, a cosponsor of the American Clean Energy and Security Act (ACES) and Democratic House member from Massachusetts, noted, "I am aware of the economic arguments for a carbon tax, but politics is the art of the possible, and I think cap-and-trade is possible."[23]

There was also a *symbolic* reframing of the ultimate purpose of the proposal. Climate change mitigation was indeed a driving motivational factor but in many respects it was eclipsed by the argument that cap-and-trade could drive substantial economic growth through alternative energy development.

This represented a broad appeal to seek support from individuals who might harbor doubts about climate change but surely would not want to inhibit technological progress that might transform the American economy.

Just months into his presidency, Obama welcomed the May 2009 House endorsement of the American Clean Energy and Security Act, better known as Waxman-Markey for its cosponsors. This included a cap-and-trade program with national emission targets as well as a national renewable portfolio standard. Many of these provisions included sweeteners to particular industries or congressional districts, ranging from exemptions to subsidies. The legislation continually swelled to more than 1,400 pages upon arrival on the House floor, including 300 pages added the night before the vote. This was hardly a model bill from an economics perspective and became so complex that it proved difficult to frame politically. Nonetheless, it was able to win support in one chamber. President Obama signaled his enthusiastic reaction, eager to sign a carbon pricing bill once it passed the Senate.

That moment never arrived. One indicator of the limited political feasibility of a cap-and-trade bill in 2009 or 2010 was the very narrow House victory. Only eight Republicans supported the ACES bill and forty-four Democrats defected, leading to a 219-to-212 vote that had numerous parallels with the House vote in favor of a BTU tax sixteen years earlier. The Senate posed more daunting challenges, including its greater representation of states with strong fossil fuel interests and supermajority rules for moving legislation forward. In turn, Obama, Congress, and the nation became increasingly mired in issues other than carbon pricing. Agenda attention for cap-and-trade struggled when weighed against the competition from the Great Recession recovery process, health care reform, and foreign policy, as well as growing indications of far-reaching partisan divides on many issues.

As in the case of the BTU tax, there was growing fear that carbon pricing was a political loser. Republicans almost universally abandoned earlier support and argued that any variation on ACES would have devastating economic consequences. Many Democrats also became increasingly leery as the 2010 elections loomed and triggered memories of the backlash experienced in 1994. A groundswell of public support for climate change action never materialized, much less support for efforts to combat it through a pricing strategy. As energy policy analyst Michael Levi noted, "An economic crisis combined with intense political polarization turned cap-and-trade into a dirty word and a political non-starter."[24]

A number of last-ditch efforts in 2010 to salvage some agreement in the Senate failed. Whereas the BTU rejection ultimately led to a modest compromise over a gasoline tax hike, the demise of a carbon pricing bill did not produce any legislative alternatives before the 2010 election. This featured some parallels to the Clinton health care rejection, similarly triggering a series of scholarly and journalistic debates over whether this outcome was inevitable or reflected political blunders in designing the carbon pricing bill.[25]

House passage of ACES in May 2009 was the final time either chamber of Congress voted on a carbon pricing bill—much less approved one—through at least the end of 2015. This was also a watershed moment for state policy engagement. Not a single state legislature adopted either a cap-and-trade or carbon tax bill during this period. What once seemed a policy inevitability now appeared a daunting political stretch. The carbon pricing issue became more polarized and partisan at both federal and state levels in the United States during this period, as noted in chapter 2, continuing to confront serious political hurdles to adoption. The opponents of ACES chanted in the moments after its narrow approval on the floor of the House, "BTU, BTU, BTU...." As in 1993, imposing a price on carbon remained a heavy political lift in the United States.

The Carbon Tax Moment Never Arrives

This was not, however, a uniquely American political problem nor one confined to cap-and-trade. In the United States, no academic carbon pricing advocate has entered the political arena to attempt to secure adoption of a pricing policy through an election bid.[26] In Canada, social scientist-turned-prime ministerial hopeful Stéphane Dion set that precedent. As leader of the center-left Liberal Party, he sought election as prime minister in 2008, making a carbon tax proposal a centerpiece of his campaign. Known as the "Green Shift," Dion advanced a plan to launch a carbon tax at $10 (Canadian) per ton in 2009 and then make annual $10 increases until reaching the $40 level by 2012. Revenues would be used to reduce the rates of personal and business taxes, provide targeted tax credits, and also suspend the federal gasoline excise tax for four years.

Dion reversed gears from a 2006 party leadership bid, in which he opposed carbon pricing in favor of a "Project Green" strategy to expand federal investments in renewable energy and energy efficiency. He reached a new position for his 2008 campaign without close consultation with key advisers or polling, instead having convinced himself of his ability to sell Canadians on the idea of a carbon tax. One adviser, economist Marc Jaccard, warned Dion that such a tax was "good policy but bad politics."[27] However, Dion responded that "I believe good policy *is* good politics," confident that he could achieve both electoral and policy success through the power of the carbon tax idea and his political communication skills.[28]

History, in this case, would vindicate Jaccard. Opposition from the Conservative Party and standing Prime Minister Stephen Harper was particularly aggressive and effective in attacking the policy, with public messaging suggesting that the Green Shift would lead to major energy price increases. More surprising was a lukewarm reception from Dion's political left, including firm opposition from the leadership of the New Democratic Party and a mixed and somewhat muted reaction from a number of prominent environmental groups and foundations. These latter carbon tax opponents generally expressed strong concerns about climate change and supported nearly all policy options except a carbon price. They based their opposition on concerns over anticipated economic impact on lower-income groups. So Dion was caught in the middle and it was far narrower than expected. In 2008, his Liberal Party ultimately received only 26 percent of the national vote, the lowest total in its history, and saw its membership in Parliament plunge from 133 to only 77 seats out of 307. Dion resigned shortly after the election and there was no serious federal government effort to resurrect carbon pricing through the end of 2015.[29] Other Asian-Pacific governments, including Australia, Japan, and New Zealand, would similarly watch early prospects of carbon pricing flounder. In these cases, economist Alice Rivlin's rule of policy adoption continues to be applicable: "Perhaps there is not yet sufficient political consensus on this question to justify moves toward a policy commitment device in this area. In which case, the political battle has to be won first."[30]

Failing the Policy Launch Test

Carbon pricing did manage to pass the political adoption test in a number of jurisdictions. Twenty-three American states and four Canadian provinces followed the European Union's lead in making a commitment to carbon cap-and-trade. Despite the travails over carbon pricing in such capitals as Washington, DC, Ottawa, and Canberra, among other places, there was evidence to suggest that multiple sub-federal jurisdictions could clear an initial political adoption hurdle.

But new policies do not automatically implement. In early stages of interpretation and operation by administrative agencies they may be particularly fragile. This can hold true even when there is no immediate election or change of government. The public might have second thoughts about a particular policy shortly after adoption, especially if certain features begin to surface that had been overlooked or downplayed during the adoption process. Opponents may highlight these features following adoption, attempting either to delay implementation or scuttle the policy.[31]

Policies may prove highly vulnerable at this stage if they were not backed by broad and strong coalitional support bases during adoption. Perhaps they were never carefully vetted during an enthusiastic sweep toward adoption. This is frequently seen with policies advanced largely by a single policy entrepreneur. Elected leaders of the executive branch, such as an American president or state governor, have considerable latitude to prod the legislative chamber to respond cooperatively. These policy entrepreneurs also have substantial authority to act unilaterally through executive orders, signed statements, administrative reinterpretations, or memoranda of intent or understanding.

Use of executive power allows for rapid policy development but can also prove highly vulnerable to backlash. This occurs particularly at points where other elected officials must become engaged to operationalize and sustain the policy. In 1997, former Vice President Gore faced such backlash after achieving what initially appeared to be a major climate policy accomplishment. Despite his deep commitment to the international climate process, Gore did not originally plan to participate in Kyoto Protocol negotiations. However, he agreed to attend in the latter stages once it appeared that a deadlock was likely without dramatic intervention.

Gore ultimately played a significant role in brokering an agreement at Kyoto that was internationally heralded as a breakthrough. To get a deal he had to make significant concessions in the American bargaining position, including considerably deeper emission cuts than planned. As a result, any international accolades were offset by a firestorm of domestic political opposition. These Kyoto concessions indicated the need for a major American climate mitigation bill, most likely some form of carbon pricing, to hit carbon emission reduction targets. But there was no serious political base of support to pursue such legislation. In turn, Kyoto was rapidly deemed "dead on arrival" in the US Senate, which holds constitutional ratification authority for treaties. The Clinton administration never actively sought approval and Kyoto ultimately struggled mightily in all stages of implementation.[32] Moreover, Gore did not make Kyoto ratification or some form of carbon pricing a major emphasis in his ill-fated 2000 presidential campaign. So the initial American commitment had substantially dissolved by the time President George W. Bush formally pulled the plug in 2001.

The second stage of the policy life-cycle thus poses the following question: *Is there a sufficient political foundation to allow for the initial and successful launch of a policy prior to any subsequent election or change of political leadership?* The experiences of a number of states and provinces that adopted some form of cap-and-trade confirm that this stage can create a significant stumbling block not only to short-term implementation outcomes but also to policy survival.

Policies that will impose some form of direct cost may be particularly vulnerable to scrutiny after initial adoption, a reality not confined to energy. A few years before the Clinton administration health care debacle, a far-reaching agreement was reached to expand a key area of Medicare health care support for senior citizens. This agreement extended insurance coverage for so-called catastrophic cases in which highly extended and expensive care proved necessary. Under previous Medicare coverage, there was a gap that could leave seniors vulnerable to prolonged illness and staggering bills, jeopardizing their financial security.

The Medicare Catastrophic Coverage Act of 1988 was designed to remedy this shortcoming through the biggest legislative expansion of Medicare since its 1965 adoption. This legislation was championed by former physician and Indiana Republican Governor Otis Bowen, who had personally faced such a catastrophic coverage experience during his wife's extended illness. Bowen played a key expert role and received overwhelming support from President Ronald Reagan and members of both political parties in Congress.

The legislation looked less inviting almost immediately after its adoption. The recognition that the costs of this insurance would be covered by an increase in Medicare premiums rather than general revenue triggered a strongly negative response. This produced an oppositional coalition linking a wide range of groups representing seniors. In relatively short order, both parties reversed gear and Congress promptly repealed the legislation.[33]

Much like Gore's Kyoto experience, catastrophic care policy was effectively dead within months of adoption.

State and provincial legislators weighing the future of recent commitments to cap-and-trade worked in less-dramatic settings. But many began harboring reservations soon after their governors or premiers announced plans to join either the WCI or MGGRA, or both. Many legislators from both political parties began lamenting their lack of inclusion in the cap-and-trade policy process. They were generally not involved in high-profile executive summits and signing ceremonies and they often grumbled that they knew little about the details of official executive announcements. This might not matter if gubernatorial powers were more sweeping, but many state constitutions also accord legislators significant authority in regulatory and taxation matters.

Numerous states have constitutional provisions, including Oregon and Washington, that would likely require legislative approval of any cap-and-trade system covering their jurisdiction and connecting with others through trading. This includes legislative authorization of key design elements, such as establishment of a carbon emissions cap, a timetable for emission reductions, and components of a regulatory system to oversee the trading components. This reflects the limits of gubernatorial power in launching carbon pricing initiatives.

At the time, these hurdles seemed a mere formality. Oregon and Washington had produced a series of political leaders from both parties who expressed considerable concern about climate change. This led to a number of policies adopted in these states during the late 1990s through the mid-2000s designed to reduce carbon emissions, albeit none that used carbon pricing. Oregon and Washington also had a long tradition of Democratic Party dominance. Oregon Governor Ted Kulongoski and Washington Governor Christine Gregoire, both Democrats, were preceded and succeeded by multiple Democrats. Both also enjoyed control by majorities of their party in both legislative chambers before and after 2010, although Republicans in these states had previously supported many climate policies that lacked carbon pricing.

Despite this favorability, the anticipated slam-dunk on cap-and-trade never occurred in either state. Both Democratic and Republican legislators in these states raised sobering questions about the potential economic impact of carbon pricing, particularly at a point of growing concern about the economy. This included concerns in the Washington Senate over the possibility of "massive increases in the price of gasoline, electricity, food, and water."[34] These were specified in Senate Bill 5096, which called for Washington to formally withdraw from the WCI at the very time recession worries mounted. Similar debates and proposals emerged in Oregon.

Neither state adopted legislation to officially abandon their governor's cap-and-trade commitment, but such a step was not necessary to achieve the same effect. Despite repeated efforts by Kulongoski and Gregoire to secure support, their legislatures would not budge. The Washington House and Senate adopted different bills calling on the State Department of Ecology to further analyze greenhouse gas reduction measures and report back to the legislature, but failed to reconcile differences even on this bill.[35] This precluded any steps toward implementation. Neither governor formally withdrew from WCI, hopeful of a shift in future fortunes. But the Oregon and Washington cap-and-trade commitments withered from legislative neglect, despite stable Democratic Party control of both chambers.[36]

Legislators in other states and provinces also struggled with these issues, though not all had to pursue a formal approval process for cap-and-trade to move forward in some fashion. Some legislative opponents of carbon pricing began to circulate resolutions calling for abandonment of both the WCI and MGGRA, citing many of the same economic concerns that surfaced in Oregon and Washington.[37] In other instances, concerns were raised about funding to cover staff expansion and launch new administrative systems to oversee trading programs alongside growing state fiscal concerns linked to the economy. This broached the challenging issue of how to establish appropriate governance of cap-and-trade for carbon emissions, given mounting media reports about early implementation problems with the EU cap-and-trade system. This emerged as a particular concern in Canadian provinces with little or no prior history with this policy tool, including application to sulfur dioxide emissions, and led to resistance within some ministries.

For many states and provinces, the idea of constructing a regulatory apparatus to manage carbon emission trading entered the tricky political terrain between the production and use of energy and its environmental consequences.[38] Most states and provinces retain separate energy and environmental agencies or ministries, with little operational history of working cooperatively across traditional boundaries. So thinking through the financing and design of new administrative units proved challenging, particularly for jurisdictions that lacked California's substantial staffing commitment and experience in operating such programs through its formidable Air Resources Board and related agencies.[39] These types of political and administrative hurdles made it difficult to launch policies after governors made initial cap-and-trade commitments. It tended not to lead to dramatic decisions whereby states or provinces formally terminated their recent vows to sign up for regional collaboration. Indeed, those kinds of steps would be more common and more visible in the next stage of the process.

Failing the Electoral Transition Test

The majority of states and provinces that adopted cap-and-trade survived the policy launch test. States like Oregon and Washington struggled to enact essential authorizing legislation; others discovered that it took considerably more time and preparation than anticipated to move from legislation to actual launch of cap-and-trade. It was still possible, however, that these states could eventually move forward. By 2010, most state and provincial commitments remained in place up to the point of the next crucial policy life-cycle test—namely, the ability of a policy to endure beyond the first election or leadership change following adoption.

Elections can often become a referendum on a policy adopted during an incumbent's term in office. This is particularly likely if there is close association between the policy, its political advocates, and controversy surrounding it. In such cases, a particular executive or legislative majority might face repudiation at the polls, especially if combined with other controversial policy steps. After initial creation, a policy likely remains in preliminary stages of implementation and may be susceptible to attack during an election cycle and, pending the results, after the votes are tallied. Carbon pricing policies might prove particularly vulnerable if they are perceived as elevating energy consumption costs in the absence of tangible and offsetting benefits.

A bureaucracy hostile toward a new policy may take steps to delay implementation and may even make the policy appear feckless to the public. Oppositional interest groups may seize upon elections as opportunities to redouble their efforts to throttle the policy. If a policy has been championed by a leading official, such as a governor or premier, their departure from office or a very narrow victory can unravel a supportive coalition. Indeed, key elements of the legislative coalition adopting the policy, assuming there was some form of statute, can be wiped away in short order, possibly due to public dissatisfaction with their earlier handiwork.

This may be a far more common phenomenon in democratic systems than is traditionally recognized. Long-standing assertions that policies can approach "immortality" and defy rejection or emaciation after adoption have now been weakened by political science advances on the longer-term survivability of governmental policies and institutions. One careful study of major American domestic policy initiatives across eight policy domains concluded that 42 percent of them were "fully or partially over-turned or modified subsequently."[40] Many of these major shifts appear to have occurred or begun within a single election cycle following adoption. Another major study examining a larger set of US policies over a longer time period corroborated that there was a surprisingly high rate of "policy termination."[41]

Sub-federal governments are not immune from this type of policy rejec-tion, although this has received limited scholarly attention. The voluminous political science literature on state policy diffusion focuses primarily on bandwagons that begin in one state but then expand.[42] Policies often spread to bordering neighbors, cluster in regions, and then extend across much or all of the country. This "horizontal diffusion" process may trigger "vertical diffusion" whereby the federal government ultimately embraces some form of these state policies on a national basis.[43] Diffusion studies acknowledge that some policies can stall, with the pace of expanded adoption slowing or even stopping. There may also, however, be more instances than are generally acknowledged of "reverse diffusion," whereby one or more states abandon initial policy commitments. It is possible that state policy rever-sals occur in clusters, perhaps through national opposition campaigns that blanket state capitols with tailored versions of the same core message. Such a shift may markedly reduce the number of states sustaining a policy and may serve to deter other states from considering adoption.[44]

This type of reverse bandwagon effect might be particularly possible at points where major partisan shifts occur in state legislatures or executive positions such as governor and attorney general. Many statehouse seats are up for electoral reconsideration every two years, and twenty-one states impose some form of statutory term limits on legislators. Nearly all gov-ernors and other elected executives face some form of term limitations, most commonly after a pair of four-year terms. This can create numerous opportunities to repudiate incumbents, either during election cycles or when their names can no longer be placed on the ballot.

State-level elections in 2010 provided a strong test of political support for the cap-and-trade commitments made previously in twenty-three states. A mixture of Democratic and Republican governors championed cap-and-trade adoption in prior years but nearly all of them relinquished office by 2010. In the case of MGGRA, all six governors who signed the pact in 2007 had left office by January 2011, along with their appointed energy and environ-mental department heads. These departures were linked to term limits, electoral defeat, retirement, pursuit of the presidency, or federal indictment. Similar leadership transitions were under way in other states and provinces that had made initial commitments to cap-and-trade in previous years. Among US state legislatures, nearly two-thirds of the 7,368 seats were up for election in 2010. If not a referendum on cap-and-trade, this election would at minimum provide a pivotal test of whether there was a broad political base of support to sustain those policies.

The third stage of the policy life-cycle thus poses the following question: *Can the policy survive a subsequent election that delivers a change of leadership or partisan control of government?* The two years following the 2010 elections would suggest that the political foundation underpinning cap-and-trade was quite thin and vulnerable to leadership change. There was a major partisan shift from Democratic to Republican control in many states, with a net Republican gain of 680 legislative seats and six governorships. In some instances, this shift toward Republican control reflected significant opposi-tion to cap-and-trade.

But opposition was not confined to Republicans. In some instances, Democrats either retained a governorship (Illinois and Oregon) or wrested it away from a Republican (Minnesota) while still abandoning cap-and-trade. In other cases, a state shifted from a Republican governor who sup-ported cap-and-trade to a Democratic successor who continued to support the policy (Connecticut, Maine, and Vermont). While 2010 brought a par-tisan electoral tidal wave, this partisan shift alone was not the sole driving force behind shifting state cap-and-trade participation. During the same period, Canadian provinces also demonstrated that varied forms of partisan control can lead to similar shifts toward policy termination.

Between the 2008 and 2012 elections, thirteen states would abandon cap-and-trade, leaving only ten states engaged, as reflected in table 2.2.

Three of the four provinces pledged to cap-and-trade also reversed course during this period, although in a quieter and less formalized manner. There was no standardized election timing across provinces and fewer shifts in partisan control, despite the similar outcomes. No state or province reversed its position and restored cap-and-trade through the end of 2015. No new state or province came close to adopting cap-and-trade (or carbon taxes) during this period.

This shift reflects rapidly changing political views on cap-and-trade, underscoring a classic political problem facing policy reforms that impose significant costs on specific constituencies in the broad public interest. In these cases, the public may simply not be aware of the policy or grasp its broader consequence. But any imposed costs are likely to be visible to distinct stakeholders. They are likely to further fuel their efforts to thwart the policy, whether through a direct assault or a series of steps that slow implementation and ultimately undermine the policy. It may also be possible for organized foes to frame these potential problems and build a broader base of opposition.

Any form of legislation that imposes costs through creation of new taxes, increased tax rates, or reduced tax preferences runs considerable political risks. These may be particularly significant in cases where any offsetting benefits are difficult to discern or prove unconvincing despite political framing. John Witte's classic analysis of the politics of the American federal income tax remains a powerful reminder of the political sensitivity to tax-related changes. Indeed, Witte and other tax politics scholars were somewhat taken aback when Congress adopted far-reaching tax reform in 1986 that promised broad benefits in exchange for loss of targeted tax preferences. Therefore, he was not terribly surprised when its base of political support disintegrated not long after adoption.[45]

The case of the Tax Reform Act (TRA) may represent the ultimate contemporary example of the expert path to policy adoption. It demonstrated the ability of a powerful economic idea to garner a broad, albeit temporary, base of political support and adoption. In this instance, diverse tax experts persuaded a coalition of Republicans and Democrats to support significant across-the-board reductions in federal income tax rates. In exchange, those alterations would be revenue-neutral on the federal budget given simultaneous elimination of numerous individual and corporate tax subsidies. The support base for the Tax Reform Act was quite diverse, ranging from

President Ronald Reagan to Democratic Senate champion Bill Bradley. It ultimately steamrolled intensive interest group opposition.[46] This experience has been widely referenced as a model for any legislative "grand bargain" linked to some form of tax increase or creation, including potential applications to carbon pricing adoption.

This was perhaps the ultimate feel-good political moment for tax policy in the last quarter of the twentieth century: A powerful policy idea trumped interest group preference in search of the broad public good. But it was short-lived, followed by sustained efforts to undermine the legislation through ongoing proposals and subsequent bills adopted during the next three presidencies to reverse key provisions. There was no formal repeal of the Tax Reform Act. But as political scientist Eric Patashnik noted, the process of extended opposition would serve "to bleed the reform to death, one nick at a time."[47] For all of its initial promise, the TRA remains a cautionary tale on the political feasibility of sustaining high-minded reform that lacks a sufficiently strong political foundation and constituency base to endure electoral transitions.

Cap-and-trade followed a somewhat similar path at the state and provincial levels from 2010 to 2012, but with multiple reversals in the same policy window. It lost more than half of its early adopters in the United States and Canada within a few years after adoption. In some instances, the withdrawal was gradual and lacked a single, definitive act. Oregon and Washington did not experience any significant shifts of partisan control in either branch, and Washington's Gregoire continued to press for adoption of supportive legislation. But neither of the states' Democrat-dominated legislatures budged on this issue in 2011 or 2012, leaving cap-and-trade to quietly die.

Noisy Exits and Quiet Fades

Partisanship was more evident in other jurisdictions, often moving quickly and decisively against cap-and-trade after a leadership change. Arizona set the pace. A gubernatorial control shift occurred just before the 2010 election when Democrat Janet Napolitano resigned to join President Obama's administration as secretary of homeland security. Arizona's constitution does not allow for the election of a lieutenant governor, meaning that any vacancy in the governorship elevates the sitting attorney general into that role. In this case, Attorney General Jan Brewer, a Republican, became governor and subsequently won election to a full term in November.

Brewer acted almost immediately to reverse cap-and-trade. Her issuance of Executive Order 2010–06 formally ended Arizona's support for the policy, saying that this was necessary to prevent cap-and-trade from "imposing costs on Arizona's economy" that would "cost investment and jobs in Arizona." This effectively halted state involvement with cap-and-trade and did not require any legislative action. Department of Environmental Quality Director Benjamin Grumbles confirmed the decision but also noted that the state was not formally withdrawing from the WCI. Instead, he noted that Arizona still wanted to pursue other climate-friendly goals with neighboring jurisdictions, including collaboration on more popular, politically feasible renewable portfolio standards and energy efficiency requirements. "Green and grow is our approach now," said Grumbles.[48]

A series of states would follow Brewer's lead over the next two years, usually following transition in the governor's office. There was no longer state incentive to take early actions to reduce emissions, given the 2010 death of federal carbon pricing legislation and subsequent electoral reversals in Congress. When explaining their withdrawal decisions, many governors cited concern about potential economic harm from carbon pricing and doubts that their reduction efforts would have any benefit. This reflected growing concerns about the lingering recession and also the increasingly partisan antipathy of Republicans toward carbon pricing.

In New Mexico, both Democratic and Republican gubernatorial candidates raised concerns about cap-and-trade during the 2010 campaign to succeed WCI enthusiast governor Bill Richardson. Republican Susana Martinez was particularly outspoken and moved with Brewer-like speed to reverse the state's cap-and-trade commitment upon taking office. She first suspended any administrative rulemaking on climate change for her first ninety days in office, using that time to fire and replace the entire State Environmental Improvement Board that had just approved WCI cap-and-trade membership rules. Martinez claimed that participation in the WCI process "would impose a new energy tax on businesses and families" in New Mexico.[49] "Cap-and-trade regulations passed during the Richardson administration put the state (at) an uneven disadvantage," confirmed Jim Winchester, communications director of the New Mexico Environment Department.[50]

Like Arizona, New Mexico used this departure to pivot toward active development of alternative energy sources. Whereas Arizona focused on renewables, particularly solar, New Mexico sought to revive and expand its historic natural gas production through hydraulic fracturing.[51] Every other WCI state governor, except California's, followed suit in repudiating cap-and-trade. In Montana, Democratic Governor Brian Schweitzer backpedaled from early support and also opposed federal cap-and-trade and carbon regulation. He faced considerable pressure from fossil fuel interests and a Republican legislature. In Utah, Gary Herbert withdrew his state from WCI in 2010 during his first year as governor. His predecessor, Republican Governor Jon Huntsman, was an early supporter but concluded later that the regional effort was "probably long-term unsustainable."[52]

A similar conclusion emerged from capitols around the Midwest that had once joined forces to launch the MGGRA, but without the drama of some of their Western counterparts. In the East, opposition to cap-and-trade was not as pronounced. But that did not stop New Jersey Republican Governor Chris Christie from joining the oppositional chorus to cap-and-trade. He repeatedly attacked New Jersey's engagement in the Regional Greenhouse Gas Initiative (RGGI) under Democratic predecessor Jon Corzine as a "tax" that was increasing electricity costs and could imperil economic recovery. Christie also characterized cap-and-trade as a "failure" that was not having any impact on carbon emissions.[53] Christie carried through in 2011 with his threat to withdraw New Jersey from RGGI without legislative approval.[54]

Similar sentiments emerged from three of the four provincial cap-and-trade partners, who tended to backpedal quietly rather than issue bold condemnations. This may be partly attributable to the lack of turnover of provincial premiers, reflecting reluctance to self-criticize their earlier actions. Nonetheless, the ultimate outcome was for every pledged cap-and-trade participant from Canada, except Quebec, to abandon its commitment by the end of 2012. For Ontario, participation in cap-and-trade was hammered by opposition forces in a 2011 election as a threat to economic recovery. Ontario's Liberal Party survived, but narrowly and with only a minority government remaining. The government became especially mired in the high costs and political tensions surrounding its provincial plans to expand wind energy and to phase out all operating coal plants.[55] So Ontario quietly slid away from its earlier pledge to continue implementing cap-and-trade.

Manitoba acknowledged that it lacked the staffing capacity and resources to fully engage in cap-and-trade. It also lost interest in the policy after realizing that opportunities to secure carbon reduction credits for expanded hydro capacity were frowned upon by California authorities, thereby minimizing anticipated economic benefits. British Columbia also drifted away from cap-and-trade by 2012, after several years of developing regulations to establish trading system linkage with California and other WCI partners. Much like New Mexico, British Columbia had growing political support for expanded natural gas production that discouraged continued engagement in cap-and-trade negotiations, given potential threats to extractive industries.

Beyond North America, other continents were not immune from these pressures. In Europe, Italy sought to become an environmental tax leader in 1998 by adopting a carbon tax, but it faced fierce political opposition and was repealed in less than one year. France has had a dizzying on-and-off engagement with carbon taxes at least since the idea surfaced in the 2007 presidential election. This has included reversals of early steps due to political opposition and constitutional complications before efforts to relaunch the idea in the mid-2010s.

In Asia, both Australia and New Zealand would also experience carbon tax repeals. Australia's Kevin Rudd became the leader of his center-left Labor Party in 2006 and was eager to make climate change a central plank in a subsequent campaign for prime minister. He was extremely confident that he could navigate the expert path and sell the carbon price idea politically, first to voters in an election and then to Parliament. Public concern about climate change appeared to be increasing during an extended and historic drought known as the "Big Dry." Rudd won a significant election victory in 2007 and immediately ratified the Kyoto Protocol, promising to follow with an aggressive carbon pricing proposal (see table 3.1). He declared climate change to be "the defining challenge of our generation" and a "top priority of the new Australian government."

After internal leadership debates, Rudd and Labor embraced cap-and-trade in 2008 through a proposed Carbon Pollution Reduction Scheme (CPRS) rather than a carbon tax. This built on earlier experimentation with cap-and-trade by the Australian state of New South Wales.[56] Much like the American experience with cap-and-trade, the proposed legislation was adopted in the Australian House of Representatives in 2009 but struggled in the Senate, where it faced opposition from coalition partners on the right (seen as too stringent) and the Green Party on the left (seen as too weak).[57] Rudd responded through use of the pluralist and partisan paths, brokering numerous CPRS adjustments in attempting to construct a more viable and partisan coalition.

Rudd feared intensifying industry and partisan opposition to cap-and-trade amid growing signs of recession, having failed in numerous attempts to achieve a workable compromise.[58] He was also embroiled in a battle with the coal and other mineral extraction interests over a major proposed increase in severance taxes on industry "super profits." As a result, the prime minister ultimately decided in 2010 to postpone further consideration of the legislation until 2013, giving him time to regroup politically and start afresh after anticipated reelection. However, later that year Rudd was ousted from his position after a brutal battle for power with fellow Labor Party member and Deputy Prime Minister Julia Gillard.

Gillard lacked Rudd's fervor for carbon pricing and vowed not to adopt a carbon tax in seeking her own electoral mandate. She ultimately needed to shift her position to secure coalition government support from the minority Green Party after a closely fought election. This led to the narrow and contentious adoption through the 2011 Clean Energy Act of a carbon tax that would eventually transition toward a cap-and-trade system. However, the backlash against that tax and her negotiated settlement with mineral industry leaders over extraction taxes helped destabilize the Gillard government. This created a window for Rudd to return to power in 2013 against the increasingly unpopular Gillard. He pledged a more rapid transition away from a carbon tax toward cap-and-trade with the intent of providing price relief for Australians unhappy with price hikes linked to the tax.

The Labor Party carbon pricing soap opera, however, finally ran out of time, with its loss of power linked in large part to an "axe the tax" movement led by Liberal Party leader Tony Abbott. Any prospect of bipartisan support for carbon pricing dissolved with Abbott's election as party leader, with some parallels to Republican opposition to any carbon pricing discussion after the 2008 elections. Decrying carbon pricing as a "wrecking ball across the economy" and a "giant new tax on everything," Abbott became prime minister in a 2013 election and oversaw prompt repeal of the Clean Energy Act.[59] The Australian carbon pricing experiment was then replaced with renewed commitment to a Direct Action Plan that emphasized more modest and politically palatable steps, including financial incentives to firms that undertook voluntary emission reductions.[60]

Australian greenhouse gas emissions increased 7.5 percent in the first two years after carbon pricing repeal and were expected to continue rising beyond 2020. After prolonged drought and more than a half-decade of political

Table 3.1
Australian carbon pricing policy timeline.

June 2007	Prime Minister John Howard announces that federal government will introduce an Emissions Trading Scheme (ETS).
November 2007	Labor Party wins the election and announces plan to ratify Kyoto Protocol, set up a national ETS, and cut Australia's emissions by 60 percent by 2050.
December 2007	Prime Minister Kevin Rudd ratifies the Kyoto Protocol.
December 2008	Prime Minister Rudd introduces details of cap-and-trade ETS titled Carbon Pollution Reduction Scheme (CPRS) to go into effect July 2010.
June 2009	CPRS bills pass in House of Representatives.
August 2009	Senate votes down CPRS bills.
December 2009	Acting Prime Minister Julia Gillard announces that revised and amended CPRS will be future federal policy.
April 2010	Prime Minister Rudd announces that CPRS will go into effect in 2012 rather than 2010.
June 2010	Gillard replaces Rudd as prime minister.
July 2010	Gillard rules out carbon tax policy as an interim measure.
February 2011	Prime Minister Gillard introduces carbon tax plan, titled 2011 Carbon Price Framework, that is to transition into ETS after a few years.
November 2011	Gillard's carbon tax plan passes in the Senate.
July 2012	Gillard's carbon tax (as part of the Clean Energy Act 2011, derived from the 2011 Carbon Price Framework) begins operation.
June 2013	Rudd returns as prime minister.
July 2013	Rudd announces prospective changes to Clean Energy Act to terminate fixed-cost phase and move directly to ETS.
September 2013	Tony Abbott replaces Rudd as prime minister.
November 2013	Prime Minister Abbott introduces legislation to repeal the Clean Energy Act.
March 2014	Repeal legislation is passed in the House but blocked in the Senate.
July 2014	New Senate votes to repeal the Clean Energy Act.
October 2014	Senate passes Prime Minister Abbott's Direct Action Plan.
September 2015	Malcolm Turnbull replaces Abbott as prime minister, agreeing to maintain Direct Action Plan.

Sources: John Taberner and Zorzetto, "A Short History of Climate Change Policy in Australia," August 2014, https://www.nela.org.au/NELA/Documents/HSF-Short_History _of_Climate_Change_Policy_in_Australia.pdf; "Carbon Pricing Mechanism: About the Mechanism," *Australian Government Clean Energy Regulator*, May 11, 2015, http://www .cleanenergyregulator.gov.au/Infohub/CPM/About-the-mechanism; "Carbon Tax: A Timeline of Its Tortuous History in Australia," *ABC News*, updated July 16, 2014, http://www.abc .net.au/news/2014-07-10/carbon-tax-timeline/5569118.

control by a party committed to carbon pricing, Australia finally launched a policy. However, it floundered during political transition and was reversed in short order. This reflected many parallels to initial cap-and-trade commitments made by various American states and Canadian provinces that were abandoned after a subsequent election and leadership change.

New Zealand experienced its own carbon price ups and downs that paralleled the Australian and North American experiences. Adoption in 2005 of a $15 per ton carbon tax under Prime Minister Helen Clark was reversed within months after minority parties backed away from initial support through a multiparty coalition. A cap-and-trade program was approved three years later but the resulting New Zealand Emissions Trading Scheme was loaded with exemptions, allocated allowances at no charge, and experienced considerable market volatility. Critics contended that it lacked a fixed emissions cap and did not fully meet the definition of a cap-and-trade program.[61] There were, however, ongoing reform efforts in the 2010s designed to create a more functional system, including a mid-decade review.

Failing the Managerial Adaptation Test

An added disincentive to pursue carbon pricing was the troubled experience of the EU Emissions Trading Scheme (ETS), which initially received international acclaim. Borrowing heavily from the US experience with cap-and-trade for sulfur dioxide emissions, the ETS was celebrated for successful adoption of large-scale carbon pricing. It was widely thought to usher in a new era of political support for cap-and-trade that would further prompt other developed nations to embrace carbon pricing and eventually spread it across the globe. Some contended that Europe was so forward-thinking on issues such as carbon pricing that it should be renamed the "Environmental Union."[62]

The ETS successfully passed the political test of initial policy adoption and survived the policy launch test with the opening of a continent-wide trading system in 2005.[63] This was followed by an ability to endure multiple political transitions, both in Brussels and in the capitols of the participating EU member states during its first decade of operation. Few of the early political champions of ETS remained in elected office by the end of 2015 and yet the system continued to operate. Consequently, it demonstrated that carbon pricing could advance at least this far along a policy life-cycle, maintaining sufficient political support to continue operations into its second decade.

This was really only the beginning, however. Much more was expected of ETS, reflecting widely held assumptions that carbon pricing systems would operate effectively if political leaders could somehow muster the political courage to establish them. Policy advocates relentlessly argued that the American sulfur dioxide case could easily be replicated for carbon. Implementation feasibility and system management received little consideration. Expectations included successful policy management over time and demonstrated ability to reduce emissions in a cost-effective manner.

The ETS was also thought to be exceptionally well suited to take advantage of global flexibility provisions established by the Clean Development Mechanism (CDM) through the Kyoto Protocol. Supporters also believed that it would be able to choose among emerging global cap-and-trade partners as the European approach diffused to other continents. All of this reflected widespread confidence that any emerging problems could easily be remedied and that citizens would rally behind the considerable environmental and economic benefits anticipated from emissions trading. ETS was heralded as a "new grand experiment" in carbon pricing and as the "cornerstone and flagship" of European climate policy.[64]

Cap-and-trade, however, proved substantially more challenging than its European adherents anticipated. The ETS struggled mightily during its first decade of operations from 2005 through 2015. Rather than a model worthy of diffusion, it serves as an example of how not to operate carbon pricing, filled with management stumbles and an inability to secure a political fix. During its first decade of operation, scholarly and journalistic analysts of ETS concluded that it was a "farce,"[65] "marginalized,"[66] "fail[ed] wretchedly,"[67] an example of "what not to do,"[68] "dead or at least undergoing a serious crisis,"[69] and offered "salutary lessons on how not to handle some of the most salient governance dilemmas."[70]

The ETS serves as an important reminder that even policies designed to tap into economic power require careful attention to the design of governing institutions, the cultivation of capable staff, and the flexibility to make adjustments after initial launch. Elected officials rarely get all elements of policy design right the first time. Policy studies are littered with examples of policies that struggle upon moving into full operation, requiring midcourse adjustments and sustained managerial stewardship.

It remains enormously difficult in many contexts to address this challenge. As Americans have seen in the past decade with federal health care and financial regulation reforms, implementation can prove vastly more complicated than envisioned. Essential political support can wane in the interim, especially if managerial foibles undermine confidence in the policy by key constituents and the general public. Such challenges may be particularly great for climate policy, given the contentious intersection of energy use and environmental protection. As political scientist William Lowry noted, these two policy spheres have very different political and related governing systems, frequently producing major governance collisions.[71] Governments routinely divide their energy, transportation, agricultural, and environmental portfolios into separate policies and governing institutions. Climate change policy necessitates considerable collaboration and integration across these and other traditional boundaries.

The late Nobel Laureate Elinor Ostrom noted that creating effective institutional arrangements to govern "common-pool resources" can be profoundly challenging, albeit not impossible. Ostrom emphasized the importance of such key elements as disclosure and transparent release of vital information, promotion of familiarity and trust among key actors, and application of sanctions in the event of any noncompliance.[72] Policy professionals who serve in government agencies can play a central role in developing these features, thereby transforming legislation into workable policy. For emerging policy problems, this may require recruiting professionals with new technical and disciplinary skills as well as creating organizations to allow them to work effectively together. Over time as they standardize operational routines, these professionals can create a clear set of expectations for compliance. They can also go farther, managing political controversies that may arise and mobilizing client groups to provide a constituency to sustain policy support.[73] All of this occurs through a multiphase evolution that can take a number of years.

But this does not happen easily, especially in a new and complex arena like climate change. There will be adjustments over time, perhaps including significant modifications in policy as lessons are learned from early performance. Consequently, public managers will either need to be given the latitude to make those adjustments or to return the policy to the political shop floor for modification and amendment. Without that adjustment capacity, policies may struggle, losing credibility and support and perhaps leading to termination.

The fourth stage of the policy life-cycle thus raises the following question: *Can political supporters of the policy establish management systems that effectively implement the policy, including capacity to make adjustments or modifications necessary to allow the policy to continue to operate effectively over time, thereby enduring politically and building constituent support?* The first decade of ETS provides reminders that this question is more difficult than was widely anticipated at the point of its political adoption or policy launch. Many of the problems that surfaced in the first years of ETS implementation were not resolved after a decade and have endured. This has not led to political reversal of ETS but instead undermined effectiveness and has prompted European leaders to increase consideration of alternatives to carbon pricing. ETS also provides a sobering real-world case experience when matched against soaring claims by proponents on the merits of cap-and-trade.

At the same time, the ETS has proved resilient in terms of political survival, has experienced some management maturation over time, and might further evolve in its second decade of operation given late-stage reforms. Indeed, there were some important signs of far-reaching internal reforms in the mid-2010s that might enable the ETS to finally approach its potential. This suggests the possibility that political survival can provide time for extended operations and policy learning from early failures that ultimately lead to constructive adaptation. The ETS might then follow the example of other policies whereby policy professionals were able to work collaboratively over time with political leaders to fashion credible reforms that could finally produce higher levels of policy performance.[74] Consequently, the ETS is best portrayed as an uneven case rather than an abject failure after its first decade of operation.

The European Union clearly had numerous political advantages in moving forward on carbon pricing in the early 2000s. It built a foundation of new environmental policies and governing institutions in the 1980s and 1990s to address a series of continent-wide environmental problems. Many achieved considerable success in securing collaboration across member states.[75] The EU also had an impressive history as a carbon pricing pioneer, with five northern European nations using carbon taxes since the early 1990s, as discussed further in chapter 4. Carbon pricing had strong political support across multiple political parties in many member states that sought an international leadership role on climate change.

However, the EU chose not to build on its carbon tax experience and, instead, selected cap-and-trade. This followed a prolonged political conflict in which many environmental groups expressed considerable reservations about cap-and-trade. The decision was driven by political factors rather than analytical ones. Since cap-and-trade was not a tax, it did not require unanimous votes among the participating member states for adoption or adjustment.[76] It gave political leaders more latitude to make carbon pricing decisions without giving each nation an effective veto. In terms of international politics, selecting cap-and-trade was perceived as a way to accelerate American engagement in the Kyoto Protocol, thereby triggering further diffusion that might evolve into the global system leaders hoped to attain.[77] This would ultimately enable Europe to become a central political broker on climate change, rather than a peripheral player.

These decisions did not trigger the political backlash seen a half-decade later in the United States, Canada, and Australia. But ETS implementation proved unexpectedly rocky in its early years and did not ease over time. There were stunning stumbles during ETS's first decade of operation, reflected in a sequence of major plunges in emission allowance prices (see figure 3.1). An initial collapse in the first three years of ETS operation was largely shrugged off as reflecting a "learning by doing" phase.[78] But a second plunge resulted in a drop in the price per ton from nearly 30 euros in 2008 to less than 10 euros in 2009. Prices remained low through the end of 2015, trading between 5 and 10 euros per ton for most of that period. This fell far below estimates, triggering a search for explanations and concerns about longer-term system viability.[79] These fluctuations reflect a series of ETS structural and political problems that largely persisted into its second decade.

Analysts have continually concluded that the ETS has regularly allocated an excessive number of allowances, putting more into circulation than actual emissions warrant.[80] This pattern first emerged in the earliest stages of implementation, linked to declining rates of carbon emissions given the economic contraction as well as the flood of CDM offset credits that were available until they were prohibited after 2013.[81] There was no immediate political remedy to this problem and management institutions lacked the authority to make adjustments and absorb these surplus allowances. It was expected that this problem would fade over time but it has persisted. A 2015 study projected a surplus of 2.6 billion European Allowance Units (EUAs) in the ETS by 2020, undermining its aspirations to evolve into a global model of a successful emissions trading system.[82]

Political pressures on the EU to delay the shift from fossil fuels diffused down to national and subnational authorities. As political scientist Inger

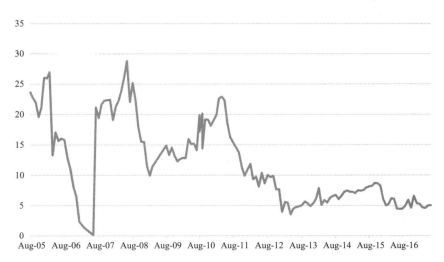

Figure 3.1
Spot price (in €/metric ton) for carbon allowances in the EU ETS, 2005–2017.
Source: "Carbon Emissions Futures Historical Data," investing.com, accessed June 28, 2017, https://www.investing.com/commodities/carbon-emissions-historical-data#.

Weibust explained, the European Union operates a very decentralized version of federalism or multilevel governance, lacking many of the coordinating provisions common in formal federations such as the United States, Canada, and Australia.[83] In the case of the ETS, initial design weaknesses in the continental system were compounded by delegation of authority to individual member states, many of which faced considerable political pressure to make compliance as flexible as possible.[84] At the same time, most EU member states had no prior cap-and-trade experience and only belatedly established their own policies and management systems. They began ETS engagement with little reliable data on their historic carbon emissions and were not prepared to credibly track future releases, much less oversee all key components of a carbon trading system that would require collaboration across a continent-wide policy network.

Nations such as Poland have commonly been singled out for noncompliance and resistance to reforms, reflecting their enduring dependence on coal as a primary source of electricity. But compliance issues have also dogged EU member states with greater histories of commitment to environmental protection and active ETS support. Germany, for example, has long struggled to reduce its surplus allocations, even after a negotiated adjustment with the European Commission for 2008–2012 that tightened the emissions cap and expanded allowance auctioning. Tensions included growing German reliance on coal as a nonintermittent alternative to nuclear power, which was being phased out in reaction to Japan's Fukushima disaster. Other nations presented somewhat different puzzles, each with unique challenges to making needed cap-and-trade modifications for increased ETS effectiveness. As political scientist Vivian Thomson observed, "the ETS's over-allocation problems persist."[85]

The problems did not end with allocations. ETS was hit by a wave of cyber crimes in the early 2010s, one of which led to temporary closure of the system. In the Czech Republic, a bomb threat created a diversion that led to electronic permit theft. In Austria, Denmark, Greece, and the United Kingdom, cyber thieves stole security codes and pilfered millions of euros of trading certificates.[86] EU and member state governing authorities were widely criticized for lax security procedures.

In turn, allegations of "windfall profits" by the very firms expected to pay for carbon pricing has continued to dog the ETS and its credibility. ETS's heavy reliance on free allocation of allowances rather than auctioning did not deter firms from passing along costs to customers, thereby swelling profits.[87] This raised questions of equity and fairness, triggering proposals for expanded use of auctioning techniques that produce revenue for government, but which faced considerable industry opposition. Further questions of equity arose in attempting to designate proposed carbon offsets as compliance options. Concerns about this matter soared when offsets were used with much higher frequency than anticipated in many nations and oversight of international offset projects proved challenging.[88]

All of this might have been written off as a decade of necessary growing pains had ETS not been heralded as a transformational policy that would follow the lead of the American sulfur dioxide experience and provide a global model for carbon pricing. Solid evidence of a demonstrable ETS impact on reducing emissions in a cost-effective way might also have helped. European carbon emissions have declined in past decades, with a drop of 18 percent from 1990 to 2015. But this decline began long before ETS and is likely more attributable to a series of recessions and sluggish economic growth than to cap-and-trade. In turn, a wide range of other continental, national, and subnational policies promoting renewable energy and energy efficiency have likely had a greater impact.[89] This left the one-time poster child of cap-and-trade challenged by the need to make essential managerial and political adjustments.[90]

However, the ETS continued to operate, fending off various setbacks and likely playing some role in continental emission reductions. This raised the question of whether a more robust rebound might be possible in its second decade of operation and beyond as leaders attempted to fashion a series of major reforms in the mid-2010s—most notably, the adoption in 2015 of a Market Stability Reserve that could make automatic adjustments to better link allowance allocation with actual emission levels. If successfully implemented, the reserve could foster a more robust trading system and "lead to a gradually increasing carbon price and smoother policy interaction."[91] It was intended to be phased in over succeeding years and had no obvious impact on allowance prices in 2016 and 2017. In turn, the European Union's commitment to the ETS was shaken by the Brexit decision of the United Kingdom, one of its leading supporters but potentially the first member state to withdraw from the cap-and-trade program. The ETS also continued to face periodic challenges from coal-centered nations such as Poland.[92] Nonetheless, the creation of the reserve and related reforms suggested continued potential for ETS maturation during its second decade, made possible by sustained political support during its earlier years.

Failing the Performance Test

It is not inevitable that carbon pricing policies will flounder during any of the political or managerial stages of the policy life-cycle. It is politically possible that a carbon tax or cap-and-trade system could be adopted and operate largely as intended over a decade or more without major disruptions and upheavals. In one such North American case, this path was followed, leading to claims by elected officials that this jurisdiction was developing a model worthy of wide diffusion.

This case featured a solid political foundation that endured subsequent election cycles and transitions in elected political leadership. It benefited from substantial investment in the development of reliable data systems on carbon emissions and expansive efforts to make that data publicly available in a user-friendly format. A generous budget was created to hire talented policy professionals to staff new and expanding governmental units devoted to carbon pricing in the larger context of climate policy. This led to rapid transition from policy adoption to initial implementation in only four months. In turn, the institution created to oversee operations was allowed to make some midcourse adjustments as proved necessary based on early results.

The proponents of this system claimed a role in global leadership in the fight against climate change by developing the world's first version of carbon pricing with a hybrid approach. This entailed the creation of alternative compliance paths featuring both carbon tax and cap-and-trade options. Rather than pick only one of these heralded alternatives, both were embraced as viable routes to compliance. Regulated parties could pick their preferred option or even consider a more traditional performance standard if they were so inclined.

This hybrid policy was essentially designed for a two-part political game, reflecting goals that varied depending on the political level that was being addressed. In the internal game, the policy was carefully tailored to maximize local political support. Geared directly to the unique economic and energy contexts of the jurisdiction, the policy offered maximal flexibility and minimal implementation burdens to regulated parties. These included modest compliance costs and the possibility that those costs would eventually be returned as allocated benefits. This internal political game was complemented by an external game focused on audiences outside the boundaries of the jurisdiction, who generally viewed it with disdain as a climate outlaw given its substantial role in oil and gas production. In this latter case, political leaders of this jurisdiction proved eager to tell the story of how they were taking the lead in adopting a "world class" system of carbon pricing while much of the rest of the world was wringing its hands on the issue.

In the outside game, elected officials wanted their new policy to garner outside respect and even influence other governments to emulate their steps. They saw their policy as so innovative and promising that it should not be disturbed by policies potentially adopted at higher governmental levels. This campaign continued across multiple elections and heads of state, featuring extensive use of advertising and lobbying paid for with government funds. It was a bold step on carbon pricing, contended its architects, and the world should take note.

This pioneering carbon pricing strategy also offered a possible path out of a difficult political threat to one of this government's core industries. The Canadian province of Alberta did indeed have a major carbon emissions problem. At the point of adopting carbon pricing, Alberta generated more than 30 percent of Canadian carbon emissions despite a population that constituted less than 15 percent of the Canadian total. The province had long embraced development of oil and gas as a cornerstone of its economic well-being and was eager to tap massive oil sands deposits in remote areas to become an even larger player in continental and global energy development.

Oil and gas extraction from oil sands (originally known as tar sands until an aggressive industry and government effort to change the common term) is an energy-intensive process, far more so than most conventional drilling or hydraulic fracturing. Oil sands development promised a massive expansion of provincial energy production for Canadian consumption and exports. But it faced withering attacks from external opponents about the substantial carbon footprint of production while also facing vigorous political opposition to proposed pipeline development necessary to ship oil sands products over long distances to refineries and population centers. These challenges threatened future fossil fuel development aspirations.

Alberta faced blistering national and international condemnation for its oil sands development, particularly given projections that carbon emissions would continue to grow rapidly with expanded oil and gas development. Political and industrial leaders in particular feared that Canada's initial embrace of the Kyoto Protocol could derail their plans. Alberta's premier Ralph Klein loudly and repeatedly denounced Kyoto ratification plans as comparable to "signing a mortgage for a property you have never seen and for a price that you have never discussed."[93] He recruited a prominent predecessor, Peter Lougheed, to lead the assault on Kyoto by naming him chair of Alberta's Kyoto External Advisory Committee. This included a charge to "advise Alberta on the merits of writing its own laws to protect the province from the effects of the accord" and make the case for this approach aggressively in the province, across the nation, and internationally.[94]

Klein decried Kyoto ratification as "the goofiest, most devastating thing" ever considered by a Canadian government.[95] He raised questions about its constitutionality if provincial concerns were not addressed and made veiled threats of withdrawal from the federation if its terms were not met. This did not stop ratification, although it remained highly uncertain how Canada would implement its carbon emission reduction commitment. Indeed, succeeding federal governments would flounder on this issue, creating a vacuum for provincial policy innovation. Consequently, Klein and his political allies doubled down on a "made in Alberta" approach. If put together in an appealing and compelling manner, this might be a way for Alberta to thwart future federal or international pressure to impose a certain type of climate policy. It could instead pursue its own strategy, which it would frame as bold and innovative.

Carbon pricing offered a crucial political answer to this puzzle. It was designed in such a way that Alberta truly appeared to be a national, continental, and global pioneer in tapping the best of both carbon pricing policy options. But it was loaded with exceptions, exemptions, and loopholes that allowed for a carbon tax and cap-and-trade system to operate but only through a pricing strategy that proved nominal at best. Emission reductions might be marginal, but politically, the policy was framed in a way that suggested the province was truly on a de-carbonization path. In short, the carbon pricing policy might well clear all political hurdles to adoption and sustained implementation but accomplish essentially none of its climate protection goals.

This experience raises the question of whether carbon pricing might be used for symbolic purposes, enabling a government to look good politically through use of a heralded policy tool while not really accomplishing anything. This leads to a final question concerning a policy that endures for a considerable period of time in a policy life-cycle: *Can the policy surmount all of these previous political and managerial hurdles and also demonstrate empirically a significant reduction of greenhouse gas emissions in a cost-effective manner? In particular, can it set performance goals linked to reduced emissions and achieve these in a cost-effective manner over time?* The Alberta case offers a sobering indication that carbon pricing may clear all political and managerial paths addressed earlier in this chapter and yet have virtually nothing to show for it in terms of environmental performance after nearly a decade of operation.

This reflects a larger concern about environmental policies that may endure multiple seasons of political change but largely "drift" along rather than deliver measurable benefits. Such policies likely had little if any environmental performance impact over time, but this did not necessarily trigger significant public outcry or lead to significant reform.[96] In the United States, the Toxic Substances Control Act (TSCA) was heralded in 1976 as a major step toward reducing risks from a wide range of toxic chemicals.

Its adoption followed a series of major chemical release episodes internationally and in the United States. Industry became relatively comfortable
with the procedures of TSCA and experienced some protection against litigation through compliance. It also welcomed formal constraints in TSCA
that restricted states from taking unilateral steps to impose more rigorous
oversight. However, the legislation was widely recognized as having serious
shortcomings, leaving many chemicals with limited review or regulatory
oversight. Decade after decade, TSCA continued to drift, until a major revision was passed with bipartisan support in 2016.

Similar concerns have been raised as states have attempted to use their
considerable jurisdiction to regulate oil and gas drilling using hydraulic
fracturing and horizontal drilling techniques. Federal legislation generally
defers to state prerogative in this area, preserving enormous state latitude
to design their own oversight of risks to air, land, water, and public health.
Many states have simply fallen back on their established statutes and institutions that oversee conventional drilling practices, including some that have
remained in place for decades. The new technologies, however, involve a great
many new risks, ranging from groundwater contamination to the release
of methane, a greenhouse gas, into the atmosphere. This reflects the highly
decentralized deployment of large numbers of drilling operations, substantial
use of water and chemicals in extraction, and extremely deep exploration
involved in unconventional drilling. States have struggled mightily to make
adjustments to this new extractive era, particularly in instances in which
policy had drifted for an extended period but comfortable relationships have
emerged between regulatory agencies and regulated industries.[97]

These types of concerns offer an important reminder that the sheer
political survival of a policy over an extended period does not automatically mean it is delivering intended public benefits. As Ann Carlson and
Robert Fri have noted, "Policies may sometimes be durable simply because
they are weak or ineffectual and thus generate little opposition."[98] Carbon
pricing policies need not be exempt from this pattern. This could emerge
as a significant point of concern once evidence on policy performance has
been gathered over time, leading to the question of whether there was any
public or environmental benefit to be derived from continued operation of
the policy.

All of these concerns apply to Alberta's venture into carbon taxes and
cap-and-trade. A centerpiece of Alberta's strategy was a redefinition of

how carbon emissions are measured. Rather than address actual emissions, Alberta instead focused on the "carbon intensity" of emissions, weighed as a ratio of economic activity. Under this reframing, Alberta could contend that it had been reducing its carbon emission intensity since the 1990s, whereby emissions had declined when measured as a proportion of economic activity (measured in terms of intensity), if not in the aggregate. This metric approach could then facilitate the launch of a carbon pricing system with a goal to reduce carbon intensity rather than actual emissions. In 2002, the province announced "the beginning of a 50-year initiative to dramatically reduce carbon emissions," albeit one measured in terms of intensity.[99]

Alberta established new public management units to take the lead in implementation, including Alberta Climate Change Central, Energy Solutions Alberta, and the Alberta Energy Research Institute to launch this half-century effort. Emissions reporting began promptly as the province prepared to launch its novel hybrid carbon pricing system. The Specified Gas Emitters Regulations (SGER) was put into operation for domestic electricity generation and major industrial plants in 2007, offering distinct options for meeting future carbon intensity reduction targets. Newer facilities would be exempt for their first three years of operation, further softening any impact on emissions.

The carbon tax compliance path entailed payment of a $15 (Canadian) per ton contribution to the Alberta Climate Change and Emissions Management Fund (CCEMF), which would allocate funds for various carbon reduction projects in the province. The cap-and-trade compliance path involved purchasing Government Emission Performance Credits that had been earned by firms that had exceeded their intensity reduction targets. It could also entail purchasing Government Offset Credits for approved offset projects located within the province. Finally, firms could comply by demonstrating improved energy efficiency of their operations as measured in intensity terms.[100]

The SGER did not experience many of the profound managerial problems that bedeviled the EU Emissions Trading Scheme. There was early recognition that intensity targets would be reached earlier than anticipated and so the province adjusted these accordingly in 2008, agreeing to a nonbinding plan to stabilize actual emissions by 2020 and to begin to reduce them thereafter.[101] Carbon prices did not fluctuate wildly or crash suddenly, the government faced no cyber attacks on the trading system, and there were no lamentations about excessive allocation of allowances. Alberta was a model of carbon pricing stability compared to the European Union.

However, there were considerable concerns that the policy was little more than a symbolic gesture. Offsets were used with far greater intensity than anticipated, in part because the province offered extremely generous terms for projects established before its carbon pricing system was even in place. More than 80 percent of the approved offsets during the first three years of SGER operation were for projects such as wind turbine siting and expanded low-till agricultural practices that had been undertaken in the five years before carbon pricing began.[102] This pattern continued into the second half-decade of SGER operation, supplemented by "double offset credits" for certain types of projects. Between 2007 and 2012, more than half of SGER compliance was handled through these mechanisms.

Aspirations that tax revenues collected in the CCEMF would support projects that reduced emissions were dashed by a series of setbacks with initial projects. Most of the funds were concentrated into a small set of initiatives directly linked to complying facilities. They included projects intended to capture and store carbon dioxide below the ground, create underground pipelines to attempt to increase oil extraction efficiency, gasify coal below ground, and improve efficiencies in oil sand operations. All of these were quite expensive and highly unproven, leading to allegations that the fund was essentially a cycled payment process that let industry use most of its tax revenues for its own research and development projects. As one study noted, this allocation method would "reduce the effective carbon price that they [oil and gas producers] pay."[103] In any event, a number of these projects faced setbacks and even cancellation, leaving little indication after a decade that there had been any consequential environmental gain from the use of these funds.[104]

Multiple studies examining SGER conclude that its overall impact on carbon emissions has been largely negligible or even nonexistent. These studies note that SGER features so many loopholes that it imposes a price on less than 10 percent of total Alberta emissions[105] and costs approximately three cents per barrel of extracted oil.[106] Canada's Ecofiscal Commission concluded in a detailed 2015 study that SGER compliance costs in 2012 were only 77 cents per ton. As the Commission report concluded, Alberta's carbon pricing system "has led to minimal emissions reductions, partly due to its limited stringency."[107] A 2014 study found that the policy had no significant impact on annual emissions or emissions intensity.[108] As David McLaughlin, one of Canada's leading experts on carbon pricing and a former director of the National Round Table on Energy and the Economy, noted in 2016, the Alberta carbon pricing system "hasn't reduced a single ton of emissions yet."[109]

More than a full decade after the launch of the process that led to carbon pricing, Alberta's next era of provincial leaders endorsed the policy. Premier Alison Redford continued to campaign on the merits of the SGER as a pioneering model of carbon pricing. Much like Klein in the early 2000s, she praised this effort in the United States in 2013 in seeking support for completing the proposed Keystone XL Pipeline that was crucial to expanded oil sands development. Alberta is "leading the way" on carbon pricing, she wrote in a *USA Today* op-ed. "We have a $15 price per ton on carbon for those who do not meet legislated limits. We take the revenue generated from this levy and direct all the money into a clean technology fund."[110]

Alberta officials contended that the SGER had been so successful that they would consider expanding it in coming years with higher prices, though working within the same intensity targets as the original. This message was clearly aimed at American audiences to attempt to build a pipeline partnership. It also extended those claims within Canada, contending that its approach to carbon pricing was so successful that it should be embraced as a model for federal policy.

The Alberta case indicates that it is possible to devise a carbon pricing policy that works well politically and is managed without turmoil, even over an extended period of time. But that does not mean that it produces a consequential impact on carbon emissions reduction. More robust cases are not easy to find but do exist, as we will consider in the next two chapters.

4   When Carbon Taxes Work

It is tempting to survey the cases discussed in chapter 3 and dismiss carbon pricing as a political nonstarter. Initial policy adoption is challenging, probably a long shot at best in many settings. Even ideational backers giving their strong support must confront the harsh reality of trying to persuade political officials to embrace near-term energy price increases for which they may later face electoral wrath. Surmounting steep adoption hurdles opens up further challenges, including policy launch. Subsequent elections and leadership changes may lead to policy reversal. Carbon prices that manage to run those gauntlets then must demonstrate an ability to meet environmental performance and cost-effectiveness expectations in a reasonable period of time if they are to serve any role beyond symbolism. As we have seen, the first decade and a half of the twenty-first century is littered with carbon pricing initiatives that either crashed-and-burned upon introduction, suffered significant and even decisive setbacks following adoption, or survived but accomplished little.

But that is not the end of the story. This period also demonstrated that carbon pricing can be more than a solely ideational exercise in climate policy in an imaginary world free of political realities. In a small set of cases, each of the hurdles identified and explored in chapter 3 were cleared. Both carbon taxes and cap-and-trade in these instances were adopted politically. They then proved resilient throughout their first decade of operation. This entailed launching policy in a timely way, then securing confirmation through subsequent elections and leadership changes that did not impair policy implementation. They created adaptive management systems capable of phasing-in requirements and making needed adjustments as unanticipated challenges arose.

Over time, these carbon prices sustained and expanded their base of political support. Proponents relied heavily on strategic allocation of pricing revenues to pursue other policy objectives and to build an expanding constituency. This enabled constituents to experience tangible policy benefits in the near term rather than wait for longer-term benefits that might defy precise measurement. These cases transform our conventional definition of political cost-imposition through carbon pricing. They demonstrate that the sustained allocation of benefits to designated recipients can build a supportive coalition that grows over time rather than contract once the sticker shock of initial costs are realized.[1]

After an initial decade of operation, these policies demonstrate promising performance outcomes, measured in estimates of impact on emissions and the economy. Multiple studies emerged to provide a chorus of encouraging empirical evidence regarding performance. They confirmed that these policies occupied solid political, managerial, and economic ground and could serve as a model for emulation elsewhere. The jurisdictions that adopted them might serve as a formal partner for others wanting to take a collaborative step.

There were indeed limits to these policies. None produced a climate mitigation silver bullet with a carbon price set so high that it dramatically reduced consumption of carbon-based fuels. The emerging prices for these carbon taxes and cap-and-trade auctions were relatively low and were supplemented by other policies. There was no evident political appetite to increase these prices significantly over time and replicate the tobacco pricing experience, so they tended to work alongside other climate policies and complement them rather than replace them with a demanding carbon pricing regime. They gave every indication of being politically durable. Diffusion to other jurisdictions, whether through replication elsewhere or formal integration across governments, appeared plausible politically by the end of 2015, albeit with many uncertainties.

Nonetheless, these cases demonstrate the classic limitations of a small-N sample. It is increasingly common to dismiss such cases in the policy sciences; they may point to outlier examples rather than indicate a more representative base to consider more generalizable principles that could guide policy development. Did an entrepreneurial leader take political risks and assemble a one-time-only coalition to gain support? Did adoption hinge on a unique window of opportunity, whether a localized episode that heightened public concern about climate change or unusual political timing? Did low-emission and low-cost energy alternatives emerge that would have been developed in the absence of pricing policies? All of these would be appropriate questions to apply to this small set of cases.

That said, it would be unfair to examine the politics of carbon pricing while dismissing cases such as British Columbia's carbon tax and the Regional Greenhouse Gas Initiative's nine-state cap-and-trade system as a pair of flukes. Despite the considerable differences in their design and geographic location, both demonstrate the possibilities of navigating each of the policy life-cycle hurdles that have confounded other carbon pricing experiments. Neither are textbook examples of how carbon pricing would work in an ideal economic scenario, but both offer numerous insights into how carbon pricing ideas can evolve into politically feasible and administratively viable operations. By the end of 2015, as further discussed in chapter 7, these examples demonstrated that carbon pricing might have a viable political path forward.

In turn, other cases began to emerge during this period that demonstrated similar promise. There was no identical counterpart to British Columbia, and yet other North American jurisdictions began to find some political traction either with an explicit carbon tax or a policy that used a different label but essentially achieved similar results through a "fee," a "charge," or an equivalent mechanism. In cap-and-trade, a unique partnership emerged from the wreckage of the Western Climate Initiative, pairing California and Quebec in the novel launch of a trading system between sub-federal jurisdictions from different nations.

Carbon taxes receive primary consideration in this chapter, which explores the conditions under which such taxes in British Columbia and beyond were adopted and have been sustained across each stage of the policy life-cycle for over a decade. It is followed by a chapter that explores cap-and-trade, through a review of the Regional Greenhouse Gas Initiative and emerging supplemental cases. In both instances, other precedents helped pave the way in designing and implementing new policy, just as these in turn may serve as stepping stones for expanded carbon pricing development elsewhere.

The Nordic Path to Carbon Taxes

Energy taxes were largely confined to individual fuels, most notably gasoline, until a quintet of northern European nations adopted cross-cutting carbon taxes in the early 1990s. Initial adoption by Finland and the

Netherlands in 1990 was followed by Norway and Sweden in 1991 and Denmark the following year.[2] This reflected a period of growing concern in these nations about climate change and other environmental risks as well as a period in which environmentally focused parties began to experience some electoral success.[3] These taxes built on an established tradition of high national consumption tax rates that included transportation fuels and other consumable goods, but went further to address the carbon content of all fossil fuels across multiple sectors.[4]

These taxes proved durable politically and remained in place more than a quarter-century after adoption. There was no major effort to repeal or reverse them without a carbon pricing substitute, although they were frequently adjusted over subsequent decades. One significant change involved phasing out some important applications of the taxes as the European cap-and-trade system expanded coverage into overlapping economic sectors, often serving to reduce actual carbon prices given the numerous ETS limitations discussed in chapter 3. These taxes generally moved rapidly into implementation upon adoption, measured in months rather than years. Many of these tax rates range from $15 to $75 per ton (translated into American dollars) of carbon dioxide across fuels (see table 4.1). Both nominal and real tax rates tended to be highest in Sweden, exceeding $100 per ton for each fuel source.[5] There were also exemptions in Sweden for emissions from such industrial processes as coke ovens, blast furnaces, lime kilns, cement production, and refineries, with considerable parallels to exemption patterns in other Nordic cases.[6]

Revenue was targeted in these nations for such purposes as reducing personal income or payroll taxes, supporting government programs, or underwriting other environmental objectives.[7] In Finland, for example, all carbon tax revenues were placed into the general budget, whereas the Netherlands used funds to reduce individual and business taxes and also to support accelerated depreciation of environmental equipment purchases.[8] The taxes were widely thought to have helped reduce greenhouse gas emissions in these nations from where they would have been without the tax.[9] In Sweden, emissions dropped 24 percent between 1990 and 2014, despite 60 percent gross domestic product growth. Reductions were greatest in areas directly impacted by the tax, such as heating fuel for households and services.[10]

Table 4.1
Nordic carbon tax rates.

	Carbon Content	Denmark	Finland	Netherlands	Norway	Sweden
Coal	26		$58.09	$6.02	$17.33	$122.04
Heavy Fuel Oil	21.5	$26.25	$73.09	(not covered)	$46.78	
Light Fuel Oil	19.95	$25.95	$67.34	(not covered)	$54.50	
Diesel	19.6	$23.75	$85.07	(not covered)	$53.53	$144.40
Gasoline	19.3	$25.41	$86.15	(not covered)	$53.79	$135.52
Natural Gas	14.5	$23.71	$65.62	$156.67	$47.22	$140.67

Note: Carbon tax rates by fuel type, in USD/tonne of CO2.

Sources: Erick Lachapelle, "Energy Security and Climate Change Policy in the OECD: The Political Economy of Carbon-Energy Taxation" (PhD diss., Graduate Department of Political Science, University of Toronto, 2011), https://tspace.library.utoronto.ca /bitstream/1807/29780/1/Lachapelle_Erick_201106_PhD_thesis.pdf. IEA Energy Prices and Taxes: Second Quarter 2017 Country Notes, http://wds.iea.org/wds/pdf/EPT _countrynotes.pdf; US Energy Information Administration, "Carbon Dioxide Emissions Coefficients by Fuel," February 2, 2016, https://www.eia.gov/environment/emissions /co2_vol_mass.php.

The political path to carbon tax adoption was eased through concessions to industries thought particularly vulnerable to international competition or susceptible to migration elsewhere. This is evident in the considerable variation in actual tax rates depending on the particular source to which it is applied, contrary to a purer model of carbon taxation that imposes rates closely linked to actual carbon emissions. In Norway, for example, fossil fuels used in aviation, process industries, and on-land gas and oil production received favored treatment as reflected in significant exemptions.[11] Taxation of offshore oil and gas production was a long-standing topic of political controversy given debates over its possible transition into the ETS and industry claims that significant taxes would undermine its competitiveness.[12] The Norwegian government kept offshore production within the realm of carbon taxation rather than shifting it fully into continental emissions trading, however, and approved a major increase in its carbon tax rates in 2012.

The issue of concessions and exemptions would also compromise subsequent efforts to develop carbon taxes in other EU member states. Both the

United Kingdom and Germany developed their own versions of these taxes in the following decades, though these were considerably more modest in scope. In the United Kingdom case, most of its annual "climate change levy" could be erased by firms that met negotiated energy efficiency targets or purchased EU Emissions Trading Scheme (ETS) allowances. In the German experience, there were substantial exemptions for energy-intensive industries. In both cases, concerns about disrupting some sustained use of coal was a significant concern, leading toward favored treatment status despite coal's high carbon content.[13]

Alongside the lack of significant diffusion beyond the initial surge of adoption in the early 1990s, the EU's decision to move toward cap-and-trade via the ETS further marginalized carbon taxes. Nonetheless, the Nordic cases have continued to receive considerable attention in carbon tax conversations, albeit not with the frequency or visibility of the American sulfur dioxide case in cap-and-trade deliberations. They demonstrated that it is possible in at least some political contexts to adopt and sustain such a tax. In British Columbia, this model ultimately proved far more attractive than cap-and-trade or regulatory options.

Carbon Taxation Comes to North America

British Columbia seemed destined to adopt nearly every climate policy option except carbon taxes during the first decades of the twenty-first century. Its signature industry of forestry faced a profound threat from an insect that proliferated under warmer winters linked to climate change. Its premier city, Vancouver, began to confront far-reaching risks from its massive development in areas with low sea level and it ranked among the world's major cities at greatest risk from climate change. The province had a strong reputation for environmental concern and policy innovation. A center-left political party with a significant following made climate change mitigation a focal point of its efforts to secure an electoral majority and other parties were on board to do something.

Carbon taxes, however, seemed a real stretch. British Columbia experimented with cap-and-trade in pilot programs, and political leaders were clearly smitten by the possibility of working closely with other states in the Pacific Northwest, such as Washington and Oregon.[14] California held a particular allure, as it developed a wide range of climate policies, sought cross-border partners, and offered a global stage for climate summits with its high-profile governor. In California, just about every policy imaginable was under consideration or had been adopted by mid-decade, as will be discussed in the following chapter. But, as further discussed in chapter 6, carbon taxes were essentially ruled out in California for political reasons. To the north, there was clearly no groundswell in British Columbia between 2000 and 2007 to adopt a carbon tax.

British Columbia, though, is also known as a bit of a quirky and unpredictable place, both politically and culturally. It has frequently hosted fringe political parties that have no counterpart in other Canadian provinces and yet often rise to power.[15] Independence from the rest of Canada, particularly the central and eastern regions, has long been a central concern,[16] although it has not moved to the extremes of Quebec and its formal exploration of secession in past decades. Nonetheless, British Columbia possesses an enduring political streak that reveres independence to chart its own course. As Premier Gordon Campbell explained in 1996, he viewed "British Columbia as the West, Alberta, Saskatchewan, and Manitoba as the Near East, Ontario and Quebec as the Mideast, and everything past that as the Far East."[17] So it was not obvious just how such a polity might address climate change.

One additional factor that has dominated British Columbia politics is economic dependence on natural resources, including timber cultivation, energy production, and mineral extraction. British Columbia produces more lumber for export than all other provinces combined.[18] Its historic reliance on abundant hydro power has created the possibility of major exports of carbon-free electricity. The province is also a major Canadian producer of fossil fuels, reflecting large natural gas and coal deposits. In 2016, for example, British Columbia ranked second only to Alberta in natural gas output and produced considerably more than all remaining provinces combined.[19] Moreover, there was promise of significant discoveries of additional natural gas, suggesting that British Columbia could become an ever-bigger source of this prized commodity, particularly if it expanded use of hydraulic fracturing techniques to extract it and liquification techniques to export it.[20] British Columbia also ranked second to Alberta in coal production, responsible for about 40 percent of national output from its operating mines in the 2000s.

A carbon tax offers an interesting option, allowing British Columbia to reduce its own use of fossil fuels and related greenhouse gas emissions without killing the golden goose of fossil fuel extraction and export. Much like energy-producing US states and their severance taxes (discussed in chapter 2), the province produced significant revenue from royalties on the extraction of natural gas, coal, and oil. So drilling generated a substantial amount of economic development and government funds in the province, particularly in the northeastern region where most natural gas supplies were located. But at least two-thirds of the energy extracted in British Columbia is consumed in other provinces or nations, especially given the dominant role of hydro and the province's limited need for coal or natural gas for power.[21] A provincial carbon tax might be imposed on fossil fuels used to facilitate extraction operations, but not on their postproduction consumption elsewhere. In turn, it would not interfere with existing royalties that rivaled those already in operation in other provinces, such as Alberta, or severance taxes in other states, such as Alaska. Consequently, such a tax offers a way to achieve internal carbon emission reductions while not necessarily discouraging continued fossil fuel extraction for export.

But there was a big catch. A carbon tax of any size would still impose higher prices on British Columbia's citizens and so could face considerable political opposition. Even a major exception for energy extraction would not hide this fact. This may explain why the carbon tax idea had no significant or visible political support beyond the academic and think tank communities between 2000 and 2006. The political party most engaged on climate change policy, the center-left New Democrats, actively endorsed numerous climate policy steps. They were on record, however, as being strongly opposed to carbon taxes, fearful of their possible impacts on lower-income residents as well as the anticipated political backlash. Instead, they supported a wide range of regulations and subsidies related to energy efficiency and renewable energy. Without a serious base of political support, carbon taxation increasingly appeared to be one policy path that British Columbia would not take.

Carbon Tax Adoption

Enter Gordon Campbell as an unexpected carbon tax policy entrepreneur. Such an entrepreneur uses a position of political leadership to champion a particular policy idea or cause. This person does not necessarily invent the idea but rather embraces and advances it, even if such a step entails political risks. Policy entrepreneurs were common in climate policy development during earlier periods of policy formation in American states when organized interests were not as engaged as they were in later periods.[22] But Campbell would be uniquely successful in North America and globally as a carbon tax policy entrepreneur.

By 2007, Campbell embraced carbon taxation as a central plank of his Liberal Party strategy. There was not an obvious political benefit to this and his endorsement occurred after he had won reelection as premier of British Columbia in 2005. As premier and in his previous roles as head of the Liberal Party in opposition and as Vancouver mayor, Campbell was not known as a champion of environmental causes, much less climate change. Instead, his signature issue was fiscal responsibility, whereby he relished tax rate cuts and balanced budgets far more than domestic policy innovation. Governing from the center-right, he had not previously embraced any form of carbon taxes in his many prior electoral bids, including 2005.

Nonetheless, Campbell nodded repeatedly and approvingly in February 2007 as Lieutenant Governor Iona Campagnolo read the Throne Speech that the premier had authored (see table 4.2). Campagnolo revealed a dizzying array of new climate initiatives, including creation of a new Climate Action Secretariat in the provincial government, establishment of tailpipe emission standards in concert with California, plans for a low-carbon fuel standard, new energy efficiency standards, and even plans for a proposed hydrogen highway that would stretch along the West Coast. There were also a series of hints that a coming tax reform would be linked to all of these policies. "[The reform] will look for new ways to encourage overall tax savings through shifts in behavior that reduce carbon consumption," explained Campagnolo.[23]

Within months of the Throne Speech, Campbell and his leadership team rolled out plans for a carbon tax that would ultimately reach $30 (Canadian) per ton on carbon dioxide emissions. It applied to all fossil fuels used in the province under the banner of "revenue neutrality," whereby all revenues would be returned to British Columbians through rebates and tax rate reductions. Thirteen months after the Throne Speech, the world's biggest carbon tax outside of northern Europe was adopted. Five months after adoption, it began operation.

It would be a vast overstatement to suggest that this carbon tax was a one-man show. However, it is difficult to envision a similar outcome under any other premier, whether a Liberal or New Democrat. As a recently reelected

Table 4.2
British Columbia carbon tax timeline.

February 2007	Speech from the throne sets climate change as B.C.'s top priority.
February 2008	Carbon tax adopted in provincial budget.
July 2008	B.C. implements carbon tax; rate starts at $10/ton (Canadian).
February 2009	Government introduces grant for northern and rural homeowners.
May 2009	B.C. Liberals win reelection to thwart "axe the tax" proposal from New Democratic Party.
July 2009	Rate increases to $15/ton (Canadian).
July 2010	Rate increases to $20/ton (Canadian).
March 2011	Clark succeeds Campbell as B.C. premier.
July 2011	Rate increases to $25/ton (Canadian).
February 2012	Government announces carbon tax review in 2012 budget; provides exemption for greenhouse growers.
July 2012	Rate increases to $30/ton (Canadian).
February 2013	Government extends exemptions for greenhouse growers and adds exemption for agriculture.
May 2013	B.C. Liberal Party wins provincial election; carbon tax rate and coverage frozen for five years, or until other jurisdictions implement comparable approaches.
November 2014	Liquefied Natural Gas Income Tax Act passes amid LNG push.
March 2017	Prosperity Fund created when Budget Measures Implementation Act passes.

Source: The Pembina Institute, *The B.C. Carbon Tax: Backgrounder* (Drayton Valley, AB: Pembina Institute, 2014), http://www.pembina.org/reports/lessons-bc-carbon-tax-pembina-institute-112014.pdf.

premier, Campbell had a strong political base that was not encouraging him to take a potentially risky step in climate policy. He faced no constitutional pressures to step down, given the absence of formal term limits, and so he would have to face future voters with this tax on his record in the subsequent election. Nonetheless, he ultimately used this tax to help propel him to a third consecutive electoral victory in 2009.

No other political leader, in North America or beyond, played such a central role in carbon tax adoption between 1995 and 2015. What compelled Campbell to take a step that seemed so contrary to political norms observed in other cases, including ones where there was some support for carbon pricing?[24] At least five factors appear to have contributed to this decision, each of which reflects some idiosyncratic elements that could limit the prospects for following this path to carbon taxation in other jurisdictions.

First, Campbell had a political incentive to think boldly about climate change given the saliency of the threat to British Columbia forests posed by the mountain pine beetle. The gradual shift toward warmer winters in the province eliminated the extreme cold necessary to keep this insect under control. Between 1982 and 2002, it became increasingly clear that forests were under growing threat due to the proliferation of the beetle, with an estimated loss of 300 million trees valued at an estimated $6 billion.[25] Continued seasonal shifts served to expand the areas where the beetle could thrive, infecting nearly 80 percent of British Columbia forests by 2007. The Canadian Forest Service estimated in 2008, the year of carbon tax adoption, that 80 percent of mature pine forests in British Columbia might be destroyed within five years.[26] Given the substantial and historic role of the timber industry in the provincial economy and the dramatic photos illustrating the rapid change in forest color and health, British Columbia had tangible measures of climate change impacts to trigger public support for the new policy.

Second, worries about forestry health in British Columbia surpassed those about the province's economic health in 2007. There were no obvious signs of recession at the time and the province's 4.2 percent unemployment rate was well below national averages. There were concerns about escalating housing prices, but British Columbia appeared distant from major turmoil about the economy. This afforded Campbell considerably more latitude to advance climate policy that would increase the price of energy than many counterparts would later face when mired in recession.

Third, Campbell had a strong ideational network of allies, including members of his leadership team and locally based academic experts. He began to study publications about climate change and carbon taxation well before making any public endorsement.[27] This clearly reflected his broader desire to shift taxation away from labor and toward consumption. The idea of revenue neutrality worked well with his larger goal of containing provincial expenditures and deterring deficits. Campbell had some strong colleagues in his inner circle, most notably Finance Minister Carole Taylor, who helped design the policy and shepherd its early implementation.[28] Campbell also remained in close contact with California Governor Arnold Schwarzenegger and state officials, ultimately placing British Columbia into the Western Climate Initiative, despite his primary focus on carbon taxes rather than cap-and-trade. His bold steps gave him an almost-immediate star quality in environmental policy circles, reflected in heroic treatment when he ventured to California or other meetings on climate change.[29] Consequently, carbon taxation quickly transitioned from a political risk to a legacy-making issue.

Fourth, there were significant personal dimensions at play in his decision to become a carbon tax champion. Campbell faced a huge public embarrassment in 2003 with a drunk driving charge during a Hawaii vacation, including media coverage that would be any politician's nightmare. Evolving into a climate change entrepreneur helped reduce the damage from this event as he reclaimed moral high ground. In turn, Campbell was clearly moved by a trade mission to China, where he observed profound air quality problems.[30] He also often spoke openly about how becoming a grandfather for the first time made him think more about taking responsibility on intergenerational issues such as climate change.[31] Some observers have described Campbell's transition as a "conversion on the road to Damascus" or "finding religion."[32]

Fifth, there may also have been significant strategic considerations in play for Campbell. Some have likened his carbon tax step to a Nixon-to-China moment, where an astute politician on the right sees a unique opportunity to do the unexpected and gain politically from taking this step. Campbell had been outflanked on climate change by the New Democrats previously and had a reason to fear that this might heighten his difficulty in winning a third term following his 2005 reelection. His support not only of climate policy but the specific tool of carbon taxation served ultimately to marginalize the New Democrats and even open them to charges of hypocrisy on climate protection when they came out in opposition to the proposal. Ironically, in 2009 he campaigned against the New Democrats as "one of the most anti-environmental parties in the country," due to their opposition to the carbon tax that he had championed.[33]

Launching the Tax Seamlessly

Simplicity of policy design can mightily assist timely policy launches. Clear statutory construction provides direction to implementing agencies and illuminates intent, making it clear to multiple constituencies. Relatively straightforward policy tools can reduce the need to create new administrative structures to interpret and operationalize the policy. Policy simplicity may also obviate the need to recruit, hire, and deploy substantial new staff who would otherwise need to take considerable time to assemble work teams and complete rounds of regulatory development. A sound constitutional foundation can also deter or deflect potential legal challenges that consume time and funding. Years of inertia can be compressed into months of constructive engagement.

Carbon cap-and-trade has generally represented the antithesis of simple or transparent policy design. Such bills have often been drenched in complexity and confusion. The sprawling American Clean Energy and Security Act likely faced a massive administrative launch process and possible years of delay had it been adopted. Cap-and-trade programs launched at the state level have required many years of interpretation and administrative preparation to begin operations, as discussed in chapters 5 and 6. This phenomenon has also been evident in Canada and beyond, frequently leading to long lags in initial implementation and creating policy launch problems that not only delay matters but can serve to undermine political support for the policy in the long interim.[34] One could, of course, envision carbon taxes that were so laden with complex provisions and favors to numerous special interests that implementation could also face extended delays.

In vivid contrast, the British Columbia carbon tax had a smooth and nearly seamless administrative launch. Five months after passage, its Carbon Tax Act was fully operational and being applied to nearly two dozen variants of fossil fuels (see table 4.3). This reflected the relative simplicity of the carbon tax as a policy tool in comparison to cap-and-trade. But it also stemmed from a remarkably clear and orderly statute that totaled ninety pages. The legislation followed a straightforward path toward easy interpretation and rapid implementation that was based on established legal precedents. There might be a future political backlash but the initiation of the carbon tax would be smooth and enable it to advance to the next stage of the policy life-cycle.

The carbon tax built directly on the foundation of long-established excise taxes for gasoline and diesel motor fuels as well as provincial sales taxes. According to the Carbon Tax Act, "a retail dealer must collect the tax imposed by this Act at the time of selling fuel to a purchaser."[35] In turn, "a person who sells fuel is deemed to be an agent of the government and as agent must levy and collect tax."[36] This meant that the province "essentially

Table 4.3
British Columbia carbon tax fuel rates by type (in $Canadian).

Fuel	Units for Tax Rates	July 1, 2008 to June 30, 2009	July 1, 2009 to December 31, 2009	January 1, 2010 to June 30, 2010	July 1, 2010 to June 30, 2011	July 1, 2011 to June 30, 2012	July 1, 2012 to June 30, 2018
Liquid Fuels							
Gasoline	¢/liter	2.34	3.51	3.33	4.45	5.56	6.67
Light Fuel Oil	¢/liter	2.69	4.04	3.84	5.11	6.39	7.67
Heavy Fuel Oil	¢/liter	3.15	4.73	4.73	6.3	7.88	9.45
Aviation Fuel	¢/liter	2.46	3.69	3.69	4.92	6.15	7.38
Jet Fuel	¢/liter	2.61	3.92	3.92	5.22	6.53	7.83
Kerosene	¢/liter	2.54	3.81	3.81	5.22	6.53	7.83
Naphtha	¢/liter	2.55	3.83	3.83	5.1	6.38	7.65
Methanol	¢/liter	1.09	1.64	1.64	2.18	2.73	3.27
Gaseous Fuels							
Natural Gas	¢/cubic meter	1.90	2.85	2.85	3.80	4.75	5.70
Propane	¢/liter	1.54	2.31	2.31	3.08	3.85	4.62
Butane	¢/liter	1.76	2.64	2.64	3.52	4.40	5.28

Ethane	¢/liter	0.98	1.47	1.47	1.96	2.45	2.94
Gas Liquids	¢/liter			2.48	3.30	4.13	4.95
Pentanes Plus	¢/liter			2.64	3.52	4.40	5.28
Refinery Gas	¢/cubic meter	1.76	2.64	2.64	3.52	4.40	5.28
Coke Oven Gas	¢/cubic meter	1.61	2.42	2.42	3.22	4.03	4.83
Solid Fuels							
Low Heat Value Coal	$/ton	17.77	26.66	26.66	35.54	44.43	53.31
High Heat Value Coal	$/ton	20.77	31.16	31.16	41.54	51.93	62.31
Coke	$/ton	24.87	37.31	37.31	49.74	62.18	74.61
Petroleum Coke	¢/liter	3.67	5.51	5.51	7.34	9.18	11.01
Combustibles							
Peat	$/ton	10.22	15.33	15.33	20.44	25.55	30.66
Tires - Shredded	$/ton	23.91	35.87	35.87	47.82	59.78	71.73
Tires - Whole	$/ton	20.80	31.20	31.20	41.60	52.00	62.40

Sources: British Columbia Ministry of Finance, "Tax Schedule," 2010, http://www.sbr.gov.bc.ca/documents_library/shared_documents /carbon_tax_rates_by_fuel_type_from_jan_2010.pdf; *Carbon Tax Act*, S.B.C. 2008 c. 40, s. 14, http://www.bclaws.ca/Recon/document/ID /freeside/ 00_08040_01#part14.

deputizes every fossil fuel retailer as a tax collector, requiring the collection of the tax at the retail-sales level."[37] Tax collection and remittance procedures require fuel sellers to pay a security identical to the tax payable on the final retail sale, with consumers then required to pay the tax through their purchase.[38]

Under this arrangement, the tax is moved well downstream whereby extracted fossil fuels transition into a refined product ready for retail use. Gasoline service stations apply this tax on the transportation fuels that they sell whereas natural gas suppliers apply it to monthly customer bills.[39] As a result, the tax is "clearly shown on households' bills for natural gas for home heating and gasoline for vehicles."[40]

None of this was particularly new, but rather an expansion of an established tax collection system common to Canadian provinces and American states. In British Columbia, gasoline excise and provincial sales taxes were launched shortly after World War II and the province had considerable experience in adjusting rates over subsequent decades. This was reflected in some modest increases in provincial gasoline taxes in the decade prior to carbon tax adoption as well as provisions for larger cities such as Vancouver and Victoria to insert their own taxes into the mix.[41] Adding measures reflecting fossil fuel combustion and production of carbon dioxide would be different than adjusting existing gasoline tax rates. Yet they would prove relatively straightforward given the clear marching orders provided by the legislation.

These changes did not require any consequential ministry costs, staffing additions, or administrative reconfigurations. The 2008 provincial budget noted that this taxation system was adopted in part because it "minimizes the cost of administration to government and the compliance cost to those collecting the tax on the government's behalf."[42]

In contrast to the carbon tax, the remainder of the British Columbia climate strategy entailed separate legislation that necessitated a major reorganization of the provincial government to address the wide range of new tasks. This included integration of separate units into a new Climate Action Secretariat. The Secretariat would be located within the Ministry of Environment but would have its own deputy minister, budget, and human resources staff, "with sufficient authority to provide effective coordination of a range of policy tools."[43] It provided direct support to a cabinet committee on climate action that was chaired by Premier Campbell. The Secretariat was modeled closely after the complex climate governance system developed in California in the Schwarzenegger administration.[44]

This reorganization required considerable time for developing new routines, particularly to implement more complicated policies such as low-carbon fuel standards. Substantial staff time was also invested in possible adoption of a cap-and-trade program for sources not covered under the carbon tax, in conjunction with the Western Climate Initiative, but the province ultimately backed away from this option. Despite a steady pattern of budget and staff cuts in environmental and energy ministries during the 2000s, provincial budgets attempted to protect governmental resources for those elements of the climate plan that were more administratively complex and costly than the carbon tax. This was necessary to complete the lengthy processes of launching many new climate programs.

In vivid contrast, the carbon tax went almost immediately into operation, located not in the heavily publicized Climate Action Secretariat but rather the more staid Ministry of Finance. There were no significant organizational changes required in the ministry to operationalize the tax. Some additional econometric modeling to determine the impact of the tax on various industries and groups was secured from outside experts.[45] The Ministry also provided detailed annual reports on the tax revenues and related tax reductions implemented for public review and use by elected officials in overseeing compliance.[46]

But these adjustments were modest in comparison with the start-up challenges of other climate policies.[47] There were no significant glitches or gaps in the administration of the tax. In turn, carbon tax implementation also benefited from the early mentorship of one of its architects, Finance Minister Carole Taylor. Neither she nor her successors would ever be docked up to 15 percent of salary in the event of carbon tax implementation failures, an option that was authorized in the legislation.

The launch of the carbon tax was also eased by a clear, five-year phase-in strategy. The tax was immediately applied to all fossil fuel sources but only at a tax rate of $10 (Canadian) per ton on carbon dioxide emissions from combustion. This rate gradually increased by $5 per ton annually until reaching $30 per ton in 2012. As a result, the tax as applied to gasoline climbed from 2.34 cents per liter in 2008 to 6.67 cents per liter in 2012, which translated at the end point to approximately 27 cents per gallon if applied in the United States.[48] Other fossil fuels experienced similar phase-ins, as outlined in table 4.3, which draws directly from the tax table included in the Carbon Tax Act.

This phase-in process made it possible to fully operate all facets of the tax and familiarize constituents while gradually increasing tax rates and tax reduction allocations. There were no reported administrative problems with this phase-in and some experts felt that it helped establish public confidence in the tax following adoption. As Taylor noted, the lower initial rate allowed British Columbia to "get the principle accepted" without triggering the concern that might have followed a more rapid increase or the price volatility that has proved common under cap-and-trade.[49]

Politically Sustaining the Tax

The path from Canberra to Trenton is littered with carbon pricing cases that achieved initial adoption and launch but then faced sudden reversal after an election and resulting leadership change. Such political transitions are inevitable and represent a major challenge to enduring the policy life-cycle. This type of political reversal appeared to be a real possibility in British Columbia, following the adoption and rapid implementation of its carbon tax. The Liberal Party and Premier Campbell faced a likely electoral challenge in either 2009 or 2010. This followed not only legislative approval but also initial stages of imposing the tax and beginning to increase its rate.

There were numerous reasons the 2009 election had the possibility of going poorly for the Liberals. It is very difficult to win three consecutive terms in any political system, and the last time the Liberals had succeeded in doing so in British Columbia was between 1933 and 1941. Campbell had already served longer than any premier in more than a quarter-century and may well have been to the right of the provincial electorate on a range of issues. Moreover, the British Columbia economy faced considerable turbulence toward the end of the 2000s, with particular concerns about a potential housing bubble in prominent markets such as Vancouver.

There was also the potential vulnerability of being the champion of a policy that would markedly increase the costs of using fossil fuels amidst a global recession. Campbell's chief opponents, the New Democrats, made the tax a focal point in their electoral strategy. They maintained a strong commitment to climate change mitigation if elected but proposed a wide range of alternative policies alongside repealing the carbon tax. Indeed, their campaign became widely known for its "axe the tax" pledge, which emerged as one of the signature campaign issues where a fundamental policy difference emerged between the major parties.

It was not difficult to envision British Columbia going the way of other jurisdictions, whereby shifting political power culminated in the reversal of an initial carbon pricing commitment. However, Campbell and his Liberal Party allies approached this issue quite differently than other jurisdictions. First, they made some modest adjustments in the tax and its revenue allocation plans that improved its political prospects without abandoning core tenets of the policy. This allowed them to put the tax into operation very quickly but take some highly visible steps prior to the election to alter a few provisions that proved particularly controversial. Second, they made no bones about the fact that the carbon tax would increase energy prices but actively sought to offset concerns by emphasizing the immediate and enduring benefits. This provided important leverage, as the revenue neutrality provisions suggested that any reduction or elimination of the carbon tax would also entail a loss of linked tax reduction benefits.

Third, Campbell and his colleagues decided to double down and run on the carbon tax as a central plank in their bid for a third term. They decided to portray the New Democrats as hypocritical on climate change, unwilling to take the one step that was likely to have the greatest impact. This differed markedly from election campaigns in numerous other jurisdictions during this period. In these cases, officials linked to a carbon price through cap-and-trade tried to obscure or downplay any costs rather than acknowledge them up front. But they also struggled to identify concrete and immediate benefits that the policy could deliver. As a result, they failed to embrace carbon pricing as a bold policy move that included not only real costs but also tangible payoffs in the short term as well as additional ones over the longer haul.

Politically Targeted Adjustments

No one likes to pay taxes, but the initial reaction to the British Columbia carbon tax was particularly hostile from several constituencies who alleged unfair treatment and anticipated harm. In these cases, the province made accommodations before the May 2009 election, either through a tax rebate, tax credit, or tax exemption. Many citizens in the agricultural industry, for example, contended that the tax would threaten their way of life, given their need to use considerable fuel to cultivate their crops and transport them to market. They also contended that their remote locations required more driving than urban residents and thereby made them especially vulnerable to an energy tax. Provincial authorities had not anticipated this vociferous rural backlash, as their economic analyses prior to adoption had found that rural residents would not be particularly threatened by the tax. Rather than quibble over likely impacts, the government responded with a Northern and Rural Homeowner Benefit in 2009, providing a tax rebate up to $200 (Canadian) for these citizens and also reduced property taxes for farms. Local governments also expressed concerns about possible carbon tax impacts on their operations and secured a carbon tax rebate in 2009.[50]

None of these adjustments had a significant effect on total revenues produced by the tax or on its impact on fossil fuel use. These changes reflected sectors with relatively small amounts of total fossil fuel use and a small portion of the provincial population. But these changes did provide a way to allow the government to use its oversight of both tax rate application and tax benefit distribution to address some constituency concerns that arose following adoption without undermining the general principles of the tax. Liberal Party officials could thus argue that they had preserved the key provisions of the tax, noting both its environmental benefits but also broader contributions to fiscal and economic reform. As Environment Minister Mary Polak noted, "What I decided to do was talk about straight economics. So I said 'I don't care whether you're pro- or anti- on climate change. If you're a conservative, you should be in favor of consumption taxes over income taxes.'"[51]

Building a Constituency through Allocations

It is rare for government leaders to follow the adoption of a carbon pricing policy by providing very visible accounts of how much the new pricing system was expected to cost residents, especially prior to a first election review. However, this became a central part of the British Columbia strategy, including detailed breakdowns of the average annual cost to vehicle drivers with different fuel economies or of various industries that used considerable amounts of fossil fuels. Finance Minister Taylor was front and center in these public briefings. She pulled no punches in acknowledging that fossil fuel prices would increase promptly once legislation was passed and then continue to climb annually through at least 2012.

Taylor offset this bad news with a two-part strategy to claim credit for a pair of distinct benefits expected to stem from the carbon tax. On the one hand, she played the green card of environmental commitment, emphasizing the Liberal Party's willingness to take a bold step to address climate change with no parallel among Canadian and American jurisdictions. "We've promised you green and today we've delivered green," she explained while sporting a green suit and shoes at a major event explaining the imposed costs due to the carbon tax.[52] This promise was backed by a review of anticipated environmental benefits, both to the climate over time but also relating to other expected gains from improved air quality. These, of course, are hard to quantify with precision and cannot be allocated quickly to coincide with near-term election cycles.

That, however, was only part of the package. The carbon tax emphasis on revenue neutrality was not merely a rhetorical prop. Instead, the authorizing legislation was every bit as specific about promised tax benefits as the costs being imposed. The carbon tax thus promised rapid distribution of new tax credits as well as rate reductions in established personal and corporate taxes. All of this could be packaged as a transition toward consumption taxes while shifting away from taxing labor and income.

Taylor was masterful in ensuring that this would not be an ethereal or academic exercise. Instead, she helped devise the plan to establish these tax benefits and maximize awareness of their pending arrival during the brief interlude between legislative adoption and initiation of the tax. These steps included a new and permanent Climate Action Tax Credit that would appear on provincial income tax statements and assist low-income individuals and families to offset the costs of new carbon taxes. Provincial income tax rates were also reduced. For example, the two lowest income tax rates would be cut by 2 percent in 2008, followed by a 5 percent cut the following year. On the corporate side, the general corporate income tax rate declined from 12 to 11 percent at the point the carbon tax went into effect in mid-2008. In turn, the small business corporate income tax rate dropped from 4.5 percent to 3.5 percent at the same time.

These and other tax adjustments were highlighted immediately following the announcement of the tax, with the goal of building public support by accentuating the real and immediate economic benefits. The province also attempted to capture public attention by making a one-time Climate Action Dividend Payment of $100 (Canadian) available to every citizen who resided in the province at the end of 2007. This dividend was "intended to help British Columbians make lifestyle changes to reduce the cost of fossil fuels."[53] But it was also designed for political consumption, allocated one month before the tax began to impose costs in order to demonstrate the offsetting effects of immediate benefit allocation. As Environment Minister Polak explained, "If you tell someone he's going to save $100 on his income taxes, he probably doesn't remember how much he paid last year anyway."[54]

Taylor championed this approach by insisting, "We want to bring the benefits first."[55] These benefits continued to be calculated by the Ministry of Finance and announced annually. They would also be posted on a provincial website in adjoining columns that identified revenue received from the carbon tax alongside details that highlighted offsetting tax cuts. Over time, this would serve to chronicle all of the uses of the more than $7.1 billion in tax reduction allocations linked to the carbon tax between 2008 and 2015.

Provincial officials further used these steps to accentuate broader benefits to provincial residents and businesses. This reflected the ways in which the tax reductions improved British Columbia's overall tax competitiveness in comparison with other provinces. As a result, the province has claimed the lowest tax rate on personal income below $119,000 of any Canadian jurisdiction. Officials also routinely highlighted corporate income tax rates that tied with Alberta and New Brunswick as the lowest in Canada.[56]

The combination of these individual and collective benefits made possible through the adoption of a carbon tax flipped the conventional understanding of such a tax as a burden. Instead, it made the benefits immediate and tangible, something no recipient would likely want to relinquish. As previously noted, any prospects to repeal the carbon tax threatened immediate loss of those very benefits. One prominent observer of this process noted that any move to thwart the carbon tax would "unmake the omelet" of tax reduction.[57] Campbell and his party bet heavily on the assumption that voters would want to protect this policy creation.

Policy Affirmation via Subsequent Election

Campbell and the Liberals focused on their plans to ease British Columbia through recession as their primary 2009 campaign theme. There was a commitment to operate a fiscally sound and economically stimulating 2010 Winter Olympics and complete a new, state-of-the-art convention center in Vancouver. There was also a major legislative proposal, the Recognition and

Reconciliation Act, which intended to recognize aboriginal rights and title to land without proof of claim, offering a possible path to reducing legal and political battles over land development. In Campbell's words, this proposal was designed to "create certainty on the land base" while also advancing reconciliation between the province and aboriginal groups.[58]

The carbon tax was also a significant part of this strategy, with a framing that combined its environmental virtues with its potential economic stimulus through personal and corporate tax cuts. On the one hand, Campbell and his allies argued that the carbon tax would send a clear price signal unlike that of any other Canadian or American government in favor of developing alternatives to fossil fuel–based energy. On the other hand, they relentlessly emphasized immediate tax reductions that were expected to provide visible economic benefits across the province. As Campbell explained during a campaign press conference, "There's an old observation that says you can be for improving the environment, or for improving the economy. I think what we're proving is that you can be both. Green technologies are expanding in British Columbia; thousands of people are involved in that work. Independent power projects are creating brand-new clean alternative energy across the province, while they create over 1,100 jobs in rural communities all over British Columbia."[59]

Campbell also used the carbon tax as a wedge issue to peel away voters from the New Democrats. The New Democratic Party (NDP) was conventionally seen as the pro-environmental party with credible electoral prospects, unlike the more marginal Green Party that continually struggled to win any legislative seats. It preceded the Liberals in power with a pair of victories in the 1990s. The NDP held thirty-three of seventy-nine seats in the provincial legislature and appeared poised to mount a significant challenge to the Liberals, given their long tenure in power and growing economic concerns. Some members quietly favored the carbon tax but capitulated when party leader Carole James and her allies decided to actively oppose it. They instead proposed a repeal-but-replace package that combined elimination of the tax with a mixture of alternatives that included a Green Bond program, a moratorium on private power projects, and possible engagement in cap-and-trade with the Western Climate Initiative. The NDP did not challenge the carbon tax on climate protection grounds but rather on economic terms to "recast themselves as tax-fighters determined to rescind the controversial carbon levy."[60]

Campbell and his British Columbia Liberals, however, had already adopted the tax policy and could point to its early rebate and tax cuts. They transformed carbon taxation coupled with tax reform from a potential albatross into a political strategy that weakened opposition from the political left. As economist Shi-Ling Hsu explained, "Notable environmental groups and figures scolded the NDP for its position, and clearly helped the Liberals to siphon off some traditional NDP voters."[61] Indeed, the Liberals picked up support from a wide range of environmental groups that would normally support the NDP. The nonpartisan Conservation Council launched an "anybody but James" campaign reflecting the NDP leader's opposition to the carbon tax. In turn, the party trailing the NDP in support from the left, the Greens, endorsed the tax and offered an option on the left for NDP loyalists unhappy with the party's carbon tax stance.

In the end, it is not clear that the carbon tax was a decisive factor in the vote, given limited exit polling and overall results that were quite comparable to 2005. But Campbell won a third term, receiving 45.8 percent of the vote and a net gain of three legislative seats (from forty-six to forty-nine) from the 2005 election. The NDP polled 42.1 percent and lost two seats, followed by the Greens at 8.2 percent and still no seats. Carbon tax supporters could sum the Liberal and Green totals and note that at least 54 percent of British Columbia voters backed a party that wanted to sustain the tax. In his victory speech, Campbell proclaimed affirmation for his politically risky climate strategy. He noted, "To others who may have looked at this possibility with trepidation and said this can't be done, it should be done and it must be done for our children and grandchildren."[62]

The election results unleashed recriminations among New Democrats, beginning with James's prompt resignation as party leader. Aspiring leadership successors lamented the "axe the tax" strategy in vowing to shift their party toward full support for the tax. According to provincial legislator John Horgan, "We misread the public mood on the carbon tax. We collectively made a mistake in the 2009 election by opposing the carbon tax."[63] Legislator Mike Farnworth explained, "I think we made a mistake in the last election. We as a party got it wrong. We were out of touch with the majority of British Columbians and I think that is one of the key reasons why we lost the election."[64]

After the election, political opposition to the tax effectively ended in the province, although there would be a significant question about where it might head after reaching the $30 per ton cap in 2012. Campbell and his team secured a third term and continued to implement the tax. The premier would not serve a full term due to subsequent controversy that was not connected to climate policy. But he maintained his national and global reputation as the political conservative who showed that a carbon tax was politically feasible and successful.[65]

Evidence of Performance

Once the political status of the carbon tax was resolved after the 2009 election, implementation continued with a series of rate increases that ran through 2012. British Columbia thus offered the first consequential carbon tax since the Nordic cases of the 1990s to surmount the policy life-cycle of initial adoption, launch, and survival through a confirming election. Upon reaching its peak rate in 2012, the province clearly had the highest carbon price, measured in costs per ton, of any new carbon tax or cap-and-trade policy adopted anywhere in the world since those earlier northern European taxes.[66] It also provided considerable evidence, based on its first seven years of operation, that it was capable of achieving many of its initial performance expectations. Quite unlike the hybrid pricing mechanism that was developed in neighboring Alberta, British Columbia passed early tests of evidence on its environmental and economic impacts.[67]

Several major studies were published between 2012 and 2015 using a mixture of methods to attempt to assess carbon tax impact on greenhouse gas emissions. They concluded that the tax reduced transportation fuel or natural gas use or both between 5 to 18.8 percent during different subsets of this period.[68] For example, Stuart Elgie and Jessica McClay concluded in a 2013 study that British Columbia's per capita consumption of multiple transportation fuels covered by the tax declined 17.4 percent between 2008 and 2012. They noted that overall Canadian fossil fuel use increased 1.5 percent during this period, despite lower economic growth outside of British Columbia. Moreover, British Columbia surpassed any of the larger provinces in this reduction level and passed Ontario to have the lowest rate of per capita fuel use of any province by 2013. No such differences were found between British Columbia and the remaining provinces for aviation fuel, which was not covered by the carbon tax.[69]

One American study by a team of scholars firmly opposed to carbon taxes and other climate mitigation policies argued that some of the reductions were attributable to the relatively easy access many British Columbians have to neighboring Washington for cheaper fuel purchases.[70] Approximately 70 percent of provincial residents live within 100 kilometers of the American border, far higher than the percentage within that distance from Alberta. This created the possibility of expanded "fuel tourism." However, Washington gas prices had also climbed during this period, following back-to-back gas tax increases in 2003 and 2005 that gave the state one of the highest rates per gallon in the United States. Indeed, these dual tax increases added 14.5 cents per gallon, equivalent to a $16.53 per ton tax on carbon emissions and the biggest gas tax increase of any state in the 2000s.[71] Gas costs were especially high in the western part of the state, closest to the dominant concentration of British Columbia residents, due to limited access to refinery capacity. Other studies question whether such purchases or other energy policies could have played a significant role in reducing British Columbia consumption.[72] There is no opportunity for significant cross-border purchases of natural gas for commercial and residential use and yet this fuel experienced comparable reduction rates.[73] Some studies contend that the impact of these reductions increased in later stages when the tax rates peaked.

The tax has had little demonstrable effect on the British Columbia economy thus far.[74] This suggests the lack of a major boost that Campbell and others had anticipated but also no evidence of any adverse impacts. Some sectors, such as cement, may have been negatively impacted but this has been offset by growth in other areas, suggesting a relatively neutral economic impact from the initial years of carbon pricing.[75] This may reflect the fact that the carbon tax generates less than 5 percent of total provincial government revenue. It thus likely has a limited effect on the overall economy, particularly given offsetting tax reductions.

The British Columbia economy grew at a slightly higher rate than the rest of Canada during the first five years of carbon tax implementation, although this cannot clearly be linked to the tax program.[76] But there is solid evidence that British Columbia has been successful in designing measures to reduce any risk that a consumption tax on carbon fuel use could be regressive, with harmful effects on low-income or rural residents. This is a common concern in discussion of a carbon tax but appears to have been eliminated in the British Columbia case given revenue allocation provisions that have been particularly attentive to these constituents.[77]

The British Columbia carbon tax has also demonstrated impressive results in two other settings: public opinion and global media coverage.

One longitudinal study of public opinion on the British Columbia carbon tax shows increasing support over time. Support generally stood below 50 percent during its early years but reached 58 percent in November 2011 and 64 percent in December 2012.[78] A 2011 Pembina Institute poll found a 69 percent tax approval rating.[79] This is consistent with political scientist Erick Lachapelle's 2015 findings that British Columbia support for carbon taxation is higher than residents of any other province in Canada.[80]

However, public sentiments were modest in comparison to the way in which the British Columbia carbon tax was portrayed in American and international media coverage and by global economic leaders. Major American media outlets regularly offered stirring accounts and *The Economist* declared the tax "a roaring success."[81] In turn, the province's experience was regularly cited in Canadian media discussion of carbon pricing, usually held as the model for such a policy. Accolades also rolled in from leaders of such institutions as the World Bank and the United Nations.[82] In a representative comment, Organization for Economic Cooperation and Development (OECD) Secretary General Angel Gurría declared, "British Columbia's carbon tax is as near as we have to a textbook case, with wide coverage across sectors and a steady increase in the rate."[83]

Troubles in Carbon Tax Paradise

Even textbook cases have their issues. The British Columbia carbon tax did indeed run the gauntlet of politics, management, and performance that scuttled so many other carbon pricing initiatives. Its political standing was solidified through the 2009 election, reflected in the fact that all major parties supported its continuation in the next election four years later. The tax continued to operate through the end of 2015, largely as designed at its outset and moving smoothly toward a long-term path of durability.

Nonetheless, this model case began to confront some significant limitations in the years following the 2009 electoral endorsement. None of these threatened its continued operation, but they combined to place constraints on its impact over subsequent years, underscoring the challenges facing longer-term implementation of any carbon pricing policy. This began to raise questions about whether British Columbia would best be characterized as a robust carbon pricing experience or one filled with promise that endured politically but began to drift as it entered a more advanced age.

Entrepreneurial Exit

Premier Campbell appeared poised in May 2009 to build on his latest electoral triumph and cement British Columbia's climate policy legacy through its carbon tax. Ever fascinated with the subject of tax policy, Campbell decided to use his electoral mandate to push for another major tax reform, though this one resulted in his political undoing. It had been widely rumored leading up to the 2009 election that Campbell and the Liberals were considering a major shift in the provincial sales tax structure. The Provincial Sales Tax (PST) was established in 1948 and, as in many other provinces, was coordinated with the federal Goods and Services Tax (GST). By 2009, the PST rate was 7 percent and the tax produced about 15 percent of British Columbia's government revenue, more than three times that of the carbon tax. The PST was collected on most commercial goods but only a limited number of services, unlike the more expansive reach of the federal GST.

In British Columbia, like other provinces and American states, there were growing questions about taxing services, especially since their role in most economies was expanding dramatically. In theory, an expanded tax would allow for greater equivalency in the tax treatment of goods and services; it could make possible some tax relief on goods if a service tax were introduced. This might also lead to the development of a provincial value-added tax system that better matched the federal GST. A value-added tax considers layers of increased value as various commodities evolve into a final product, an approach that has received considerable support from economists as a possible alternative to more traditional taxation.

Despite the rumors, Campbell and the Liberals were adamant during the campaign that some form of new Harmonized Sales Tax (HST) that expanded service coverage was not part of their agenda. However, they quickly pivoted after the May election and introduced an HST proposal within two months. This tax had considerable support from some sectors of the business community, as the proposed reform would actually reduce rates on such purchases as new homes and alcohol. At the same time, a much longer list of items would now be included in the provincial tax program, including entertainment, dry cleaning, newspapers and magazines, taxi rides, and much more.

Campbell may have thought he could work his tax reform magic once again, following the carbon tax playbook and its emphasis on benefits that offset added costs. The Liberals thus pushed through HST reform in July 2009. However, Campbell was sorely mistaken and never recovered from the public perception that he had concealed plans long enough to secure election and then proposed expansive new taxes on a host of common purchase items. His public approval ratings plunged, moving into single digits in early fall 2010 and culminating in his resignation on November 3, 2010.[84] Despite this taxation drama, the carbon tax quietly chugged along and was not an issue.

Campbell's resignation coincided with a direct democracy campaign to reverse HST adoption. This reached the ballot in August 2011 and led to a decisive rejection of the tax, by a margin of 54.7 percent to 45.3 percent. It appeared that this verdict paved the way for a transition to an NDP government in the next election, though one did not have to be scheduled for several years. The new NDP leadership developed a platform that included not only support for the carbon tax that they had earlier opposed but also proposals to expand its rate and scope. This included extending the coverage of the carbon tax to methane that was either flared or released during extraction. In addition, the NDP proposed taking some of the new revenue anticipated from an application of the carbon tax to methane and investing it in alternative energy projects.

The party also registered strong opposition to proposed expansion of pipelines for shipping natural gas. This proved quite politically salient as increased drilling appeared likely given the advent of hydraulic fracturing and horizontal drilling. Expanded use of fracking technology opened up vast new possibilities for tapping the substantial Duvernay, Horn River, and Montney Basins shared by British Columbia and Alberta that had long been dismissed as irretrievable.

The Transition

The Liberal Party remained in power despite Campbell's departure and ultimately turned to Christy Clark as the next premier. She had considerable political experience, having entered the provincial legislature in 2001 and serving for a time as deputy premier and cabinet minister under Campbell. In 2005 she lost a bid to become mayor of Vancouver and shifted into a new career as a radio talk show host. Clark emerged as the new premier in 2011 and unveiled a "family friendly" agenda that placed a major emphasis on new economic development strategies. This included support for expanded natural gas drilling and pipeline development. Clark viewed these as job-creation strategies rather than possible sources of increased greenhouse gas emissions, contrary to a more cautionary stance from the NDP.

Clark took no steps to reverse the provincial carbon tax and allowed it to increase to its statutory cap of $30 per ton. She often boasted of the province's bold leadership on this topic, particularly in settings with other premiers or state governors. But she rejected any proposals to further increase the tax or expand it to cover methane, countering the NDP tax increase proposal with a plan to cap rates at their 2012 level for at least five years. Clark also backed away from consideration of extended cap-and-trade coverage to sectors of the economy exempt from the carbon tax.

Perhaps her boldest initiative relevant to energy pricing was designed to reduce electricity costs. In this case, the dominant provincial utility, BC Hydro, proposed a 30 percent rate increase in 2011 over a three-year period. Whereas Campbell had treated BC Hydro as a major ally in transitioning toward a next-generation energy economy that would be increasingly reliant on hydro and other renewables, Clark seized the rate increase proposal as a reflection of poor management and an assault on her family-focused agenda. She opposed the increase and ultimately settled for a much smaller one, drawing considerable attention to her opposition to higher energy prices.

All of this seemed transient, as Clark and the Liberals appeared destined to lose power to the NDP when elections were announced in May 2013. The NDP and its new leader, Adrian Dix, boasted a double-digit lead in public opinion polls and felt that they could now outflank the Liberals on climate change given their plans to expand rather than eliminate the carbon tax. But the Liberals ultimately won a victory that was in many ways comparable to 2009, holding a legislative majority. Clark actually lost her bid to win a seat but won a by-election that was created to allow her to remain as premier. She could thus claim her mandate to prevent any further increase in the carbon tax while also continuing to pursue policies that might mitigate its effectiveness.

Revenue Negativity

Revenue neutrality was a core component of the British Columbia carbon tax from its outset, whereby every dollar of tax revenue would be returned to the citizenry through the tax system. In practice, the tax produced less revenue than anticipated, leading to deficits once revenue reallocation was complete. These deficits exceeded $1 billion out of $6.1 billion in total revenue collected between 2008 and 2015.[85] However, the province was on a path to restore neutrality as revenues rose with annual tax rate increases through 2012 before slowing in later years (see table 4.4).

This path was undermined by a series of decisions between 2012 and 2014 to make statutory adjustments that collectively created a large structural deficit that is projected to continue into the future. There are exemptions from the tax for greenhouse growers and gasoline and diesel used in farming, thereby reducing the total amount of revenue being generated. There has been a small set of relatively modest tax credits adopted since 2012 including a Children's Fitness and Art Credit, a Small Business Venture Capital Tax Credit, and a Tax Training Credit.

Far more significant, however, has been transfer to the carbon tax ledger of existing tax credits that benefit particular industries. These have included an Interactive Digital Media Tax Credit in fiscal year 2013, a Film Incentive Tax Credit and Production Services Tax Credit in fiscal year 2014, and a Scientific Research and Experimental Development Tax Credit the following year (see table 4.4).[86] Collectively, these other credits increased revenue reallocation by $442 million (in Canadian dollars) in fiscal year 2015, greater than that year's entire carbon tax deficit. Future projections show a continuing structural deficit linked to these provisions.[87]

This reflects the type of targeted "tax expenditure" that often follows broad tax reform and can ultimately undermine its public support.[88] In this case, these new and transferred credits have been allocated to specific business constituencies, dramatically altering the earlier balance between personal and business tax relief that was a central part of the package promised to British Columbia citizens. Chronic revenue negativity may further work to deter future rate increases, given the likelihood that additional revenue would be used to reduce the fiscal imbalance rather than provide new benefits. This fiscal reality may further undermine any serious consideration of the NDP proposal to use some tax revenues for purposes linked to energy transition or climate change.

Table 4.4

British Columbia carbon tax revenue and disposition (in millions of $Canadian).

	FY 2009	FY 2010	FY 2011	FY 2012	FY 2013	FY 2014	FY 2015	FY 2016*	FY 2017*	FY 2018*
Carbon Tax Revenue	**306**	**542**	**741**	**959**	**1,120**	**1,222**	**1,198**	**1,216**	**1,234**	**1,252**
Individual Benefits										
Low Income Climate Action Tax Credit	106	153	165	184	195	194	193	192	195	195
Income Tax Bracket Reductions	107	206	207	220	235	237	269	283	288	302
Northern and Rural Homeowner Benefit			19	66	67	69	83	83	83	84
Seniors' Home Renovation Tax Credit					49	22	0	1	2	2
Children's Fitness and Art Credit					9	8	8	8	8	8
Small Business Venture Capital Tax Credit					3	3	3	3	5	5
Tax Training Credit—Individuals					10	11	9	9	20	20
Total Personal Tax Benefits	**213**	**359**	**391**	**470**	**546**	**522**	**565**	**579**	**601**	**616**
Business Benefits										
Corporate Income Tax Reduction	65	152	271	381	450	200	216	218	236	250
Small Business Corporate Tax Reduction	35	164	144	220	281	240	250	257	265	277

Industrial Property Tax Credits		54	58	68	68	43	23	24	21	21
Farm Property Tax Credits			1	2	2	2	2	2	2	2
Interactive Digital Media Tax Credit					26	63	37	33	45	45
Scientific Research and Experimental Development Tax Credit							82	131	150	160
Film Incentive Tax Credit						88	78	106	90	90
Production Services Tax Credit						66	265	385	310	310
Tax Training Credit—Businesses					7	8	6	5	10	10
Total Business Tax Benefits	100	370	474	671	834	710	959	1,151	1,132	1,169
Total Designated Revenue Benefits	313	729	865	1,141	1,380	1,232	1,524	1,730	1,733	1,785
Net Revenue	-7	-187	-124	-182	-260	-10	-326	-514	-499	-533
Individual Share of Benefits	68%	49%	45%	41%	40%	42%	37%	33%	35%	35%
Business Share of Benefits	32%	51%	55%	59%	60%	58%	63%	67%	65%	65%
Tax Rate per Metric Ton (in CAD)	$10	$15	$20	$25	$30	$30	$30	$30	$30	$30

Note: Forecast.

Source: British Columbia Ministry of Finance (various years).

Exempting Extraction

Clark's premiership maintained a sizable gap left by the carbon tax as she attempted to promote expanded fossil fuel production in a province that was receiving global acclaim for its carbon tax leadership. The vast majority of coal and natural gas produced in the province had long been shipped to other provinces or nations for ultimate use, reflecting British Columbia's modest population and massive reliance on hydro. Like all other provinces that produce fossil fuels, British Columbia collected royalties on these nonrenewable natural resources at the point of extraction (comparable to state severance taxes on gas, oil, or coal, as discussed further in chapters 7 and 8).[89] But the provincial carbon tax was only applied to energy used to extract those fossil fuels and not their eventual use, as long as that occurred outside the province. In turn, both royalties and the carbon tax exempted methane, a greenhouse gas that is thirty times more potent per unit than carbon dioxide for the first century after its release. Drilling for oil and gas is a major source of methane in British Columbia, where it can be flared or vented into the atmosphere during drilling.[90] Consequently, despite its carbon tax and climate leadership, British Columbia provided considerable economic incentives to sustain and expand drilling for fossil fuels.

This reality was not unique to the Clark era in British Columbia politics. The Campbell regime also had to contend with significant Liberal Party representation in fossil fuel–producing legislative ridings (or districts). Natural gas has also played a far larger role than coal in the British Columbia economy in recent decades, but it was largely concentrated in fields located in a pair of legislative ridings in the Northeast. In contrast, coal has a lesser economic role but was produced in eight ridings. Five of these seats were held by Liberals when the carbon tax was adopted. Four of these members held cabinet positions, including the Energy, Mines, and Resources file. As political scientist Erick Lachapelle observed, coal is more "geographically dispersed across the province" and so tends to "cover more ground, so to speak, in that coal is actively mined" in multiple ridings.[91] A number of these districts are comparatively low in population and are potential swing seats.[92]

The enduring political clout of fossil fuel extraction threatened carbon pricing development, much as it has in other jurisdictions such as California and even Norway. In such cases, there is a potential political path to carbon pricing but enormous risks from applying these policies on industries that extract fossil fuels for export. British Columbia demonstrated one way to navigate the situation through a carbon tax that addressed nearly 80 percent of total provincial CO_2 emissions but left significant gaps in coverage for particularly sensitive local industries. This explains tax exemptions for fuels used in forestry and farming as well as non-combustion carbon dioxide used in lime production, a critical element in cement manufacturing. Fossil fuel extraction also fits this pattern, reflected in the generous exemption of extracted natural gas, coal, and methane from the carbon tax.[93]

The province thus sidestepped a potential point of political contention, though reserving the option of applying later regulation, emissions trading, or expanded royalties to either fossil fuel extraction or methane releases. But this appeared far less of an issue at the point of carbon tax adoption in 2008 than a half-decade later, since fossil fuel extraction seemed likely to decline given anticipated transition toward renewable sources in British Columbia and elsewhere. Campbell thus did not formally try to restrict coal or natural gas development but characterized the carbon tax as a key tool in giving the province a lead role in accelerating that transition.

All of that changed under his successor. Clark viewed much-expanded natural gas extraction as a "once in a generation" economic development opportunity. This reflected a growing realization that British Columbia might have a far greater natural gas supply than anticipated, particularly through expanded use of hydraulic fracturing technology that had already begun to be used in the province. By the early 2010s, it became evident that British Columbia possessed "massive" natural gas reserves spread across multiple ridings that could be extracted via fracking, with deposits that represented half of Canada's total shale gas supplies.[94] Indeed, projections of its total gas reserves grew between 16 to 40 percent in 2013 alone.[95]

Natural gas production in the province quietly began to increase around 2000, growing at a rate of 3.4 percent annually alongside a 3.1 percent annual decline in the remainder of Canada.[96] These reductions were influenced by political decisions in Quebec, Newfoundland, and Nova Scotia to restrict or ban drilling, despite considerable natural gas supplies.[97] As a result, the British Columbian role in Canadian natural gas production grew steadily, from 12.2 percent of total national output in 2000 to 27 percent in 2013. This symbolized a major expansion of drilling in the province, reflected in nearly 20,000 wells and more than 100,000 kilometers of pipeline.[98] Projections from the Conference Board of Canada anticipated that

British Columbia was on pace to become the nation's dominant natural gas producer between 2013 and 2025.[99] These projections further anticipated that the province would eventually eclipse fossil fuel powerhouse Alberta, produce more than four times the total amount from all other provinces combined except Alberta, and contribute nearly half of total national output over that period.[100]

The carbon tax extraction exemption would be inconsequential if much of the newly produced natural gas were consumed in British Columbia and thereby covered by the tax. No one, however, anticipated that outcome, given the continued productivity of established hydroelectricity supplies, expanding supply of other renewables, and the ongoing reliance on imported oil and gasoline for transportation. But it was also uncertain whether there was significant demand in either Canada or the United States for natural gas, given the American version of the fracking boom that began to flood continental natural gas markets in the late 2000s.

Premier Clark promptly opened an entirely new approach to British Columbia energy policy with a focus on natural gas exports. She offered a plan to transform the province into an international hub for development of liquefied natural gas (LNG) and exports to Asia. Clark contended in the 2013 campaign and after her victory that the province could become a global leader in this area. This would require British Columbia to develop the capacity to transport the gas to newly constructed plants that would transform it into liquid form suitable for oceanic shipment. Clark and a provincial Natural Gas Workforce Strategy Committee envisioned the creation of five major LNG terminals along the province's Pacific Coast and major pipeline expansion to allow for major gas transfers to these hubs.[101] Officials also began to prepare for training and recruitment of an anticipated 75,000 new skilled jobs associated with full pursuit of LNG potential.[102]

Clark portrayed this step as a transformational opportunity. "We can be the second-largest exporter (to Qatar) of liquefied natural gas in the world," she stated in 2013. "When we reach our potential, it will have the same impact on Canada's national economy that the oil sands in Alberta have had."[103] Her campaign floated the idea of a new $100 billion Prosperity Fund, a sovereign wealth fund that would draw on expanded royalties or a possible new natural gas export tax to help ensure a long-term fiscal future for British Columbia.[104] Clark also argued that this natural gas development could have salutary environmental effects in places such as China, particularly if natural gas replaced coal use and thereby produced a net reduction in greenhouse gas emissions. "They need it, we've got it. It's a perfect marriage," she explained during a 2013 trade mission to China.[105]

However, the export tax plan never materialized and royalties declined, along with the plunge in natural gas prices in the province and globally in the mid-2010s. This reflected earlier political decisions to impose royalties on the basis of current value rather than volume of energy extracted, contrary to the practice in many American state severance taxes.[106] The revenues being secured from natural gas drilling in British Columbia actually were declining in the very years that drilling expanded and the idea of British Columbia evolving into a global LNG export leader was being cultivated.[107] Think tank studies emerged that challenged the viability of the Clark plan, especially given global demand uncertainty, the absence of any established LNG terminals, steep infrastructure development costs, and mounting political opposition to pipeline siting.[108] By 2017, the British Columbia Prosperity Fund was created, but its lone funds had come from general revenue transfer given the absence of LNG production that could be taxed. Indeed, a Liquefied Natural Gas Income Tax was approved in 2014 but failed to produce any revenue for the Prosperity Fund during its first years of operation.

Limited Diffusion

British Columbia continued to win international accolades for its carbon tax, with far less attention devoted to its significant omission of exported fossil fuels. Clark and other Liberal leaders expressed their continued support for the carbon tax, albeit at levels capped in 2012. They frequently claimed credit for the province's leadership role in demonstrating the possibilities of such a climate policy option.

In turn, British Columbian officials continued to be struck by their global notoriety and the frequency with which they are consulted by other jurisdictions about the tax and how it was feasible to adopt and sustain it. "We hear from people all over the world, including many Asian delegations and a lot from Australians," explained a senior provincial official. "We also get lots of inquiries and invitations to speak from American states."[109]

But there is little evidence that the British Columbia carbon tax has unleashed a process of policy diffusion. Liberal Party campaign director

Mike McDonald noted during the 2013 election that "B.C. is a world leader and remains committed to the carbon tax as a way of (incentivizing) people to choose cleaner forms of energy and reduce their carbon consumption. At the time it was introduced it was believed other jurisdictions would follow B.C.'s leadership position, but to date that has not happened to the extent expected."[110]

British Columbia officials often bemoaned the reluctance of other jurisdictions to emulate their policy. Jock Finlayson of the Business Council of British Columbia lamented that, contrary to expectations, "we are dancing alone" in North America on this issue and that "an ever-increasing made-in-B.C. carbon tax isn't sustainable if other provinces and states decline to follow the same path."[111] Indeed, any diffusion of this heralded model or development of other forms of carbon taxation remained modest through the end of 2015.

Several American states, including Massachusetts, Oregon, and Vermont, floated carbon tax proposals. Some of these proposals were modeled in part after the British Columbia tax but all of them stalled politically. A number of emerging policies billed as carbon taxes ultimately involved modest fees applied only to a single source such as coal use or transportation fuel, as occurred in Manitoba, India, and Slovenia. Other jurisdictions have announced plans for major carbon taxes but ultimately established them at nominal levels (Chile, Japan, Mexico, and Portugal), eliminated them in favor of other policies (Australia and New Zealand), withdrew them without substituting other policies (Italy), or took long pauses after initial adoption to decide whether or not to go forward (South Africa and France).[112] Many of these plans were adopted in the mid-2010s and so were only beginning to navigate the policy life-cycle by the end of 2015. Nearly all were set initially at equivalents of less than $5 (Canadian) per ton and lacked clear plans for future increases.

More common have been policies that technically entail carbon pricing but operate almost in a stealth fashion. These tend to utilize some term other than "tax" to describe what they are doing. Such phrases as "levy," "fee," "social benefit charge," or "public good charge" substitute for taxation, in order to soften the political blow. In turn, they are generally set at very low levels, between one to $3 per ton, and tend to be used to fund governmental climate policy operations or to support particular alternative energy projects. They are set at such a level that they cannot realistically be expected to have much, if any, impact on energy use behavior, much like the Alberta Specified Gas Emitters Regulations (SGER) program discussed in chapter 3. Instead, they allow for collection of small amounts of revenue to help cover climate-related costs.

Quebec, for example, launched a "carbon levy" in 2007, set at a level of 0.8 cents (Canadian) per liter of gasoline, equivalent to about 3 cents (US) per gallon. The levy was never intended to operate as a major carbon tax like British Columbia's and it was continued after Quebec made a full commitment to cap-and-trade in collaboration with California (see chapter 5). Instead, it was explicitly intended to cover climate program operations. It generated $975 million (Canadian) during its first five years of operation and funded approximately 2,000 clean energy projects around the province.[113] This policy has some parallels to a similarly named "climate change levy" established in the United Kingdom in 2001, which was never intended to match the ETS in scope of coverage or carbon price level.

No American state has ever adopted a carbon tax, despite the flurry of legislative proposals in the 2010s. However, at least eighteen states have adopted their own versions of the Quebec levy, through a series of fees and charges that were added to electricity bills. Oregon created a 3 percent "public-purpose charge" on all power bills, whereas Michigan imposed a $3 monthly "surcharge" on electricity users. Both states allocated these funds to various energy efficiency and renewable energy programs.[114] As energy policy scholar Sanya Carley noted, it is a "cross-subsidizing mechanism that taxes regular electricity consumption and subsidizes energy efficiency."[115] The most aggressive of these efforts involves electricity bill surcharges in Texas that have directly covered a massive expansion and upgrade of state transmission capacity, a case discussed further in the final chapter.

None of these policies can be directly compared to British Columbia's carbon tax or the Nordic cases from the early 1990s. Far more than a matter of nomenclature, they impose far too modest a price to realistically have much, if any, effect on consumption. Many of these policies do not discriminate between the different carbon impacts of various fossil fuels or distinguish between electricity generated by fossil fuels and renewables. Instead, their intent is to establish a small added charge on electricity use that can then underwrite energy transition programs.

A significant exception to this general pattern of aversion to launching and sustaining consequential carbon taxes is Ireland. Its harsh fiscal crisis in 2008 and 2009 triggered a desperate search for new government revenue. This was linked to a proposed bargain with the International Monetary Fund, the European Commission, and the European Central Bank to secure an infusion of additional financial support if new funds could be generated domestically. As Ireland weighed various new taxation options, the idea of previously discussed environmental taxes resurfaced as one of the more palatable choices.

Green Party participation as a minority partner in the Irish government helped advance the idea of a carbon tax, leading to 2010 adoption. Much like the British Columbia tax adopted two years earlier, it cut across a wide range of fuels, including petrol, heavy oil, auto-diesel, kerosene, liquid petroleum gas, fuel oil, natural gas, coal, and peat.[116] The tax was set at a rate of 15 euros per ton, equivalent at adoption to about $20 (American) versus a British Columbia tax conversion rate at that time to $24. Ireland also launched a related set of environmental taxes, including nonrecycled trash that was weighed at the street curb for taxation, and yearly vehicle registration fees proportional to vehicle emissions.

Unlike the British Columbia case, there was no revenue neutrality and commensurate tax reduction. Instead, the new carbon tax and other environmental taxes produced fresh revenue that was placed directly into the general budget along with a number of other new taxes, helping to reduce massive deficits and deter the need for increasing other taxes.[117] These taxes enabled Ireland's politicians to make the case at the international and continental levels that they had taken steps to address their fiscal disarray and that they should thereby qualify for bailout support. This created a rough parallel with British Columbia, in that any reduction of the Irish carbon tax necessitated an income tax increase under the terms of the agreement.

The Irish carbon tax went into operation rapidly and produced approximately 1 billion euros during its first three years of operation, covering approximately one-fourth of the required revenue increase. The International Monetary Fund recommended in 2012 that Ireland should "expand the well-designed carbon tax" and its vehicle taxes to produce additional revenue.[118] The rates were increased to 20 euros per ton in 2011 and 2012, and subsequently remained stable through the end of 2015.[119]

The arrival of the tax has coincided with a substantial drop in domestic greenhouse gas emissions, a decline of more than 15 percent between 2008 and 2012. It remains unclear how much of this reduction was due to the carbon tax as opposed to the economic contraction and other factors, although the significant rebound of the Irish economy has not produced a reversal of the emission reductions. Eamon Ryan, Ireland's energy minister from 2007 to 2011, observed, "We are not saints like those Scandinavians— we were lapping up fossil fuels, buying bigger cars and homes, very American. We just set up a price signal that raised significant revenue and changed behavior. Now, we're smashing through the environmental targets we set for ourselves."[120]

Iceland and Switzerland offered some parallels to Ireland, reflecting additional support among some European nations to follow the original Nordic model and establish their own carbon taxes. Iceland decided to join its Nordic neighbors with a 2010 tax that was adopted on a temporary basis and set at one half the ETS price. However, this tax became permanent two years later and was increased to match the full ETS price. This was linked to other efforts to better address environmental concerns through tax reform and placed revenue into the general budget. Switzerland adopted a carbon tax in 2008 with an initial rate equivalent to $10.86 per ton. It was steadily increased and reached $87 per ton in 2016, with revenues allocated to a combination of business tax cuts, rebates, and investments in renewable energy. Firms were allowed to make voluntary reduction commitments as an alternative to paying the tax. Both taxes retained political support and faced no significant managerial challenges through 2015.

These cases represent important complements to British Columbia, demonstrating the potential for carbon taxes to be adopted and then move through subsequent stages of implementation while delivering intended results. By the second half of the 2010s, there were further possibilities that the carbon tax diffusion process might accelerate in both North America and beyond, as will be discussed in the final chapter. Cap-and-trade also passed through a somewhat similar evolution between 2000 and 2015, with a small set of cases demonstrating its potential as a carbon pricing option.

5 When Cap-and-Trade Works

Cap-and-trade had a different political trajectory than carbon taxes. Far more jurisdictions in North America and beyond would give cap-and-trade serious agenda consideration, reflected in far-reaching auditions and hearings before legislative bodies. These frequently transitioned into initial policy adoption. By 2010, more than half of all Americans and Canadians lived in a state or province that had adopted cap-and-trade. These governments then took the remarkable political step of forming cross-unit agreements, whereby twenty-seven separate policies were blended into three regionally based partnerships. This took place without any federal pressure or incentives to take these steps. These developments occurred alongside major new cap-and-trade commitments by the European Union and Australia.

At this point, cap-and-trade appeared to have left carbon taxes in the political dust of carbon pricing. Prospects for future diffusion, both horizontal and vertical, seemed boundless. But then the bottom fell out as of the mid-2010s, as discussed in chapters 2 and 3. The majority of states and provinces that had adopted cap-and-trade reversed gear; no others came close to adoption. Two of the three regional partnerships imploded and the early track record from cap-and-trade experiments in Europe and Asia were dismal. As a result, cap-and-trade shifted from center stage to the political fringe of legislative bodies in North America and elsewhere.

In this process, cap-and-trade was transformed from the golden child of policy innovation into a poster child of governmental smoke and mirrors. It was vilified in many circles as a stealth form of a tax, one that piled numerous regulatory provisions atop a de facto increase in energy costs. Indeed, the moniker of "cap-and-tax" was actively promoted as an alternative to "cap-and-trade" in public debates. Public opinion surveys demonstrated substantial public uncertainty over just what cap-and-trade entailed and found at best a hedging base of support for it.[1] Cap-and-trade proponents struggled to explain why policies that they had so enthusiastically promoted so frequently struggled or evaporated in practice. Consequently, any ideational allure for cap-and-trade as an intriguing policy idea seemed to fade once tested in the arena of politics.

Even the world's flagship cap-and-trade case began to wobble by 2010. The much-trumpeted American experience with cap-and-trade for sulfur dioxide had been employed routinely in making the case that this tool could address climate change. But its demonstrated effectiveness began to lag in the late 2000s and the trading market largely ground to a halt by 2010. This reflected the fact that although major emission reductions set in Title IV of the 1990 Clean Air Act had been achieved, the program required legislative adjustments and updates if it was to attain significant additional reductions in releases.

Such an option was not politically possible in subsequent Congresses, given partisan and regional divides. In turn, a major attempt by the US Environmental Protection Agency (EPA) during the George W. Bush presidency to create a new interstate trading program through the Clean Air Interstate Rule (CAIR) was overturned by federal courts. CAIR was found to have exceeded its authority under the Clean Air Act in a case brought by several states and utility companies.[2] A more modest alternative to CAIR, developed by EPA under President Barack Obama, withstood court scrutiny but was largely limited to intrastate trading and unable to stave off a system collapse. As a result, the vaunted trading program began to languish. This was reflected in plunging allowance prices whereby coinage proved sufficient to cover the costs of an allowance (see figure 5.1).[3]

Unlike the European Emissions Trading Scheme (ETS), however, the sulfur dioxide program was effectively managed and produced substantial emission reductions at relatively low cost. It operated successfully for two decades before encountering a midlife slump.[4] Its plunge in allowance prices, moreover, was driven by very different factors than the ETS. It has generally retained a reputation as an environmental policy "living legend" and continues to serve as a role model for cap-and-trade initiatives.

As in the carbon tax case, however, policy reversal and shaky performance were not the lone outcomes for carbon cap-and-trade, despite enduring problems in Europe. There was not a single jurisdictional case of relative

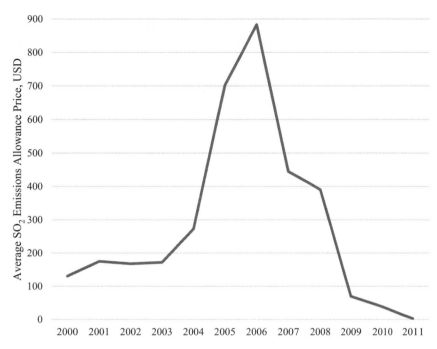

Figure 5.1
Average prices of US sulfur dioxide emissions allowances, 2000–2011 (weighted, dollars/ton).
Source: "Average Prices for Spot Sulfur Dioxide Emissions Allowances at EPA Auction Sets New Lows," *EIA Today in Energy*, May 11, 2011, https://www.eia.gov/todayinenergy /detail.php?id=1330.

success to compare with British Columbia but rather nine, reflecting the states that proved resilient, having pioneered North American adoption of carbon cap-and-trade in a few individual state cases and then transitioned into a regional trading zone, the Regional Greenhouse Gas Initiative, or RGGI for short. Much like British Columbia, all of these jurisdictions found ways to secure initial political support. In many instances, they drew from key policy entrepreneurs such as governors and agency heads. But they found ways to build broader political bases, reaching across political parties in many instances and also securing legislative branch support.

Some policy analysts derided RGGI as a "toy" or a "joke" of a cap-and-trade system. It focuses only on one sector, electricity, and its allowance price per ton of emissions during its first seven years of operation averaged less than one-fifth that of the British Columbia carbon price via taxation between 2010 and 2015. RGGI functions in a region that has less reliance on coal than most other parts of the United States, historically dependent on a mix of hydro, nuclear, natural gas, and oil sources. This region featured a much lighter carbon footprint in the electricity sector than most states long before RGGI began operations.

Few RGGI states possessed known fossil fuel reserves and none permitted significant drilling for oil or natural gas. Three of these states (Maryland, New York, and Vermont) were the only ones in the nation to place a formal moratorium or ban on all hydraulic fracturing, although New York alone has significant production potential. None has severance taxes for extraction, reflecting their lack of engagement in this area, thereby enabling them to avoid the carbon complications of reducing local emissions while producing fossil fuels that were exported elsewhere, unlike British Columbia and California. The RGGI states had also begun to make major investments in the 1990s and early 2000s to expand renewable energy and promote energy efficiency, putting them on a path to further reduce their use of fossil fuels well before cap-and-trade began. Consequently, the Northeast states entered into RGGI with a rate of per capita emissions well below the national average, and so any reductions driven by cap-and-trade would only build on a low-emission base.

But it is not accurate to dismiss RGGI as a symbolic case. Much like British Columbia, RGGI has demonstrated an ability to build a solid political foundation and sustain it through shifts of political leadership and partisan control over more than a decade. It has proved able to maintain operations across multiple state boundaries during periods of considerable economic upheaval and major transitions in energy alternatives for electricity. RGGI has regularly surmounted the kinds of political disruptions and public management problems that have so plagued the ETS and damaged the cap-and-trade brand internationally. In turn, this cap-and-trade system has found ways to make essential adjustments to allow for extended tightening of its overall emissions cap and make longer-term reductions possible. After its initial years of operation, it offered solid evidence of having a consequential impact on emissions and no adverse economic impacts, in many respects rivaling British Columbia's carbon tax.

Moreover, RGGI pioneered two important features of cap-and-trade that may have longer-term consequences in any future development of this carbon pricing tool in North America or beyond. First, it represents the first sustained experiment for any cap-and-trade program to operate across multiple jurisdictional boundaries over time in the absence of any central government requirements or incentives to pursue this course. RGGI represents a voluntary policy decision taken in concert across nine sovereign states, each acting collectively after an internal political decision to pursue collaboration and then maintain that agreement over time. These states include Connecticut, Delaware, Maine, Maryland, Massachusetts, New Hampshire, New York, Rhode Island, and Vermont. RGGI reflects a bottom-up approach that has endured, contrary to other multi-unit partnerships that have floundered. This represents a significant foundation of trust established between these states, their lead executive agencies, and key stakeholders. It thus offers a model for jurisdictions in other federations or multilevel systems to consider.

Second, RGGI created an unprecedented approach to the distribution of emission allowances that may permanently change cap-and-trade operations. Before RGGI, cap-and-trade conventionally allocated allowances to emission sources at no charge, gradually reducing the pool of allocations to tighten the emissions cap for a specified area. Trading then occurred with these freely distributed allowances, presumably achieving the most cost-effective option for compliance. In contrast, RGGI launched what political scientist Leigh Raymond has characterized as a "revolution" by auctioning nearly all of its allowances to the highest bidder and generating revenue that could be applied to related climate protection goals. This reflected a strong political commitment to reframe allowances as a "public resource, not a private one, to be used for public benefit."[5]

RGGI also produced revenue that individual state governments would receive quarterly and could then apply to various initiatives. Whereas British Columbia pledged to return all revenues (and then some) to the citizenry through tax credits and rate reductions, RGGI states placed most of their auction funds into energy efficiency and related programs designed to further reduce greenhouse gas emissions. This created a direct link between the imposition of a carbon price through allowance purchase and use of that revenue as a public benefit. Much like the British Columbia case, this approach would offer a way to use carbon pricing revenue to build a constituency to sustain support for the program.

The Northeastern Path to Cap-and-Trade

As in the sale of real estate, the location of a multijurisdictional cap-and-trade program may be quite significant in determining its success. Consequently, the American Northeast may have been one of the most politically and managerially favorable settings for attempting a multistate regional program in the United States or anywhere else. This reflects a long-standing economic interdependence and penchant for operating what political scientist Daniel Elazar described as a "sectional confederation."[6] This is reflected in a high level of northeastern state participation in interstate compacts, including regional pacts that only involve some subset of their members. As political scientist Ann Bowman has noted, states such as Maine, Maryland, New Jersey, and Vermont rank among the nine states most likely to participate in interstate compacts, followed closely in these rankings by states such as Connecticut and New York.[7]

Interstate compacts require a binding policy agreement or pact among multiple states, leading to a formal request that Congress delegate policy authority to them collectively.[8] State proponents of the cap-and-trade system that would become RGGI were interested in this model but realized that it would be politically unlikely to secure congressional support. Instead, they decided to move forward without any federal endorsement and built on a large and dense set of regional governance organizations. Some of these established entities focused either fully or partially on environmental and energy issues and contributed directly to the establishment of RGGI. Political scientist Jorgen Knudsen has compared RGGI's regional cohesion to Europe's Nordic countries, noting that both have "network constellations" that aided the "formulation and execution" of climate strategies, including those linked to carbon pricing.[9] The states and provinces that attempted to form the Western Climate Initiative (WCI) and the Midwestern Greenhouse Gas Reduction Accord (MGGRA), by contrast, lacked this kind of regional solidarity.

Perhaps the most significant regional body that facilitated RGGI development was NESCAUM, the Northeast States for Coordinated Air Use Management. This organization was established in 1967 to develop unified air quality strategies for six New England states, adding New York and New Jersey in the subsequent decade. It includes every RGGI state except Delaware and Maryland and is empowered to address "the entire spectrum of air quality issues." NESCAUM covers both industrial and transportation sector emissions and expanded in the 1990s to address greenhouse gases. It routinely seeks to create cross-state regional strategies and represent regional interests at the federal level. "NESCAUM precedes the creation of EPA and it has engaged a range of topics, from reducing the volatility of summer gasoline to (nitrogen oxide) budgeting and mercury emission reductions," explained Christopher James, official of the Connecticut Department of Environmental Protection. "We are small states and we are used to working together and NESCAUM has been a big part of that."[10]

New England and the larger Northeast have an established history of active and sustained collaboration across state borders on issues including higher education, criminal justice and law enforcement, and dairy production and pricing. Likewise, northeastern regional engagement on environmental policy has taken many forms, including repeated formal endorsement of California standards, once they are approved, via a federal waiver to tighten tailpipe emissions from new vehicles. This reflects unique powers granted only to California through the Clean Air Act, but with the proviso that other states can join that state to create a "bandwagon effect." This commonly unites states from both coasts and then leverages federal standardization based on this state-based approach.[11] Northeastern regionalism is also reflected in a cap-and-trade system under the auspices of the twelve-state Ozone Transport Commission (OTC), nine members of which were involved in accepting a federally delegated charge in the 1990 Clean Air Act Amendments to develop a "model rule" to address its pernicious ground-level ozone problems.[12] This resulted in a series of interstate strategies in the 1990s and 2000s that included a regionally based trading system for nitrogen oxides that led to significant emission reductions with high compliance levels and no discernible signs of adverse economic impacts.[13]

These types of experiences tended to promote unusual levels of familiarity among officials across state boundaries and to bridge conventional divides between environmental protection and energy generation functions. Such engagement was further promoted by ongoing energy and environmental working groups of the Coalition of New England Governors, representing seven states that engaged in many partnerships with neighboring Canadian provinces. This created an unusually broad network of officials from differing jurisdictions and areas of expertise, including cap-and-trade through the OTC delegation. "All the staff involved in this process were very familiar with (nitrogen oxide) and the acid rain budget and many had worked together before," explained Chris Nelson of the Connecticut Department of Environmental Protection. "These are pretty sharp people and they are fun to work with. It means we have a nice atmosphere to be collaborative and everyone believes in what they are doing."[14]

Cap-and-Trade Adoption

This foundation provided fertile ground for development of cap-and-trade proposals by environmental groups and policy entrepreneurs within state governments in the Northeast. It facilitated a rapid process of political adoption across jurisdictions, the first step in the policy life-cycle. Alongside a blizzard of state climate action plans and policies around the nation in the late 1990s and early 2000s, two states took unilateral steps to launch cap-and-trade for power plants within their boundaries. A number of carbon pricing proposals had emerged in Massachusetts but Republican Governor Jane Swift decided to preempt those by incorporating carbon dioxide emissions from six major power plants into a multi-pollutant rule to curb air emissions. "The new, tough standards will help ensure older power plants in Massachusetts do not contribute to regional air pollution, acid rain, and global warming," explained Swift in announcing the world's first cap-and-trade system for carbon dioxide in April 2001 (see table 5.1).[15]

New Hampshire followed less than a year later by adopting the first legislation in the world to establish cap-and-trade for its electricity sector. This reflected ideational exploration of policy options from the mid-1990s that included state agency officials, environmental groups, and interested legislators. Democratic Governor Jeanne Shaheen signed the Clean Power Act into law in May 2002, after it received broad bipartisan support in the legislature. It required that three operational power plants using fossil fuels reduce their emissions by about 3 percent from 1999 levels by 2006 and then achieve additional reductions that would put them on a pace to match reduction targets set under the Kyoto Protocol. Much like the administrative action in Massachusetts, New Hampshire integrated carbon emissions into a larger package that cut across air pollutant categories.

Shaheen used the New Hampshire action to try to compel similar steps by other jurisdictions. "Pollution does not respect state boundaries," she noted. "Other states and the federal government must follow our lead so

Table 5.1
Regional Greenhouse Gas Initiative timeline.

May 2001	Massachusetts establishes regulations to reduce CO_2 emissions from six coal plants.
August 2001	New England governors and Eastern Canadian premiers adopt the Climate Change Action Plan aimed at reducing greenhouse gas emissions.
July 2002	The Clean Power Act becomes law in New Hampshire, calling for reduced CO_2 emissions through a cap-and-trade program.
September 2003	Eleven northeastern US governors meet to discuss the development of a regional cap-and-trade program to address CO_2 from power plants.
December 2005	The governors of Connecticut, Delaware, Maine, New Hampshire, New Jersey, New York, and Vermont sign a memorandum of understanding (MOU) outlining plans to implement RGGI; Massachusetts and Rhode Island decline to sign the MOU.
August 2006	The seven MOU signatory states publish a Model Rule to provide a set of regulations to form the basis of each state's CO_2 Budget Trading Program.
January 2007	Massachusetts and Rhode Island sign the MOU and commit to RGGI.
April 2007	Maryland signs the MOU and commits to RGGI.
September 2008	RGGI's first auction of CO_2 emission allowances held.
December 2008	RGGI states issue a revised Model Rule with consistencies among state rules.
January 2009	The first CO_2 Budget Trading Program compliance period begins.
May 2011	Governor Chris Christie announces plans to withdraw New Jersey from RGGI in 2012.
December 2011	First compliance period ends.
January 2012	Second compliance period and first program review begin.
February 2013	Program review results and updated Model Rule released with a 45 percent reduction in the 2014 CO_2 emissions cap and subsequent annual 2.5 percent cap reductions through 2020.
December 2013	Updated Model Rule adopted with proposed adjustments.
December 2014	Second compliance period ends.
January 2015	Third compliance period begins with lowered CO_2 emissions cap.
January 2016	Second program review begins.

that downwind states like New Hampshire have clean air."[16] The legislation acknowledged the limited scope of focusing on only three power plants located within the state. In the design of its cap-and-trade system New Hampshire allowed these plants to reach their reduction targets by reducing their generation or improving their fuel efficiency. But it also allowed them to purchase emission credits from neighboring states that had achieved required reductions on their own.[17]

The inclusion of cross-state credit options formally raised the possibility of multistate collaboration on cap-and-trade, one that might build on prior regional examples. This also coincided with the implementation of electricity deregulation across much of the Northeast. Such restructuring created the possibility of a more uniform regional electricity market alongside division of traditionally merged energy production and distribution functions into separate organizations. It potentially weakened opposition to electricity-sector carbon pricing. Only electricity generators would be required to obtain allowances under cap-and-trade. At the same time, "wires only" distributors might welcome the push for greater energy efficiency, especially if their efforts would be subsidized with revenue from allowance auctions.[18]

These issues were not lost on other leaders across the Northeast, though the idea of integrating a set of small and independent cap-and-trade programs into something bigger had particular appeal in Albany. New York was the largest electricity producer and consumer in the region and its actions would loom large in other states given the substantial cross-border movement of power. New York Republican Governor George Pataki decided to use that leverage in 2003. He invited ten gubernatorial counterparts to begin to explore the viability of a northeastern regional cap-and-trade strategy, providing a key stepping stone to the formation of RGGI three years later.

Pataki likely had several motivations for taking this step. New York had been actively exploring a range of climate policies, including plans for a renewable portfolio standard and expanded energy efficiency standards. Environmental groups were routinely pushing Pataki and other state leaders to continue moving forward on these and related policy fronts.[19] Cap-and-trade represented one additional way to expand the state's efforts, and state action might position New York and the region for influence in the design of a much-anticipated federal policy in the near future, much as the Empire State had shaped the design of sulfur dioxide cap-and-trade on a national scale in 1990. Pataki also seemed to have a Gordon Campbell–like personal interest in climate change and policy design. This was reflected in his extensive public talks on climate change and subsequent coeditorship of a book on the subject with former Iowa Democratic Governor Thomas Vilsack.[20]

There were also political considerations at play. Pataki had won reelection in 2002 and, perhaps like Campbell, was looking to longer-term considerations. One stretch option was the presidency, using his base in Albany to make his case as a moderate Republican who might combine fiscal conservatism with a market-based approach to an issue such as climate change. Leadership of a multistate cap-and-trade agreement might provide further evidence of his ability to lead beyond the confines of state boundaries.

This led to prolonged negotiations between these states, once governors met and expressed broad support for the idea of a regional trading system. This included extensive meetings between working groups dominated by state environmental protection and energy officials, building on strong relationships forged in prior venues for collaboration. The policy development process also involved rotating meetings that combined public hearings with working group sessions. These were jokingly referred to as a traveling show dominated by "RGGI Roadies."

These meetings explored all dimensions of creating a multistate trading system, ranging from agreement on metrics for emissions to the organizational details involved in putting together a multistate partnership with some kind of central coordinating unit. Connecticut's lead environmental official, Gina McCarthy, noted during a public meeting in Hartford that "there is a lot of work to be done before this kicks off and this is not an easy process, in many ways. We're not sure how many bites of the apple we'll get at this and so we want to get it right."[21]

Launching Cap-and-Trade

The governors of Connecticut, Delaware, Maine, New Hampshire, New Jersey, New York, and Vermont approved core agreements for a regional system on December 20, 2005, two years after Pataki's initial proposal. These governors would be drawn from both political parties, a pattern that would continue in subsequent years (see table 5.2). This agreement then led to a memorandum of understanding that included a framework for a model rule that could guide RGGI implementation. It began a process that would include key steps necessary to launch RGGI in a credible manner and thereby navigate the policy launch stage of the policy life-cycle that would confound other carbon pricing efforts. This would be considerably more complex and time-consuming than the British Columbia case (three years versus five months), reflecting the heavier management lift involved with cap-and-trade.

The memorandum became RGGI's founding document and its signatories made clear that they "wish to establish themselves and their industries as world leaders in the creation, development, and deployment of carbon emission control technologies, renewable energy supplies, and energy-efficient technologies, demand-side management practices, and increase the share of energy used within the Signatory States that is derived from secure and reliable sources of Energy."[22] Central figures in this regional process have continued to lay claim to national, continental, and even global leadership in establishing RGGI as a model for carbon emissions trading, as did McCarthy when she served as EPA administrator from 2013 to 2017. Even after several years of operation and a declining emissions trend, RGGI states collectively would rank twentieth in the world in comparing their emissions with other nations. They would place immediately behind Italy and France in global rankings.[23] These states represented 16 percent of American gross domestic product as of 2012 but only 7 percent of total national carbon dioxide emissions from energy consumption.

Each state had to subsequently complete a formal review to authorize its participation, either through legislation or a rule-making procedure. The coalition would formally expand, as the memorandum allowed. Massachusetts and Rhode Island pulled back from their initial support for RGGI membership in 2005 but remained active in negotiations and returned to the fold in 2007. Maryland was a relative latecomer to the deliberations but joined later in 2007. Other jurisdictions, including Pennsylvania, the District of Columbia, and the Canadian province of New Brunswick, remained as official observers, reserving the option to pursue membership at a later time.

RGGI ushered in a cap-and-trade system for carbon dioxide emissions on all power plants that generate more than half of their electricity from burning fossil fuels and produce more than 25 megawatts of power annually.

The formal cap went into operation in 2009, set at a level of 121.3 million short tons of carbon dioxide, which was "approximately equivalent to 1990 emissions."[24] This level would be maintained through 2014, when the emissions cap was set to decrease by 2.5 percent annually through 2018. Such a phased reduction schedule would bring 2018 emissions 10 percent below 1990 levels.

Brokering Political Adjustments

These provisions were designed after prolonged interstate negotiations, and they reflected political considerations needed to deter state defections. Indeed, the 2009 cap and its maintenance through 2014 was in many respects quite modest, given plausible emission declines even in the absence of such a policy. Nonetheless, it proved necessary politically to secure broad support and ease concerns about capacity to meet targets in the near term. Many other aspects of the RGGI development and launch process also required deft political maneuvering to sustain multistate and stakeholder coalitions. Bars of Ivory brand soap were jokingly awarded to state agency officials at regional meetings, reflecting their occasional insistence on "pure" decisions regarding cap-and-trade design rather than tempering them to assuage political calculations. Public management sensitive to political realities helped ease the launch process for cap-and-trade.

Even a provision as seemingly straightforward as allocating the annual carbon dioxide emission budgets among states served as a venue for political bargaining. Under the final allocation plan, states with the lowest overall emissions were allowed to increase them slightly during initial years of operation. In contrast, states with the largest overall emissions generally accepted initial allocations somewhat below baseline levels. This emerged as a political compromise, whereby larger states agreed to assume a somewhat disproportionate share of the overall responsibility for emissions reductions, which helped placate smaller states with few sources and potentially less latitude in securing reductions.

RGGI architects also attempted to navigate among a range of diverse stakeholders, many of whom stood to lose or gain financially depending on the design of various cap-and-trade provisions. This resulted in a complex set of early-reduction credit, trigger, safety valve, and offset provisions. Each of these were designed in part to maintain implementation flexibility and political support from various constituents. In the case of early-reduction credits, utility producers who would be covered under cap-and-trade insisted that they receive flexible and favorable terms for any emission reductions that they achieved between the 2005 memorandum of understanding (MOU) signing and the 2009 trading system launch. Credits offered formal recognition of these steps, leading to allowances that would be issued in addition to the overall state allocation. In these instances, credited reductions likely would have occurred without adoption of cap-and-trade and so limited the program's future impact on emissions.

Triggers and safety valves reflected a complex set of formulas whereby any future allowance price increase above anticipated levels could lead to greater compliance flexibility. This could entail formal extension of compliance deadlines or more liberal use of offsets to compensate for excessive emissions. Offset options included methane capture from landfill gas, end-use energy efficiency, and afforestation strategies to sequester carbon. Offsets that were generated within RGGI boundaries were to be approved on a ton-for-ton basis, whereas those generated outside "shall be awarded one allowance for every two CO_2 equivalent tons of certified reduction."[25] Generators could use offsets to cover up to 3.3 percent of their reported emissions for any compliance period, although this could be increased under the trigger provisions.

Offset use could also be expanded under the safely valve features, which could be invoked if allowance prices exceeded $7 per ton, set in 2005 dollars and adjusted thereafter for inflation. If the safety valve threshold was surpassed, RGGI allowed for both expanded offset use and more favorable terms for those generated outside its regional boundary. At that point, offsets could also be considered that were generated outside of the United States.

Crafting Governing Institutions

Even the organizational design and physical location of RGGI headquarters featured political overtones. The founding RGGI memorandum of understanding announced that the program would be managed through a "regional organization with a primary office in New York City." But there were no particulars beyond this statement, thereby making it a major topic for negotiation among the regional partners. The express reference to a New York City location seemed to rule out a formal role for NESCAUM, given its base in Boston. But a number of smaller states thought NESCAUM would be the logical lead agency, given its established expertise, the high costs of operating an office in New York, and the absence at that point of any mechanism to generate revenue to cover administrative costs. They also thought that a central NESCAUM role might foster greater coordination between the emerging cap-and-trade program and other climate policies that were being adopted in states around the region.

This preference would collide with the strong desire of Pataki administration leaders to create a new nonprofit organization that would be based in their flagship city. They noted the symbolic ties to the New York financial markets hub, arguing that a new regional entity could take shape in that setting. New York also offered generous financial terms, covering most of the operational costs for at least the initial three years and possibly longer. Under this plan, there would be no formal links with NESCAUM, even though it had been working for a number of years on a regional registry for greenhouse gas emissions and its own demonstration program for greenhouse gas credit trading.

As a result, RGGI, Inc. was unveiled in New York City in July 2007. It was led by an executive director who oversaw a staff of five other full-time policy professionals. This staff featured expertise in running all aspects of the emissions trading process, including allowance tracking and offset oversight. It also handled external communications and financial management. Other functions, such as auditing and reporting on transactions, would be handled in part through consultant contracts. The organization supported an executive board consisting of members nominated by the governors of each member state. RGGI, Inc. would also host ongoing meetings of various multistate working groups as well as periodic hearings around the region. It replaced the initial model that featured a multistate committee, a website, and a series of rotating meeting locations.

Smoothing Asymmetries amid Early Exits

The tensions between larger and smaller states would continue to emerge during early stages of launching RGGI. This reflected New York's outsized role, which included greater staff representation in various working groups than any other state. At times, this contributed to a perception among some states that New York had become too dominant in many areas of program design. These concerns were compounded when Massachusetts withdrew from RGGI in 2005, as it was widely seen as a close second to New

York, with sufficient clout and resources to offset any asymmetries emerging from New York leadership.

Massachusetts's withdrawal was particularly surprising given the state's earlier development of its own cap-and-trade program and very active and enthusiastic support for RGGI during its formative stages. Republican Governor Mitt Romney and his commonwealth development secretary, Douglas Foy, repeatedly cited RGGI as one of many Massachusetts climate protection initiatives that had made it a national leader on the issue. Foy and his lead RGGI staffer, Sonia Hamel, advanced positions that their governor initially supported but ultimately rejected. In particular, Romney insisted on a firm price cap on electricity rates, whereby additional allocations would be made available if these caps were exceeded. But Foy and Hamel had already agreed with New York and other states to avoid such a cap, while instead inserting various triggers and safety valves. At this point, Romney decided to pull the plug, and Rhode Island Republican Governor Donald Carcieri, who closely adhered to the Massachusetts position throughout the deliberations, followed suit.

The Massachusetts legislature subsequently considered enactment of a state agreement to return to RGGI. Romney floated a plan to expand the existing state cap-and-trade program, albeit with a firm cap on electricity prices. But neither made much progress leading up to the November 2006 elections. Romney's pivot may have been linked to his own evolving political agenda, once he decided not to seek a second term amid increasingly negative poll results in Massachusetts and growing reports of 2008 presidential ambitions. This shift enabled Romney to make a case to a potential national audience that he was receptive to market-based approaches to climate change but more sensitive to possible rate increases than his anticipated presidential race rival, New York's Pataki.

This political theater and resulting departure of such a large portion of the entire RGGI membership before completion of the final details of trading raised questions about the durability of this regional program. Initial defection might snowball into a full system collapse, much as would occur in the West with the WCI and in the Midwest with the MGGRA. But remaining RGGI states and their fledgling organization were able to adjust quickly to the withdrawal of Massachusetts and Rhode Island. They also prepared for the possibility of an exit by one or more other members such as Connecticut or New Hampshire, where some elected officials expressed reservations about sustaining RGGI membership. They quickly adjusted the program to eliminate any allowances from Massachusetts and Rhode Island and also moved to fill emerging gaps created in staff working groups. In turn, they made clear that the door was left open to departing states for a return at any future point. As a result, RGGI continued to move forward during its formative years. The program remained on schedule with all subsequent deadlines for launching North America's first carbon cap-and-trade program, despite the political disruptions.

Politically Sustaining Cap-and-Trade

Subsequent elections among the RGGI states would not provide a Gordon Campbell–like endorsement of carbon pricing. Indeed, cap-and-trade was not a major consideration in most states holding 2006 elections, the first major test of RGGI's potential political prospects following its creation. No major party embraced RGGI repeal as had the New Democrats in trying to oust Campbell in British Columbia (see chapter 4), and there was no evidence of voter backlash against gubernatorial sponsors of emissions trading in these state elections. In turn, three of the elections served to bolster or expand the regional program. Collectively the first set of statewide elections after RGGI adoption were affirming and supportive of the program, allowing for steady transition toward full implementation (see table 5.2). Unlike other carbon pricing cases, RGGI smoothly cleared this significant hurdle in the policy life-cycle.

Seven of the original nine state members held elections for governor in 2006, including the two states that had departed in 2005. There were five races where incumbents were reelected, generally with large margins. These races included three Republicans, Jodi Rell of Connecticut, Carcieri of Rhode Island, and Jim Douglas of Vermont. Douglas was reelected decisively despite having supported full auctioning of allowances in 2006. Carcieri's initial support for RGGI and subsequent decision to have Rhode Island withdraw along with Massachusetts did not harm his reelection bid, although his margin of victory was considerably narrower than in his prior election. Successful incumbents also included two Democrats, John Baldacci of Maine and John Lynch of New Hampshire. And 2006 was generally a good year nationally for Democrats in state legislative elections; the region's biggest shift occurred in New Hampshire, where Democrats gained control of

Table 5.2

Regional Greenhouse Gas Initiative state governor partisanship, 2000–2017.

States	2000	2001	2002	2003	2004	2005	2006	2007	2008	2009	2010	2011	2012	2013	2014	2015	2016	2017
Connecticut	R	R	R	R	R	R	R	R	R	R	R	D	D	D	D	D	D	D
Delaware	D	D	D	D	D	D	D	D	D	D	D	D	D	D	D	D	D	D
Maine	I*	I*	I*	D	D	D	D	D	D	D	R	R	R	R	R	R	R	R
Maryland	D	D	D	R	R	R	R	D	D	D	D	D	D	D	D	R	R	R
Massachusetts	R	R	R	R	R	R	R	D	D	D	D	D	D	D	D	R	R	R
New Hampshire	D	D	D	R	R	D	D	D	D	D	D	D	D	D	D	D	D	R
New Jersey	R	R	D	D	D	D	D	D	D	D	R	R	R	R	R	R	R	R
New York	R	R	R	R	R	R	R	D	D	D	D	D	D	D	D	D	D	D
Rhode Island	R	R	R	R	R	R	R	R	R	R	R	D	D	D	D	D	D	D
Vermont	D	D	D	R	R	R	R	R	R	R	R	D	D	D	D	D	D	R

*While he identified as an Independent during his governorship, Maine Governor Angus King was a former Democrat and caucused with the Democratic Party while serving as a US Senator.

Sources: "Former Governors' Bios," *National Governors Association*, 2015, accessed July 5, 2016, http://www.nga.org/cms/FormerGovBios; "Current Governors," *National Governors Association*, 2015, accessed July 5, 2016, http://www.nga.org/cms/governors/bios.

both legislative chambers. Lynch would remain a strong advocate of RGGI in later years, when some opposition to cap-and-trade surfaced in the legislature and Republican membership increased.[26]

But there were three other races that resulted in the election of new governors, all of whom indicated strong support for RGGI. In Massachusetts, Democrat Deval Patrick won a four-way race to replace outgoing Romney. During a debate, Patrick responded to a question about options for addressing climate change by noting that: "First of all, I think we ought to join the Regional Greenhouse Gas Initiative. That was a regional approach to the generation of greenhouse gases, to the causes of global warming; it was something that was negotiated during this administration and then right when it was time to sign, if I understand it correctly, the administration walked away and I think that's a mistake. When I'm governor we will join it."[27] Patrick honored this commitment quickly after his inauguration, returning Massachusetts to the RGGI fold and restoring its active engagement in all aspects of cap-and-trade development and implementation. This prompted Rhode Island's Carcieri to again follow Massachusetts in rejoining after his reelection bid was successful.

In New York, Democratic Attorney General Eliot Spitzer won an overwhelming victory to replace the retiring Republican Pataki and made clear that he would pursue full development of RGGI as a key part of his climate change strategy. Spitzer and his advisers had ranked among the first public officials to endorse auctioning in 2006.[28] But more significantly, another Democrat, Martin O'Malley, became Maryland's governor by defeating Republican incumbent Bob Ehrlich. The Ehrlich administration had monitored RGGI developments as an observer but had balked at becoming a full member until Ehrlich agreed in 2006 under political pressure to join. O'Malley campaigned in part on a more aggressive state approach to climate change, formally enrolling Maryland into RGGI in April 2007 and becoming an outspoken advocate for the program.

The 2008 elections did not involve as many governors and all three incumbents won reelection. This included Douglas in Vermont and Lynch in New Hampshire, reflecting their two-year election cycles, as well as Democrat Ruth Ann Minner in Delaware. So this pair of 2006 and 2008 elections served to politically sustain much of the original gubernatorial alliance that had helped foster RGGI. Swing 2006 elections in Massachusetts and Maryland helped bolster the program. Indeed, the only election during the first five years after RGGI that damaged cap-and-trade was Republican Chris Christie's victory over embattled Democratic incumbent Jon Corzine in 2009. RGGI was not a significant campaign issue, although Christie removed New Jersey from the regional program after his victory, as discussed in chapter 3.

Building Political Support for Auctions

The 2006 elections also provided a political foundation for a defining set of decisions that would be taken before the next voting two years later. This reflected one piece of unfinished business in the original design of RGGI; namely, the process for allocating emission allowances. As noted previously, up to that point conventional practice in cap-and-trade called for government distribution of allowances without cost, thereby triggering a trading process to minimize overall compliance costs. The idea of auctioning at least some of the allowances surfaced during the creation of RGGI, although no formal decision on it was taken through the memorandum of understanding, leaving it for subsequent consideration.

Environmental groups championed this idea, particularly if auction revenues could then be concentrated on other carbon-friendly projects such as energy efficiency. State political and appointed officials were somewhat cautious about this approach. They were mindful of potential political backlash that could be linked to such a form of cost imposition, particularly if auction prices proved to be quite high. With the notable exception of Vermont, this issue was not resolved before the 2006 election, although auctioning gained tremendous political momentum immediately afterward. Many states saw bills authorizing auctioning introduced shortly after the elections, with adoption of some version in seven states between May 2007 and July 2008. Two other states, Connecticut and New York, instead adopted auctioning through regulatory rule-making (see table 5.3).

No two states designed identical auction plans within the confines of a regional system. Maine, for example, enacted legislation to allow sale of all its allowances "at public auction" while also creating a state Energy and Carbon Savings Trust "to receive, hold, bank and expend revenue resulting from the sale of allowances."[29] Massachusetts, following Patrick's lead, decided to auction 99 percent of its allowances and devote all funds to energy efficiency programs.[30] Maryland, in contrast, decided only to auction

Table 5.3
Regional Greenhouse Gas Initiative revenue allocation.

State	Auction Adoption	Percent to Efficiency or Renewables	Percent to Rebates	Cumulative Allowances Sold	Cumulative Proceeds
Connecticut	2007	93%	0%	53,718,424	$165,176,146
Delaware	2008	75%	15%	27,751,842	$91,691,799
Maine	2007	100% <$5/ton	100% >$5/ton	25,827,664	$79,566,813
Maryland	2008	56.5%	40%	170,667,164	$519,512,121
Massachusetts	2008	100%	0%	135,645,449	$415,724,857
New Hampshire	2008	100% <$6/ton	100% >$6/ton	34,660,280	$109,180,023
New Jersey	2008	60%	20%	48,483,770	$113,344,551
New York	2008	100%	0%	311,973,151	$951,630,295
Rhode Island	2007	Not determined by rule	Not determined by rule	15,649,598	$52,511,855
Vermont	2006	100%	0%	6,216,274	$18,944,036

Sources: Leigh Raymond, *Reclaiming the Atmospheric Commons: The Regional Greenhouse Gas Initiative and a New Model of Emissions Trading* (Cambridge, MA: MIT Press, 2016), 46; Regional Greenhouse Gas Initiative Inc., "Cumulative Allowances and Proceeds," accessed July 11, 2016, http://www. rggi.org/market/tracking/public-reporting/54-co2-auctions -tracking-a-offsets/Auction-Results/207-cumulative-allowances-a-proceeds-by-state.

80 percent of its allowances and designated 40 percent of the proceeds to customer rebates. Nonetheless, more than 90 percent of total RGGI regional allowances between 2008 and 2014 would be auctioned, with the remainder either allocated for free or retired.[31]

Despite these variations, auctioning represented a sea change for cap-and-trade, moving relatively quickly and with unanimity across multiple jurisdictions. The RGGI experience helped establish auctioning as an alternative in any future cap-and-trade initiative, reflecting a strong political commitment to reframe allowances as a public resource.[32] These steps were propelled by strong support from environmental groups even in the face of vigorous industry opposition. A coalition representing regional utilities noted in a public statement that "it is clear that the balance promised in the multi-state process has been lost."[33] They warned of future steep increases in regional electricity prices and lamented that future auctions "have a good chance to be manipulated by outsiders and a better chance to increase regional costs with few benefits."[34]

These decisions collectively set an alternative precedent from the one established in British Columbia—namely, designating most of the auction revenue for environmentally related purposes rather than returning money to taxpayers. The RGGI states never seriously explored revenue-neutrality through combinations of tax credits, contrary to British Columbia. There was considerable discussion of returning revenue through some form of a rebate following the initial $100 (Canadian) rebate in British Columbia, as well as some discussion of adhering to the precedent of the Alaska Permanent Dividend Fund and its annual allocation of a royalty check to all Alaskans.[35] Aside from those portions of RGGI revenue allocated to rebates in Maryland, New Jersey, and Delaware (see table 5.3), the vast majority of auction funds would be directly linked to supplemental programs to further accelerate the transition from fossil fuels.

Using Auctions to Build Constituency Support

Quarterly auctions began in September 2008 and would quickly play a far greater role in sustaining and building political support than had been anticipated. The launch of RGGI coincided with the full onset of the Great Recession. This triggered a substantial plunge in electricity demand regionally at the very point that RGGI's new carbon emission caps became operational. Combined with the expansion of state renewable energy programs and the growing availability of natural gas through hydraulic fracturing from neighboring Pennsylvania that could be substituted for coal and cut emissions, the region faced the prospect of steep electricity demand reduction without cap-and-trade. Indeed, regional electricity-sector emissions stood 34 percent below the established RGGI cap by 2009, the very point at which a reliable baseline was essential to allow for successful implementation.

It was not politically feasible to achieve a near-term agreement to markedly reduce the emission cap to reflect this sudden and unanticipated shift. There were also significant questions as to whether electricity demand might rebound if the economy regained strength, despite the broader energy transition. So RGGI faced the possibility of beginning operations with essentially no consequences, largely a perfunctory exercise that transpired well below any real emissions cap. And its emissions price might have fallen to negligible levels given the likely flood of allowances available for pursuit via sealed bids.

Auctioning and one other administrative feature bought the program invaluable time and also gave it a mission through the generation of revenue for alternative energy promotion. Even at very low price levels, the quarterly auctions produced revenue that would be reallocated to each state on the basis of its emissions. So RGGI began, in many respects, to function far less like a conventional cap-and-trade system and far more like a de facto carbon tax that employed auctioning to generate revenue for reallocation.

As a result, the inclusion of auctioning for nearly all RGGI allowances gave the program a significant reason to move ahead despite the cap collapse, rather than to simply bide time in hopes of some future political agreement to adjust the cap or for a rebound in electricity demand.[36] Auctioning continued to produce low overall bids, many hovering at or just above a formally established minimum bid price. This so-called reserve price or price floor was included in the initial RGGI agreement as a hedge against any potential price collapse. The initial reserve price was set at $1.86 per ton, and many subsequent auctions registered prices just pennies above that level, particularly between 2010 and 2012 (see figure 5.2). About 40 percent of total allowances were withdrawn from the market in this period, lacking any bidder and thereby retired.[37] This was only a fraction of the size of a carbon price that was realistically capable of driving major behavioral changes in fossil fuel use. But it was sufficient to allow RGGI and its auctioning process to make a credible start, avoid EU ETS pitfalls, and generate significant revenue for participating states.

Such a low initial price might also have featured a strategic benefit. It allowed for the development of operational cap-and-trade expertise and revenue generation but also kept auction prices very low before any subsequent adjustments might be made to tighten the system. This bought time to refine program management but also opened an opportunity for states to allocate revenues adroitly and build constituency support through distribution of immediate benefits. RGGI states promptly and vocally demonstrated how auction funds could support a range of climate-linked projects, thereby building a political base with each allocation. As was true in the British

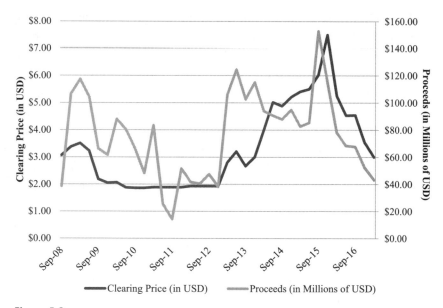

Figure 5.2
RGGI proceeds and clearing price, 2008–2016.
Note: Includes allowances purchased by compliance entities and their affiliates.
Source: "Auction Results," *Regional Greenhouse Gas Initiative*, accessed July 11, 2016,
https://www.rggi.org/market/co2_auctions/results; Regional Greenhouse Gas Initiative,
Various Market Monitor Reports, 2016, https://www.rggi.org/market/co2_ auctions
/results/auctions-1-32.

Columbia case, this experience indicated that carbon pricing could not
only impose costs but also deliver near-term and demonstrable benefits to
garner constituency support.[38]

RGGI generated more than $2.5 billion through its first thirty-five auc-
tions running through March 2017 (see figure 5.2). RGGI, Inc. and its state
constituents regularly framed the auction process as one that delivered significant benefits that included climate mitigation but also provided other
tangible environmental and economic benefits. The nonprofit oversight
agency routinely reports auction results and attempts to quantify all plausible beneficial impacts to date. A 2015 RGGI report explained that "the
investment of RGGI proceeds through 2013 is projected to return more
than $2.9 billion in lifetime energy bill savings to more than 3.7 million
participating households and 17,800 businesses."[39] It also broke those
investments down by state. Maryland, for example, used RGGI funds to

support 11,880 energy efficiency upgrades in low- and moderate-income residences and assisted 5,206 families and 2,011 businesses to install new renewable energy systems. In turn, Rhode Island used RGGI funds to enable sixty-seven nonprofits and community buildings to receive comprehensive efficiency upgrades, while Maine used RGGI proceeds to help retail customers to purchase over 1.9 million high-efficiency lightbulbs.[40] The list of recipients only expands over time with the completion of additional quarterly auctions.

The program also publicizes enthusiastic statements from each state's lead environmental agency official on the impacts of these funds, usually in a press release that accompanies each auction results report and then broader publications. For example, Delaware's top environmental official noted after a 2013 auction that state "reinvestment of auction proceeds in energy efficiency programs has not only avoided carbon pollution, but helped businesses and families reduce their electricity bills, and workers find jobs weatherizing homes, retrofitting outdated industrial equipment, and constructing more energy-efficient buildings."[41] A senior Connecticut energy official celebrated a 2016 auction by declaring that this process has "enabled a virtuous cycle of benefits."[42]

RGGI, Inc. also publishes an ongoing set of "success stories" that portray individual families, government agencies, or businesses that have benefited from direct auction fund support.[43] Such stories have included a profile of a New Hampshire family restaurant that slashed its energy costs due to an energy efficiency grant and a Delaware city that purchased hybrid vehicles for use by public officials through RGGI auction dollars. Media accounts of RGGI frequently accentuate these kinds of cases, putting a personal touch on the argument that carbon cap-and-trade can deliver tangible benefits, in vivid contrast with media coverage of the European version of cap-and-trade.

Adjusting the Cap

Auctioning afforded cap-and-trade a distinct new focus and also helped overshadow RGGI's initial failure to establish an emissions cap that was roughly commensurate with actual releases. But the much-anticipated rebound in electricity demand never occurred and so the gap between the official regional cap and actual regional emissions has remained enormous, thereby undermining program effectiveness and credibility. Indeed, the experience of the EU ETS loomed large, given its prolonged political struggles to better connect its emissions cap and related allowances to actual emissions.

The RGGI memorandum of understanding established periodic program review periods whereby necessary adjustments could be made. These could draw on technical input from program staff and advisers but would not be a purely administrative adjustment. Instead, these changes would require a series of political decisions that would then be implemented by RGGI, Inc. and member states. This would entail a regional agreement by the participating states that would then have to be ratified by each statehouse, either through new legislation or regulatory revision. The Clean Air Act failed to provide such an adjustment provision for its sulfur dioxide trading program, thereby limiting its longer-term effectiveness.

This raised the question of whether RGGI's early political feasibility could be parlayed into a second major agreement across political jurisdictions. Any new plan would likely impose considerably more political and economic pain than the original version by tightening the emissions cap and likely increasing compliance costs of purchasing auction allowances. By 2013, all but one of the original set of governors who had joined forces to establish RGGI were no longer in office. That one exception, John Lynch, was entering the final year of his four-term rule in New Hampshire. This meant that an essentially new team of political officials, backed by new sets of agency heads, would have to convene and correct a major error made by their predecessors. Political benefits in this case were likely greatest on a legacy basis for former governors; their successors would have to make the decisions and face near-term consequences for any problems.

The political complexity of this transition was compounded by the fact that RGGI was largely benign in its early operations. The auction price was quite low and unlikely at that level to cause any major reactions or upheavals. Yet it had quietly found a way to extract revenue from electric utilities and apply that either to popular alternative energy programs or return funds to customers through rebates. This created considerable political temptation to dodge the cap issue and allow it to hover without a fix. This might have been particularly tempting during 2011 and 2012, following the collapse of federal deliberations over carbon pricing and backlash against early cap-and-trade commitments in other states and abroad.

Despite these factors, the RGGI political coalition held together during this second round. This reflected broad support from a set of governors and legislatures that had increasingly shifted toward Democratic control. During a period in which Republicans gained considerable control in many states, Democrats actually expanded their influence in the Northeast. Between 2011 and 2013, the key period for RGGI cap adjustment, all but one state was governed by a Democratic governor (see table 5.2). Five of these states also featured full Democratic control of both legislative chambers during a period where the party's political fortunes were generally on the decline at the state level. This reflected a growing pattern of partisan divide over climate change in American state politics and further suggested that RGGI revision took place in an increasingly partisan context. It was lodged in one of the few areas in the nation with a substantial concentration of political authority in the hands of the major party that has become most likely to be receptive to engagement on carbon pricing.

Nonetheless, there was no great public clamor to increase the carbon price in the region and public opinion analysis revealed some doubts as to whether many residents in the Northeast even realized RGGI was in operation more than five years after its launch.[44] Moreover, there was significant opposition from regional electricity providers, and the national organization Americans for Prosperity pursued an active campaign in opposition to cap tightening. The association's spokesperson Steve Lonegan argued that regional electricity customers "are going to be walloped thanks to this diktat from a bunch of unaccountable bureaucrats to cut the emissions cap almost in half."[45]

But RGGI countered with its own coalitional supporters, including environmental groups but also a consortium of over 225 businesses in the region with a financial stake in promoting expanded transition from fossil fuels. These firms lobbied RGGI and joined forces in submitting a July 2011 letter to regional governors seeking a tighter RGGI cap. It noted that "we are companies that believe strong clean energy and clean air policies create jobs and stimulate economic growth," further arguing that "improving RGGI will provide still more cost-effective benefits."[46] RGGI Inc. and state agency staff convened more than a dozen stakeholder meetings, webinars, and learning sessions during the two-year review period, and these generally produced strong support for cap tightening. The Boston-based Analysis

Group reported in early 2013 that its analyses concluded that a significant cap reduction would have only a small impact on regional electricity bills.[47]

This would ultimately be a political decision, and governors increasingly began to rally around the idea. New York's Democratic Governor Andrew Cuomo chose to build on Pataki's earlier work and endorsed cap tightening during his 2013 State of the State address. This followed a period of extensive flooding in New York City from Superstorm Sandy. Cuomo characterized RGGI expansion as a path toward climate mitigation while also announcing a number of efforts to try to protect the New York coasts and subways from future storms linked to the changing climate. Other governors also expressed support for the cap alteration during this period. Supporters were further emboldened by President Obama's 2012 reelection and the possibility of using RGGI to ease regional compliance with anticipated federal application of the Clean Air Act to electricity-sector carbon emissions.

These forces converged in February 2013, leading to an agreement by the nine RGGI states to undertake a major reduction in its emissions cap, one that went well beyond the original level and required additional reductions through 2018. This reduced the cap by 45 percent from its original 2014 target, from 165 million to 91 million tons per year, followed by subsequent reductions of 2.5 percent per year from 2015 through 2020. This collective decision altered the original RGGI model rule and each state then had to adjust its own related statutes and regulations to allow for regional implementation. Additional adjustments were made to the RGGI market, including permanent withdrawal of any unsold allowances from previous years for potential purchase in order to further tighten supply. The new cap would begin operation in 2014, following the completion of the original model rule that ran through 2013.

The initial allowance auction following this announcement took place in March 2013, with a clearing price increase to $2.80 per ton from the $1.93 level of December 2012.[48] The initial response from economists was that this was a strong signal of an increasingly robust carbon market in the Northeast, "like the flip of a switch" in the words of one analyst.[49] Allowance prices trended upward in subsequent years, reaching $6.02 in September 2015 and $7.50 in December 2015 before declining during the next two years (see figure 5.2). RGGI Inc. and member states heralded this development as a milestone step in correcting an initial design flaw. They projected that allowance prices would continue to climb in auctions during the late 2010s, generating additional revenues for energy efficiency and renewable energy projects through state government reallocation.

The revisions in the original RGGI design were not confined to cap adjustment. In particular, the states tried to ensure constituents that any cost increases would be contained through a price ceiling known as a cost containment reserve (CCR). This replaced the original model rule plan to allow increased offset use in the event that prices soared. Under the CCR, RGGI would hold supplemental allowances for release into the market if prices exceeded certain limits. This began at $4 per ton in 2014, growing steadily to $10 per ton in 2017 and increasing 2.5 percent annually thereafter.[50] The CCR was not intended to serve as a formal price cap, contrary to the $1.86 reserve price. But it was designed to flood the market with expanded allowance supply in the event of a price surge, in order to suppress that price growth.

Preparing for the Future

This revised agreement helped launch RGGI into its second half-decade of operation, with a solid political and organizational foundation and a possible path toward an increasingly robust carbon pricing regime. It clarified key design questions through 2020, with the prospect of another program review round prior to that date. In turn, RGGI leaders further raised the issue of whether it might serve as a model and perhaps a hub for much-expanded cap-and-trade operations under the Obama administration's Clean Power Plan.

This plan reflected the administration's decision to abandon efforts for a legislative route to carbon pricing following the 2010 and 2012 elections, due to a lack of political support. Instead, it drew on authority of the 1990 Clean Air Act Amendments to consider carbon dioxide as an air contaminant, using a separate legislative title from the one that had been used to establish cap-and-trade for sulfur dioxide emissions. With this reframing, aided by a 2007 US Supreme Court decision, the US Environmental Protection Agency established a plan in 2015 to require all states to reduce carbon emissions from their electricity sector. But the emerging Clean Power Plan would give them enormous latitude to design their own approach to reducing their emissions, with the goal of producing a net reduction of approximately

30 percent from 2005 levels by 2030. Each state would be required to submit a state implementation plan to EPA for approval, including specifics on what policies they would adopt to achieve these targets. The list of options included cap-and-trade and carbon taxes, although EPA clearly viewed the "trading ready" option as the superior approach and was inclined to impose that on any state that failed to cooperate with the agency in the planning process.

The implementation of the Clean Power Plan was deterred by a Supreme Court stay in 2016, but the Obama EPA remained committed to it in the event of a favorable final ruling by the judiciary after the November elections. RGGI was mentioned at least a dozen times in White House documents explaining the Clean Power Plan, and EPA administrator (and former RGGI architect) Gina McCarthy routinely described RGGI as a model for what other states might consider.[51] These developments were not lost on RGGI leaders, including political officials and state agency heads, who sought highly favorable terms for their program in any evolving federal Clean Power Plan. They further argued that RGGI, especially after its program review and model rule revision, was poised to accept additional state partners and become the hub of a far larger regional or even national trading system. Forty-one congressional representatives from RGGI-based districts called on the EPA in 2014 to use the program as a national model.[52]

These officials noted that their states had already achieved significant emission reductions and were set under the recent revisions to cover much of the ground being sought under the Clean Power Plan (CPP). Individual states and RGGI, Inc. aggressively advanced these messages after a draft EPA rule was issued in 2014 and with the issuance of a final rule that was somewhat more favorable to RGGI states. They submitted a detailed report to EPA in November 2014, making the case for RGGI to take center stage in any future federal discussion of cap-and-trade in the electricity sector. The report asserted that "RGGI is a near-perfect match for the CPP…. The particular relevance of the RGGI program is that it provides an off-the-shelf model that is well-aligned with the goals and structure of the CPP. In order to ensure that other states can take advantage of the opportunity provided by the RGGI model, the EPA should provide strong support for states that implement RGGI-like programs or become participants in RGGI, an outcome that would be welcomed by the RGGI states."[53] As a result, the prospects for considerable diffusion of the RGGI approach beyond its founding states appeared considerably greater by the end of 2015 than the British Columbia carbon tax.

Cap-and-Trade Performance

The future of RGGI and its possible expansion through an emerging federal system will be explored more fully in chapter 8. But the program stands alone in North America and internationally in carbon cap-and-trade. It cleared each of the political and managerial hurdles that either thwarted or impaired other cap-and-trade proposals. This involved more than six years of full operation through the end of 2015. It included more than thirty carbon allowance auctions, endurance through multiple political and leadership changes among its nine members, and a major political revision to address initial design shortcomings. Contrary to cap-and-trade cases discussed in chapter 3, RGGI successfully navigated multiple stages of the policy life-cycle.

RGGI also avoided the types of sudden and lasting price spikes and fundamental market performance failures that plagued the EU ETS or the midlife crisis that impaired the heralded US sulfur dioxide system. By mid-decade, no other carbon cap-and-trade system in the world could approach this record, and RGGI had demonstrated that cap-and-trade could indeed be a durable policy despite the absence of any central governing authority. "You have a group of states, they are close to each other and have a natural sort of interaction, that's important," said Vermont's administration secretary, Justin Johnson. "But it's also important to know that they are very different, they have different political flavors, different governors that have changed over time.... At the end of the day, RGGI works. It works very well."[54]

But what exactly has RGGI accomplished during that period? Does it have a record of performance to match its demonstrated political resilience and adaptability over its first decade of existence? Or is this another stalking horse, like the Alberta Specified Gas Emitters Regulations (SGER), rather than the real deal? RGGI has attempted to answer these questions on multiple occasions, usually pointing to some combination of regional emission reductions from the power sector and a summary of its alternative energy investments. In a typical example, RGGI's 2014 press release announcing its report to EPA on the Clean Power Plan heralded the program's "regional success in reducing carbon emissions by 40 percent, while injecting more than $1.6 billion into state economies."[55]

As in other contexts, RGGI, Inc. and its state partners have been very effective in chronicling its positive impacts. But any review of its performance through the end of 2015 is somewhat uneven, reflecting in part the fact that its cap adjustment only became operational toward the end of this period. There have indeed been several very positive analyses of RGGI performance, both in terms of environmental and economic impacts. These provide some tangible evidence that desired performance outcomes have begun to be obtained, but they must be qualified by acknowledgment of some enduring uncertainties and likely limits, at least to this point in time.

RGGI electricity-sector emissions have declined markedly since 2005, as indicated in figure 5.3. This decline was far greater than in any other region

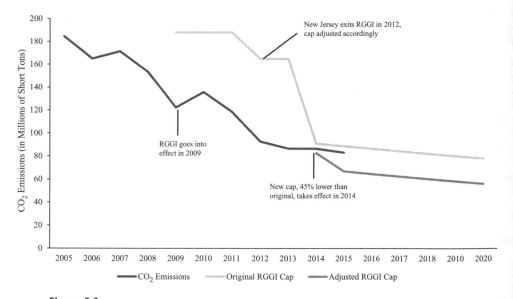

Figure 5.3
RGGI CO_2 emissions cap vs. actual emissions.
Sources: Regional Greenhouse Gas Initiative, *Summary Level Emissions Reports*, accessed July 12, 2016, https://rggi-coats.org/eats/rggi/index.cfm?fuseaction=search .rggi_summary_report_input&clearfuseattribs=true; Regional Greenhouse Gas Initiative, *The RGGI CO_2 Cap*, accessed July 12, 2016, https://www.rggi.org/design/overview /cap; Regional Greenhouse Gas Initiative, *Historical Emissions 2000–2008*, accessed July 12, 2016, https://www.rggi.org/historical_emissions.

of the United States or Canada and has been confirmed in a number of studies.[56] Some analyses have attributed a good deal of this reduction to RGGI. One particularly enthusiastic study contended that the "announcement effect" that RGGI would begin operations in the Northeast had a substantial impact on subsequent electricity generation. This assessment estimated that approximately one-half of the region's reductions were linked to the creation of this cap-and-trade program. In other words, with all else held equal, "the region's emissions would have been 24% higher without the program."[57]

This would represent a very powerful effect on emissions, unlike anything seen in the impact of cap-and-trade announcements in other states or internationally. But there may well have been substantial mitigating factors in the RGGI case that do not negate any program impact but serve to qualify more far-reaching claims. Many observers argued in 2009 and 2010 that the plunge in regional emissions was primarily attributable to the recession and suppressed demand for electricity, high coal and oil prices that deterred their extended use, and the expanded availability of a cleaner alternative from natural gas being produced via hydraulic fracturing in neighboring states such as Pennsylvania. Environmental organizations such as the Sierra Club, Environment Northeast, Environment America, and Environmental Advocates of New York, among others, called attention to these factors in the years following RGGI adoption, often lamenting the fact that the RGGI emissions cap had fallen more than 30 percent below actual emission levels. They gave no indication that the emission reduction was linked to the announcement of RGGI and instead contended that a major cap adjustment would be needed before cap-and-trade could have any consequential impact in the region.[58]

Coal and oil had long been used commonly for electricity in the Northeast United States, although both had declined as sources during the decade before 2005. This pattern continued in subsequent years, evident in their decline from 33 percent of total regional electricity in 2005 to 11 percent in 2014. This reflected decisions to formally shut down numerous operational coal plants, as was commonly occurring in other regions lacking a cap-and-trade program. This included a 2013 announcement that the region's largest coal plant, Brayton Point in Massachusetts, would close, despite having received more than $1 billion in pollution control upgrades in previous years.[59] A Conservation Law Foundation report concluded that the facility faced flattening demand linked to the economy and improved energy efficiency, growing competition from natural gas, and increasing coal prices, converging to create a perfect storm that made the plant decreasingly viable. Oil had lingered as an electricity source longer in the Northeast than any other region but ceased to be competitive and was increasingly phased out.

The dominant transition was to natural gas, with regional use increasing from 25 percent of total electricity in 2005 to 39 percent in 2014.[60] Nuclear and renewables use also grew during this period, reflecting a significant electricity transition that reduced carbon emissions, alongside overall declining electricity demand. The significant expansion of renewables may likely be linked to a range of state policies, including some form of a renewable portfolio standard in every RGGI state. Many of these were among the earliest to be adopted in the nation, prior to the creation of RGGI, and were among the most ambitious. New York, for example, required 30 percent of its electricity to be generated by renewables by 2015 and all but two other RGGI states set renewables targets between 20 and 40 percent.[61] Many of these policies mandated steady increases in renewables during the very period that emissions plunged and so any of these related reductions would have occurred without cap-and-trade.

In some respects, it is useful to collapse aggregate RGGI statistics into state-by-state profiles, which reflect some variation in the electricity transition story in various member states. All states in the region experienced carbon emission reductions between 2000 and 2014 but with highly varied rates, as reflected in table 5.4. In turn, the one state that formally left RGGI, New Jersey, actually had fairly stable emissions through 2008, despite any RGGI announcement effect, but these dropped in 2009 and then declined further in 2012. These latter changes occurred even though the state formally announced plans to leave RGGI in May 2011 and ended any role in carbon trading by the end of that year. At the same time, RGGI neighbors (but nonmembers) Pennsylvania and Virginia also experienced significant carbon emission reductions despite their lack of involvement in trading (see table 5.4).

The question of neighboring states further raises the issue of whether RGGI reductions can be linked to any appreciable degree to increased importation of electricity from outside the region. RGGI can only address emissions produced from generating facilities located within the boundaries

Table 5.4

Energy-related carbon dioxide emissions for RGGI and neighboring states (in metric tons of CO_2 per person).

State	2000	2001	2002	2003	2004	2005	2006	2007	2008	2009	2010	2011	2012	2013	2014	Percent Change	Absolute Change
Connecticut	12.6	12.2	11.6	12.3	12.8	12.6	11.7	11.4	10.6	10.1	10.1	9.7	9.5	9.7	9.8	-22.6%	-2.8
Delaware	21.2	20.2	19.7	20.2	19.9	20.6	18.9	19.6	18.3	13.4	13.1	14.2	15.2	14.7	14.2	-33.0%	-7.0
Maine	17.5	17.5	18.5	18.1	18.3	17.5	16.1	15.8	14.3	13.8	13.6	13.2	11.9	12.5	12.5	-28.6%	-5.0
Maryland	14.6	14.5	14.3	14.7	14.7	14.9	13.7	13.7	13.0	12.3	11.9	11.0	10.2	10.0	10.3	-29.4%	-4.3
Massachusetts	13.0	12.9	13.0	13.2	12.9	13.2	11.9	12.4	11.9	10.8	10.9	10.3	9.3	9.8	9.5	-27.1%	-3.5
New Hampshire	14.1	13.5	13.9	16.4	17.0	16.4	14.8	14.6	14.2	13.0	12.6	12.3	11.0	10.8	11.3	-20.1%	-2.8
New Jersey	14.7	14.3	14.2	14.3	14.6	15.1	14.2	15.1	14.8	12.7	13.0	13.0	11.8	12.1	12.7	-13.7%	-2.0
New York	11.2	10.9	10.6	11.1	11.2	11.1	10.1	10.4	9.9	9.0	9.0	8.4	8.2	8.3	8.6	-23.2%	-2.6
Pennsylvania	22.6	21.5	22.0	22.2	22.4	22.6	22.0	22.1	21.4	19.3	20.2	19.5	18.7	19.4	19.2	-15.1%	-3.4
Rhode Island	11.2	11.6	11.0	10.7	10.2	10.5	9.9	10.5	10.1	10.7	10.5	10.5	10.0	9.6	10.1	-10.0%	-1.1
Vermont	11.1	10.8	10.3	10.7	11.3	11.0	10.7	10.5	9.5	9.9	9.4	9.3	8.7	9.2	9.4	-15.5%	-2.7
Virginia	17.3	16.8	16.4	16.8	17.0	17.0	16.0	16.5	14.9	13.3	13.5	12.3	11.9	12.7	12.5	-27.9%	-4.8

Source: https://www.eia.gov/environment/emissions/state/analysis/pdf/stateanalysis.pdf.

of its member states, thereby raising the question of leakage from facilities in states outside the regional zone but with access to energy transmission capacity. Any regulatory attempt to impose carbon constraints on generators outside RGGI boundaries would likely confront well-established Commerce Clause constraints on efforts to impede cross-border movement of goods and services.[62] This is a potentially significant issue as the current set of RGGI states span three distinct interconnected power markets, each operated by a separate transmission entity and linked in varying degrees to many other states and Canadian provinces. RGGI has examined this leakage question and considered policy options, starting with a 2007 report and continuing through recent years.[63] It is likely that there are some limits on RGGI leakage given its growing use of imported electricity from renewable sources, most significantly Quebec hydro. However, this issue has continued to defy policy resolution and there are no accepted metrics to measure actual leakage. A long-standing hope within RGGI is to reduce leakage risks by expanding its regional boundaries, though this has yet to come to pass.

All of this has contributed to analyses that contend that the impact of RGGI on greenhouse gas (GHG) emissions may be quite limited, at least through the end of 2015. A 2015 report published by the Congressional Research Service concludes that RGGI's "contribution to directly reducing the global accumulation of GHG emissions in the atmosphere is arguably negligible."[64] However, this study also notes that the program may have had considerable indirect impact by providing reliable funding sources to all RGGI states to support energy efficiency and renewable energy transitions.[65] Alongside its set of renewable portfolio standards, all RGGI states have also maintained some form of energy efficiency resource standard (as discussed in chapter 2). RGGI states routinely receive the very highest rankings from organizations that compare state energy efficiency performance.[66] These rankings require a regular transition toward more efficient use of energy, combining regulations in most cases with a range of financial incentives for compliance. RGGI allocations have become an increasingly large source of ongoing funding for these kinds of programs, thereby likely facilitating energy efficiency gains that may reduce emissions.

During the period of RGGI operation, energy efficiency has made steady progress in the Northeast, reflected in gains that are far beyond national averages. State energy efficiency program budgets nearly doubled, adjusting for inflation, between 2009 and 2015.[67] This increase far exceeded national averages and left the Northeast with an exceptionally high rate of public expenditure per person for energy efficiency. A 2015 study concluded that energy efficiency programs saved a cumulative total of 18,934 gigawatt-hours (GWh) of electricity since the launch of RGGI auctions in 2009.[68] At the same time, collective increases among renewables, including hydro and wind, added 2,997 GWh of noncarbon electricity to the regional supply.[69]

These investments contributed to a growing consensus in various studies that the economic impact of RGGI has been a net positive for the region rather than an economic drain. A series of studies have noted net economic benefits that stem directly from reduced payments to out-of-region providers of fossil fuels. These reductions have been linked to expanded energy efficiency and increased use of locally based renewable sources. An extensive 2015 study by the Analysis Group concluded that "RGGI has produced positive economic outcomes for each RGGI state and for the region as a whole."[70] This analysis includes estimated employment impacts, measured in added job-years in each state and across the region. Program administrative costs have remained quite low.

In turn, there is no evidence to suggest that RGGI has triggered an increase in regional electricity prices. This is not entirely surprising, given auction prices over the first six years of program operation that remain far below carbon prices in jurisdictions such as British Columbia and Ireland. But it does serve to mitigate opposition concerns both at the outset of the program and during the debate over cap adjustment that cap-and-trade would dramatically elevate electricity prices and damage the regional economy. Overall electricity prices, measured in cost per kilowatt-hour (kWh), declined 3.4 percent among RGGI states between 2008 and 2015, while all other states averaged a 7.2 percent increase during this period.[71] Two states (Vermont and New Hampshire) did experience price increases during this period, but both of these increases were largely attributable to long-term purchase contracts that insulate them from wholesale price patterns, rather than RGGI operations. All other states within the region experienced electricity price reductions.[72] Most of these changes reflect a wide mixture of factors in the evolving state and regional electricity market but further underscore the mild and likely positive impact of RGGI, a unique cap-and-trade system that navigated each stage of the policy life-cycle over its first decade of operation and remained viable as it entered its second decade.

6 A Carbon Pricing Work in Progress

The Regional Greenhouse Gas Initiative (RGGI) was not the only surviving carbon cap-and-trade experiment in North America. Despite the defection of nearly all of its initial American state and Canadian provincial partners, California remained a cross-continental counterpart to RGGI, albeit on a slower timetable of implementation and with more expansive long-term ambitions. California never abandoned aspirations to rebuild a larger regional network of allies after it suffered so many state and provincial defections, as discussed in chapter 3. But it never formally delayed or waivered in its commitment to launch and sustain a statewide cap-and-trade effort even if it had to do so alone. This effort navigated the first set of political and managerial steps in the policy life-cycle and did involve one formal partner despite a national border, more than 2,500 miles of physical distance, and no prior history of collaboration on any issue. It was far too soon by the end of 2015 to assess cap-and-trade's managerial effectiveness, longer-term resilience, or performance, although it gave every indication of continuing to remain operational through 2020 and beyond.

California had always been the dominant Western Climate Initiative (WCI) partner in terms of political commitment as well as all aspects of financial and staffing leadership. It was propelled by the state's 2006 Global Warming Solutions Act, or Assembly Bill (AB) 32, that built on a suite of early state climate policies from the prior two decades. This legislation broadly authorized creation of a carbon pricing system as one of its ways to achieve its commitment to reduce carbon emissions 15 percent from 2005 levels by 2020. It was generally expected that some version of cap-and-trade would emerge through administrative actions. Unlike RGGI, California's system was only intended to begin with the electricity sector, extending to other economic sectors over time. But the state viewed carbon pricing as only one component of a large ensemble of regulatory and subsidy policies that were expected to work together to reduce carbon emissions rather than the exclusive or even dominant policy.

As California moved beyond legislative enactment to decide what carbon pricing would entail, a carbon tax was a political nonstarter. California's constitutional requirements stipulated that any new tax receive two-thirds approval in both legislative chambers, and there was political sensitivity in the legislature about adopting any new tax. Cap-and-trade thus emerged as the preferred carbon pricing option in Sacramento since it might not qualify legally as a tax even in the event of auctioning. "Regulated parties with compliance obligations, many of whom are allocated allowances for free, need not buy the allowances," explained legal scholar Ann Carlson. "An emitter subject to a compliance obligation under the cap-and-trade program could cut its emissions rather than purchase allowances at auction to cover emissions. Thus the auction could be viewed as akin to selling off of state property, not the levying of a tax."[1] Cap-and-trade could be created under the terms of the 2006 legislation without adoption of additional statutes and so appeared to offer a politically and legally safe path. It served to add carbon pricing to an exceptionally large and complex maze of competing programs that had been designed previously to reduce state emissions.

The 2006 California legislation arrived at a high-water mark of political concern over climate change in the state, reflecting growing patterns of drought and concerns about long-term water availability for its growing population and expansive agricultural sector. The state had begun policy development on climate change in the late 1980s, following an incremental and ongoing pattern of policy adoption in the following decades. In 2002, the state adopted pioneering legislation, AB 1493, to require a steady reduction in carbon emissions produced by newly manufactured car and truck engines that built on decades of efforts to tighten regulatory standards on tailpipe emissions that began in the 1940s.[2]

California would have a unique advantage in translating a political mandate into policy implementation, given its strong and long-standing commitment to environmental protection. Scholars have long noted California's willingness to take bold environmental policy steps before other states or the federal government. This has reflected strong concerns over environmental risks to public health and sensitive ecosystems.[3] It has produced pioneering efforts in such areas as air quality, land-use planning, environmental impact assessment, and toxic substances control. It also reflected a pattern of considerable support over time from both political parties, including many Democratic and Republican governors.

Part of that consensus was linked to shared preference for policies that did not impose direct and traceable costs through taxation or other forms of pricing emissions, even though these policy ideas were long familiar in state political and academic circles. AB 1493 and all other California climate policies prior to 2006 had sidestepped carbon pricing. If anything, they attempted to avoid alternatives that might have led to more cost-effective outcomes, such as transportation fuel pricing through taxation to reduce emissions from that sector. California had for decades championed aggressive efforts to reduce emissions from the vehicle sector that contributed to severe and enduring air quality problems but eschewed taxation or any policy that might actually discourage driving and potentially endanger economic development.[4] Instead, the state preferred the blunter instrument of performance standards in engine manufacturing, with any costs (and political blame) harder to trace and easier to shift elsewhere.

California had relatively few vehicle manufacturing and assembly jobs, so its requirements for investments in new emissions control technologies could be imposed on firms based largely in other states and nations. Any actual increases to cover the costs of those technologies would likely be added to new vehicle purchase prices but could not be traced directly to the state's regulatory policy, thereby enhancing its attractiveness to California political supporters. Even the 2006 legislation that opened the door to carbon pricing was quite vague in policy details, reflecting a rush to achieve a political outcome through adoption that could provide statewide and international notoriety through dramatic signing ceremonies in multiple locations. This provided a strong political boost to supporters, including primarily Democratic legislators and Governor Arnold Schwarzenegger in his bid for a full term after initial election in 2004 to fill a recall vacancy.

But Schwarzenegger used his powers of legislative interpretation to embrace cap-and-trade after his election victory as a major component of California's climate strategy. He authorized the state's formidable California Air Resources Board to begin work on the design of a cap-and-trade system and personally led an effort to build a multijurisdictional coalition that included considerable cultivation of alliances with neighboring governors and provincial premiers, including British Columbia's Gordon Campbell. But it also entailed hosting global climate summits in Hollywood and other enticing locations, with an effort to draw participation from leaders in international politics, business, and entertainment. This type of symbolic exercise led by a California governor did not begin or end with Schwarzenegger, but he used his celebrity status to take it to a new level. All of this suggested that California was rapidly ascending into a role of regional, national, and global leadership on climate change and carbon pricing. Schwarzenegger and allies repeatedly contended that they were designing a novel carbon pricing experiment that might transform national and global energy markets.

For a time, California did build a coalition to operate cap-and-trade beyond the boundaries of a single jurisdiction, following to some extent the earlier playbook produced by RGGI. But all facets of the WCI process were dominated by California, allowing other willing states to ride along at minimal expense and potentially get in on the ground floor of this venture. This worked for a short time but, unlike RGGI, began to unravel as the potential program launch in 2012 neared, the possibility of securing state advantage in federal legislation evaporated, and both state governors and provincial premiers began to harbor reservations. It is not clear that California could have done anything differently to sustain the WCI coalition, given the internal state political dynamics discussed in chapter 3. But its coalitional dominance discouraged any RGGI-like exploration of more flexible provisions or broader constituency-building efforts that might have helped sustain it.[5]

Political Resilience amid Frontal Assault

Even California's commitment to continue pursuit of cap-and-trade was not guaranteed at this juncture. Along with its flagging state and provincial partners, California cap-and-trade also faced fundamental tests of political resilience four years after legislative adoption. AB 32 had been forged through a coalition between a Republican governor and predominantly Democratic legislature eager to establish themselves and their state as climate policy leaders while also positioning themselves for political advantage heading into 2006 state elections.

But a pair of 2010 developments posed significant political threats to the resilience of cap-and-trade policy. They included another gubernatorial election that threatened cap-and-trade and a statewide ballot proposition designed to reverse state climate policy. The campaign to succeed Schwarzenegger featured two candidates with very distinctive stands on cap-and-trade. Republican Meg Whitman sought to distance herself from the increasingly unpopular Schwarzenegger on a few salient issues, most notably cap-and-trade. Whitman vowed if elected to freeze program implementation for at least one year to allow for careful review of long-term commitments. In contrast, Democrat Jerry Brown embraced full pursuit of cap-and-trade and all elements of AB 32. These factors combined to pose a significant political challenge to cap-and-trade in California, particularly given the central role of the governor in implementing the 2006 legislation. This arrived at the very point of political transition following policy adoption that had led to reversal of cap-and-trade support elsewhere, including some states that shared a physical border with California and were heavily engaged in cross-border trade in electricity and commerce.

Unlike its WCI partners, however, California decisively demonstrated political resilience in surmounting both the gubernatorial-level challenge and a separate ballot proposition during that year. Climate policy was hardly the lone issue in the former election, but Brown never relinquished his lead and coasted to a third term with a 54 to 41 percent victory.[6] Democrats also retained sizable majorities in both legislative chambers, in what was a very strong Republican year in many other states, including some WCI partners. Brown would also roll to reelection victory four years later, and he subsequently elevated climate change and California's ongoing cap-and-trade commitment into a major theme in his 2015 inaugural address and final term in office.[7]

Direct democracy, however, posed an even more direct and fundamental challenge to the future of California cap-and-trade. The state's extensive use of ballot propositions for environmental policy and many other policy issues is well-established.[8] The 2010 ballot was no exception and featured an up-or-down vote on Proposition 23, a "yes" vote on which would have placed AB 32 into a prolonged freeze unless there were substantial and sustained reductions in statewide unemployment. Opposition forces contended that cap-and-trade further threatened a declining California economy and so could only be considered after a demonstrated period of robust economic performance, thereby likely scuttling the program if adopted.

Public opinion broke decisively against the ballot proposition during the middle of the fall and never wavered significantly. This resulted in a clear rejection of Prop 23 by a 61-to-39 percent margin, suggesting that, at least in California, cap-and-trade had endured initial transition of political leadership and a frontal opposition campaign. These were steeper hurdles than any RGGI state faced, as no direct democracy campaigns ever reached the ballot in that region. California could thus continue moving toward cap-and-trade implementation having cleared these political hurdles four years after initial policy adoption.

Launching Cap-and-Trade

California's enduring commitment to pioneering environmental protection efforts went beyond bold legislation. It also included strong political backing for the development of a series of exceptionally large and highly professional agencies to put policies into operation. Sixteen separate state departments, agencies, or commissions were integrated into the California Climate Action Team through a 2005 executive order, including the California Environmental Protection Agency (CalEPA), the California Energy Commission, and the California Public Utilities Commission. One unit of CalEPA that has considerable autonomy, the California Air Resources Board (CARB), has loomed particularly large in any policy linked to air pollution for many decades. It was given and has retained a formative role in defining and implementing cap-and-trade and many other provisions of AB 32.[9]

In many respects, CARB may be the governmental agency most prepared anywhere in the world to address carbon cap-and-trade, due to its large staff, range of expertise, and extended involvement with other experiments using some form of emissions trading beyond participation in the federal sulfur dioxide program. In 2016, it maintained a staff of 1,365 employees with a $581 million budget, all focused on air and related climate issues. In contrast, during the same year the US EPA had a total staff of 15,408 employees and a budget of $8.2 billion, stretched across regional and specialized program offices, sharing much of its funding with states and localities through grant programs and being responsible for a full range of national programs alongside air quality and climate issues.

In turn, CARB has had active and sustained leadership from a formidable agency leader, Mary Nichols. Nichols has been the most visible and influential American air quality administrator of the past half-century and served as CARB director from 1979 through 1983 and then 2007 through 2017. She also held related positions in California and the EPA during years when she was not at the helm of CARB. In 2014, former Schwarzenegger climate adviser Susan Kennedy asked: "Would cap-and-trade have happened without Nichols? Nope. I think it was tenuous enough that I think the legislature would have killed it."[10]

Consequently, AB 32 was handed over to a unique agency and a leader with formidable resources and technical and political skills to interpret and implement cap-and-trade. They had considerable latitude to make administrative adjustments and, in essence, create a trading program that was not sketched in the September 2006 legislation. More than six years would be needed to complete these tasks, leading to the launch of California's version of cap-and-trade in November 2012. This followed an extended trial run period that was intended to detect and address any problems that might emerge once the program formally began operations.[11]

This resulting program included a number of flexibility provisions in its design, largely reflecting CARB handiwork.[12] These provisions were generally designed to ease implementation both administratively and politically. They acknowledged the uncertainties involved in launching carbon trading and also built in part upon some lessons that emerged from earlier experience in the European Union as well as in RGGI. California's version of cap-and-trade was designed to be phased in gradually through an expansion over time in the number of entities that were required to participate. The program began with a primary focus on electric utilities, much like RGGI, but expanded in 2015 to address some transportation-sector emissions linked to use of gasoline and oil in vehicles.

CARB accepted the RGGI precedent of auctioning but pursued a more cautious and gradual path for it. This began in 2012 with auctioning of only 10 percent of total allowances, allocating the remainder at no charge. This would increase over time through 2020, when the legislative mandate for the program ended and its future would have to be reconsidered.

The initial statewide auctions went smoothly and largely uneventfully, with no signs of the glitches that occurred with the Emissions Trading Scheme (ETS) in Europe or pricing volatility. The carbon price gradually increased from an initial base of $10.09 per ton to $14 per ton before settling in between those levels by 2015. CARB prepared to deter potential auction price fluctuations that might either impose an unusually steep initial cost or lead to a plunge in purchase prices. At one end, it established an Allowance Price Containment Reserve, a pool of additional allowances that could be made available to the market if permit prices exceeded specified levels, thereby creating a price ceiling of sorts to guard against potential price spikes. At the other end, CARB created a "price floor," beginning at a rate of $10 per ton during its first year, before rising at a rate of 5 percent annually, plus inflation. Collectively, these provisions were designed to increase California's prospects of making a smooth transition into an era of carbon cap-and-trade.

CARB also developed a set of five protocols to facilitate the use of offsets in either California or other states and nations as an alternative path to compliance. RGGI had also created offsets but capped their potential use at 3.3 percent of total emissions and defined them much more narrowly. In contrast, California allowed offsets to be used to cover up to 8 percent of total reductions, and its offset market would prove quite active. CARB designed separate offset approvals for such projects as methane reduction from coal mining and dairy digester equipment, reduction of ozone-depleting substances from various appliances and equipment, and carbon capture and sequestration (CCS) from forests. The state also explored extending offset status to controversial geological sequestration of carbon.[13]

Incremental Expansion

California also made some progress in reversing its pattern of losing trading partners. Although none of the states that left the Western Climate Initiative returned to the cap-and-trade fold, the Canadian province of Quebec agreed to create a program and attempt to link it with California. This was ironic in many respects, given the distance of more than 2,500 miles between the two jurisdictions and the fact that Quebec borders four RGGI states (New York, New Hampshire, Vermont, and Maine). Indeed, electricity has long moved frequently back and forth between Quebec and portions of RGGI. Nonetheless, Quebec ignored repeated RGGI overtures to instead pursue partnership with California.

Quebec officials contend that they already have made a less carbonized path possible for the Northeast with hydro-based electricity exports, and further observe that they would be happy to export even more in the future. The province produces 96 percent of its electricity from hydro and offers some of the lowest electricity prices in North America, less than half the price per unit of power in the Boston and New York areas. Consequently, it has an exceptionally high rate of electricity consumption and uses electricity for numerous purposes such as heating in more than 80 percent of residences. As a result, Quebec is a prodigious consumer of electricity, but most of it has little or no carbon content.[14]

A long-standing cornerstone of Quebec politics has been expansion of hydro given its extensive reserves. Consequently, carbon pricing for electricity in neighboring jurisdictions, such as RGGI states, might make its hydro power even more attractive in the future. But it would not need to join RGGI to expand these exports, so it had little interest in joining this regional program. Quebec instead found considerable attraction in a California partnership that would include other sectors under cap-and-trade and provide possible access to its expansive offsets market.

Linkage with California also provided a more dramatic political stage than RGGI for Quebec, allowing it to use its step toward cap-and-trade to assert its climate policy leadership and quasi-independence from the rest of Canada on a larger stage. Such a high-visibility partnership might also give Quebec more recognition within Canada and beyond as a climate change and carbon pricing leader, as it resented being overshadowed by the notoriety afforded the British Columbia carbon tax. The province had previously adopted a wide range of climate mitigation policies and used a modest carbon levy to cover many related costs.[15] Unlike British Columbia and California, Quebec also decided to place a moratorium on drilling for fossil fuels through hydraulic fracturing.[16] It thus promised minimal emissions from its hydro-centered energy development sector, although it began to backpedal on this after the 2014 election of a Liberal Party government led to approval for some fracking and governmental financial support for expanded delivery of liquefied natural gas to remote areas.

Overall, Quebec's carbon emissions per capita remained among the lowest in North America, reflecting both its noncarbon electricity base and relatively low emissions in other sectors such as transportation. But it was able to sustain negotiations with California and pursue regulatory development during 2011 and 2012, leading to formal and mutual establishment of linkage in 2014. "By adopting this regulation, Quebec acquires the means to achieve the transition toward a green, sustainable and prosperous economy," said Pierre Arcand, Quebec's minister of Sustainable Development, Environment, and Parks in announcing the agreement.[17]

American states and Canadian provinces lack constitutional authority to enter into treaties, so this bilateral partnership was formalized through a memorandum of understanding. Both California and Quebec have considerable experience in pushing the boundaries of state and provincial regulatory authority in their respective federal systems. However, they have minimal prior engagement working with each other on any policy issues and operate in entirely different electricity generation markets. Unlike neighboring RGGI states, this makes for an alliance among relative strangers, further reflected in linguistic differences, given Quebec's requirement for submission of cap-and-trade documents in French, and asymmetries, given California's dominant role in most aspects of this relationship.

This relationship gave the Western Climate Initiative a new lease on life, emerging from its hiatus to serve as the primary oversight body in designing and implementing the cross-jurisdictional trading program. WCI, with staff and funding provided by California and CARB, received authority to manage contracts, coordinate transactions, operate the system's joint auction process, and maintain an emissions registry and technical support office. As a result, there was far less of the shared governance system established through RGGI, thereby creating significant dependence on California expertise and resources to make the system work.

Early auction practices went smoothly, although one early round faced technical glitches with system log-ins that led to a five-day auction delay. Undersubscription of Quebec allowances became a major concern, reflected in relatively low bid prices that were either lodged on the auction price floor or hovered just above it. Nonetheless, there were none of the kinds of management problems that have continually plagued the EU ETS. Quebec officials heralded their collaboration as a significant carbon pricing breakthrough and as a model for other Canadian provinces. California officials argued that the partnership vindicated the viability of their cap-and-trade system after the earlier loss of all partners. As Nichols asserted in 2014, "We are pleased and proud that California is showing the world how to make cap-and-trade work to reduce pollution and create jobs."[18] Governor Brown and CARB Director Nichols sought to build on this bilateral agreement through recruitment of additional partners, including the courting of American and Mexican states and Canadian provinces.

Uneven Performance

California's launch of cap-and-trade was simply too new to reach any significant conclusions about its impact on emissions and the economy by the end of 2015, much less the performance of the expanded system that involved Quebec. Some early indicators were quite encouraging, reflecting a continuing trend of stable or declining greenhouse gas emissions in California throughout much of the first decade and a half of the twenty-first century. During the 2010s, California remained the most populous state but second to Texas in terms of total greenhouse gas emissions. During this period, it ranked only behind New York and the District of Columbia in maintaining the lowest emissions rate on a per capita basis.

California emissions from sectors covered under cap-and-trade fell 3.8 percent during its first year of operation in 2013; there was no change during that year in emissions not covered by the cap.[19] Considerable growth in the state economy complemented this development, building on a major upsurge in the California economy that began in 2010–2011. A major study of this early performance argued that the advent of cap-and-trade had not deterred this economic expansion and may indeed have helped fuel it in part with continuing growth in clean-technology sectors.[20]

It remained inconclusive, however, as to just how much of the recent reductions could be linked to the implementation of cap-and-trade or any earlier policy "announcement effect," as has been argued in the RGGI case. There are literally dozens of other California climate programs with likely overlapping effects, and the state anticipates achieving greater emissions reduction through 2020 via its renewable portfolio and energy efficiency standards combined than it does from cap-and-trade (see table 6.1). This raised the possibility that other programs, many with a broader base of political support, might increasingly "crowd out" the presumably more cost-effective reductions produced by cap-and-trade implementation. This possibility continued during the period in which extensions of cap-and-trade and other climate policies were being considered for extensions and expansions. For example, during 2015 through 2017, legislators introduced bills that would require California to procure between 50 and 100 percent

Table 6.1
California AB 32 greenhouse gas reduction strategies.

Regulation	Expected CO_2 Reduction (in Million Metric Tons of CO_2)
Cap-and-Trade	23
Low Carbon Fuel Standard	15
Energy Efficiency and Conservation	12
33 percent Renewable Portfolio Standard	12
Refrigerant Tracking, Reporting, and Repair Deposit Program	5
Advanced Clean Cars	3
Reductions in Vehicle Miles Traveled (SB 375)	3
Landfill Methane Control	2
Other Regulations	5
TOTAL	80

Source: Mac Taylor, *The 2016–2017 Budget: Resources and Environmental Protection* (Sacramento, CA: Legislative Analyst's Office, 2016), http://www.lao.ca.gov /reports/2016/3354/resources-analysis-021616.pdf.

of its electricity from renewable sources, possibly eclipsing cap-and-trade in future emission reductions from that sector.

Moreover, two sets of concerns began to emerge in examination of the California case that raised some reservations about how much impact cap-and-trade was actually having. First, ongoing debates about the reliability of offsets in delivering impacts commensurate with actual emission reductions took new shape in 2014 when CARB decided to invalidate a large number of offsets from an Arkansas-based chemical incinerator project. This facility was operating in violation of federal permits, raising questions about the environmental integrity of its operations. CARB also began to investigate other offset cases, including a project for destroying methane from Indiana livestock operations, while beginning a review of its offset protocols in other areas such as forestry.[21] Second, CARB levied fines in 2014 against seven firms for either late or inaccurate emissions reporting or confidentiality violations that involved disclosure of information about auction participation and bidding to third parties. Such disclosure is formally prohibited to deter collusion among auction participants. An additional fine was levied against the City of Riverside for submitting an auction bid that exceeded CARB's assessment of its ability to pay for any allowances it acquired.[22]

Neither of these steps represented the kind of deep flaws or corruption of the ETS case. Indeed, they may well reflect healthy CARB oversight of early-stage compliance issues. However, they served to demonstrate the complexities of maintaining a credible cap-and-trade market, even prior to expanding it to include Quebec and potentially other jurisdictions over time. In contrast, RGGI has not had any experience with these kinds of fines and did not use offsets during its more extended period of operation through the end of 2015.

A more searching concern, however, addressed the question of whether California was achieving a good deal of its emissions reduction through substitution of electricity imports from other states or provinces. The Commerce Clause places significant limits on a state's ability to control imported goods and services, including commodities like electricity. California has imported about one-fourth of its total electricity from other jurisdictions in recent years. Approximately one-third of this imported electricity came from the north, particularly hydro power from Oregon, Washington, and British Columbia. But the remaining two-thirds came from the Southwest, including three large coal-powered plants in Arizona, New Mexico, and Utah. In comparison, California only relies on coal for less than one-half of 1 percent of the electricity that it generates within its boundaries. Its reliance on coal when weighing both internally generated power and imports increases to 6 percent.[23]

California has attempted to use various regulatory strategies to deter electricity imports derived from fossil fuels, but this raises not only legal concerns but also questions as to whether they can actually be implemented technically to deter leakage. It is theoretically possible that there can be paperwork agreements to import only those sources of power from utilities that are not linked to coal or natural gas. But these may ultimately mean nothing in terms of net regional generation and so may simply be a form of so-called resource shuffling. Economist Danny Cullenward has argued that California is particularly ripe for extensive resource shuffling given its substantial dependence on imported electricity and the design of its cap-and-trade system. He sees a strong likelihood that this form of emissions trading "merely rearranges which party on the western electricity grid is legally responsible for consuming the carbon-intensive resources, without reducing net emissions to the atmosphere." Instead, under his interpretation, "The liability for those emissions simply 'leaks' to the unregulated party."[24] CARB has maintained a formal prohibition against resource shuffling, but Cullenward and an influential set of environmental economists have questioned whether this step can or does have any impact in practice.[25] As economist Severin Borenstein has noted, "It turns out as much as California would like to make reshuffling illegal...you can't really make it illegal. There is going to be an immense amount of simply relabeling what comes into California as the cleaner stuff."[26]

Constituency Unrest

As in the RGGI case, the inclusion of auctioning created the possibility of producing revenue from cap-and-trade. This might be applied toward related aspects of the state's clean energy agenda or directed to other purposes, as was the case with the revenue-neutral approach under the British Columbia carbon tax. California projected annual auction yields of up to $1 billion during its initial operations and considerable expansion thereafter. This created a potentially large pool of revenues that could be put to constructive use. It might also serve to further bolster program constituency support, as was so significant in the RGGI and British Columbia cases in building on initial political support.

One stable and seemingly popular revenue use involves the return of funds from auctioned allowances held by investor-owned utilities to ratepayers. These take the form of dividends that are included as credits on their electricity bills. This arrangement has some parallel to Maryland's dividend system under RGGI and has been in place since a 2012 decision by the California Public Utilities Commission.[27] It is managed through separate auctions that are also administered by the state and began to produce dividends in 2014. There has been some interest among legislators in expanding this approach, possibly building on Alaska's dividend model for returning oil extraction royalty revenue.

However, California has continued to struggle to establish a clear and compelling plan for all remaining revenue allocation, even after the first dozen rounds of auctioning were completed.[28] There was no statutory language on auctioning, much less allocation in AB 32, leaving considerable room for ongoing political jockeying over revenue use. Numerous elected officials and interest groups have continually promoted a potpourri of proposals for alternative funding uses in recent years, with the absence of a clear plan serving to divide such potential program supporters as environmental justice groups, local governments, and energy efficiency and renewable energy firms. As Schwarzenegger's chief climate advisor, Terry Tamminen, noted, "It's a land grab and everyone's going to have their tin cup out."[29]

Brown's return to the governorship included his commitment to allocating at least one-fourth of total auction revenue to his pet project of high-speed rail across much of the state. After initial support in a 2008 ballot proposal and an infusion of federal funds in conjunction with economic recovery stimulus spending, high-speed rail proved increasingly controversial and fell far behind schedule and budget needs. Brown's intervention provided the project with some new revenue but tarnished politically the reputation of auction allocation. This step also triggered numerous complaints from other constituents that sought their own share of the proceeds.

Each allocation shift by Brown or the legislature would then trigger new complaints and produce new claimants, essentially the opposite of the constituency-building process that was so successful in RGGI and British Columbia. Ultimately, legislation adopted in 2012 specified portions of revenue use, including a pair of bills that set aside funds for "disadvantaged communities."[30] However, the lack of clear definition of that term in statute only compounded political consternation, expanding divides among various regions and communities in California, each of which thought that they should receive a larger share of these funds.

Initial years of allocation have reflected significant year-to-year shifts across possible spending options, as noted in table 6.2. This has been compounded by great variability on expenditures within these broad categories. San Diego County official Ron Roberts lamented that "there's no real guideline, and virtually everything qualifies" for cap-and-trade funds. "If I keep my tires filled with air, I'll get better gas mileage. So I guess we should supplement air pumps at every gas station. That works; whether it makes sense or not, I don't know." CARB board member Daniel Sperling noted that "we really need to make this performance-based as much as possible. It really lends itself to just getting politicized too much."[31]

Brown further inflamed these concerns when in 2013 he announced plans to borrow $500 million from the initial auction to curb California's

Table 6.2
California cap-and-trade revenue expenditures (in millions of USD).

Program	2013–14	2014–15	2015–16[a]
High-Speed Rail	—	250	600
Affordable Housing and Sustainable Communities	—	130	480
Transit and Intercity Rail Capital	—	25	240
Transit Operations	—	25	120
Low Carbon Transportation	30	200	90
Low-Income Weatherization and Solar	—	75	70
Agricultural Energy and Operational Efficiency	10	25	40
Urban Water Efficiency	30	20	20
Sustainable Forests and Urban Forestry	—	42	—
Waste Diversion	—	25	—
Wetlands and Watershed Restoration	—	25	—
Other Administration	2	10	31
TOTALS	72	852	1,691

a. Based on the California Legislative Analyst's Office revenue projection for 2015–2016.

Source: Mac Taylor, *The 2016–2017 Budget: Resources and Environmental Protection* (Sacramento, CA: Legislative Analyst's Office, 2016).

expanding budget deficits. State officials announced that the loan would be short-term and funds would be repaid with interest. However, this hardly inspired confidence in a state with a diminished credit rating, a recent history of severe fiscal problems, and no announced plan for fund repayment. Environmental activist Van Jones described this as a "heartbreaking disappointment," insisting that "you cannot steal from poor people and the planet and get away with it in California."[32]

Environmental justice groups continued to assert their view that carbon trading might well concentrate a disproportionate amount of remaining carbon and related emissions in regions with a large presence of low-income and racial minority residents. They saw subsequent reallocation of revenues to such constituents as essential to "climate justice" and remained strongly opposed to established revenue allocation patterns, reflected in their continuing legal challenges to cap-and-trade.[33] They routinely argued that both the legislature and executive agencies such as CARB tended to deflect rather than engage seriously their concerns. The California Environmental

Justice Alliance called for the state to abandon cap-and-trade in favor of a carbon tax after release of a 2016 study that showed elevated pollution levels in minority and low-income areas since the advent of emissions trading, possibly linked with high utilization of offsets from out-of-state projects. In 2017, CARB's Environmental Justice Advisory Committee voted to oppose extension of cap-and-trade beyond 2020, though the board remained steadfast in its support for extending the existing cap-and-trade system.

In turn, officials from California's legislative branch increasingly sounded concerns over a perceived lack of executive branch transparency and coherence in revenue allocation. "If we were in corporate America and the CEO presented and had approved an expenditure plan of $3 billion and we spent year over year $1, $2, or $3 billion without having a clear set of goals and objectives that produce a positive result for the business enterprise, the CEO would get fired, or at least get an F for a grade," lamented Democratic State Senator Richard Roth in a 2016 hearing.[34] A series of reports by the California Legislative Analyst's Office (LAO) confirmed these problems and further questioned whether many of these expenditures were simply subsidizing emissions reductions that were already being achieved through cap-and-trade or other state programs. The LAO sought greater transparency from Governor Brown and CARB on expenditures and endorsed the creation of an external advisory board to guide investment in a more coherent and strategic direction.[35] Additional LAO studies criticized the high costs of many emission reduction programs supported with auction revenues. These ranged from a low of $4 per ton (for loans to expand recycling and organic foods) to a high of $725 per ton (for pilot vehicle fleets for disadvantaged communities).[36]

This question of revenue allocation continued to dominate discussion of cap-and-trade's future by the end of 2015 and beyond. It would have to be confronted in any political extension of the program beyond 2020. CARB's deep technical prowess aided many areas of program operation but also produced an aura of arrogance and dismissiveness in the eyes of many constituents, complicating development of trust and credibility in this area. Contrary to British Columbia and RGGI, carbon pricing revenue use in this case clearly divided potential constituencies rather than united them behind the program, creating significant political challenges in considering longer-term program expansion or extension. However, a complex legislative compromise struck in 2017 offered promise in addressing some of these concerns while extending cap-and-trade through 2030.

Sustaining Extraction

California's approach to carbon pricing has also exempted some sectors that produce considerable emissions and could expand markedly in future decades. Despite its expansion of cap-and-trade beyond its initial focus on electricity to transportation fuels, the state has approached fossil fuel extraction with pause. Much like British Columbia, a major fossil fuel production industry receives fairly favorable regulatory and tax treatment under carbon pricing. This issue has received far less political, journalistic, and scholarly attention than the advent of California's cap-and-trade and related carbon protection regime.

Nonetheless, the possibility of sustained or expanding oil and gas production in California in coming years through hydraulic fracturing has created a climate policy paradox of sorts for political leaders. Many state officials espouse global moral leadership in their support of carbon pricing, but they have struggled to extend its application to fossil fuel production. Consequently, oil and gas will primarily be exported and charged against the carbon ledger of other jurisdictions at the point of final fuel use. This reflects California's ongoing love-hate relationship with fossil fuels and political protection for their production. Cap-and-trade as designed in California does not focus on energy extraction and the state retains an unusually modest severance tax and fee system on fossil fuel production.

Oil development began in California during the latter stages of the Civil War and has never relented. The state remained a leading state for total production and has ranked behind only Texas, North Dakota, and Alaska during the last decade in oil output. Overall California production increased after 2010, although the state share of national output fell amid a surge in production from other regions (see figure 6.1). Discoveries of vast shale oil deposits in the early 2010s created the possibility that California might ultimately become the nation's largest producer. The Monterey/Santos shale play falls beneath a vast swath of territory across multiple inland counties in the central part of the state. These areas have generally had higher rates of unemployment and more stagnant economic growth than major hubs such as Los Angeles, San Francisco, and San Diego. Oil production has remained a central part of the inland economy, and the spectre of vast additional

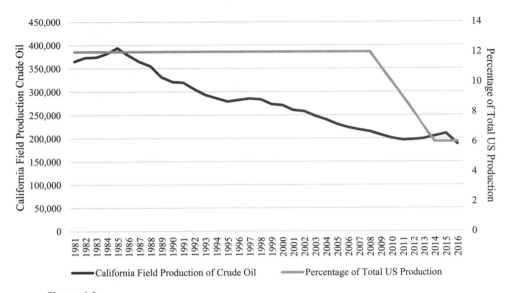

Figure 6.1
California oil production, 1981–2016.
Note: Production values in thousands of barrels of crude oil.
Sources: US Energy Information Administration (EIA), "U.S. Field Production of Crude Oil, Annual," accessed July 13, 2016, https://www.eia.gov/opendata/embed .cfm? type=chart&series_id=PET.MCRFPUS1.A; EIA, "California Field Production of Crude Oil," accessed July 13, 2016, https://www.eia.gov/dnav/pet/hist/LeafHandler .ashx?n=pet&s=mcrfpca1&f=a.

deposits that might be tapped via expanded use of hydraulic fracturing and horizontal drilling has considerable appeal in those parts of the state given its economic development potential.

The economic promise of these deposits reached unparalleled heights in 2011 when the US Energy Information Administration announced that "the largest shale formation is the Monterey/Santos play in southern California, which is estimated to hold 15.4 billion barrels or 64 percent of the total shale oil resources" in the United States.[37] This estimate suggested that California possessed an oil resource that was more than four times the size of either the vaunted Bakken shale play in North Dakota and Montana or the massive Eagle-Ford play in Texas, although it did not assess the technical, economic, and political feasibility of its active development.

One might have expected the state's political leadership to extend the deep concern about climate protection to the arena of fossil fuel drilling. This might have included following the path of other jurisdictions such as

New York and Quebec in eschewing economic development opportunity in favor of a moratorium or ban on drilling. Some environmental groups and Hollywood celebrities have pushed for such steps, but they have been generally rebuffed.[38] In response, Governor Brown has tempered his customary moral opprobrium directed at those who do not aggressively address climate protection by noting that "the fossil fuel deposits in California are incredible, the potential is extraordinary." As a result, he has argued that "we want to get the greenhouse gas emissions down, but we also want to keep our economy going. That's the balance that's required."[39]

California has attempted to strike such a balance through the incremental reform of existing oil and gas industry regulations to address expanded fracking activity, much like other major extraction states such as Texas, North Dakota, and Pennsylvania.[40] It has avoided major new legislation on fracking and instead relied primarily on regulatory modifications by its lead oversight agency for overseeing oil and gas extraction, the Department of Oil, Gas, and Geothermal Resources (DOGGR). This effort has received considerable criticism from environmental groups, reflecting DOGGR's dual mission of environmental protection alongside energy production. This agency has struggled mightily in developing a strategy to reduce major methane releases from drilling operations, including four formal delays in promulgating proposed rules.[41] The state's overall methane and related natural gas record received international attention in early 2016, when a 112-day leak from the blowout of a wellhead connected to a massive underground storage system for gas was characterized as "the worst accidental discharge of greenhouse gases in US history."[42]

Brown and many state political leaders have sustained support for this gradual regulatory transition while keeping open the possibility of major expansion of the Monterey/Santos play in the future, particularly if oil prices and demand rebound. Brown in 2015 rejected any effort to cap drilling in California, noting that reducing carbon dependence is not a "matter of snapping your fingers, and to just instantly kill an industry, with the trivial impact on climate change, does not seem to me the wise way to go." In turn, he contended that the state cannot "let third-world countries do the oil production so that Californians can drive around, even in their hybrids. We have to shoulder our part of the responsibility."[43]

California has also approached the issue of severance taxes on extraction gingerly, leaving it with only a modest "assessment" rather than a tax, one that imposes a charge of 1.4 cents per barrel or 10,000 cubic feet of natural gas and uses those revenues to cover DOGGR administrative costs.[44] It also has authorized county governments that host drilling to establish their own ad valorem taxes tailored to mineral withdrawal. There are some parallels between the California approach and Pennsylvania's use of an "impact fee" structure on natural gas extraction that covers state government oversight costs, although that method also produces some local government revenue.[45] All other oil- and gas-producing states maintain severance taxes, as discussed in chapter 2, most at rates significantly higher than the California assessment.

Dozens of political attempts have been made in California between the early 1990s and mid-2010s to develop a severance tax system and rate comparable to those of other major extraction states, but all have failed. This has reflected California's supermajority requirement for adoption of new taxes as well as sustained opposition from political leaders representing energy-producing jurisdictions away from the coasts and strong industry groups, including the Western States Petroleum Association and, in more recent years, Californians against Higher Oil Taxes.[46] Severance tax opponents have argued that the state already levies very high income and sales taxes and that any additional tax burden focused on extraction might deter further energy development, given the expanding opportunities for extraction linked to fracking. As a result, despite its continuing high rates of oil production, California has derived from its oil and gas assessment some of the lowest total revenue yields of any state that produces fossil fuels.[47] It routinely receives a fraction of the revenue from oil production than other states that actually generate less output.

The California approach to extraction underscores a further political paradox of carbon pricing. Jurisdictions most receptive to a carbon tax or cap-and-trade are not necessarily eager to impose similar pricing constraints on their energy extraction industries, given opportunities to boost their economies through the export of those commodities. This also means that official measure of much of the greenhouse gas emissions from fossil fuel use will shift from the jurisdiction where it is produced. In turn, jurisdictions least receptive to carbon taxes and cap-and-trade are often quite willing to impose steep taxes on extraction and sustain them over time. But they do not act because of concern for climate change and emission reduction. Instead, they are attracted by the economic development advantage of imposing a tax that will largely be applied to purchases made by consumers who live and work elsewhere. Indeed, every government that allows both use and production of fossil fuels also picks its politically preferred energy taxation and carbon price battles; none maintain a perfect moral position of attempting to eliminate the production and use of fossil fuels across the board. This dynamic also applies elsewhere, including Australia and the European Union, and is further explored in subsequent chapters.

Extraction would be only one of a series of challenges facing California as it weighed possible next steps on carbon pricing. Like British Columbia and RGGI, California proved successful in gaining political support to adopt carbon pricing, launch a cap-and-trade program, and weather some significant political threats in its early years. It was too early at the end of 2015 to assess performance. In turn, numerous questions swirled around longer-term policy implementation and whether auction revenue could build a broad political base rather than divide competing constituents. Nonetheless, it provided another example that carbon pricing could clear many hurdles in the policy life-cycle and transition into a durable system over time.

7 Carbon Pricing Lessons

Imagine a drop in American greenhouse gas emissions that peaked in 2005 but then fell back below 1995 levels by 2015 (see figure 7.1). This occurred despite substantial population growth and economic expansion. Reductions would be especially significant in the electricity sector. By 2015, the United States produced about the same amount of power as in 2005 but that generation released 19 percent lower carbon emissions.[1] This reflected significant shifts in the mix of sources that Americans used for energy. Coal use for electricity plunged during this period from more than one-half to less than one-third of total power generated, with further declines highly plausible during the next decade. A much cleaner fossil fuel, natural gas, served as the primary replacement source, although it was supported by considerable expansion of wind, solar, and other renewables. Established noncarbon sources such as nuclear and hydro remained significant, although very little new capacity was added.

The United States also emerged from this decade as a far more fuel-efficient nation, producing each dollar of gross domestic product with significantly less carbon emissions than before. This reflected regulatory changes in the tailpipe emissions of cars and trucks, building and appliance performance efficiency, and many other policies promoting greater energy efficiency. An American president celebrated this achievement in August 2015, noting that "over the past decade, even as our economy has continued to grow, the United States has cut our total carbon pollution more than any other nation on earth."[2]

Any forecast produced in 2005 that projected such massive shifts within a decade would have likely assumed that a federal carbon price had been adopted and was a central driver behind this transformation. Some

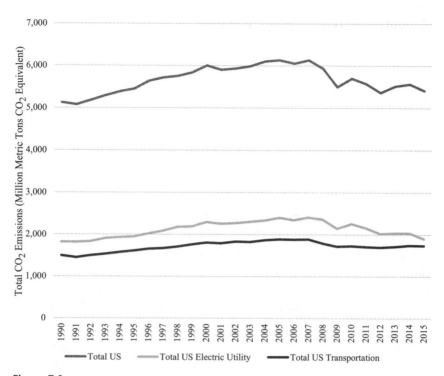

Figure 7.1
US greenhouse gas emissions, 1990–2015.
Source: US Environmental Protection Agency, "Greenhouse Gas Inventory Data Explorer," last modified April 30, 2015, https://www3.epa.gov/climatechange/ghgemis sions/inventoryexplorer/chartindex.html.

form of cap-and-trade or a carbon tax would be necessary to unleash market forces to begin to reverse the steady expansion of American use of fossil fuels and related carbon emissions across prior decades. As we have seen, that American carbon pricing step never occurred, aside from cap-and-trade experiments launched and sustained in ten states that already had per capita emission rates well below national averages. Nonetheless, data from the US Environmental Protection Agency confirms that the United States had achieved just such an emissions reduction record.[3] American greenhouse gas emissions had declined 12 percent by 2015 from 2005 levels, despite significant population and economic growth (see table 7.1). Indeed, 2015 emission levels from the electricity sector reached the lowest levels since 1993, the year Congress rejected a BTU tax proposal.[4]

Table 7.1
US greenhouse gas emissions, 1990–2015.

Year	Total US Carbon Dioxide Emissions	Total US Electric Utility Carbon Dioxide Emissions	Total US Transportation Carbon Dioxide Emissions
1990	5,123.04	1,820.82	1,493.76
1991	5,074.49	1,818.19	1,447.60
1992	5,178.58	1,831.54	1,496.85
1993	5,292.61	1,906.90	1,532.41
1994	5,385.92	1,931.23	1,576.98
1995	5,450.92	1,947.92	1,609.86
1996	5,636.30	2,020.99	1,654.30
1997	5,713.36	2,088.39	1,670.14
1998	5,753.82	2,177.38	1,706.64
1999	5,834.23	2,190.51	1,761.06
2000	6,001.36	2,296.88	1,805.46
2001	5,902.71	2,257.91	1,789.43
2002	5,934.95	2,272.67	1,830.64
2003	5,990.73	2,304.16	1,822.26
2004	6,105.43	2,335.89	1,867.14
2005	6,131.83	2,400.87	1,887.03
2006	6,051.50	2,345.28	1,882.63
2007	6,130.63	2,411.90	1,886.07
2008	5,932.98	2,360.08	1,791.80
2009	5,495.70	2,145.66	1,716.97
2010	5,699.93	2,258.40	1,728.27
2011	5,569.52	2,157.69	1,707.63
2012	5,362.10	2,022.18	1,696.75
2013	5,514.02	2,038.12	1,713.00
2014	5,565.50	2,038.02	1,742.81
2015	5,411.41	1,900.67	1,736.38

Note: Emissions in million metric tons of carbon dioxide equivalent.

Source: US Environmental Protection Agency, "Greenhouse Gas Inventory Data Explorer," last modified April 30, 2015, https://www3.epa.gov/climatechange /ghgemissions/inventoryexplorer/chartindex.html.

These results did not indicate that America had moved into automatic pilot heading toward the continuing levels of decarbonization necessary to increase the prospects of deterring the worst impacts of climate change. Nor did they mean that the United States had necessarily created a model that could or should be emulated by other nations of the world in pursuit of those goals. A wide range of federal, state, and local policies were adopted with broad and sustained political support and played a consequential role. New technological breakthroughs and applications were also important factors. But so was the most devastating economic recession since the 1930s, which was responsible for the bulk of those reductions achieved between 2007 and 2009.[5]

But many of these changes appear to be enduring; an initial emissions rebound as modest economic recovery took hold yielded to sustained reductions in the 2010s. Popular state policies supporting renewable energy and energy efficiency appeared to have continued momentum going forward. New clean technologies will continue to mature and proliferate. Coal was likely to be increasingly marginalized, although there are few signs that natural gas or oil were on a similar path. Renewables and energy efficiency likely have continued momentum going forward.

So what happened to carbon pricing? And does it have a political and policy future in the United States? Or elsewhere? Carbon pricing has indeed proved far more challenging politically than was anticipated or acknowledged in prior decades. As we have seen, this reflects an American political story but also a global one. That said, the economic and environmental case for adding some form of a credible carbon price remains, both to sustain and accelerate any recent carbon emission gains. This chapter begins by reviewing why carbon pricing has proved so difficult politically in the United States and beyond. But it also considers some of the lessons from the more politically and managerially successful carbon pricing experiments thus far. This review includes ways to actually build political support while confronting the unenviable task of imposing price increases on familiar and visible commodities.

The Limits of Predicting the Future

The enormous political challenge of embracing carbon pricing was compounded by at least three mistaken assumptions that had evolved into conventional wisdoms in policy circles as climate change reached national and subnational agendas. First, expectations that the historic Montreal Protocol on Substances That Deplete the Ozone Layer, which was adopted with broad international support in 1987, would provide a road map for additional global partnerships foundered against the challenges of carbon. "Montreal" would become synonymous with a profound international environmental achievement that featured regulation alongside an integral taxation component.

Indeed, this initiative may also have delivered greater carbon reduction benefits than any other climate policy developed in subsequent decades, including carbon pricing policies. This was achieved through a far-reaching reduction of chlorofluorocarbons, a highly potent greenhouse gas.[6] It was understandably tempting to see the ozone accords as a stepping stone toward an even bigger international bargain on climate, but this was never realistic. The ozone case featured advanced chemical alternatives that were ready for deployment, with considerable economic incentives for some nations such as the United States to take an early and active role. The ozone threat was also more immediate with its risks easier to explain than climate, making the case for aggressive near-term action more compelling politically.

In contrast, "Kyoto" would largely be a bust, despite all of the inflated hopes surrounding the 1997 agreement and prolonged efforts to resurrect it into a viable international regime that would employ some form of carbon pricing globally. Nations routinely backtracked on initial emission reduction commitments, without consequences beyond moral opprobrium. The Kyoto process is a disappointing tale on the challenges of building and sustaining international coalitions, though it remains quite remarkable that so many national or subnational governments found ways to take constructive emission reduction steps through unilateral policy development, despite considerable Kyoto failures.

Second, hopes that the pioneering American use of emissions trading for sulfur dioxide might provide a path toward a national or international embrace of carbon pricing also collided against political reality, as discussed in chapters 2 and 3. In retrospect, the American sulfur dioxide experience would prove more of a flukish case rather than a reliable model for carbon. It featured an unusual political advantage of an alternative and domestically available coal source with low sulfur content, technically feasible emissions abatement technology, and flexible transportation arrangements for coal shipment in the era of rail deregulation. It also benefited from legislation that was carefully crafted and had a broad base of political support across partisan lines and multiple branches and levels of government.

This case would be trundled out repeatedly as a model to guide climate policy across dozens of congressional hearings and international discussions that downplayed its unique features and distinct political appeal. But early cap-and-trade experiments applied to carbon emissions proved far more difficult to adopt than had been anticipated by proponents. Political opposition was formidable in many polities, even when promising political coalitions assumed power. There was little evidence of any public groundswell of support for carbon pricing. Those policies that were adopted proved considerably more difficult to launch and sustain through subsequent election cycles and leadership changes. Political opposition often mounted after adoption rather than melted away. Managerial capacity to make essential adjustments and provide credible policy oversight was assumed to be automatic in such market-based policies. But this, too, proved far more challenging than anticipated.

Third, the widespread expectations in the late 1990s and early 2000s that any transition toward carbon pricing would be eased because the world was thought to be approaching "peak oil" would prove wildly inaccurate. This presumption of steady declines in fossil fuel availability led to common expectations that governments in the United States and beyond would actively seek alternatives on national security grounds. Natural gas and oil were deemed increasingly rare and expensive to provide amid that anticipated scarcity. This would leave considerable reserves of coal nationally and internationally, but its many negative externalities might well marginalize it as America and the world embraced diverse renewable alternatives and more efficient use.[7]

But the advent of hydraulic fracturing and horizontal drilling from abundant shale supplies, led by technological transformation in the United States and with potential expansion to many corners of the globe, radically altered that thinking. The era of fracking set aside the common expectation that fossil fuels were fading away and could be easily elbowed to the margins of energy use by carbon pricing. Instead, any future carbon pricing would have to confront the possibility of expanding fossil fuel supplies and plunging costs in using them. This would test public appetites to support the application of pricing tools to commodities that increasingly appeared to be readily available and stable or declining in price, thereby enabling citizens to keep more money in their pockets.

These factors combined with the enduring reality that carbon pricing is simply a difficult political lift in virtually any context. It asks citizens to accept immediate and ongoing increases in the price of familiar and essential commodities. These commodities have facilitated significant economic growth and have never been deemed illegal to use by any government in the world. Instead, citizens are asked in carbon pricing regimes to take a leap of faith. They are expected to accept the proposition that immediate sacrifice in the form of higher prices will somehow translate into a future benefit, perhaps one that may only be tangible for future generations rather than those paying the costs in the near term.

All of these factors combined to undermine the serious advancement of a promising policy tool. Excessive and exaggerated use of prior examples (ozone depletion via Montreal and sulfur dioxide emissions via the Clean Air Act) turned them into caricatures rather than models, vastly oversimplifying the ease with which they could be applied to carbon. Projections that natural gas and oil supplies were disappearing proved aspirational and ignored emerging technological advancement. The political path toward adopting carbon pricing at international, national, or subnational scales would prove substantially more complicated than proponents envisioned. Indeed, we have seen the numerous political challenges facing carbon pricing, not just in initial stages of adoption but also during advanced stages of management and adjustment to inevitable transitions between political parties and elected leaders. The earlier presumption that carbon pricing policies would just self-implement if political actors could somehow muster the courage to make an initial adoption lies in tatters, as demonstrated in the earlier chapters. At the same time, the last two decades of experience are not only littered with carbon pricing failures, but also include some promising experiences that can offer insights, if not an exact blueprint, into where carbon pricing might head constructively in future decades.

Building a Political Base That Can Endure

The political adoption of carbon pricing can benefit mightily from effective policy entrepreneurs, well-placed champions who hold prominent elective office such as a governorship or premiership or head a key government agency. Such entrepreneurs have demonstrated considerable ability to not only grasp the idea of carbon pricing but also to frame it as a compelling option for a particular jurisdiction to pursue. They have often found creative ways to use executive powers to launch policy formation, including some efforts that cut across jurisdictional boundaries.[8]

But entrepreneurs have their limits, and more durable carbon pricing initiatives have built a broader and more enduring political base. Such a base needs to expand over time rather than contract or collapse when the entrepreneur leaves the stage or other stakeholders become more active. The Gordon Campbell experience in British Columbia demonstrated the possibility of pursuing carbon pricing via a center-right party eager to advance a climate protection agenda while outflanking its most significant party opponent, which occupied the center-left. Campbell clearly positioned British Columbia to adopt what remains one of the few consequential carbon prices (measured in dollars per ton) established anywhere in the world in the last two decades.

The British Columbia premier relied on a solid coalition of leaders within his Liberal Party and generally strong support from a range of environmental and industry groups. The tax endured through subsequent elections, actually expanding support from rival parties and benefit recipients over time. There was no real question that it would prove durable through a shift of power to the succeeding premier, Christy Clark. However, she was less enthusiastic about it than her predecessor, being far more interested in expanding natural gas extraction and export than increasing the carbon tax rate. Clark also rejected proposals to increase the tax, despite a small increase in greenhouse gas emissions between 2011 and 2014 and concerns about provincial ability to hit future reduction targets.

The Regional Greenhouse Gas Initiative (RGGI) features numerous parallels, with multiple policy entrepreneurs and strong environmental group support at its outset, but also capacity to sustain and expand a supporting coalition over time. Unlike the Western Climate Initiative (WCI), the Midwestern Greenhouse Gas Reduction Accord (MGGRA), and other short-lived pricing experiments, RGGI was built to last. There was considerable buy-in across partisan lines, including active early support from Republican governors such as New York's George Pataki. The executive branch role was crucial in policy development, but legislatures were frequently drawn in and have generally continued to play supportive roles, despite near-total turnover of all key elected and appointed officials since the dawn of cap-and-trade in the Northeast United States. As in British Columbia, environmental groups and some industry groups would remain supportive and help see RGGI through important transitions that prepared it for a credible albeit limited role over time.

Being Realistic about Policy Goals

In an ideal world, a carbon price would be linked to the social cost of carbon. Such a robust price would then drive emission reductions across all economic sectors and lead to full compliance with Paris accord pledges. But no government in the world, regardless of its fervor for confronting climate change, has approached that level of commitment via either a carbon tax or cap-and-trade in the past two decades. Instead, the more enduring carbon pricing initiatives have set far more modest goals, giving them a part within an ensemble of policies rather than exclusive standing on center stage. This is reflected in the relatively modest carbon prices established in recent decades, headed by British Columbia. These remain far below most estimates of the social cost of carbon, including the ones employed in Canada and the United States. Many other carbon pricing mechanisms, including RGGI, the European Union's Emissions Trading Scheme (ETS), and the California-Quebec programs, place a firm cap on price and in practice generally fall well below even that level (see table 7.2).

Table 7.2
2015 actual carbon prices (in USD).

Carbon Pricing Scheme	Price per Ton
British Columbia	$23.28
California/Quebec	$12.77
European Union	$7.34
Ireland	$23.20
Regional Greenhouse Gas Initiative	$6.11

Sources: "Carbon Price," *California Carbon Dashboard*, accessed July 14, 2016, http://calcarbondash.org/; "Auction Results," *Regional Greenhouse Gas Initiative*, accessed July 11, 2016, https://www.rggi.org/market/co2_ auctions/results.

All of these mechanisms have been designed to ease transitional adjust-ments and minimize the chances of a political backlash related to cost imposition. Political leaders have been mindful that carbon pricing was sold to constituents not only as a needed climate protection step but also for its modest impacts on their lifestyles and pocketbooks, even in climate-focused polities such as California. Consequently, the kinds of carbon prices that are likely to be politically feasible can play a number of constructive roles but may well need to avoid high levels or broad application if they are to prove politically feasible and sustainable.

Political leaders have taken great pains to phase in pricing over time. This was reflected in the staged increase of the British Columbia carbon tax, which has remained unchanged since reaching its peak in 2012. RGGI found ways to adjust its emissions cap and thereby produce a real, albeit quite modest, increase in its auction price. California has managed to expand its total coverage through a phased-in process that added sectors in 2015, nine years after authorizing legislation. Such steps reflect careful consider-ation of political sensitivities to price increases, even in cases such as British Columbia, where all revenues are required to be returned to the public via tax reductions and credits.

No carbon price adopted and sustained to date has been designed as the exclusive mechanism for achieving climate protection goals. Instead, durable carbon taxes and cap-and-trade programs operate alongside a wide range of other policies with overarching goals. Policies such as renewable portfolio standards, energy efficiency resource standards, and tailpipe emis-sion controls, among many others, have been adopted with far broader political bases. Cross-partisan political support has generally proved easier to secure and sustain over time in such cases, further reflected in the fact that these kinds of policies have faced far fewer of the policy reversals after initial adoption than we have seen in carbon pricing. They routinely receive a higher level and more ideologically diverse base of support in public opin-ion surveys, regardless of level of government, than any form of carbon tax or cap-and-trade.[9] They often have considerable appeal in jurisdictions that would be highly unlikely politically to adopt carbon pricing unless they were coerced to do so. Jurisdictions that have active carbon pricing policies tend to have the largest number of supplemental policies and set the most ambitious targets for them, serving to further marginalize any singular role for carbon pricing. This experience is reflected not just in North America but also Europe and Asia.

It seems highly unlikely going forward that policies that do not employ carbon pricing are likely to be jettisoned in favor of an all-out pursuit of a robust pricing regimen. Constituency and general public support for these alternative policies suggest that they are likely to be the most popular and durable climate policies going forward, despite the important reminders from economists that at least some forms of carbon pricing would likely be more potent if freed from an entourage of complementary policies.

Revenue Use and Constituency Building

The inevitable political caution about triggering public opposition with a carbon price that is set too high or a cap that is set too stringently generates another important question to guide policy development: Are carbon prices intended to stimulate far-reaching behavioral change in energy consumption, or are they intended to produce revenue necessary to support various climate protection goals?[10] These options need not be mutually exclusive. Nonetheless, the enduring political caution about going too far with any carbon pricing regime suggests continued likely limits politically on what they might entail going forward. If this holds into the future, it will place significant constraints on what carbon prices can accomplish in driving major behavioral change. Even broad Paris emission reduction commitments can hardly be expected to supersede national and subnational political considerations and reverse inevitable reservations about imposing steep costs. This suggests that the issue of revenue generation to pursue other climate goals may loom considerably larger in the future as a leading attribute of carbon pricing than many purist proponents would prefer.

Perhaps one of the biggest surprises to date in examining design elements that have contributed to more durable and effective carbon pricing experiments is the strategic role of revenue allocation. This issue has long been studied from an economics perspective, particularly in the case of carbon taxes. This analysis frequently explores the best tax structure and revenue allocation plan from an overall economics perspective or in weighing economic impacts across various income groups. But it tends to ignore consideration of factors that might expand or shrink political support. Indeed, the political ramifications of pursuing various ways to use revenue to actually build or expand policy constituency support have gone largely ignored by scholars. There are, however, emerging lessons from expanding practice, particularly now that the RGGI experience has revolutionized cap-and-trade by turning it into a revenue-producing policy via auctions rather than earlier iterations that allocated allowances without cost.[11]

The net proceeds from existing carbon taxes and cap-and-trade programs remain quite modest as a total percentage of governmental revenue. And they continue to be overshadowed by revenues generated by energy extraction taxes, such as state severance taxes in the United States or royalties in much of the rest of the energy-producing world. Table 7.3 demonstrates that annual severance tax revenues are significant, totaling over $11 billion in fiscal year 2015, despite major declines from prior years due to reduced oil and gas prices. These severance taxes or royalty equivalents continue to produce vastly more revenue than all carbon pricing policies combined in the United States, Canada, and other nations—a topic we revisit later in this chapter. But carbon pricing revenue from cap-and-trade has increased in recent years. This could expand significantly in the future if established policies expand or new ones are adopted, raising a host of political and policy questions related to revenue use.

Both British Columbia and RGGI have found ways to use carbon-pricing revenue to provide visible public benefits that their citizens find tangible and can embrace politically. The revenue-neutrality provisions in the British Columbia carbon tax have routinely returned funds through a sustained set of benefits, as was discussed in chapter 4. They began with a small rebate check but have expanded through reduced individual and corporate tax rates. Political champions of the tax have routinely reminded the public of these benefits alongside claims of overall economic enhancement and environmental protection through this policy. Over time, constituencies have formed that have come to appreciate and expect these benefits. They would likely oppose any effort to reduce the tax rate or repeal the tax, fearful of benefit decline or loss, alongside those who would continue to support the tax solely on emission reduction grounds.

RGGI has built a different kind of constituency through targeted allocation of most auction revenues to a range of projects that assist residents and businesses to become more energy efficient. States have been masterful in chronicling and claiming political credit for these RGGI "success stories"

Table 7.3
Actual annual carbon price revenue, 2008–2015 (in USD).

Carbon Pricing Scheme	2008	2009	2010	2011	2012	2013	2014	2015
British Columbia Carbon Tax[a]	—	234 M	415 M	567 M	734 M	842 M	918 M	918 M
Regional Greenhouse Gas Initiative Auctions[b]	145 M	349 M	283 M	175 M	168 M	448 M	367 M	436 M
North Dakota Severance Taxes[c]	792 M	827 M	1.1 B	1.9 B	3.2 B	2.5 B	3.5 B	2 B
California/Quebec Auctions[d]	—	—	—	—	56 M	477 M	437 M	2.6 B
Texas Severance Tax[e]	4.1 B	2.3 B	1.7 B	2.7 B	3.7 B	4.6 B	6 B	4.0 B
All US State Severance Taxes[f]	17.8 B	13.4 B	11.1 B	15.6 B	17.0 B	17.2 B	17.5 B	11.6 B

a. British Columbia Ministry of Finance (various years).
b. "Auction Results," *Regional Greenhouse Gas Initiative*, accessed July 11, 2016, https://www.rggi.org/market/co2_auctions/results.
c. Robert McManmon and Grane Nülle, "State Severance Tax Revenues Decline as Fossil Fuel Prices Drop," *U.S. Energy Information Administration*, last modified January 12, 2016, http://www.eia.gov/todayinenergy/detail.cfm?id=24512; Rachel L. Hampton and Barry G. Rabe, "Leaving Money on the Table: Pennsylvania Exceptionalism in Resisting Energy Severance Taxes," *Commonwealth* 17, no. 1 (2017): 10–11.
d. California Environmental Protection Agency, Air Resources Board (CARB), *Annual Report to the Legislature* and various Joint Auction Reports.
e. Hampton and Rabe, "Leaving Money on the Table."
f. Department of Commerce, US Census Bureau, "Quarterly Summary of State and Local Taxes," https://www.census.gov/govs/qtax/; Hampton and Rabe, "Leaving Money on the Table."

that have been made possible through carbon pricing, as was discussed in chapter 5. Each RGGI state has cultivated a long list of constituents who have received some portion of the auction bounty. These rosters have only expanded and diversified as auction prices began to scale upward gradually after the 2014 emissions cap adjustment.

Such strategic uses of revenue offer tangible benefits, transforming the politics of carbon pricing from its traditionally ethereal discussions about possible future climate benefits from early action. It remains extremely difficult to make a clear and compelling case as to how global temperatures will differ in 2030 or 2050 if a particular nation or state adopts a carbon tax at $20 or $80 per ton or cap-and-trade designed to reduce electricity sector emissions by 20 or 80 percent over the next decade. But that political calculus on perceived benefits changes markedly when a British Columbia premier can point to a website outlining tax reductions and credits, or a RGGI state governor can host a media event celebrating the latest recipients of energy efficiency grants. Revenue use has thus helped solidify and expand the base of support for these programs, independent of any particular claims of emissions reductions. Indeed, as discussed in chapter 5, RGGI might well have collapsed politically after its first years without revenue allocation from auctions to sustain it and thereby set the stage for essential cap adjustment.

But revenue allocation entails more than just tossing money around in the hope that it curries favor. Indeed, there is growing political science literature examining ways in which more durable federal programs have systematically built constituency support through their use of funds, although most of this work has focused on social welfare programs rather than energy or environmental protection.[12] Such linkages are not forged easily and require a credible and sustained approach. Failures can lead to policy reversals, including termination or downsizing, and these setbacks are likely more common than is generally recognized.[13] California has demonstrated that the lack of a coherent revenue allocation plan that is credibly implemented can divide its political base of support for cap-and-trade. Expanded revenue production in recent years has only intensified ongoing political battles over who gets what share of the proceeds. Other governments have also struggled with this very issue, including the ETS system and the prolonged soap opera of Australian carbon pricing proposals, as discussed in chapter 3.

The Political Wisdom of Extraction Taxes

The American experience with severance taxes may offer one of the most compelling examples of how imposing a price on extraction of fossil fuels can be linked to an advantageous long-term strategy for revenue use that sustains long-term support for the tax. Much severance tax revenue is placed directly into general funds, thereby allowing for reduction of other taxes to sustain existing governmental operations. But many states have also found ways to require that some portion of their revenues be placed into designated funds supported exclusively by the severance tax. These funds can help guard against fiscal boom-and-bust cycles of energy development while also deterring the corruption common in petro-states around the world.[14] Such funds also allow designation of potential beneficiaries from interest on investments. This process can build a constituency to support the policy against temptations to spend all of the principal for short-term ends.

Seven states have established sovereign wealth funds, formal trusts with constitutional protections that guide investment and allocation, removing revenues from ongoing battles over use and sending clear signals to the public on allocation; they have proved remarkably durable and politically popular, operating in many cases over numerous decades.[15] States such as Texas and Wyoming rely heavily on trust fund revenue to support educational programs from kindergarten through college.[16] Alaska has long maintained a trust fund that provides enormously popular annual dividend checks to every state resident, presenting some parallels with the British Columbia experience.[17] Several states that have expanded fracking operations in recent years have begun to follow this pattern, most notably North Dakota, as we will examine in chapter 8.

This tax-and-trust nexus has helped make severance taxes remarkably impervious to proposals to cut tax rates in states that have adopted them. The dramatic expansion of drilling operations and related plunges in oil and gas prices triggered an outcry from energy producers in states around the nation to cut tax rates markedly or eliminate them entirely. These laments were frequently combined with threats to close operations and migrate to friendlier states if tax rates were not slashed. But states have generally proven resilient in maintaining these taxes on fossil fuels, though their overall yields declined after 2014 as prices plunged nationally and globally (see table 7.3).[18] The few states that made deep tax rate cuts, such as Oklahoma and Mississippi, did not have trust funds, instead spending all severance tax revenue immediately through the general fund. They gambled that they could navigate short-term fiscal challenges by producing new revenue through reduced tax rates, though with little evidence that this has occurred. Some states have strategically kept rates low (Ohio), refused to adopt such a tax (Pennsylvania) to encourage drilling, or allowed local government to decide whether to establish a tax (California).[19] But these cases remain exceptional against national patterns among severance tax states, including those with trust funds that have maintained significant rates.

Consequently, there are clearly opportunities to use energy tax revenue to build and sustain political support for placing some form of a price on carbon. Durable policies have found ways to connect costs with plans for some type of linked use. Numerous options might be considered in future carbon pricing regimes, including linked allocation to storage and transmission for next-generation energy, energy research and development, climate adaptation costs, broader tax reform, and support for workers in the fossil fuel sector whose livelihoods might be adversely affected by carbon pricing.[20]

Taking Policy Management Seriously

Much of the early advocacy for carbon pricing in the United States and beyond featured a type of hubris that an initial act of policy adoption courage would be sufficient to launch and sustain it across various stages. Hearings in Congress and state legislatures were remarkably silent about the details of governance, including the design and staffing of governmental agencies that would have to operationalize carbon pricing and make needed adjustments along the way. This pattern was also reflected in political debate over carbon pricing in Canada, Europe, and Asia. Instead of careful design of public management systems to guide implementation, the implicit assumption was that carbon pricing would largely self-implement, much as had appeared to be the case in earlier policies such as Nordic carbon taxes and American sulfur dioxide cap-and-trade.

One rude awakening for carbon pricing proponents has been evidence that clarity in initial design, policy placement into appropriately staffed and structured organizations, and capacity for adaptation may well determine whether pricing policies succeed or fail over time. Carbon pricing implementation has proved considerably more difficult than anticipated, whether correcting fundamental problems in Europe's ETS design or overcoming second thoughts during launching periods, as happened in cases from Australia to New Jersey. Public officials serving energy production and environmental protection departments generally have little common history with one another; they often work for organizations that operate at cross-purposes rather than practice sharing of resources, data, functions, or missions. Other policy specializations also may have to be consulted and integrated, whether transportation (to deal with vehicle use and efficiency) or agriculture (for biofuels and carbon offsets from cultivating crops or forests).

The general track record of forced marriages of governmental units across traditional policy boundaries is not good. Public health and health services delivery, for example, should be closely meshed and yet often collide. Prior efforts to integrate public management around new and complex challenges often face far-reaching problems not anticipated in early stages, such as the governance challenges that endure in the era of homeland security. Public management scholar Donald Kettl has identified numerous policy arenas in which the complexity of the issues and emerging policies are so great that ultimately performance lags and issues arise of governmental competence to deliver on initial promises.[21] Kettl has also noted that these kinds of challenges are hardly eliminated by reliance on market mechanisms such as carbon pricing.[22]

These challenges differ depending on the form of carbon pricing being adopted. Carbon taxes that follow the policy playbook of jurisdictions such as British Columbia and Ireland pose relatively modest public management challenges. These have featured clear and straightforward descriptions of policy design and intent in authorizing legislation. They build on decades of experience with commodity taxation and rely principally on a small set of policy professionals based in finance departments. Consequently, their full implementation has not required massive new staff hiring or governmental reorganization. These policies have also made the transition from policy adoption to formal launch in a matter of months, with clear mechanisms to allow for adjustments through a phasing in of tax rates (British Columbia) or amendments to increase them after early operation (Ireland). These carbon taxes also lend themselves to performance management metrics, including relatively clear indicators of how much revenue is being generated and how it is being allocated. Emerging analyses of these cases have demonstrated their capacity to reduce emissions while having a net neutral or slightly positive economic impact. The relative simplicity and transparency of implementation has also been evident in the far more common use of severance taxes on energy extraction, further demonstrating that energy-focused taxes present relatively modest public management challenges.

Cap-and-trade, however, has received far more serious consideration politically in North America and beyond in past decades, in large part because it has been seen as presenting an easier political path than the more explicit costs linked with new taxes on carbon. But recent experience with cap-and-trade has demonstrated a considerably higher degree of public management complexity than taxation, including the challenge of integrating functions across energy development and environmental protection. Transition from adoption to launch has been measured in most cap-and-trade cases at more than a half-decade rather than months. It has also necessitated larger staffing expansion and organizational oversight efforts.

These problems need not be insurmountable, as reflected in the RGGI case examined in chapter 5. This multistate network navigated key design features and made major midcourse adjustments, although it drew heavily on an unusually deep and established body of policy professionals and governing institutions with previous experience in many core functions. As in the carbon tax cases, performance indicators have begun to emerge for RGGI and are generally encouraging on both environmental and economic grounds. In California, cap-and-trade implementation has been highly resource-intensive and complex, even after losing all initial state partners. Classification and implementation of offset provisions, as discussed in chapter 6, have been labor-intensive and riddled with conflicts. But the vaunted California Air Resources Board has a substantial body of expertise with most key facets of cap-and-trade and related work across policy sectors, with a generous base of resources and staff. It is likely able to continue to absorb Quebec and any other new partners into advanced stages of implementation, despite some enduring concerns addressed in chapter 6.

But these American state cases remain largely exceptional, given the considerable challenges of launching and sustaining cap-and-trade elsewhere. Other states, most Canadian provinces, and many governments from Asia, Europe, Africa, and Latin America lack this depth of professional experience and capacity to navigate the many complexities involved in implementing carbon cap-and-trade in a credible manner. Cap-and-trade has also struggled to garner and maintain public confidence, as reflected in very mixed verdicts in most surveys of public opinion.[23] Future cap-and-trade proposals will need to acknowledge and address these challenges, just as carbon taxes will have to confront the political optics of their blunt imposition of higher prices on familiar commodities.

Taking Federalism Seriously

One additional surprise in the evolution of climate change policy and carbon pricing proposals over past decades is how fundamentally wrong early projections were in assuming that a few large national governments would dominate the field, with the expectation that this would lead to the development of a global pricing regime. Instead, carbon pricing has moved forward in fits and starts, with a number of small nations or subnational governments taking lead roles rather than carbon superpowers. This has resulted in considerable early policy experimentation, with a number of reversals but also some successes in sustaining policy through stages of adjustment and into advanced implementation. In contrast, a great many other governments have balked at any form of carbon pricing or reversed course after initial exploration. This new reality of highly varied responses and policy preferences is reflected in the policy architecture linked to the Paris accords. In this case, individual nations are encouraged to make their own emission reduction pledges but have enormous latitude in allocating responsibility for them across internal jurisdictions.

Climate change policy has thus become a far more decentralized arena than was ever envisioned during Kyoto or other early international climate deliberations. In these instances, states, provinces, and localities were commonly depicted as bit players that would quickly yield to a more integrated and unified set of national and global policies that would employ some form of carbon pricing. RGGI, WCI, and MGGRA states would be preempted by Congress; British Columbia and Quebec would yield to Ottawa; New South Wales and Victoria would be woven into a national plan established in Canberra; Germany and the United Kingdom would harmonize policies with other member states under European Union auspices. Whether or not national systems of government were formally federated or engaged in some kind of multistate governance, climate change would invariably be increasingly centralized in this earlier perspective, creating a broad and expanding platform for carbon pricing.

But this bottom-up approach has proved remarkably durable, now spanning decades in many cases, both with pricing and other kinds of policies.[24]

And this approach does not appear likely to dissolve anytime soon. Indeed, the very initial stages of developing carbon pricing policies in more unitary systems such as China, Japan, and South Korea appear to rely heavily on more localized experiments within various municipalities, states, and provinces. Even more recent efforts emerging in the United States and Canada to try to move toward some form of a national carbon pricing system eschewed legislation that would impose centralized authority and uniform policy design. Instead, they were designed to provide enormous latitude to individual states and provinces to design policies that worked for their political and economic systems while remaining broadly congruent with federal aspirations.

This suggests enormous opportunities to tap creative approaches from more localized jurisdictions, ones that might diffuse across boundaries. But such an approach also poses enormous challenges for any central government to foster innovation alongside imposing possible sanctions for resisting compliance or failing to produce credible policies. Climate change thus becomes a classic example of a policy challenge that will require design principles that at best lead to a "robust federation." Rather than an intergovernmental arrangement rift with battles over authority, sub-federal shirking of responsibilities to the nation, or burden-shifting across jurisdictions, political scientist Jenna Bednar's vision of a robust federal system is one that is "strong, flexible, and resilient."[25] As she has noted, "a robust federation needs firm constraints, upholding the distribution of authority between federal and state governments. It needs a method to recover from error, and a way to deliberate, experiment, and ultimately adjust the distribution of authority."[26]

It is doubtful that any federal or multilevel government had met the letter or the aspiration of that definition by the end of 2015, the period of primary focus in this book. But new permutations of federalism and carbon pricing were converging in new ways at this point, offering new twists on earlier experimentation with carbon taxes and cap-and-trade, as reflected in developments in the United States and Canada but also beyond. They also proceeded alongside additional policies that imposed some form of a price on either extraction of carbonized energy sources, commercial or residential use of electricity, or even long-term energy planning. This reflected the highly decentralized form of policy development that defied earlier models but set the stage for possible next steps in carbon pricing.

8   A Second Act for Carbon Pricing?

Despite all of its political struggles, carbon pricing appeared to catch a second wind toward the end of the 2010s. This was evident in a wide range of new carbon pricing proposals from North American governments but also from relative newcomers to the idea from Asia, Africa, and South America. It was further reflected in the December 2015 Paris climate accords, which supplanted the Kyoto quest for the "one best system" of an international treaty in favor of a more loosely structured set of national emission reduction pledges. Under the Paris mechanism, individual nations or federations would declare their future emission commitments but then determine their own preferred policy path to achieve them. Governments could select some form of carbon pricing or opt for other carbon reduction alternatives. They could achieve these reductions unilaterally or in collaboration with other governments.

All but 9 of the 195 participants in the Paris process submitted their Intended Nationally Determined Contribution pledges prior to the completion of negotiations. None of these would be formally binding although the Paris agreement established accountability measures, periodic reporting procedures, and mechanisms to ratchet up emission reduction pledges in the future. This was aimed at a goal of limiting global warming to two degrees Celsius with a stretch goal of containing any increase at or below 1.5 degrees. As a result, Paris emerged as far more than a symbolic step, instead presenting a test of whether a more decentralized international climate governance regime might work and perhaps place carbon pricing on center stage. Hope sprang eternal for another transformational climate policy experience, although enormous uncertainties remained about domestic political capacity to honor futuristic Paris commitments that would cross many decades and election cycles.

The chorus of support for carbon pricing during the Paris deliberations was led by international economic organizations. The International Monetary Fund released a report coinciding with the Paris meetings that noted: "For reducing carbon emissions, carbon pricing (through taxes or trading systems designed to behave like taxes) should be front and center."[1] The World Bank echoed this view, with one of its leaders explaining that a "robust, predictable" carbon price "is key to ultimately reaching the collective ambition and goals that we all want."[2] World Bank president Jim Yong Kim noted that "There is a growing sense of inevitability about putting a price on carbon pollution."[3]

It was hardly surprising that organizations such as the International Monetary Fund and the World Bank would take such active roles in calling for carbon pricing as a linchpin in meeting future emission reduction targets. They had long advocated such steps and clearly hoped that a proverbial policy window for them was reopening. But what was striking about the Paris meetings was the sheer size and diversity of the chorus of world leaders who endorsed or replicated these kinds of statements. This included numerous national and subnational heads of state from nations in Africa, Asia, Europe, North America, and South America, many of whom shared a stage and expressed their support for an expanded role for carbon pricing in their own national climate strategies going forward. This action overlapped with the launch of the Carbon Pricing Leadership Coalition, representing more than twenty governments and corporate leaders from over ninety firms. These steps did not translate immediately into the adoption of new policies or the expansion of existing ones. But they suggested that it was premature to relegate carbon pricing to the periphery of policy debate, plausible only in a handful of exceptional cases that defied the political odds.

These endorsements coincided with a flurry of other nations taking formal steps to adopt some form of carbon tax or cap-and-trade. Such diverse nations as China, Chile, India, Japan, Mexico, Portugal, South Africa, and South Korea, among others, showed some signs of carbon price policy development between 2014 and 2017, albeit with significant limits. Most of these policies appeared quite modest or even experimental in scope and some faced significant implementation delays. Initial prices were generally set at nominal levels, often without clear expansion plans. Many included generous exemptions that in some cases entirely excluded certain fossil fuels from coverage. In turn, these nations had little if any prior history of using these policy tools and were only beginning to consider long-term political and management challenges to successful operation. These new steps might constitute a base for expanded efforts in the future but they might also be largely symbolic, garnering international accolades while not actually accomplishing much. Nonetheless, their mere consideration or adoption in multiple settings further suggested that carbon pricing in various forms may have a viable political future, albeit likely in a supportive role alongside other policies rather than an exclusive one.

These emerging policies can build on the lessons from those instances in which carbon pricing has proved most successful to date. Future exploration of cap-and-trade would be wise not only to avoid the pitfalls of rejected policies in the United States, Canada, and Australia, and the protracted struggles of the EU Emissions Trading Scheme (ETS). It should also consider those design features that have made the Regional Greenhouse Gas Initiative and the California-Quebec partnership so relatively durable and functional. Future exploration of carbon taxation should consider why it has been so difficult to replicate the 1990s successes among Nordic countries, but also why British Columbia and Ireland have been able to perform so well in more recent times.

This chapter considers possible next steps in carbon pricing development, while staying mindful of what may be plausible politically rather than envisioning an economically ideal policy that could never realistically be adopted in a democratic political system. The chapter will review the future political viability of carbon taxes and cap-and-trade, explore alternative carbon pricing policies that deviate a bit from these standards, and offer options that might provide greater political feasibility. This discussion will draw from the real-world experience of energy extraction taxes and royalties as well as fees on energy use, including ones embraced by American states that have been able to raise revenues to address negative externalities and promote longer-term energy transitions.

This allows for consideration of a range of ways in which various forms of carbon pricing might accelerate essential transitions in the way we produce and use energy, possibly with significant policy differences across various continents, nations, and states. In turn, we will examine existing gaps in policy, where no pricing systems are in place and existing regulations are notoriously porous, such as the release of methane, a potent greenhouse gas, from sloppy fossil fuel extraction and distribution processes. This entails the waste of a nonrenewable natural resource that produces considerable climate and environmental harm while deriving no benefit from energy production. Current policies tread very cautiously on this wasteful behavior for fear of upsetting energy producers and distributors. Growing recognition and concern about this practice may present new opportunities for creative application of carbon pricing to methane releases as opposed to the current admixture of regulatory and voluntary approaches.

We will also consider the increasingly likely political reality that any carbon pricing strategies in the coming decades will need to complement rather than supplant other policies that retain substantial political support. The idea of multiple and overlapping policies threatens inefficiency from an economics standpoint. But this reflects political realities that tend to favor nonpricing policies and shows little appetite for dismantling them in order to give carbon pricing exclusive standing.

This chapter will also explore the politics of revenue allocation from any future carbon price, building on recent experience that suggests that this can play a significant role in fostering a loyal constituency and sustaining political support over time. One option is using carbon pricing not only to send a price signal but also provide a financial bridge to coming energy transitions. This reflects consideration of carbon pricing from a "silver buckshot" perspective. This approach views pricing as one of a series of policy weapons to confront climate change rather than the lone option. It could combine the impact of some form of price to deter consumption with financial support for other climate-friendly policies that retained broader bases of political support. This kind of support might help make the political case to sustain carbon pricing and expand its scope over time.

A Second Act for Carbon Taxes?

Carbon taxes remained conspicuous in the frequency with which they continued to be embraced and promoted by economists based in think tanks, the academy, and environmental groups. This was reflected in innumerable reports, papers, workshops, policy dialogues, conferences, op-eds, and blogs emanating from major American and Canadian cities. In many cases, these efforts cut across traditional ideological lines. One economist even went so far as to abandon more scholarly analysis and instead take the case for carbon taxes into more popular venues, such as comic books, stand-up comedy routines, and advocacy for carbon tax adoption through direct democracy. A former Republican member of Congress from South Carolina traveled the United States to promote carbon taxes, with an aggressive campaign that focused on recruiting conservative students on college and university campuses to the cause.[4]

The British Columbia case would be routinely referenced in these discussions, a poster child of political courage and policy efficacy. One think tank report concluded that the adoption of a comparable tax at the $30 per ton level in the United States in 2020 would cut energy-related greenhouse gas emissions by 8.5 percent in that year. This would produce an estimated $150 billion in revenue, with the possibility that it could cover 30 percent of the anticipated federal budget deficit for 2020.[5] In many respects, the British Columbia experience became the gold standard of carbon tax adoption, durability, and performance in North America and beyond, whether or not proponents had spent much time examining the case, the unique political factors that had made it possible, or its limitations.

Public opinion surveys held out nuggets of optimism that carbon taxes might have a political base of support, though remaining a tough sell in comparison with most other climate policy options. Economist David Amdur directed a 2014 National Surveys on Energy and Environment (NSEE) study that found public opposition of 61 percent overall to a proposed carbon tax in the United States, with particularly strong opposition among self-identified Republicans and Independents and an even divide in views among Democrats.[6] This opposition only grew if the survey question added an estimated 10 percent increase in energy costs due to the tax. The study also found, however, that some proposed uses of the revenue from such a tax could move the needle of support significantly. Using funds to reduce deficits had only marginal effect and increased opposition from Democrats. But allocating revenues for either tax rebates or development of alternative energy programs produced narrow majority support (see table 8.1). These findings have been largely replicated in subsequent NSEE surveys.

Rejections in the Washingtons (DC and State)

But would any of this advocacy by economists and other policy analysts or maneuvering of survey questions to create unique scenarios ever lead anywhere in terms of adoption and sustained implementation of a carbon tax?

Table 8.1
Public opinion on carbon tax with different uses of revenue.

	Base Case (No Cost, No Revenue Use)	Increases Cost by 10%	Revenue Used for Deficit Reduction	Revenue Returned with Income Tax Rebate	Revenue Used for Renewable Energy R&D
All Americans					
Support	34	29	38	56	60
Oppose	61	68	56	28	37
Republicans					
Support	15	10	34	43	51
Oppose	81	87	63	53	47
Independents					
Support	37	31	34	52	54
Oppose	59	67	60	44	43
Democrats					
Support	47	41	39	65	70
Oppose	47	56	55	28	25

Source: David Amdur, Barry G. Rabe, and Christopher Borick, "Public Views on a Carbon Tax Depend on the Proposed Use of Revenue," *Issues in Energy and Environmental Policy*, no. 13 (2014), http://closup.umich.edu/files/ieep-nsee-2014-spring-carbon-tax.pdf.

Or were the handful of durable carbon tax cases from prior decades destined to remain flukes that attracted intensive scholarly review but never diffused elsewhere? Few world leaders returned home from their carbon pricing exhortations in Paris to champion active pursuit of carbon tax or cap-and-trade adoption or expansion of existing policies. President Obama celebrated the Paris agreements as a historic step but outlined no plan to adopt a carbon price of any sort through new legislation.

The Democratic Party debated the inclusion of a carbon tax in its 2016 platform at the behest of supporters of Senator Bernie Sanders, but ultimately decided to refrain from an endorsement. Sanders did embrace this option in his primary campaign, though he never outlined a credible political path to adoption by Congress in the event he won the presidency. The party's nominee, Hillary Clinton, vowed to build on the climate legacy of her predecessor, Barack Obama, but removed a carbon tax from her menu of proposals very early in her campaign. "We have done extensive polling on carbon tax. It all sucks," wrote Clinton campaign chair John Podesta in an email that went public through WikiLeaks.[7] No serious Republican candidate evinced support for any form of carbon pricing, reflecting the major shift within the party since the 2008 election. Nominee Donald Trump questioned whether climate change was real and demonstrated no interest in considering any form of a carbon tax. Only third-party candidates, Libertarian Gary Johnson and the Green Party's Jill Stein, indicated support for such a step.

Carbon taxes retained a political pulse in some portions of the legislative branch in America, at least insofar as a few members of Congress and state legislators introduced bills that looked a good deal like the one British Columbia adopted in 2007. Several members of Congress routinely introduce some form of a carbon tax in every legislative session. Senator Sheldon Whitehouse, for example, first introduced the American Opportunity Carbon Fee Act (S.1543) in 2014. This would set an initial rate of $45 per ton that increased annually by 2 percent. All resulting revenue would be returned to the public in the form of tax cuts and credits. Whitehouse also indicated receptivity to swapping the tax as a replacement for President Obama's proposed regulation of carbon emissions through the Clean Air Act.[8]

At least nine carbon tax bills were introduced by state legislators between 2013 and 2016 and one ballot proposition on this topic went to the voters in November 2016 (see table 8.2), each proposing different rates and revenue use plans. In New York, for example, state assembly members Kevin Cahill and Barbara Lifton introduced a proposed "Tax on Carbon-Based Fuels" (A08372). This bill declared that "a market-based solution such as a carbon tax has been embraced widely by economists, including those in New York State."[9] It proposed a tax that would begin at $35 per ton and increase $15 per year until it reached $185 per ton. The legislation was intended to play a central role in enabling New York to reach its goal of reducing its carbon emissions by 80 percent from 1990 levels by 2050. Revenues would be deposited into a new Carbon Dioxide Emissions Fund, with 60 percent returned to "very low to moderate income residents of the state" and the remainder "to support the transition to one hundred percent clean energy in the state."[10]

All of these federal and state proposals were introduced by Democrats, followed by initial flurries of media attention and speculation that these might lead to an American transformational breakthrough on carbon taxes.

None received a serious hearing, much less any legislative vote, but they demonstrated at least some political receptivity to keeping the carbon tax idea alive on political agendas if more opportune moments arose in the future. Versions of these bills were reintroduced in five states after new legislatures convened in 2017, four from states in the Northeast that were already participating in the Regional Greenhouse Gas Initiative (RGGI).

There was also speculation during the run-up to the 2016 presidential election that a Hillary Clinton victory with significant Democratic coattails in Congress might lead to some form of a "grand bargain." Under this scenario, a carbon tax would be woven into a much larger political deal involving far-reaching tax reform and a shift toward a more market-based approach to climate change, even though this was not endorsed during the long campaign. Grand bargain proponents often noted possible parallels with the 1986 Tax Reform Act discussed in chapter 3. Any such speculation ended with Clinton's loss to Trump, reflected in the new president's aggressive reversal of a number of regulatory climate initiatives that had been launched by President Obama. A postelection effort to launch a revenue-neutral carbon tax by a coalition of Republican Cabinet members and academics, led by former secretaries of state George Shultz and James Baker, received a burst of media coverage. Baker claimed that "we happen to believe that this will make America great again," but he and his colleagues were summarily dismissed by the Trump administration and ignored by Congress.[11]

The November 2016 election was also consequential for carbon taxes given developments in the state of Washington, as the tax pioneered nine years earlier in British Columbia showed some promise of migrating across its southern border. State political leaders inclined toward some form of carbon pricing had struggled mightily over the prior decade in securing political approval, as discussed in chapter 3. This included repeated failures by two Democratic governors, Christine Gregoire and Gary Locke, to gain legislative support to proceed with full engagement in the Western Climate Initiative, as discussed in chapter 3. Another Democratic governor, Jay Inslee, was elected in 2012 and sought to position Washington as a national leader on climate change through a series of policy proposals that included cap-and-trade. But Inslee also failed to secure legislative support for carbon pricing or regulations that would establish a statewide emissions cap.

This prolonged political stalemate appeared to be broken in 2016 by an unanticipated political champion, an economist best known for his unique work in carbon tax comedy. Yoram Bauman had coauthored a book in the 1990s, *Tax Shift*, that may have played a modest role in shaping thinking about a carbon tax in British Columbia and Washington.[12] But he gained far greater notoriety for his subsequent comic books and stand-up comedy routines that included pitches for carbon taxation. Bauman and his allies in a group known as Carbon Washington rode this visibility to lead the battle to bring a carbon tax to the ballot for the first time in any political system. They secured sufficient petition signatures to place Initiative 732 on the November 2016 ballot. This called for a carbon tax that began at $25 per ton and would increase at a 3.5 percent annual rate until reaching a level of $100 per ton during the 2030s.

This ballot proposition offered simultaneous reductions in a mix of personal and business taxes, including cuts in the state sales tax from 6.5 to 5.5 percent. It would thus follow the British Columbia playbook as a model of revenue neutrality. As Bauman explained, "The basic premise of our policy is that you spend a few hundred more for fossil fuels and a few hundred less for everything else, and that's going to save the world."[13] Supporters included environmental groups such as Audubon Washington and the Citizens Climate Lobby and climate luminaries such as actor Leonardo DiCaprio, former NASA scientist James Hansen, and former Energy Secretary Steven Chu.

However, this initiative failed to build a broader constituency base and ultimately went down to a withering 59 to 41 percent defeat. A key dividing line involved competing views among potential supporters about how to use the money produced by the tax, much as would snarl California's efforts in implementing cap-and-trade (as discussed in chapter 6). Bauman's embrace of tax cuts triggered significant opposition from a number of environmental, labor, faith-based, and minority groups. They mounted a counterproposal for an alternative carbon tax ballot proposition that would divide revenue between low-carbon energy development and support for members of minority communities and workers in energy-intensive industries who might be harmed economically by the tax. This group faced challenges in meeting its petition signature threshold and ultimately suspended its effort to add an alternative carbon tax proposal to the November ballot.

Table 8.2

State carbon tax proposals, 2013–2016.

State	Bill	Year	Starting Tax Rate (per Ton)	Annual Increase	Ceiling Rate (per Ton)	Revenue Use	Status
California[a]	SB-1156	2014	Not specified	Not specified	Not specified	Rebates	Withdrawn
Massachusetts[b]	H.2532	2013–2014	$5	N/A	N/A	Transportation and tax cuts	No action
Massachusetts[c]	S.1786	2015–2016	Not specified	Not specified	Not specified	Renewable energy, transportation, and rebates	No action
Massachusetts[d]	S.1747	2015–2016	$10	$5	$40	Rebates	No action
New York[e]	A8372/S6037	2015–2016	$35	$15	$185	Rebates and renewable energy	No action
Rhode Island[f]	H.7325	2016	$15	$5	Not specified	Rebates, energy efficiency, and renewable energy	No action
Vermont[g]	H.506	2013	$10	N/A	N/A	Tax cuts	No action
Vermont[h]	H.412	2015	$10	$10	$100	Tax cuts and renewable energy	No action
Vermont[i]	H.395	2015	$50	$10	$100	Rebates and energy efficiency	No action
Washington[j]	I-732	2016	$25	3.5%	$100	Tax cuts and rebates	Rejected

a. California Carbon Tax Law of 2014, SB-1156, California Legislature 2013–2014 Session, http://leginfo.legislature.ca.gov/faces/billNavClient.xhtml?bill_id=201320140SB1156.

b. Bill H.2532, 188th Massachusetts General Court, https://malegislature.gov/Bills/188/House/H2532.

c. Bill S.1786, 189th Massachusetts General Court, https://malegislature.gov/Bills/189/Senate/S1786.

d. Bill S.1747, 189th Massachusetts General Court, https://malegislature.gov/Bills/189/Senate/S1747.

e. A08372, New York State Assembly 2015–2016 Session, http://assembly.state.ny.us/leg/?default_fld=&bn=A08372&term=2015&Summary=Y&Memo=Y&Text=Y.

f. H 7325, Rhode Island General Assembly, January 2016 Session, http://webserver.rilin.state.ri.us/BillText/BillText16/HouseText16/H7325.pdf.

g. H.506, Vermont General Assembly 2013–2014 Session. Paper copy on file with author.

h. H.412, Vermont General Assembly 2015–2016 Session. Paper copy on file with author.

i. H. 395, Vermont General Assembly 2015–2016 Session. Paper copy on file with author.

j. Initiative Measure No. 732, March 20, 2015, http://sos.wa.gov/_assets/elections/initiatives/FinalText_779.pdf.

Its members divided on the issue of whether to embrace the revenue-neutral model that did go to the voters, thereby weakening a core base of potential support for what would have been the first carbon tax adopted in the United States.

Opposition surfaced from industry groups such as the Association of Washington Business, Puget Sound Energy, Kaiser Aluminum, and Koch Industries. But it also emerged from the Sierra Club as well as carbon price enthusiasts like Governor Inslee, who worried that a revenue-neutral approach would in practice produce revenue-negativity. If tax revenues ultimately proved lower than tax cuts, as has been the case in British Columbia (as discussed in chapter 4), Washington's chronic fiscal problems would only be exacerbated. In the end, Bauman and his supporters never assembled a viable coalition to secure a ballot victory, despite operating in a state that has long viewed itself as a national leader on environmental protection and climate mitigation and has voted for every Democratic presidential candidate since 1988.

New Steps in Alberta and Ottawa

Carbon tax adoption did, however, occur elsewhere in the Americas in the mid-2010s. Chile and Mexico established carbon taxes, albeit with numerous exemptions and set at low rates that were comparable to other new taxes emerging in Asia and Africa.[14] A far more substantial tax was adopted in 2016 by a most unlikely source, the government of Alberta. As discussed in chapter 3, Alberta had long been synonymous with climate controversy—from aggressive oil sands development to pioneering use of a largely feckless carbon tax to try to deflect external criticism of its steadily increasing carbon emissions. Alberta continued in the early 2010s to defend its policies across Canada and in periodic visits by its leaders to the United States in search of support for Keystone XL Pipeline development.[15] This included defenses of its unique carbon pricing system and occasional proposals for incremental adjustments going forward.

Through the middle of 2015, Alberta had been governed continuously by Progressive Conservative Party leaders for more than four decades, with the most significant threats coming from maverick parties to its political right. But a collapse of oil prices and the Alberta economy created an opening for the center-left New Democratic Party to win a surprise victory in May 2015 that elevated Rachel Notley into the role of premier. Notley and the New Democrats campaigned heavily on the province's fiscal woes and the need for leadership transition from multigenerational control by one political party. They also argued that Alberta needed to rethink its long-standing intransigence on climate change and energy policy.

Indications were that they would pursue some form of carbon pricing if elected. But this took place alongside more pointed criticisms of the way in which Alberta Conservatives had collected and allocated royalty revenues from drilling for oil and gas. The New Democrats were not proposing any slowdown in drilling and, in fact, openly hoped for an increase in oil prices once they took control to increase production and boost the provincial economy. They also actively supported proposals to expand their ability to export oil through major pipeline development or expansion efforts to the south (Keystone XL), west (Kinder Morgan, Trans Mountain, and Northern Gateway), and the east (Energy East).

But the New Democrats also argued that Alberta Conservatives had been too timid in setting royalty rates and too prone to using revenues from extraction for immediate political purposes rather than to pursue long-term economic security and reduced fossil fuel dependence. Notley championed the idea of a major royalty review process in the province, one that might lead to larger revenues and could be linked to reforms in long-term invest-ment and allocation of those funds. This built on growing concerns that the Alberta Heritage Fund, established in the 1980s to create a long-term endowment once oil and gas extraction declined, had floundered in com-parison to other sovereign wealth fund models such as Norway and Alaska in terms of fiscal integrity.[16] As in the United States, a campaign to increase taxes on energy extraction can pay political dividends.

Notley and the New Democrats rode their fiscal reform package to a surprising victory and began a process of examining carbon pricing and royalty reform options. In May 2016, they adopted a carbon tax, labeled as a "carbon levy," with some striking similarities to British Columbia's sys-tem. The new Alberta tax was intended to replace the earlier carbon pricing mechanism; it was scheduled to begin at $20 per ton in 2017 and increase to $30 per ton the following year. The tax was passed strictly along party lines as a postelection mandate, with vehement opposition from Conservatives and far-right Wildrose Party representatives in the provincial legislature. Revenue allocation was to be divided between rebates to low- and middle-income families, investments in renewable energy, energy efficiency, and mass transit; a small business tax cut; and transition costs for coal plant phaseout. The New Democrats also continued to explore royalty reform, with plans to launch new approaches to revenue collection and investment in 2017.[17]

Opposition to the tax was palpable, evident in a 2016 rally at the provincial capital in Edmonton that featured chants of "lock her up." These borrowed directly from American campaign attacks against Hillary Clinton, applying them to Premier Notley for her role in carbon tax adoption. One legislator opposed to the tax characterized it as a form of "genocide" that would destroy life for many Albertans if sustained. This suggested a potentially rocky political road for the new carbon tax, particularly given the 2017 unification of the Progressive Conservative and Wildrose parties into the United Conservative party and the traditional conservative dominance of Alberta politics.

Nonetheless, Notley and the New Democrats claimed that these steps positioned Alberta for a less volatile fiscal future, one less dependent on current oil and gas prices while remaining a global player in fossil fuel production. "We don't control the policies of Saudi Arabia or Iran," she said after her election victory. "So we therefore have to manage the hand that we've been dealt, while working to diversify our economy and working to reduce our dependence on a single product and a single price."[18] The new Alberta leaders also argued that implementing a carbon tax alongside royalty reform could prepare the province for a less defensive and more credible role in national and international energy and climate policy deliberations. They linked proposed reductions in greenhouse gas emissions with improvements in increasingly severe air quality problems around the province and opportunities to expand development of renewable energy sources such as wind, along with continued pursuit of oil and natural gas.

The Notley Government further used its carbon tax adoption to position itself for effective negotiations in an evolving federal government strategy on climate that reflected a major federal leadership shift in October 2015. Five months after the Alberta election, Liberal Party leader Justin Trudeau defeated Conservative incumbent Stephen Harper to become prime minister. Trudeau campaigned in part on a more aggressive approach to climate change, although he did not move beyond broad endorsement of some form of carbon pricing in collaboration with ongoing provincial efforts. In office,

Trudeau and the Liberals launched a process of intergovernmental bargaining that resulted in the December 2016 announcement of a Pan-Canadian climate framework. This called for the creation of a carbon pricing system that would begin at $10 per ton (Canadian) in 2018 and rise gradually to $50 by 2022. However, each province and territory would be free to design its own tax or cap-and-trade system and would be able to keep all revenue generated within its borders, as long as its policy met federal standards.

This gave Alberta a chance to join forces with British Columbia and Quebec, claiming that they had already made commitments to significant carbon pricing systems that could be applied to meeting federal targets. These negotiations remained a work in progress during 2017, given a lack of unanimity among provincial and territorial leaders. Saskatchewan premier Brad Wall was particularly outspoken in his opposition, describing the Trudeau plan as "treachery" that would "siphon" $2.5 billion from the province. He instead called on the federal government to fund carbon capture technology with funds previously designated for international aid. Provinces with a carbon price, such as Alberta, retained a far easier path to compliance than those without one. This increased the potential political viability of the new Alberta carbon tax, if it could serve to satisfy a federal mandate, although it continued to face stiff opposition in the province.

The Washington and Alberta experiences demonstrated that it remained possible to advance carbon tax proposals that were more than symbolic, including adoption in the latter case. But they also underscored their fragility and the challenge of constructing a supportive coalition that could endure inevitable political challenges. Neither Washington nor Alberta triggered any bandwagon effect or policy diffusion to other states and provinces, although the flurry of new (albeit modest) carbon taxes in some other nations during the mid-2010s offered a new test of the idea's viability beyond North America. The Obama administration did take a modest administrative step toward a carbon tax in 2015 by announcing that a state could adopt one as an option for compliance with a new federal regulatory strategy designed to reduce electricity-sector emissions. However, that strategy clearly favored cap-and-trade over carbon taxes and all other carbon reduction policies, representing an important test of the political future for this alternative form of carbon pricing.

A Second Act for Cap-and-Trade?

Cap-and-trade has demonstrated greater capacity for initial political adoption than carbon taxes, due in part to its greater ability to conceal costs from public view. It has also experienced political roller coasters in many contexts, as was discussed in chapters 2 and 3, ranging from reversals of initial adoption in many states and provinces to prolonged implementation challenges in settings such as the European Union. In some contexts, such as the US Congress and the Australian Parliament, it is difficult to see any path toward legislative embrace of carbon cap-and-trade in the coming decade given its uneven political history and a strong and enduring base of political opposition.

Nonetheless, cap-and-trade continued to move forward in a number of ways after 2015, and has demonstrated some capacity for additional diffusion and expansion. China and South Korea have taken steps to launch their own versions of cap-and-trade, albeit with numerous questions concerning their scope, capacity to facilitate extensive trading, long-term management capacity, fit with other policies, and likely impact on emissions. Both conceptually and through formal linkages, these efforts might build on the relatively successful cap-and-trade systems that have been launched and sustained along both American coasts. The RGGI states initiated steps to review their progress to date and developed plans to pursue further emission reductions after reaching their 2020 statutory end point. They launched a series of regional hearings on the topic in 2016 and 2017, with leaders from most member states visible in their endorsement of further tightening of the emissions cap and sustained operation of the auction allowance system through 2030.

All of the RGGI states have examined cap-tightening options in concert with a number of other established climate policies that might be expanded or extended, including a number of established ones addressing renewable energy and energy efficiency. As in the prior decade, New York has loomed large in this regard, setting a 50 percent renewable energy target by 2030 through its portfolio standard and making major investments in large renewable projects, including offshore wind. Other states have also followed with new commitments to renewables and energy efficiency programs. Cap-and-trade was treated as an important member of this policy ensemble given its anticipated ability to further reduce electricity-sector emissions and generate revenues for future energy transition alongside these other policies. But there were no serious discussions in any RGGI state about abandoning or weakening these other policies to enable cap-and-trade to assume a more central role in driving emission reductions.

California also considered possible cap-and-trade expansion beyond the 2020 boundary established in the 2006 Global Warming Solutions Act, in concert with its new trading partner, Quebec. As discussed in chapter 6, California faced more implementation challenges than RGGI and remained in relatively earlier stages of implementation. Executive orders by governors Brown and Schwarzenegger set longer-term emission reduction targets, although many questions persisted about state ability to reach them in the absence of new legislation. The California Air Resources Board (CARB) began in 2012 to outline possible next steps for the state, including tightening of the state emissions cap and cap-and-trade program extension. These discussions intensified after significant declines in the auctioning price and volume of auction activity.

The California legislature began to actively explore possible next directions in 2017. This reflected some sentiment to substitute a carbon tax for cap-and-trade, given expanded Democratic margins in the legislature after 2016 elections and growing opposition to cap-and-trade from environmental justice groups. This opposition reflected enduring concerns about possible incentives under a trading program to sustain high-emission facilities in predominantly low-income and minority areas of the state. This was linked to concerns that insufficient auction revenue was being allocated to such communities. But there were enormous political hurdles involved in any shift toward a carbon tax, including vigorous support by Governor Brown and CARB for cap-and-trade.

As a result, California focused instead on a longer-term commitment to its existing cap-and-trade program, culminating in a set of new statutes adopted in July 2017. Governor Brown sought a two-thirds vote to thwart any future legal challenge against a carbon price and secured eight Republican cross-over votes to produce a supermajority despite some Democratic defections. This new-found coalition delivered preferential treatment for refineries, manufacturers, and farmers but provided a political base that extended the program through 2030 while delegating many core implementation issues to CARB and future legislatures. Brown was joined by his Republican predecessor, Schwarzenegger, in a signing ceremony and used the agreement to further signal his commitment to providing an alternative form of American political leadership to Donald Trump on carbon pricing.

Trading Ready and the Clean Power Plan

These state developments, however, appeared likely to be overshadowed by a far more ambitious federal plan to reduce electricity-sector emissions. This plan was designed to allow for the reintroduction of cap-and-trade on a potentially larger and even national scale. After the collapse of congressional negotiations in 2010, there was no serious federal legislative consideration of cap-and-trade. This was reflected in the fact that all of the new congressional proposals related to carbon pricing in subsequent years involved long-shot options involving carbon taxes. However, President Obama had frequently warned during 2009 and 2010 that any failure to produce a consequential climate protection statute would compel him to consider unilateral action. Testing his authority under the 1990 Clean Air Act Amendments, the president would focus on such steps as the primary climate policy thrust during the final six years of his presidency.

Climate change had already reached the American political agenda by 1990 when the air quality amendments were adopted. This arrival was reflected in a number of early state policy steps and a considerable number of congressional hearings on the issue.[19] George H. W. Bush pledged to bring "the White House effect to the greenhouse effect" if he were elected in 1988, attempting to keep pace with early policy initiatives in Europe. But both President Bush and Congress largely skirted the greenhouse gas issue in completing protracted negotiations on an expansion of air quality legislation that was first adopted in the 1960s and revised twice in the 1970s. This included adoption of the vaunted cap-and-trade system for sulfur dioxide emissions and numerous revisions of controls for conventional air contaminants.[20] But the 1990 Amendments did provide some flexibility for future presidents and their Environmental Protection Agency (EPA) appointees to consider expanding the legislation's reach to address additional contaminants demonstrated by science to pose environmental and public health threats. After a prolonged political and legal battle between climate-concerned states and the George W. Bush administration, the US Supreme Court issued a ruling in 2007 that paved the way for carbon dioxide emissions to be considered under the Clean Air Act umbrella.[21]

The Bush administration balked at this option, but the succeeding Obama administration embraced it. The new president began with a major agreement in 2009 to reduce carbon emissions from mobile sources such as cars and light trucks. This was linked with a massive plan to bail out American vehicle manufacturers at their nadir while transitioning them toward cleaner production in anticipation of strong consumer demand for such products. This agreement was achieved through a major expansion of regulatory authority that included a formal integration of air quality and fuel economy standards after decades of separate operation. It resulted in substantial tightening of these provisions over the next decade, including an extension through 2025 that was announced in the final days of the Obama presidency.

Tailpipe emission regulations served to discourage further consideration of a carbon pricing strategy for the transportation sector, such as increased taxation of gasoline and oil products. Instead, it sought to achieve emission reductions through the blunter instrument of performance standards through regulation. This would ultimately add costs to the price of new vehicles and might even deter their purchase in favor of operating existing vehicles for longer periods. But any such costs would not be specified in the sticker price and would thereby not produce the political backlash that would likely follow any significant fuel tax increases.

So regulation in the transportation sector emerged as a far safer option politically than pricing, allowing state and federal political advocates to claim credit for providing cleaner and more fuel-efficient vehicle options in the future without being linked to increasing driving costs. President Obama repeatedly claimed credit for this step throughout his presidency, as did gubernatorial champions from California and other coastal states, as discussed in chapter 6. All of the states that actively supported this agreement were quite concerned about climate change but also had little vehicle manufacturing activity within their borders. Quebec and British Columbia endorsed this approach, and ultimately Canada followed suit and harmonized standards across the national border.[22] This expansion of existing policy to include carbon emissions would be firmly established in a durable Clean Air Act program and would be difficult for any subsequent president to reverse.

The application of other provisions of the Clean Air Act to other sources of carbon followed different paths, however, drawing on distinct sections of the legislation. A focus on the electricity sector was linked to state implementation plans for controlling such emissions, whereby the federal government set reduction targets but generally gave states considerable latitude to propose their own path toward compliance. Federal implementation plans would only be imposed in cases of state performance failure, reflecting a long-standing pattern of engaged federal and state bargaining over the terms of regulation.

Retrofitting this process to add carbon emissions would dominate domestic climate policy during President Obama's second term, after he achieved reelection in a 2012 campaign that said relatively little about future climate protection goals and even less about carbon pricing. It would represent a far bigger legal and political stretch of the Clean Air Act than regulation of vehicle emissions. The administration unveiled a draft version of the Clean Power Plan in 2014, conducted a massive public outreach and hearing process, and then released a final rule in August 2015. The Clean Power Plan modified existing provisions of the Clean Air Act to require a 32 percent reduction of carbon emissions from the electricity sector from 2005 levels by 2030. It would require each state to develop its own implementation plan for achieving this final milestone as well as a series of interim targets. Each state received a tailored emissions reduction target based on a complex set of federal formulas and estimates. Many of the states that had taken early steps to reduce electricity-sector emissions were given the most modest targets for future reductions.[23]

The Clean Power Plan delegated the decisions to states on how to achieve these required reductions, although it defined the menu of options that could be used to achieve them. These included carbon taxes and expansion of renewable energy and energy efficiency. But the plan also offered states the option of a "trading ready" approach that they might pursue unilaterally or in concert with other states. This might also include formal partnership in some fashion with existing carbon trading programs such as RGGI and California. The EPA generally avoided the term "cap-and-trade" even though it was clearly supporting just such an approach. This became particularly clear after the issuance of the final agency rule on the Clean Power Plan that embraced cap-and-trade as the most promising option for states to consider. There were also agency suggestions that any subsequent federal implementation plan option imposed on recalcitrant states would likely require trading.

As states began to digest the particulars of the final rule, EPA Administrator Gina McCarthy and senior officials emphasized that this policy gave
states enormous flexibility in designing their own preferred approaches to
these emission reduction requirements. McCarthy noted in a press briefing
that this would allow states' "power plants (to) use interstate trading right
away. But they don't have to use our plan. They can cut carbon pollution in
any way that makes sense for them."[24] Nonetheless, it became increasingly
clear that EPA deemed trading the superior approach. A series of think tanks
and advocacy groups began to launch seminars and workshops and issue
reports to assist states in considering compliance options. Many encouraged pursuit of the trading-ready approach and a number of states began to
consider a possible new direction for cap-and-trade.[25]

Some states responded very enthusiastically to this turn of events, particularly those that had already adopted cap-and-trade. RGGI states and
California applauded many aspects of EPA's draft rule and actively sought
further modifications to prepare them for a smooth transition into the Clean
Power Plan. RGGI states argued early in Clean Power Plan development that
they represented a "proven model" that was "extremely cost-effective" and
"provides economic benefits." These claims were used to back their requests
for highly favorable treatment under any federal plan that might position
them for expansion with other state partners, as discussed in chapter 5.[26]

Most RGGI state officials responded to the final EPA plan with effusive
praise. "This is absolutely the best of cooperative federalism," observed
Colin O'Mara, Rhode Island's lead environmental official and a RGGI board
member. "We've heard from many states informally about how the cap is
set, how allowances are handled, all those kinds of questions. We anticipate
that as states start really thinking through what compliance mechanism
makes the most sense for them, they'll recognize that RGGI is completely
plug-and-play."[27] California officials countered with comparable assertions
on their possible role as national leaders and mentors for other states on
cap-and-trade.

The Limits of Executive Federalism

But not all public officials were terribly enthusiastic about the Clean Power
Plan. In Congress, Republican leaders denounced the plan as a far-reaching
expansion of executive branch power over states taken without legislative branch consultation much less approval. They threatened extended

hearings, deep cuts in EPA funding that might impair implementation, and efforts to overturn or constrain the plan through subsequent legislation. Kentucky Representative Ed Whitfield, chair of the House Subcommittee on Energy and Power, claimed that the agency had manipulated the Clean Air Act to establish "backdoor cap-and-trade," a stealth policy that would never have been approved by any recent Congress.

In statehouses, more than a dozen states immediately sought reversal of the Clean Power Plan through the courts, arguing that this federal action exceeded the reach of the 1990 legislation. Leaders of such coal-dependent states as Indiana, Kentucky, West Virginia, and Wyoming further argued that the final rule had concentrated particularly large emission reduction burdens on them in comparison to other states. The state-led assault on the plan achieved an unexpected early victory through the issuance of a stay by the Supreme Court in February 2016. As the case proceeded through lower courts, the stay prohibited EPA from implementing the Clean Power Plan and chilled any continuing negotiation between federal and state authorities on possible compliance options. The death of Associate Justice Antonin Scalia within days of the stay further complicated the path to a final resolution, given deadlock among the remaining justices and political delays in securing the confirmation of a successor.

All of this served to place much of the Clean Power Plan into a deep freeze, with its prospects most likely contingent on 2016 election results and future court interpretations. Donald Trump and his administration wasted little time in launching a reversal of the Clean Power Plan in early 2017 through a series of statements and regulatory steps that seemingly closed the door on any introduction of cap-and-trade via executive federalism. Most state discussion of exploring cap-and-trade as a possible route toward "trading ready" compliance under the Clean Power Plan ended in 2017 following this shift in presidential support.

A Second Look in Ontario

While US states were awaiting a verdict on the Clean Power Plan, one additional Canadian province moved closer to reversing its earlier withdrawal from cap-and-trade. Liberal Ontario's premier Kathleen Wynne expressed support for some form of carbon pricing following her 2013 election and supported formal exploration of a new cap-and-trade partnership in 2015. This was seen as politically preferable to a carbon tax and allowed Wynne to build on her collaborative relationship with Quebec's premier Philippe Couillard.[28] This also positioned the province for possible leverage under the new Trudeau government, enabling it to take credit for early adoption of a policy under the Pan-Canadian climate framework under negotiation. As Wynne noted in November 2015, "We are not looking to the federal government for some kind of unilateral imposition of a standardized regime across the country. What we are looking for is support for the initiatives that we are taking province by province and territory by territory."[29]

While the Trudeau federal plan remained a work in progress, Ontario continued to move forward and began unilateral trading in 2017 with the aim of reducing emissions 15 percent below 1990 levels by 2020. This uncertainty included questions on how closely Ontario would work with Quebec and California toward trading system linkage and whether the policy would withstand strong opposition from the Progressive Conservative party amid growing uncertainty about the political future of the Wynne government.

Despite these remaining questions and after more than a decade of off-and-on deliberations over possible adoption of a cap-and-trade plan, Ontario's signature achievement in greenhouse gas emissions reduction remained its use of the blunt instrument of regulation to phase out all of its coal-burning power plants over a decade beginning in the mid-2000s.[30] This was driven largely by air quality concerns but nonetheless produced a substantial reduction in electricity-sector emissions in the province, prompting some analysts to contend that this remained North America's single largest greenhouse gas reduction initiative through the end of 2015.[31] Several other provinces joined forces with the federal government to follow this lead in accelerating coal phaseout through "capital stock turnover" when facilities reached advanced age. This would require firms to meet an emission standard either by closing these plants or converting them to natural gas. This was projected to achieve a 33 percent reduction in Canadian electricity-sector emissions from 2005 levels by 2020, followed by deeper reductions in subsequent decades, all independent of provincial cap-and-trade engagement.

Extraction Taxes as a Source of Dedicated Revenue

North America's largest prices on carbon, measured in total revenue generated, continued to be imposed by state severance taxes and provincial royalty payments. The politics of taxing extraction remained fundamentally easier to navigate than adopting carbon taxes or cap-and-trade in the vast majority of states and provinces, which continued to square with global experience. In the United States, these taxes have proved remarkably popular and durable politically. This pattern continued between 2015 and 2017, when revenues declined due to plunges in oil and gas prices but tax rates and policies generally remained quite stable despite industry pressures to downsize them.[32] There may be considerable opportunities to expand these taxes in coming years.

Political scientist Kathryn Harrison has noted the irony that most policy analysts examining climate change have focused on the production, export, and use of carbon-intensive manufactured goods rather than the production and export of fossil fuels.[33] The same applies to innumerable carbon pricing proposals introduced in North America and around the world. Imposing a tax at or near the point of extraction works politically in many jurisdictions, despite routine threats by extraction industries to relocate in search of more favorable fiscal terrain. This includes a great many political systems that likely would only establish carbon taxes or cap-and-trade through centralized political pressure and after exhausting every possible form of legal and political resistance.

The arena of extraction taxes warrants closer scrutiny, particularly in cases where the generation of revenue for climate-relevant purposes is an important factor in policy adoption. This step is a hard swallow politically for those who oppose any form of fossil fuel extraction or use, as it acknowledges some continuing production of these fuels. However, few governments around the world have demonstrated any preparedness to completely eliminate the use of these fuels or their extraction if they exist within their boundaries. Indeed, as we have seen, those governments generally seen as the most virtuous on carbon taxes and cap-and-trade have generally imposed particularly soft fiscal terms on drilling and extraction within their boundaries, including California and British Columbia. As long as the bulk of that energy is consumed elsewhere and counts against the greenhouse gas emission ledgers of other jurisdictions, climate moral superpowers such as California offer far more generous extraction tax or royalty terms than such jurisdictions as Texas, North Dakota, Wyoming, or Alberta.

This aversion to careful study of severance taxes and related tools has also tended to overlook one important development in the allocation of revenues. As discussed previously, the bulk of severance tax funds collected by states continue to be used for immediate purposes not linked to environmental protection. However, several state governments have also begun to shift their allocation and investment of some of these revenues toward longer-term purposes, including formal trust funds to ensure extended stewardship.[34] This raises the question of whether this form of carbon price can also help underwrite future energy transition costs and even mitigate environmental damages from fossil fuel extraction and use.

Norway has received the greatest global notoriety in this regard, reflected in the evolving strategy of its heralded Government Pension Fund Global (GPEG), which is funded from royalties and taxes linked to its oil and gas production.[35] Norway has long won considerable praise for its relatively light environmental footprint from oil and gas extraction, including tight restrictions on flaring since the early 1970s and overall methane release rates during drilling that stand far below global and American norms. But it has also transitioned its investment away from fossil fuels and toward renewables in the past decade as part of an active pursuit nationally of energy alternatives and sustained emission reductions. As of 2017, Norway had accumulated more than $1 trillion in assets in this sovereign wealth fund and was widely recognized as a model of excellence in terms of fiscal stewardship, transparency, and deliberative planning for long-term use.[36] Norway continues to implement a mixture of carbon taxes and cap-and-trade across various sectors, retaining a hybrid carbon pricing approach while simultaneously attempting to sustain fossil fuel production alongside reduction of its carbon footprint. It has struggled, however, in recent decades, to achieve its emission reduction targets due in large part to its expanding energy production efforts.

North America has not exactly produced a "New Norway," but there are claimants to that title. Several states such as Colorado have begun to shift portions of their severance tax revenues toward energy transition and environmental reclamation in the past decade, after oil and gas drilling expanded markedly in the fracking era.[37] But North Dakota has taken this considerably further, literally building a severance tax and revenue allocation system that is closely modeled on the Norwegian example. This policy adoption followed careful study of energy-pricing jurisdictions in the United States, Canada, and Europe and extended cross-continental diplomacy between Bismarck and Oslo on numerous aspects of policy design.[38]

North Dakota has an extended history with boom and bust cycles and economic dependence on a single commodity during various periods. There were wild fluctuations in wheat prices over many decades, oil-related busts during the 1950s and 1960s, and a major collapse in coal production in the 1970s.[39] Elected officials from both political parties were mindful of this history and joined forces over several decades to develop a set of over-lapping extraction levies that collectively imposed an 11.5 percent tax on the extracted value of oil.[40] Neither the creation nor retention of these taxes were driven by concerns about climate change, and state political leaders vehemently opposed the Clean Power Plan, characterizing it as an illegal use of federal executive authority. Instead the severance taxes reflected a broad sense of public loss from the permanent extraction of a nonrenew-able natural resource and a desire to secure long-term revenue to navigate inevitable transitions in the economy.[41] This was also informed by North Dakota's prior experience in the 1970s with increasing coal severance tax rates and applying tax revenue to pioneering land reclamation efforts fol-lowing mining, despite fierce industry opposition.[42]

Rather than pour all of the oil tax funds into immediate expenditures, various legislatures and governors developed a series of fiscal strategies to reduce near-term dependence on volatile tax revenues. They also sought increasingly to set aside substantial funds for particular environmental gov-ernance tasks and longer-term challenges once energy production waned, much like Norway as it averted resource curse challenges. A series of statutes were adopted to create separate funds for some oil severance tax revenues for such purposes as water quality protection, outdoor heritage stewardship, and energy conservation, while also increasing allocations for existing environ-mentally focused funds. The state also approved "surge funds" to increase one-time allocations to cities heavily impacted by rapid development and population expansions accompanying the oil boom, as well as substantial funds in 2015 for transportation and public safety improvements.

In 2010, the state also concluded that it should borrow even more for-mally from the Norway model and set aside at least 30 percent of total sev-erance tax revenues each year into a constitutionally protected trust fund known as the North Dakota Legacy Fund through a ballot proposition. Offi-cials decided not to make any immediate allocation decisions, despite some political pressures to do so, instead allowing for investment of proceeds through the publicly held Retirement and Investment Office. The state constitution was also modified to allow for spending designated portions of the fund in future years to address longer-term state needs.

Proposals surfaced in 2015 and 2016 that included major investments in higher education to prepare for a post-oil economy and substantial development of public health and mental health services reflecting long-term needs that may be linked to shale energy development. The state also weighed the option of funding for expanded development of non-fossil-fuel energy, reflecting its abundant wind energy that neared 20 percent of total state electricity production in 2015. North Dakota officials would continue to honor their commitment to place new revenue into the Legacy Fund, even as fiscal pressures tightened, given the declines in oil and gas prices and related severance tax revenue. They decided in 2017 to use the first available interest revenue to bolster the general fund, although there was growing receptivity toward using future funds in 2019 and beyond to support carbon sequestration technology in power plants that use lignite from North Dakota mines.

Other states have eschewed a constitutional trust fund in favor of legislation that designates severance tax revenues for immediate use in addressing negative externalities linked to drilling. Colorado, for example, passed eight separate statutes between 2009 and 2014 that allocated revenues to special funds focused on water conservation, alternative energy, forest protection, and wildfire preparedness, as well as support for administrative units linked to drilling such as the Colorado Geological Survey and the Division of Reclamation, Mining, and Safety. Colorado has also continued to allocate substantial severance tax funds back to local governments.[43] Several other states have also experimented in recent years with use of severance tax or drilling fee revenues to address related environmental concerns.

Even in California, where political officials have routinely suggested over the past decade that they lead the United States and arguably the world in their commitment to climate protection and robust carbon pricing, these ideas have begun to surface. In the summer of 2013, a bipartisan delegation of officials decided that they needed to take a field trip to meet with counterparts in Bismarck, North Dakota, to learn about a different approach to energy taxation and revenue use. California political officials have repeatedly hosted gala events that invite other leaders to California to learn about their approach to carbon pricing and to consider a partnership of some sort. Ironically, this may have been the first time that California legislators left

Sacramento to learn insights from their colleagues in North Dakota. This did not, however, launch serious consideration in California of revisiting its modest severance tax regime or developing a trust fund to guide long-term investment and use of revenues.

Extending Extraction Taxes to Methane

North Dakota failed to match its fiscal foresight with careful oversight of expanding drilling operations. During a visit to the state, retired general David Petraeus compared the vast North Dakota oil patch to war zones he had experienced; platoons of sociologists, anthropologists, and journalists have also examined the many social and environmental challenges linked to unrestricted expansion of drilling.[44] Of particular significance from a greenhouse gas perspective was dismal management of methane emissions from drilling operations, in vivid contrast with North Dakota's energy icon, Norway, where less than 1 percent of methane is lost. This included direct venting of methane to the atmosphere or flaring at the point of release that converted it into carbon dioxide. In turn, the state experienced numerous leaks in exporting extracted oil through pipelines as well as rail and truck transport, including a number of incidents that created major farmland damage and raised further questions about state oversight capacity.

Flaring from North Dakota oil fields emerged as a national issue once satellite photos were published that demonstrated bright illumination from nighttime oil operations due to widespread flaring, although critics countered that these images exaggerated any actual effects. Nonetheless, the state continued to register monthly flaring rates that exceeded 30 percent between 2011 and 2014 until it finally responded in 2014 with a set of phased regulations requiring a gradual reduction of flaring to 10 percent by 2020. Republican Governor Jack Dalrymple explained in announcing the reforms that "in the past, we have been easy on companies, and at times given them exemptions, but we're not going to do that anymore."[45]

But oil producers responded very negatively to these steps and almost immediately reported difficulties in meeting the first stages of mandated release reductions. The state responded with delays in imposing these requirements, resulting in continued high flaring rates. Industry claimed that the state had not invested in the infrastructure to allow for more efficient transport of captured methane that might be sold for profit and used for public benefit. State officials questioned whether government was responsible to provide this system but did not want to further alienate a key industry with regulations that faced such opposition. So delay continued and an industry that routinely used such terms as "world class" to describe its performance struggled to find ways to curb widespread releases of a nonrenewable resource to the atmosphere, where it contributed to climate damage. One North Dakota rancher with a direct view of natural gas flaring from her porch explained that "it's been flaring for nearly a year. It's absolutely ridiculous to be so wasteful. They're flaring gas and using diesel to fuel the pumps—it's like something Homer Simpson would do."[46]

North Dakota methane flaring rates did begin to decline significantly in 2016 and early 2017. It was not clear how much this reflected industry investment to comply with regulation as opposed to changes in the location of drilling and the growing amount of natural gas being produced in advanced stages of tapping the Bakken shale formation. Consequently, industry may have an increasing incentive to capture rather than release North Dakota methane, given its increasing size and value. But the issue of methane remained a concern, one form of fossil fuel that continued to evade severance taxation while being lost permanently, particularly once flaring rates began to increase again during late 2017.

North Dakota was not alone in this regard among major production states, although many questions remained concerning the veracity of reported state and national methane release data. A growing set of rigorous studies in 2015 and 2016 attempted to increase the accuracy of measurements, but considerable methodological debate remained, including questions over the impacts of smaller drilling operations, exempt from many governmental reporting requirements, and older drilling sites.[47] This research considered venting and flaring at the point of drilling but also began to address growing concern about releases in later stages of natural gas development, such as transportation and storage, reflected in massive releases from the nation's fourth-largest natural gas storage facility located in a California neighborhood over a 112-day period in 2016.[48] These revelations raised serious questions as to the actual levels of methane as well as natural gas releases once all sources were fully considered.

States have generally been unwilling to impose regulatory requirements on methane that are used by such global leaders as Norway, the United Kingdom, and Alberta. These governments require approval of a detailed methane capture and use plan before drilling begins and are far less accommodating toward significant methane releases than most American states.[49] The Obama administration attempted to expand federal regulatory authority, particularly for drilling on federally held lands, although its jurisdiction was challenged aggressively through litigation and the Trump administration. President Obama also struck an aspirational agreement in 2016 with leaders from Canada and Mexico to attempt to achieve a 45 percent reduction in methane emissions. However, this agreement lacked clear paths toward realizing those cuts in any of the three nations, much less the full continent, and the American part of the bargain faced even more significant challenges under President Trump.

The few states that have attempted tighter regulatory controls on methane releases have continued to face stiff industry opposition. This includes Pennsylvania, where the state Department of Environmental Protection estimates that industry loses more than $60 million annually in salable energy through leaks. Pennsylvania may also have considerably greater methane releases than anticipated from the 500,000 to 750,000 abandoned oil and gas wells scattered across the state from prior decades and generations that are not routinely monitored for releases, producing an estimated 5 to 8 percent of its total methane emissions.[50] National estimates of the cost of usable gas that is wasted exceeds $300 million per year.[51]

One of the items missing from the methane debate has been why it should be exempt from any form of taxation, whether at the state or federal level or both. Virtually all states that extract oil, natural gas, or coal tax that energy, reflected in durable severance tax rates that are often set at high levels. But escaping methane largely sidesteps this system, even though its release reflects the permanent loss of a nonrenewable natural resource and an embarrassing failure of industry and governmental performance. A few legislators in North Dakota, California, and other states have explored royalty reforms to require oil production firms to compensate land owners on drill sites for lost methane, but these have withered in the face of industry opposition.[52]

The federal government has long deferred to states in levying severance taxes. Instead, it maintains a modest system of royalties and generous leasing fees that have largely remained unchanged for decades and are particularly generous for coal.[53] There are no constitutional restrictions on either the federal government or individual states to levy a tax on methane, including one linked to either the social cost of carbon (if flared) or the social cost of methane (if vented). Nor are there constitutional constraints on any states to expand existing severance tax regimes to include methane. Much the same applies internationally under royalty provisions that ignore methane releases.

If carbon pricing has a political future, it is difficult to imagine a case that is so straightforward and compelling for using a taxation method as applying it to methane. There have been significant advances in the technology to detect and measure methane releases from oil and gas production, including new sensors, infrared cameras, imaging spectrometers, and expanded satellite use, part of a larger set of potential reforms in environmental management and a shift toward continuous emissions monitoring.[54] This could be linked with growing efforts to intensify the regulatory oversight of highly decentralized fracking operations through use of advanced technology, where Colorado has set the pace among states but has had few followers to date.[55] Methane releases from solid waste landfills might also be taxed in this way, much as they can be used as cap-and-trade offsets under RGGI. Coal bed methane from mines where safety regulations already require some level of monitoring could also be addressed.[56] Taxes applied to fossil fuel production and landfills would cover at least 65 percent of estimated national methane releases, although they are likely not administratively viable for application to the net largest remaining methane source, livestock. Revenue in these cases could be linked with longer-term considerations, ranging from alternative energy development to reduction of other taxes.

Phasing Out Fossil Fuel Subsidies

Ignoring the wasteful loss of methane represents a significant way in which federal and state governments have continued to subsidize oil and gas production. Unlike government-run energy extraction efforts that are so common globally, the United States oversees private production but sets unusually accommodating terms of operation. For methane, that means looking the other way if industry concludes it is too inconvenient or costly for them to do anything other than flare or vent it into the atmosphere. That accommodating governmental stance toward fossil fuel energy production applies to other areas, including ongoing subsidies to underwrite the costs of extraction and generous terms for leasing government land for exploration and drilling.

Governments around the world find all sorts of ways to subsidize oil and gas production as well as its purchase by citizens, attempting to keep both producers and consumers content while shielding them from the costs of their actions. This is truly a global phenomenon: the International Monetary Fund estimates that fossil fuel subsidies cost approximately $500 billion annually and the International Energy Agency contends that their elimination would produce a 6 percent reduction in global greenhouse gas emissions by 2020.[57] The G-20 Summit in Pittsburgh in 2009 produced a pledge by the leaders of participating nations that they would phase out those subsidies to promote global security and reduce emissions, although they have largely been ignored.

This global phenomenon is also a North American phenomenon. A 2015 study by the Overseas Development Institute concluded that the United States was second only to Russia in terms of the size of its overall fossil fuel subsidies among G-20 nations but that both Canada and Mexico also maintained large subsidy programs. It concluded that total American federal tax breaks and preferential treatment on royalties and leases exceed $17 billion annually from the federal government and $3 billion annually from states.[58] Mexico has taken the biggest steps in the continent to address this issue, through significant reduction of subsidies to energy consumers as part of major energy policy reforms enacted during the 2010s.

American federal tax breaks include a pair of enduring provisions created during the respective presidencies of Woodrow Wilson and Calvin Coolidge to promote American production. One allows for the immediate expensing of most drilling costs aside from those linked to equipment that will be used permanently. This includes labor costs, drill site preparation, and even drilling chemicals, mud, and sand, providing a substantial federal tax benefit that has been sustained since its creation to stimulate production during World War I. Another was established a decade later in 1926 through allowance for percentage depletion for declining resource value as extraction proceeds. This compensates developers for their need to migrate to other sites over time as fossil fuels disappear permanently at specific wells or mines. It was clearly designed for a world without the greater production siting flexibility of the fracking era. Still, additional federal subsidies include, but are not limited to, a domestic production manufacturing deduction for oil and gas, an increased geological and geophysical expenditure amortization period for independent producers, and taxation of royalty payments at the rate of capital gains rather than income. There is also a large set of specialized provisions to promote coal production, including expensing of coal exploration and development costs. These were estimated to provide between $4 billion and $5 billion of industry support annually.[59]

These tax breaks are further supplemented with generous terms for fossil fuel extraction on federal lands. Unlike most states with production, the federal government does not impose a severance tax but rather a set of royalties that have their own exemptions. Rates have remained stable and relatively modest over many decades. Federal royalties for extraction of oil and natural gas on federal land are 12.5 percent. This falls below the rate of most state royalties for drilling on state land and is only one-half of the Texas royalty rate.[60] Extraction can often proceed on public lands with very accommodating terms and low costs, quite aside from light regulatory burdens on methane release and other environmental concerns. With coal, for example, the federal government does not determine which of its lands will be opened for competitive bidding to mine. Instead, coal extraction firms approach the federal government with their own preferred spots, regularly triggering a federal auction process whereby only one firm bids for the right to develop and routinely wins with a low bid price.[61] States continue to supplement these federal policies with an array of their own initiatives to attempt to maximize production within their own boundaries, including tight constraints on local government capacity to apply its own set of land-use policies that might restrict drilling.

Many of these policies were developed to maximize production and are sustained to promote American energy security amid assumed scarcity in supply and risk of declining production of domestically produced fossil fuels. But they seem anachronistic more than a decade into the shale era, when supply projections continue to soar and production has climbed and remains high even amid price declines. Indeed, the Trump administration has proclaimed the late 2010s the era of American "energy domination," seeing expanded development and export of American oil, gas, and coal as inevitable outgrowths of the country's newfound energy abundance and technological prowess.

It thus seems strange that such a fossil fuel powerhouse would continue to need major subsidies. Congress and President Obama agreed in 2016 to a plan to phase out federal subsidies for renewable energy through the

Production Tax Credit. A similar plan was proposed by the Obama administration for fossil fuel subsidies but struggled to get traction in Congress given industry opposition. Nonetheless, this type of transition could engage both federal and state governments in moving producers away from dependency on favorable governmental treatment, perhaps shifting toward a more market-based energy policy that puts all energy sources on a more level playing field, even if resistance to an actual carbon price remained.

Electricity Pricing from an Unlikely Source

Emerging experience from American states suggests not only that extraction taxes warrant expanded review but also that there may be unique variants of carbon pricing that offer some politically promising options. These do not fully adhere to the classic textbook definition of a carbon price through a tax or cap-and-trade. But they follow these general principles in fostering transition toward less carbon-intensive energy use in the electricity sector. Nearly twenty states have established some form of a price on commercial and residential electricity consumption, eschewing the term "tax" in favor of such framing options as "public benefit funds," "social benefit charges," "climate fees," or "renewable energy surcharges," among other labels. These tend to be set at relatively low rates, comparable to new carbon taxes being launched in Africa, Asia, and Latin America since 2015. These durable state policies generally use all revenues to support either transition to expanded use of renewable sources or heightened energy efficiency. Many impose their costs on all electricity consumed, not just that drawn from fossil fuels, and so are best described as a user fee or charge on energy consumption rather than a pure carbon tax. They may constitute a "stealth" form of carbon pricing, eschewing labels like "carbon" and "tax" while largely functioning as a low-profile carbon tax.[62]

Such policies are not confined to states that actively pursue climate mitigation. Indeed, Texas would seem highly unlikely to impose any kind of a carbon price, reflected in its vehement opposition through litigation to President Obama's Clean Power Plan and its support for cap-and-trade. But it has actively promoted cultivation of its substantial wind power capacity through a series of policies over the past decade and a half, including one that involves just such a pricing provision. The state has long recognized its considerable wind potential and periodically promoted research and development in the 1970s and 1980s.[63] Nonetheless, Texas continued to rely almost exclusively on coal, natural gas, and nuclear sources for power before 2000, and it consumes more electricity than any other state.

The adoption of a renewable portfolio standard in 1999 with support from Governor George W. Bush alongside a mixture of federal and state tax incentives helped jump-start the Texas wind industry. The state long since passed the renewable targets set in the 1999 standard and a 2005 expansion, reflecting increasingly favorable market forces for wind development. The Texas Panhandle and many other north-central and western counties have exceptional wind capacity, long ranked among the most robust spots in wind potential in North America. Texas pursued this policy for multiple reasons, including a desire to diversify its electricity sources, given its limited ability to import electricity, and to begin to address significant air quality problems that stemmed from heavy reliance on coal for electricity.[64]

One enduring challenge, however, was transferring that electricity from its remote point of generation to areas where population and industry were concentrated. Texas has great technical difficulty importing or exporting electricity beyond its borders given the structure of the North American electricity grid. It faced significant limits in developing expanded wind capacity without major investments in transmission and storage. In the late 2000s, the Texas Public Utility Commission (PUC) and the Electricity Reliability Coalition of Texas (ERCOT) began to work together to develop a plan for a major expansion of transmission capacity, as authorized in 2005 legislation that also increased the state's renewable target. This ultimately led to a plan that has added more than 3,600 miles of transmission lines and upgraded switches, terminals, and substations, capable of distributing 18,500 megawatts of power throughout the state.[65]

This so-called Competitive Renewable Energy Zone (CREZ) initiative was intended to link five separate renewable energy production regions in the north and west with more densely populated areas in the central, eastern, and southern areas of the state.[66] The idea was to give Texas a state-of-the-art energy transmission system to increase reliability and capacity to further promote development and use of wind power across the state. The goal was to do this on a large scale across multiple counties and regions as part of a coordinated effort, linked with broader Texas energy development goals.

This process has helped facilitate steady growth in renewable capacity, exceeding 12 percent of total Texas consumption in 2016 and reaching 23 percent in the first quarter of 2017. This has been combined with expanded use of natural gas from fracking to offset issues of intermittency in renewable energy production. In concert, wind and natural gas expansion have produced dramatic decreases in state reliance on coal as an electricity source.[67] It has resulted in significant greenhouse gas emission reductions from the Texas utility sector, with additional reductions anticipated as wind continues to expand and coal further declines. Indeed, by 2016, Texas had greater operational wind capacity than the next three states (Iowa, California, and Oklahoma) combined and was also seeing significant increases in other renewable sources such as solar.[68]

Much of this expansion would not have been possible without significant investment in transmission and infrastructure. Many states and governments around the world would like to have such a modernized system but have not figured out how to pay for it. In the Texas case, this issue was addressed through a unique electricity pricing mechanism via monthly surcharges added to electricity bills as approved by the state PUC. It was originally estimated that the state would need $4.9 billion to complete these upgrades but this ultimately increased to $6.9 billion. This increase was due in large part to costly adjustments to initial transmission line routes given opposition to siting from many land owners, adding more than 600 miles to the original project design.[69]

No other state has approached this level of investment in transmission capacity, although versions of this charge or fee system have facilitated expanded use of renewables in a number of other states.[70] Texas has also proved capable of developing infrastructure support in other areas of energy development and use, although it has struggled like North Dakota and other states in addressing methane releases. Variations on the Texas approach to pricing might prove useful in other jurisdictions that have a strong desire to move toward renewables but face sticker shock in considering how to facilitate transmission for a more decentralized form of energy generation.

Pricing Endures in the Midwest

Carbon pricing has also entered the American climate and energy policy system through efforts to measure the social cost of carbon in state utility planning decisions. Minnesota pioneered the idea of estimating the economic effects of the environmental damage associated with various forms of electricity generation through 1993 legislation. It has subsequently used these estimates in determining future capacity expansions. This was first applied to carbon dioxide in 1997 rulemaking, producing a range of values from $0.42 to $4.27 per ton, and had continued to provide an inflation-adjusted estimated externality value for carbon dioxide in the state utility planning process.

This approach received renewed impetus a decade later through the adoption of the Next Generation Energy Act in 2007. Although Minnesota would back away from its regional cap-and-trade commitment, as discussed in chapter 3, both Republican and Democratic governors have implemented these legislative provisions to accelerate transition from substantial state dependence on coal toward cleaner alternatives. These included a requirement that the Minnesota Public Utilities Commission estimate costs on future electricity generation to comply with anticipated state and federal carbon dioxide regulations, one that might complement the earlier provisions.

The carbon dioxide values were updated in 2017, given a range from $9.05 to $43.06 per ton, and Minnesota officials have continued to explore ways to link this process with some other elements of Minnesota's climate policy portfolio, including expanded renewable portfolio and energy efficiency standards and pursuit of improved regional transmission capacity to increase hydro power inputs from Manitoba. Minnesota also channeled its early engagement in preparing for trading-ready status under the Clean Power Plan to explore possible entrance into RGGI in 2017, along with Oregon and Virginia. In 2017, Colorado built on Minnesota's experience, developing its own measure of the social cost of carbon and applying it in its oversight of utility sector investments.

A Carbon Pricing Benediction

Carbon pricing in various forms will likely play some significant role in addressing climate change in the coming decades in the United States and beyond. But its political path forward has never been easy. This is not likely to change, given the politically challenging combination of imposing immediate costs for a popular and essential commodity while offering benefits that may well be deferred and difficult to comprehend. As we have seen, carbon pricing must surmount the challenging hurdle of initial political adoption. It must also find ways to sustain and expand political support over time and be implemented with transparency, credibility, and an ability to make adjustments as circumstances change. To date, this has been a far greater challenge than proponents anticipated or have generally been willing to acknowledge. This is reflected in the many political setbacks and managerial failures of carbon pricing to date, even after initial adoption appeared to promise a bright path forward.

But those challenges can increasingly be informed not just by past failure but also by successful cases and promising ones that are emerging. These offer significant lessons on policy design, political strategy, and public management challenges to guide the next generation of carbon pricing efforts. In North America alone, there are promising examples to build on from British Columbia to the American Northeast. California may overcome early challenges and blossom into a robust system that could expand provincial partnerships from Canada and also engage other states. The European ETS may shake off more than a decade of woes, demonstrating how policy durability may offer time and sustained political support to enable reform that allows it to finally evolve into an effective cap-and-trade system. More such examples may continue to emerge as carbon pricing experiments unfold in other jurisdictions, including new initiatives in Asia, Latin America, and Africa.

It remains, however, highly unlikely that cap-and-trade and carbon taxes will be the only ways in which the world attempts to reduce greenhouse gas emissions through policy. Politics will likely continue to favor other approaches, just as disciplines other than economics will be more inclined to advance considerations other than efficiency in defining the proper terms of policy. Policy scholar Ruth Greenspan Bell is correct to contend that any future approach to the climate problem will include a diverse array of approaches and disciplines, what she has characterized as a "silver buckshot" approach, rather than rely on a single policy or body of theory.[71] Climate change policy may well be evolving toward an all-hands-on-deck approach, raising potential challenges of reconciling different ideological and theoretical views as well as competing governing institutions and policies in seeking a viable path forward.

This may well involve far more than the usual suspects from the natural, physical, and social sciences. Such disciplines as theology and philosophy have begun to increasingly weigh in on climate change mitigation and adaptation and related questions in energy policy. This is raising important questions about the fairness of various policy approaches across economic classes and among nation states at different points of economic development, just as environmental justice advocates are challenging traditional thinking about cap-and-trade in California.[72] The most prominent example of these emerging questions was the 2015 publication of *Laudato Si': On Care for Our Common Home*, by Pope Francis. This encyclical letter built on statements from prior popes and ecumenical leaders. It lamented the profound risks posed by climate change and endorsed a bold societal response that is particularly attentive to the needs of the poor and marginalized. This 176-page call to action praised those governments around the world that were beginning to make significant progress in reducing their emissions.[73] *Laudato Si'* applauded previous instances in which the nations of the world joined forces to address environmental problems, including the Montreal ozone accords and treaties to reverse the dumping of hazardous wastes in poor nations and to confront illegal trade of endangered fauna and flora.[74] Pope Francis also called for an interdisciplinary, transparent, collaborative, and participatory dialogue for decision making.[75] He did not endorse or reject any particular set of policies but noted that these would need to guide a significant transition away from excessive consumption of fossil fuels.[76] Ultimately, he noted, "Reducing greenhouse gases requires honesty, courage and responsibility, above all on the part of those countries which are more powerful and pollute the most."[77]

Popes and global religious leaders frequently issue statements on a range of issues, including climate change. But few have received such attention or generally positive acclaim as this papal encyclical. Media coverage was extensive around the world and strikingly positive. Enthusiastic endorsements rolled in from governmental, corporate, and religious leaders from around the world. Public opinion surveys suggested that Francis's message was received favorably not just among Roman Catholics but also across all religious and demographic lines in the United States. Indeed, the pope's actions appeared to play a modest but significant role in post-publication surveys on American belief in the existence of climate change, although it may have served primarily over time primarily to embolden those already concerned about climate change.[78]

But the praise was not unanimous. In Congress, Republican Senators Marco Rubio and James Inhofe contended that the pope's broad call to climate action asked too much of nations such as the United States and would ultimately harm the American economy. But criticism was particularly withering from economists who felt that the pope failed to show proper reverence for carbon pricing as the exclusive policy vehicle needed to save the planet. The encyclical never discussed the particulars of carbon taxes or cap-and-trade. But it did question the possible abuse of "carbon credits," contending that their use could foster "a new form of speculation which would not help reduce the emission of polluting gases worldwide. This system seems to provide a quick and easy solution under the guise of a certain commitment to the environment, but in no way does it allow for the radical change which the present circumstances require. Rather, it may simply be a ploy which permits maintaining the excessive consumption of some countries and sectors."[79]

Economist Robert Stavins was quoted in the *New York Times* as finding the pope's statements "out of step with the thinking and the work of informed policy analysts around the world."[80] In a subsequent column, he affirmed the accuracy of that quote and added that Francis's "misleading and fundamentally misguided rhetoric is straight out of the playbook of the small set of socialist Latin American countries that are opposed to the world economic order, fearful of free markets, and have been utterly dismissive and uncooperative in the international climate negotiations."[81] In a separate essay, economist William Nordhaus lamented that "the discussion of solutions in *Laudato Si'* provides little guidance on effective policies."[82]

It is indeed likely that Francis's Jesuit training was thin on modern econometrics and randomized controlled trials. But it is an overreach to interpret the encyclical as either embracing or endorsing any particular policy, even if the critique of possible abuse of carbon credits clearly struck a raw nerve among economists. Indeed, the Vatican issued a statement amid the controversy saying the pope did not necessarily oppose carbon pricing, cap-and-trade, or carbon taxes. Months after the publication Pope Francis stood on the White House lawn and praised President Obama's climate effort, including the Clean Power Plan and its de facto embrace of cap-and-trade. The larger thrust of the encyclical was as a broad and moral call to action, one that made sure significant reductions took place and did not harm those among us who have the most modest resources.

But the dismissal of Pope Francis for having the audacity to raise these questions is revealing in the political divides among those who want to confront climate change. It also has ignored his real-life experience in Latin America and Europe that has clearly had a profound impact on how he views the world.[83] As a cardinal in his native Argentina, Jorge Bergoglio watched a dizzying set of credits and regulations emerge around governmental efforts to promote biofuels and biodiesel as alternatives to fossil fuels.[84] These were dismal failures economically and environmentally. Upon arriving in the Vatican, Pope Francis had to confront many problems and scandals in the church, including moral misconduct of clergy and fiscal mismanagement. One of these challenges involved writing off millions of dollars in Vatican losses for a failed carbon offset scheme. This reflected an effort by Pope Benedict to reduce Vatican greenhouse gas emissions by creating a Vatican Climate Forest in Hungary and attempting to recultivate more than 600 acres of trees.[85] It was linked to efforts to expand offset markets under the evolving European carbon emissions trading system. The trees, however, were never planted, leading to litigation and a major financial loss, whereby the Vatican was suckered into "buying vague promises instead of the reductions in greenhouse gases they expect[ed]."[86] In turn, Francis might face a political upheaval in his own neighborhood if he tried to remove a popular and long-standing tax exemption that encourages fossil fuel use. Vatican employees can purchase a wide range of items without sales tax within Vatican boundaries, including gasoline.

It is true that the Vatican theoretically could adopt a carbon tax or cap-and-trade within its boundaries. As a microstate of the European Union, it might also join in some fashion with the ETS. But it is unlikely that it would want to enter the ETS unless its chronic governance problems can be finally ironed out. Francis rules out no policy option in his encyclical or subsequent statements but returns repeatedly to themes of fairness in allocating any burdens or costs. He also clearly favors a simplified life style among the affluent, reflected in his own break from papal predecessors in his selection of housing and transportation, as a way to reduce his own carbon footprint. Given these realities, the ways in which revenue would be allocated from any carbon price might well loom large in how the pope would respond to any particular carbon pricing proposal, much as it does in most public opinion surveys, legislative chambers, and ballot propositions.

Pope Francis continued to advance his case in public addresses and visits with world leaders following the publication of his book, without probing the particulars of policy. One such opportunity occurred in the Vatican in May 2017, when President Trump paid a visit. This meeting occurred amid much expectation that the president would soon make a decision about whether to keep the United States active in the Paris climate accord, having already reversed some climate policy steps taken by his predecessor. The pope made climate protection a major focal point of the meeting and gave Trump an autographed copy of *Laudato Si'*.

Trump proclaimed the meeting a great success and lavished praise on the pope, a major shift after some testy exchanges during the 2016 campaign. He also promised to read the pope's encyclical. But the book and the meeting clearly failed to have much of an impact. Trump returned to Washington, DC, and quickly thereafter withdrew the United States from its Paris commitment in a defiant Rose Garden ceremony at which he denounced the accord as a bad deal for America.

Some observers feared that this might lead to an unraveling of the Paris agreement and perhaps even carbon pricing policy. But numerous world leaders quickly denounced the move, proclaiming their steadfast commitment to Paris and pursuit of ways to meet their reduction targets. A visible and vocal array of state and local government leaders affirmed similar commitments, even launching new coalitions to facilitate multi-jurisdictional partnerships. "We're Still In" emerged as a unifying theme in these efforts. The governor of California was welcomed by the president of China as a head of state in discussing possible next climate steps, while the US secretary of energy was simultaneously assigned to meet with a lower-level official.

So it may be dangerous to overstate the impact of Trump's dismissal of the pope's advice, just as it is misleading to read the encyclical as a manifesto for or against any particular policy to reduce greenhouse gas emissions, including carbon pricing. Economists are quite right in that, in theory, market-based instruments like cap-and-trade and carbon taxes could deliver significant emissions reductions in an efficient manner. Their ideas continue to warrant a close and serious review around the world. The challenge, however, remains taking those ideas and operationalizing them given the realities of politics and public management, and making them work over time as effectively in the real world as is assumed in theory by its proponents.

Pope Francis offers a gentle reminder that carbon pricing has been a mixed blessing based on evidence to date. Any future carbon pricing regime will need to learn lessons from past failures, draw on the experience from the most effective models developed thus far, and find ways to build political support to sustain operations over time. It is no longer sufficient to assume that a promising idea like carbon pricing can be readily translated into viable, durable, and effective public policies. That idea, as we have learned, is just the beginning.

Notes

Preface

1. For an excellent overview of this field that cuts across multiple policy areas, see Eric M. Patashnik, *Reforms at Risk: What Happens after Major Policy Changes Are Enacted* (Princeton, NJ: Princeton University Press, 2008). For an excellent analysis of the extended life-cycle of an environmental policy issue, see Christopher J. Bosso, *Pesticides and Politics: The Life Cycle of a Public Issue* (Pittsburgh: University of Pittsburgh Press, 1987). For early explorations of durability on issues of energy and environment, see Ann Carlson and Robert Fri, "Designing a Durable Energy Policy," *Daedalus* 142, no. 1 (2013): 119–128.

2. Barry G. Rabe, *Statehouse and Greenhouse: The Emerging Politics of American Climate Change Policy* (Washington, DC: Brookings Institution Press, 2004).

3. For a discussion of methodological considerations of process tracing in a "cross-time case study" of climate policy in Australia, see Erick Lachapelle and Jean-Philippe Gauvin, "Against the Odds: The Politics of Carbon Pricing in Australia" (presentation, 2012 Annual Meeting of the Canadian Political Science Association, Edmonton, AB, June 13–15, 2012).

4. Jeroen van der Heijden, "Selecting Cases and Inferential Types in Comparative Public Policy Research," in *Comparative Policy Studies: Conceptual and Methodological Challenges*, ed. Isabelle Engeli and Christine Rothmayr Allison (London: Palgrave, 2014), 35–56. For an extensive discussion of this issue applied to climate policy, see Brendan Boyd, "Learning to Address Climate Change: Collaboration, Policy Transfer, and Choosing Policy Instruments in Canadian Provinces" (PhD diss., University of Victoria, 2015), chap. 4.

5. Elaine B. Sharp, "The Dynamics of Issue Expansion: Cases from Disability Rights and Fetal Research Controversy," *Journal of Politics* 56, no. 4 (1994): 919–939, doi:10.2307/2132067. For a useful application of this approach to climate policy, see Brian J. Cook, "Arenas of Power in Climate Change Policymaking," *Policy Studies Journal* 38, no. 3 (2010): 465–486, doi:10.1111/j.1541-0072.2010.00370.x.

6. Barry G. Rabe, "Beyond Kyoto: Climate Change in Multilevel Governance Systems," *Governance* 20, no. 3 (2007): 423–444, doi:10.1111/j.1468-0491.2007.00365.x.

7. The United States never ratified Kyoto; Canada ratified the protocol but failed to implement it and ultimately withdrew.

Chapter 1

1. Frank R. Baumgartner and Bryan D. Jones, *Agendas and Instability in American Politics* (Chicago: University of Chicago Press, 1993), 83–102.

2. Julianna Pacheco, "Trends: Public Opinion on Smoking and Anti-Smoking Policies," *Public Opinion Quarterly* 75, no. 3 (2011): 576–592, doi:10.1093/poq/nfr031.

3. In 1776, Smith wrote in the *Wealth of Nations* that "sugar, rum, and tobacco are commodities which are nowhere necessities of life, which are become objects of almost universal consumption, and which are therefore extremely proper subjects of taxation." See Adam Smith, *An Inquiry into the Nature and Causes of the Wealth of Nations* (London: Methuen, 1904), bk. 5, chap. 3, 474–476.

4. Richard Kluger, *Ashes to Ashes: America's Hundred-Year Cigarette War, the Public Health, and the Unabashed Triumph of Philip Morris* (New York: Alfred A. Knopf, 1996); David Kessler, *A Question of Intent: A Great American Battle with a Deadly Industry* (New York: Public Affairs, 2002).

5. Paul Cairney, Donley T. Studlar, and Hadii M. Mamudu, *Global Tobacco Policy: Power, Policy, Governance and Transfer* (London: Palgrave Macmillan, 2012), chap. 5.

6. Centers for Disease Control and Prevention (CDC), *Best Practices for Comprehensive Tobacco Control Programs–2007* (Atlanta: US Department of Health and Human Services, Public Health Service, CDC, National Center for Chronic Disease Prevention and Health Promotion, Office on Smoking and Health, 2007); International Agency for Research on Cancer, *Effectiveness of Tax and Price Policies in Tobacco Control*, vol. 13 (Lyon, France: World Health Organization, 2009); Frank Choloupka, Kurt Straif, and Maria E. Leon, "Effectiveness of Tax Price Policies in Tobacco Control," *Tobacco Control* 20, no. 3 (2011): 235–238, doi:10.1136/tc.2010.039982; Kenneth J. Meier and Michael J. Licari, "The Effect of Cigarette Taxes on Cigarette Consumption, 1955 through 1994," *American Journal of Public Health* 87, no. 7 (1997): 1126–1130, doi:10.2105/AJPH.87.7.1126.

7. Samuel Preston, Andrew Stokes, Neil H. Mehta, and Bochen Cao, "Projecting the Effect of Changes in Smoking and Obesity on Future Life Expectancy in the United States," *Demography* 51, no. 1 (2014): 27–49, doi:10.1007/S13524-013-0246-9; Jeroen van Meijgaard and Jonathan E. Fielding, "Estimating Benefits of Past, Current, and Future Reductions in Smoking Rates Using a Comprehensive Model with Competing Causes of Death," *Preventing Chronic Disease* 9 (2012): 110295, doi: http://dx.doi.org

/10.5888/pcd9.110295; Kenneth E. Warner, "Effects of the Antismoking Campaign: An Update," *American Journal of Public Health* 79, no. 2 (1989): 144–152, doi:10.2105/AJPH.79.2.144.

8. Ruth E. Malone, ed., "The Tobacco Endgame," special issue, *Tobacco Control* 22, no. 1 (2013).

9. Cairney, Studlar, and Mamudu, *Global Tobacco Policy.*

10. The amount of carbon dioxide produced in burning a fossil fuel for energy reflects its carbon content. Various types of coal produce approximately double the amount of carbon dioxide released per unit of energy generated in comparison to natural gas. Oil falls roughly between these two fuels in this regard.

11. William Nordhaus, *A Question of Balance: Weighing the Options on Global Warming Policies* (New Haven, CT: Yale University Press, 2008), 26.

12. Michael J. Graetz, *The End of Energy: The Unmaking of America's Environment, Security, and Independence* (Cambridge, MA: MIT Press, 2011), 7.

13. William Nordhaus, interview by Richard Harris, "All Things Considered," *National Public Radio*, February 11, 2014; also quoted in Environment and Energy Publishing, "Economist Says Carbon Tax Is Tough but Crucial Climate Solution," *E&E News*, February 13, 2014, http://www.eenews.net/climatewire/stories/1059994518.

14. Benjamin Hulac, "Yale to Impose Carbon Tax on Itself, Led by the Man Who Helped Invent It," *E&E News*, April 22, 2015, http://www.eenews.net/stories/1060017204.

15. Barry G. Rabe, "Can Congress Govern the Climate?," in *Greenhouse Governance: Addressing Climate Change in America*, ed. Barry G. Rabe (Washington, DC: Brookings Institution Press, 2010), 260–285.

16. Peter Howard and Derek Sylvan, *Expert Consensus on the Economics of Climate Change* (New York: Institute for Public Integrity, 2015), http://policyintegrity.org/files/publications/ExpertConsensus Report.pdf; US Government Accountability Office (GAO), *Expert Opinion on the Economics of Policy Options to Address Climate Change* (Washington, DC: GAO, 2008), http://www.gao.gov/assets/280/275448.pdf; William D. Nordhaus, "Expert Opinion on Climatic Change," *American Scientist* 82, no. 1 (1994): 45–51; Phil Izzo, "Is It Time for a New Tax on Energy?," *Wall Street Journal*, February 9, 2007, http://www.wsj.com/articles/SB117086898234001121.

17. For a more extensive discussion of supporters, see Shi-Ling Hsu, *The Case for a Carbon Tax* (Washington, DC: Island Press, 2011), 182–186.

18. Arthur Cecil Pigou, *The Economics of Welfare* (London: Macmillan, 1920).

19. Ronald H. Coase, "The Problem of Social Cost," *Journal of Law and Economics* 3 (1960): 1–44, http://www2.econ.iastate.edu/classes/tsc220/hallam/Coase.pdf.

20. Thomas Crocker, "The Structuring of Atmospheric Pollution Control Systems," in *The Economics of Air Pollution*, ed. Harold Wolozin (New York: W. W. Norton, 1966), 61–86; John H. Dales, *Pollution, Property, and Prices: An Essay in Policy-Making and Economics* (Toronto: University of Toronto Press, 1968).

21. Dallas Burtraw, "The Institutional Blind Spot in Environmental Economics," *Daedalus* 142, no. 1 (Winter 2013): 113, doi:10.2139/ssrn.2145576.

22. Gary C. Bryner, *Blue Skies, Green Politics: The Clean Air Act of 1990 and Its Implementation* (Washington, DC: CQ Press, 1995); Richard E. Cohen, *Washington at Work: Back Rooms and Clean Air*, 2nd ed. (Boston: Allyn and Bacon, 1994); Timothy J. Conlan, Paul L. Posner, and David R. Beam, *Pathways of Power: The Dynamics of National Policymaking* (Washington, DC: Georgetown University Press, 2014).

23. Cap-and-trade has also been proposed as an option for future tobacco control policy, building on its successes in prior decades with taxation. Under this approach, known as the "sinking lid" rather than cap-and-trade, governments would gradually reduce the total supply of cigarettes authorized for sale, thereby reducing demand through added scarcity and, in all likelihood, further increasing prices beyond taxation. See George Thomson et al. "Ending Appreciable Tobacco Use in a Nation: Using a Sinking Lid on Supply," *Tobacco Control* 19, no. 5 (2010): 431–435, doi:10.1136/tc.2010.036681; Nick Wilson et al., "Potential Advantages and Disadvantages of an Endgame Strategy: A 'Sinking Lid' on Tobacco Supply," *Tobacco Control* 22, no. 1 (2013): 118–121, doi:10.1136/tobaccocontrol-2012-050791.

24. Nordhaus, *A Question of Balance*, 62.

25. Jonas Meckling, *Carbon Coalitions: Business, Climate Politics, and the Rise of Emissions Trading* (Cambridge, MA: MIT Press, 2011), 2.

26. Robert O. Keohane and David G. Victor, "The Regime Complex for Climate Change," *Perspectives on Politics* 9, no. 1 (March 2011): 17, doi:10.1017/S1537592710004068.

27. Matthew J. Hoffmann, *Climate Governance at the Crossroads: Experimenting with a Global Response after Kyoto* (New York: Oxford University Press, 2011).

28. Ted Gayer (remarks, Brookings Institution Conference on Energy and Climate Change 2010: Back to the Future, Washington, DC, May 18, 2010). Many other economists have chimed in on this issue, with generally similar conclusions. For example, as Peter Orszag said at a 2007 conference, "Although both types of incentive-based approaches are significantly more efficient than command-and-control policies, studies typically find that over the next several decades, a well-designed and appropriately set tax would yield higher net benefits than a corresponding cap-and-trade approach." See Peter Orszag, "Issues in Climate Change" (lecture, Congressional Budget Office Director's Conference on Climate Change, Washington, DC, November 16, 2007).

29. Jenny Sumner, Lori Bird, and Hillary Smith, *Carbon Taxes: A Review of Experience and Policy Design Considerations* (Golden, CO: National Renewable Energy Laboratory, 2009), http://www.nrel.gov/docs/fy10osti/47312.pdf; Partnership for Market Readiness, *Carbon Tax Guide: A Handbook for Policy Makers* (Washington, DC: World Bank, 2017).

30. There are enormous variations across efforts by either government institutions or individual economists to produce an estimate of the social cost of carbon. For one American interpretation, see US Government Interagency Working Group on Social Cost of Carbon, *Technical Support Document: Technical Update of the Social Cost of Carbon for Regulatory Impact Analysis Under Executive Order 12866* (Washington, DC: US Government, 2013); William D. Nordhaus, *The Climate Casino: Risk, Uncertainty, and Economics for a Warming World* (New Haven, CT: Yale University Press, 2013).

31. Barry G. Rabe, "Racing to the Top, the Bottom, or the Middle of the Pack? The Evolving State Government Role in Environmental Protection," in *Environmental Policy: New Directions for the Twenty-First Century*, 10th ed., ed. Norman J. Vig and Michael E. Kraft (Washington, DC: Sage, 2019), chap. 2.

32. Hsu, *The Case for a Carbon Tax*, 81.

33. Barry G. Rabe and Rachel Hampton, "Taxing Fracking: The Politics of State Severance Taxes in the Shale Era," *Review of Policy Research* 32, no. 4 (2015): 389–412, doi:10.1111/ropr.12127.

34. Hsu, *The Case for a Carbon Tax,* chap. 8.

35. Sumner, Bird, and Smith, *Carbon Taxes: A Review of Experience and Policy Design Considerations*; Ian Perry, Adele Morris, and Robertson C. Williams III, eds., *Implementing a US Carbon Tax: Challenges and Debates* (New York: Routledge, 2015).

36. Hylton v. United States, 3 US 171 (1796); I am grateful to Reuven Avi-Yonah and David Ullmann for introducing me to this case and providing insights about its broader impact.

37. The most notable of these cases, known as the Heisler trilogy, was the 1981 decision in Commonwealth Edison v. Montana, which dismissed Commerce Clause challenges to Montana's decision to quadruple the rates of its long-standing tax on coal mining. See Carol Powers, "State Taxation of Energy Resources: Affirmation of *Commonwealth Edison Company v. Montana*," *Boston College Environmental Law Review* 10, no. 2 (1982): 503–564, http://lawdigitalcommons.bc.edu/ealr/vol10/iss2/5; Barry G. Rabe and Rachel L. Hampton, "Trusting in the Future: The Re-emergence of State Trust Funds in the Shale Era," *Energy Research and Social Science* (2016), 1–11, http://dx.doi.org/10.1016/j.erss.2016.06.011.

38. Roy Bahl and Musharraf Cyan, "Tax Assignment: Does the Practice Match the Theory?," *Environment and Planning C: Government and Policy* 29, no. 2 (2011): 264–280, doi:10.1068/c1045r.

39. Iowa was the first state to adopt a cigarette tax in 1921, followed by South Carolina, South Dakota, and Utah in 1923. Oregon adopted the first gasoline excise tax in 1919, followed in that year by Colorado, New Mexico, and North Dakota.

40. Charles R. Shipan and Craig Volden, "Bottom-Up Federalism: The Diffusion of Antismoking Policies from U.S. Cities to States," *American Journal of Political Science* 50, no. 4 (2006): 825–843, https://www.unc.edu/~fbaum/teaching/articles/AJPS -2006-smoking.pdf; Bruce A. Desmaris, Jeffrey J. Harden, and Frederick J. Boehnke, "Persistent Policy Pathways: Inferring Diffusion Networks in the American States," *American Political Science Review* 109, no. 2 (2015): 392–406, http://myweb.uiowa .edu/fboehmke/shambaugh2014/papers/desmarais_etal_2014.pdf.

41. Paul L. Posner, "The Politics of Vertical Diffusion: The States and Climate Change," in *Greenhouse Governance: Addressing Climate Change in America*, ed. Barry G. Rabe (Washington, DC: Brookings Institution Press, 2010), 73–98.

Chapter 2

1. As Gregory Mankiw has lamented, carbon pricing and other ideas advanced by large numbers of economists often crash against these realities. He noted that in such cases "where economists and mere muggles don't see eye-to-eye, you shouldn't be surprised to hear that I am quick to side with my fellow economists....I feel comfortable with the conclusion that, regarding these issues, economists are right and the general public is ill informed." Mankiw, "Smart Taxes: An Open Invitation to Join the Pigou Club" (paper, Annual Meeting of the Eastern Economic Association, March 8, 2008). As political scientist James Meadowcroft has noted, however, "We don't do the most efficient policy anywhere because of the mess of politics. Think of education. Think of prisons. Climate change is the same way." (Meadowcroft remarks, Canada Climate Choices Conference, Wilfrid Laurier University, Waterloo, ON, February 18–20, 2016).

2. For one attempt to compare the economic scope of these industries, see William D. Nordhaus, *The Climate Casino: Risk, Uncertainty, and Economics for a Warming World* (New Haven, CT: Yale University Press, 2013), 323.

3. Daniel C. Vock, "States, Not Just Feds, Struggle to Keep Gas Tax Revenue Flowing," *Governing*, May 18, 2015, http://www.governing.com/topics/transportation -infrastructure/gov-gas-tax-revenue-states-inflation.html.

4. Barry G. Rabe and Christopher P. Borick, "Carbon Taxation and Policy Labeling: Experience from American States and Canadian Provinces," *Review of Policy Research* 29, no. 3 (2012): 358–382, doi:10.1111/j.1541-1338.2012.00564.x.

5. Alexander Ochs, *Overcoming the Lethargy: Climate Change, Energy Security, and the Case for a Third Industrial Revolution* (Washington, DC: American Institute for Contemporary German Studies, 2008), 38.

6. For an excellent summary of why climate change constitutes a unique super-wicked problem, see Kelly Levin et al., "Overcoming the Tragedy of Super-Wicked Problems: Constraining Our Future Selves to Ameliorate Global Climate Change," *Policy Sciences* 45, no. 2 (2012): 123–152, doi:10.1007/s11077-012-9151-0. Also see Hoffmann, *Climate Governance,* 11.

7. Stephen Ansolabehere and David Konisky, *Cheap and Clean: How Americans Think about Energy in the Age of Global Warming* (Cambridge, MA: MIT Press, 2014), 77.

8. For a more detailed examination of this concept and application to multiple cases, see Leslie A. Pal and R. Kent Weaver, eds., *The Government Taketh Away: The Politics of Pain in the United States and Canada* (Washington, DC: Georgetown University Press, 2003).

9. Daniel Kahneman, *Thinking, Fast and Slow* (New York: Farrar, Straus and Giroux, 2011).

10. Martha Derthick, *Policymaking for Social Security* (Washington, DC: Brookings Institution Press, 1979).

11. Eisenhower long supported the creation of an Interstate Highway System with a sustainable funding source. This was influenced by his disastrous experience trying to move convoys of military vehicles from coast to coast after World War I and his observations of high transport mobility in Germany during World War II. His earlier interest in tolls and bonds eventually shifted toward a federal excise tax on gasoline and tires. As historian Raymond A. Mohl has noted, "the big dispute was over financing the system." See Mohl, "Ike and the Interstates: Creeping toward Comprehensive Planning," *Journal of Planning History* 2, no. 3 (2003): 244, doi:10.1177/1538513203256244; Henry Petroski, *The Road Taken: The History and Future of America's Infrastructure* (New York: Bloomsbury, 2016), chap. 4.

12. Matto Mildenberger, "Fiddling while the World Burns: The Double Representation of Carbon Polluters in Comparative Climate Policy" (PhD diss., Yale University, 2015).

13. Sixteen states impose some barrier beyond majority votes for creation of new taxes or increases in tax rates, most notably California and its requirement for two-thirds majorities in such cases. Nationally, US Senate rules create a de facto three-fifths barrier to such an approval.

14. Judith Layzer, *Open for Business: Conservatives' Opposition to Environmental Regulation* (Cambridge, MA: MIT Press, 2012).

15. Ansolabehere and Konisky, *Cheap and Clean,* 161–162.

16. The National Surveys on Energy and Environment is a partnership between the Muhlenberg Institute of Public Opinion at Muhlenberg College and the Center for Local, State, and Urban Policy at the Gerald Ford School of Public Policy at the

University of Michigan. NSEE data is posted for public use through the Institute of Social Research at the University of Michigan and the Inter-university Consortium for Political and Social Research (ICPSR) and can be found at http://closup.umich .edu/national-surveys-on-energy-and-environment/nsee-data-access.php.

17. Christopher P. Borick, Barry G. Rabe, and Sarah B. Mills, "Acceptance of Global Warming among Americans Reaches Highest Level Since 2008," *Issues in Energy and Environmental Policy*, no. 25 (2015): 1–8, http://closup.umich.edu/files/ieep-nsee -2015-fall-climate-belief.pdf.

18. Erick Lachapelle, Christopher P. Borick, and Barry G. Rabe, "Public Attitudes toward Climate Science and Climate Policy in Federal Systems: Canada and the United States Compared," *Review of Policy Research* 29, no. 3 (2012): 334–357, doi:10.1111/j.1541-1338.2012.00563.x.

19. Barry G. Rabe and Christopher P. Borick, "The Decline of Public Support for State Climate Change Policies: 2008–2013," *Issues in Energy and Environmental Policy*, no. 7 (2014): 1–10, http://closup.umich.edu/files/ieep-nsee-2013-fall-state-policy -options.pdf.

20. Iowa was the first state to adopt an RPS, followed by Minnesota in 1994 and Arizona in 1996.

21. For an overview of the political evolution of RPS policies, see Leah C. Stokes, "Power Politics: Energy Policy Change in the U.S. States" (PhD diss., Massachusetts Institute of Technology, 2015).

22. For an earlier analysis of RPS political development, see Barry G. Rabe, "States on Steroids: The Intergovernmental Odyssey of American Climate Policy," *Review of Policy Research* 25, no. 2 (2008): 105–128, doi:10.1111/j.1541-1338.2007.00314.x.

23. Most carbon pricing policies around the world have similar sets of exemptions and special considerations, although that is addressed in greater detail in later chapters.

24. Katerina Dobesova, Jay Apt, and Lester B. Lave, "Are Renewables Portfolio Standards Cost-Effective Emission Abatement Policy?," *Environmental Science & Technology* 39, no. 22 (2005): 8578–8583, doi:10.1021/es048024j.

25. James Bushnell, Carla Peterman, and Catherine Wolfram, "California's Greenhouse Gas Policies: Local Solutions to a Global Problem?," University of California Energy Institute, Center for the Study of Energy Markets (April 2007), 3, faculty.haas .berkeley.edu/wolfram/papers/local_global_040207_wtables.pdf.

26. Carolyn Fischer and Richard C. Newell, "Environmental and Technology Policies for Climate Mitigation," *Journal of Environmental Economics and Management* 55 (2008): 142–162, doi:10.1016/j.jeem.2007.11.001. For thoughtful overviews of early results of RPS implementation on carbon emissions, see Don Grant, Kelly Bergstrand, and Katrina Running, "Effectiveness of US State Policies in Reducing CO_2 Emissions

from Power Plants," *Nature Climate Change* 4 (2014): 977–982, doi:10.1038/ncli-mate2385; Samantha Sekar and Brent Sohngen, *The Effects of Renewable Portfolio Standards on Carbon Intensity in the United States* (Washington, DC: Resources for the Future, 2014), http://www.rff.org/files/sharepoint/WorkImages/Download/RFF-DP-14-10.pdf.

27. On the framing of portfolio standards to build localized political support, see Leah C. Stokes and Christopher Warshaw, "Renewable Energy Policy Design and Framing Influence Public Support in the United States," *Nature Energy* 2, no. 17107 (June 2017), doi:10.1038/nenergy.2017.107.

28. On alternative ways to frame such policies at the state level, see Barry G. Rabe, *Statehouse and Greenhouse: The Emerging Politics of American Climate Change Policy* (Washington, DC: Brookings Institution Press, 2004), chap. 1.

29. Ann E. Carlson, "Iterative Federalism and Climate Change," *Northwestern University Law Review* 103, no. 3 (2009): 1097–1160.

30. Barry G. Rabe, "Leveraged Federalism and the Clean Air Act: The Case of Vehicle Emissions Control," in *The Future of U.S. Energy Policy: Lessons from the Clean Air Act*, ed. Ann E. Carlson and Dallas Burtraw (Cambridge: Cambridge University Press, forthcoming).

31. In 2017, economist Michael Greenstone and legal scholar Cass Sunstein published a report endorsing a transition from vehicle performance standards to a cap-and-trade system for cars and trucks. It received considerable media attention but was largely dismissed as a symbolic statement and never received a serious political review. Michael Greenstone, Cass Sunstein, and Sam Ori, *The Next Generation of Transportation Policy* (Washington, DC: Brookings Institution, 2017), https://www.brookings.edu/wp-content/uploads/2017/03/es_20170327_next_generation_transportation_policy_pp.pdf.

32. Erick Lachapelle, Christopher Borick, and Barry G. Rabe, "Public Opinion on Climate Change and Support for Various Policy Instruments in Canada and the US: Findings from a Comparative 2013 Poll," *Issues in Energy and Environmental Policy*, no. 11 (2014): 1–21, http://closup.umich.edu /files/ieep-nsee-2013-fall-canada-us.pdf.

33. On the evolving role of foundations in driving policy reforms, see Megan E. Tompkins-Stange, *Policy Patrons* (Cambridge, MA: Harvard University Press, 2017).

34. One major study of multiple state climate policy options concluded that "the two most widely implemented policies examined here—climate action plans and GHG [greenhouse gas] registry/reporting—have no effect. This may be because some climate action plans are just one-off bureaucratic reports and the emissions data reported to some GHG registries are not always sufficiently publicized to mobilize local pressure on polluting plants." See Grant, Bergstrand, and Running, "Effectiveness of US State Policies in Reducing CO_2 Emissions from Power Plants." Also see

Serena E. Alexander, *From Planning to Action: An Evaluation of State Level Climate Action Plans* (PhD diss., Cleveland State University, College of Urban Affairs, 2016); Zhenghong Tang et al. "Moving from Agenda to Action: Evaluating Local Climate Change Action Plans," *Journal of Environmental Planning and Management* 53, no. 1 (January 2010): 41–62. On the question of climate action pledges and memberships in organizations with other jurisdictions, see Rachel M. Krause, "Symbolic or Substantive Policy? Measuring the Extent of Local Commitment to Climate Protection," *Environment and Planning C: Government and Policy* 29 (2011): 46–62.

35. Len Coad, *Greenhouse Gas Mitigation in Canada* (Ottawa: Conference Board of Canada, 2011); Canada's Ecofiscal Commission, *The Way Forward: A Practical Approach to Reducing Canada's Greenhouse Gas Emissions* (Montreal: Canada's Ecofiscal Commission, 2015), 2–9, http://ecofiscal.ca/wp-content/uploads/2015/04/Ecofiscal-Commission -Report-The-Way-Forward-April-2015.pdf.

36. Jacquelyn Pless, "Oil and Gas Severance Taxes: States Work to Alleviate Fiscal Pressures amid the Natural Gas Boom," *National Conference of State Legislatures*, accessed April 28, 2016, http://www.ncsl.org/research/energy/oil-and-gas-severance -taxes.aspx; Cassarah Brown, *State Revenues and the Natural Gas Boom: An Assessment of State Oil and Gas Production Taxes* (Denver: National Conference of State Legislatures, 2013), http://www.ncsl.org/documents/energy/pdf_ version_final.pdf.

37. Rachel L. Hampton and Barry G. Rabe, "Leaving Money on the Table: Pennsylvania Exceptionalism in Resisting Energy Severance Taxes," *Commonwealth* 17, no. 1 (2017): 4–32, http://dx.doi.org/10.15367/com.v19i1.131. California does not impose a statewide tax but has adopted legislation that allows counties to do so. This is discussed further in Chapter Six.

38. Barry G. Rabe and Rachel Hampton, "Taxing Fracking: The Politics of State Severance Taxes in the Shale Era," *Review of Policy Research* 32, no. 4 (2015): 389–412, doi:10.1111/ropr.12127.

39. Royalties are more common than severance taxes beyond the United States, reflecting broader experience with public control of the values associated with mineral wealth in most nations. Severance taxes apply to privately held land and related control of mineral wealth in most states, with the main exception being government-held land. For an excellent overview in the case of oil resources, see Michael L. Ross, *The Oil Curse: How Petroleum Wealth Shapes the Development of Nations* (Princeton, NJ: Princeton University Press, 2012).

40. Walter Hellerstein, "Political Perspectives on State and Local Taxation of Natural Resources," *Georgia Law Review* 19, no. 1 (Fall 1984): 31–69, http://digitalcommons .law.uga.edu/cgi/viewcontent.cgi?article=1127&context=fac_artchop.

41. Texas has regularly ranked among the top two states in oil and natural gas production on an annual basis during the 2010s. California has regularly ranked among

the top five states in oil production during this period. Hampton and Rabe, "Leaving Money on the Table," 8.

42. Carol Powers, "State Taxation of Energy Resources: Affirmation of *Commonwealth Edison Company v. Montana*," *Boston College Environmental Law Review* 10, no. 2 (1982): 503–564, http://lawdigitalcommons.bc.edu/ealr/vol10/iss2/5.

43. Political scientist Kathryn Harrison has rightly noted that this area is rich with important political science and policy questions related to climate change and carbon pricing. See Kathryn Harrison, "International Carbon Trade and Domestic Climate Politics," *Global Environmental Politics* 15, no. 3 (2015): 27–47. However, the vast majority of published scholarship on severance taxes and related issues draws almost exclusively from economics and debates the efficiency of these taxes in terms of overall energy production and remediation of damage from extraction rather than political feasibility or links with carbon emissions. Severance taxation is discussed in greater depth in chapter 5.

Chapter 3

1. Roger Karapin, *Political Opportunities for Climate Policy: California, New York, and the Federal Government* (New York: Cambridge University Press, 2016); George E. Pataki and Thomas J. Vilsack, *Confronting Climate Change: A Strategy for U.S. Foreign Policy* (New York: Council on Foreign Relations, 2008), http://i.cfr.org/content /publications/attachments/Climate_ChangeTF.pdf.

2. The polar bear issue was featured on the cover of a major report and remained the primary focal point used to gain public support for climate engagement in the province. See *Kyoto and Beyond: A Plan of Action to Meet and Exceed Manitoba's Kyoto Targets,* (Winnipeg: Manitoba Conservation Climate Change Branch, 2002), 2.

3. Timothy Sale (Minister of Manitoba Energy, Science, and Technology, Winnipeg), in discussion with the author, June 4, 2004.

4. If these early steps were taken, argued the authors, it would be possible to "take advantage of the province's central location, low-emissions economy and history as a trading hub to make Winnipeg a center for trading within Canada's domestic emissions trading system." International Institute for Sustainable Development (IISD) Task Force on Emissions Trading and the Manitoba Economy, *Realizing Opportunities: Emissions Trading in Manitoba* (Winnipeg: IISD, 2004), 9, http://www.iisd .org/sites/default/files/publications/climate_realizing_opportunities.pdf.

5. For useful background on CCX, see Matthew J. Hoffmann, *Climate Governance at the Crossroads: Experimenting with a Global Response after Kyoto* (New York: Oxford University Press, 2011), 95–100; Chicago Climate Exchange Inc. and the Province of Manitoba, *Letter of Understanding* (February 3, 2004), http://digitalcollection.gov.mb .ca/awweb/pdfopener?smd=1&did=11744&md=1.

6. Jane Gray, "Manitoba: Towards a Climate Friendly Economy" (presentation, Conference of the Reducers, Toronto, ON, May 3–4, 2003); Jane Gray (senior policy analyst, Government of Manitoba), in discussion with the author, June 3, 2004.

7. "Doer Teams Up with Gubernator over Climate Change," *CBC News* (Manitoba: CBC), September 27, 2006, http://www.cbc.ca/news/canada/manitoba/doer-teams -up-with-gubernator-over-climate-change-1.627954. Doer was hardly alone among Canadian premiers (and American governors) seeking a personal audience and photo opportunity with Schwarzenegger. Brendan Boyd concluded that premiers found this "too tantalizing to pass up as it brought a new level of attention and cache to their leadership and instant credibility to their efforts." See Brendan Boyd, "Learning to Address Climate Change: Collaboration, Policy Transfer, and Choosing Policy Instruments in Canadian Provinces" (PhD dissertation, University of Victoria, 2015), 1; Brendan Boyd, "Working Together on Climate Change: Policy Transfer and Convergence in Four Canadian Provinces," *Publius* 47, no. 4 (October 2017): 546–571, https://academic.oup.com/publius/article/3798730/Working-Together-on -Climate-Change-Policy-Transfer?.

8. Midwestern Energy Security and Climate Stewardship Summit, Midwestern Governors' Association, *Midwestern Greenhouse Gas Accord.* November 15, 2007. Paper copy on file with author.

9. "Governor Blagojevich Signs Midwestern Regional Greenhouse Gas Reduction Accord," Office of the Governor, State of Illinois (news release, November 15, 2007), http://www3.illinois.gov/PressReleases/ShowPressRelease.cfm?SubjectID=1&RecNum =6424.

10. Viveca Novak, "Pawlenty's Political Climate Change," *FactCheck.org*, January 20, 2011, http://www.factcheck.org/2011/01/pawlentys-political-climate-change/.

11. See Matthew Bramley, P. J. Partington, and Dave Sawyer, *Linking National Cap-and-Trade Systems in North America* (Drayton Valley, AB: Pembina Institute; Winnipeg: International Institute for Sustainable Development, 2009), https://www.iisd.org /sites/default/files/publications/linking_nat_cap_north_america.pdf; Three-Regions Offsets Working Group, Regional Greenhouse Gas Initiative, Midwestern Greenhouse Gas Reduction Accord, and Western Climate Initiative, "Ensuring Offset Quality: Design and Implementation Criteria for a High-Quality Offset Program," Three-Regions Offsets Working Group, May 2010, http://www.westernclimateinitia tive.org/component/remository/general/Ensuring-Offset-Quality-Design-and-Imple mentation-Criteria-for-a-High-Quality-Offset-Program/.

12. Neil Craik, Isabel Studer, and Debora VanNijnatten, eds., *Climate Change Policy in North America: Designing Integration in a Regional System* (Toronto: University of Toronto Press, 2013).

13. Ken Paulman, "Midwest Cap and Trade: Not Dead, Just Sleeping," *Midwest Energy News*, March 4, 2011, http://midwestenergynews.com/2011/03/04/midwest-cap-and -trade-is-it-dead-or-no.

14. John W. Kingdon, *Agendas, Alternatives, and Public Policies*, 2nd ed. (New York: Longman, 2003); Timothy J. Conlan, Paul L. Posner, and David R. Beam, *Pathways of Power: The Dynamics of National Policymaking* (Washington, DC: Georgetown University Press, 2014).

15. Kingdon, *Agendas, Alternatives, and Public Policies*; Ian H. Rowlands, "The Development of Renewable Electricity Policy in the Province of Ontario: The Influence of Ideas and Timing," *Review of Policy Research* 24, no. 3 (2007): 185–207, doi:10.1111/j.1541-1338.2007.00277.x.

16. Theda Skocpol, *Boomerang: Health Care Reform and the Turn against Government* (New York: W. W. Norton, 1997); David Broder and Haynes Johnson, *The System: The American Way of Politics at the Breaking Point* (Boston: Little, Brown, 1996).

17. Gore had supported a number of carbon pricing initiatives during his years in the Senate and published a best-selling book prior to his election as vice president that brought his views on climate policy to a wide audience. See Al Gore, *Earth in the Balance: Ecology and the Human Spirit* (Boston: Houghton Mifflin, 1992). I served the Clinton-Gore campaign by assembling briefing materials for debate preparation, including assignments to interpret Gore's book for senior staff. I was struck by the concern that senior Clinton economic advisers, many of whom assumed prominent roles in the administration, had about the book and its perceived political risks to the campaign and the economy if his policy ideas were adopted.

18. Dawn Erlandson, "The BTU Tax Experience: What Happened and Why It Happened," *Pace Environmental Law Review* 12, no. 1 (Fall 1994): 173–184, http:// digitalcommons.pace.edu /cgi/viewcontent.cgi?article=1528&context=pelr.

19. Michael J. Graetz, *The End of Energy: The Unmaking of America's Environment, Security, and Independence* (Cambridge, MA: MIT Press, 2011), 184.

20. Martin A. Sullivan, *Gas Tax Politics, Part 1* (Falls Church, VA: The Tax Analysts, 2008), http://www.taxhistory.org/thp/readings.nsf/ArtWeb/5DDB79194769C2BF852 574D5003C28D5?OpenDocument.

21. Posner, Conlan, and Beam, *Pathways of Power*, 200.

22. US Climate Action Partnership (USCAP), *Blueprint for Leadership: Consensus Recommendations for U.S. Climate Protection Legislation* (Washington, DC: USCAP, 2009), http://www.c2es.org/docUploads/USCAP-legislative-blueprint.pdf.

23. Markey further noted that "someone once told me that a smart man learns from his mistakes but a wise man learns from others' mistakes. We can learn from 1993

or Canada in 2008, but we should learn." Quoted in Barry G. Rabe, "The Aversion to Direct Cost Imposition: Selecting Climate Policy Tools in the United States," *Governance* 23, no.4 (2010): 583–608, doi:10.1111/j.1468-0491.2010.01499.x; John M. Broder, "House Bill for a Carbon Tax to Cut Emissions Faced a Steep Climb," *New York Times*, March 6, 2009, http://www.nytimes.com/2009/03/07/us /politics/07carbon.html.

24. Michael Levi, *The Power Surge: Energy, Opportunity, and the Battle for America's Future* (New York: Oxford University Press, 2013), 97.

25. Eric Pooley, *The Climate War: True Believers, Power Brokers, and the Fight to Save the Earth* (New York: Hyperion, 2010); Judith Layzer, "Cold Front: How the Recession Stalled Obama's Clean-Energy Agenda," in *Reaching for a New Deal: Ambitious Governance, Economic Meltdown, and Polarized Politics in Obama's First Two Years,* ed. Theda Skocpol and Lawrence R. Jacobs (New York: Russell Sage Foundation, 2011), 321–385; Theda Skocpol, "Naming the Problem: What It Will Take to Counter Extremism and Engage Americans in the Fight against Global Warming," paper for the Symposium on the Politics of America's Fight Against Global Warming, Harvard University, February 14, 2013, http://www.scholarsstrategynetwork.org/sites /default/files/skocpol_captrade_report_january_2013_0.pdf.

26. In 2016, economist Yoram Bauman led an ultimately unsuccessful effort to adopt a carbon tax in Washington State via ballot proposition. He was not an academic, however, and was best known for his work as a comedian. This case is further discussed in chapter 8.

27. As quoted in Kathryn Harrison, "A Tale of Two Taxes: The Fate of Environmental Tax Reform in Canada," *Review of Policy Research* 29, no. 3 (2012): 383–407, doi :10.1111/j.1541-1338.2012.0056 5.x; Stéphane Dion, "Carbon Taxes: Can a Good Policy Become Good Politics?," in *Tax Is Not a Four-Letter Word: A Different Take on Taxes in Canada*, ed. Alex Himelfarb and Jordan Himelfarb (Waterloo, ON: Wilfrid Laurier University Press, 2013), 171.

28. This section is greatly influenced by Kathryn Harrison's excellent analysis of the Green Shift campaign in "A Tale of Two Taxes," 383–407.

29. However, the election of Liberal Party leader Justin Trudeau in late 2015 signaled a possible reconsideration of the future of carbon pricing, albeit with many uncertainties about design and political feasibility. Dion returned to political prominence in 2015 when Trudeau appointed him to serve as minister of foreign affairs, tantamount to the US position of secretary of state. This case is further discussed in chapter 7.

30. Quoted in Richard V. Reeves, *Ulysses Goes to Washington: Political Myopia and Policy Commitment Devices* (Washington, DC: Brookings Institution, 2015), 27, https://www .brookings.edu/wp-content/uploads/2016/06/Ulysses.pdf.

31. On the prospects for "death" and "mutation" of federal domestic policies in the United States, see Christopher R. Berry, Barry C. Burden, and William G. Howell, "After Enactment: The Lives and Deaths of Federal Programs," *American Journal of Political Science* 54, no. 1 (2010): 1–17, doi:10.1111/j.1540-5907.2009.00414.x.

32. David Victor, *The Collapse of the Kyoto Protocol and the Struggle to Slow Global Warming* (Princeton, NJ: Princeton University Press, 2001).

33. On the roller coaster of the catastrophic care legislation, see Jonathan Oberlander, *The Political Life of Medicare* (Chicago: University of Chicago Press, 2003); Eric M. Patashnik, *Reforms at Risk: What Happens after Major Policy Changes Are Enacted* (Princeton, NJ: Princeton University Press, 2008), chap. 5; Posner, Conlan, and Beam, *Pathways of Power*, chap. 6.

34. For an excellent overview of this period, see Sonja Klinsky, "Bottom-Up Policy Lessons Emerging from the Western Climate Initiative's Development Challenges," *Climate Policy* 13, no. 2 (2013): 143–169, doi:10.1080/14693062.2012.712457.

35. Ronald Ezekiel and Ivan Gold, "Greenhouse Gas Cap and Trade Legislative Developments in the United States and in the Western Climate Initiative," *Climate Perspectives* (2009), http://www.fasken.com/files/Publication/fd4d089d-770a-486c -b183-b4bf303e5a8d/Presentation/PublicationAttachment/e1c8a815-6124-41c6 -9173-c0a93bbb6ee1/WCI%20Bulletin%20-%20May%202009.English.pdf.

36. Klinsky, "Bottom-Up Policy Lessons Emerging from the Western Climate Initiative's Development Challenges," 156–157.

37. In Michigan, for example, Republican State Representative Tom McMillin introduced House Resolution 277, calling for withdrawal from the MGGRA. McMillin noted that "[Michigan's] sacrifice will be for nothing and we'll watch more jobs and businesses flee Michigan to other states without cap and trade." For more, see EUP News Staff, "McMillin Proposes Withdrawal from Regional Cap and Trade Agreement," *EUP News*, May 6, 2010, http://eupnews.com/mcmillin-proposes-withdrawal -from-regional-cap-and-trade-agreement-editors-note-do-it.

38. William Lowry, "Disentangling Energy Policy from Environmental Policy," *Social Science Quarterly* 89, no. 5 (2008): 1195–1211, doi:10.1111/j.1540-6237.2008.00565.x.

39. Barry G. Rabe, "Governing the Climate from Sacramento," in *Unlocking the Power of Networks: Keys to High-Performance Government*, ed. Stephen Goldsmith and Donald F. Kettl (Washington, DC: Brookings Institution Press, 2009), 34–61.

40. Posner, Conlan, and Beam, *Pathways of Power*, 184.

41. Berry, Burden, and Howell, "After Enactment."

42. Andrew Karch, *Democratic Laboratories: Policy Diffusion among the American States* (Ann Arbor: University of Michigan Press, 2007).

43. Paul L. Posner, "The Politics of Vertical Diffusion: The States and Climate Change," in *Greenhouse Governance: Addressing Climate Change in America*, ed. Barry G. Rabe (Washington, DC: Brookings Institution Press, 2010), 73–100.

44. Barry G. Rabe, "The Durability of Carbon Cap-and-Trade Policy," *Governance* 29, no. 1 (2016): 103–199, doi:10.1111/gove.12151.

45. John F. Witte, *The Politics and Development of the Federal Income Tax* (Madison: University of Wisconsin Press, 1985); John F. Witte, "The Tax Reform Act of 1986: A New Era in Tax Policy?," *American Political Quarterly* 19 (1991): 438–457.

46. For the leading political science account, see Timothy J. Conlan, Margaret T. Wrightson, and David R. Beam, *Taxing Choices: The Politics of Tax Reform* (Washington, DC: Congressional Quarterly, 1990); for the leading journalistic account, see Jeffrey H. Birnbaum and Alan S. Murray, *Showdown at Gucci Gulch* (New York: Vintage, 1988).

47. Eric M. Patashnik, "Why Some Reforms Last and Others Collapse: The Tax Reform Act of 1986 Versus Airline Deregulation," in *Living Legislation: Durability, Change, and the Politics of American Lawmaking*, ed. Jeffery A. Jenkins and Eric M. Patashnik (Chicago: University of Chicago Press, 2012), 159; more broadly on the vulnerability of interest reforms to reversal, see Patashnik, *Reforms at Risk*.

48. John Pendergrass, "Arizona Pulls Out of Climate Initiative," *The Environmental Forum* 27, no. 2 (Spring 2010): 12. Brewer's exit from cap-and-trade was prompt and final, but climate change would remain a contentious issue during her governorship. At a later press conference during a regional governor's meeting on energy and environmental issues, a veteran Arizona reporter asked Brewer about climate change. Brewer responded, "Everybody has an opinion on it, you know, I, you know, probably don't believe that it's man-made. I believe that, you know, weather elements are controlled, maybe, by different things." Yvonne Wingett Sanchez, "Gov. Jan Brewer Chides Reporter over Question," *The Arizona Republic*, December 6, 2012, http://archive.azcentral.com/news /politics/articles/20121206gov-jan-brewer-chides-reporter-over-question.html. Brewer later punched the reporter, having asked why such a question needed to be asked in that setting. Grumbles would later serve in a similar position in a Republican administration in Maryland that remained active in cap-and-trade implementation.

49. Quoted in "Court's Order Fails to End Uncertainty over Fate of New Mexico's GHG Rule," *CarbonControlNews.com*, January 27, 2011, file 240, 3–4.

50. Quoted in Geoffrey Craig, "Six US States Leave the Western Climate Initiative," *Platts*, November 18, 2011, http://www.platts.com/latest-news/electric-power /washington/six-us-states-leave-the-western-climate-initiative-6695863.

51. David Houle, Erick Lachapelle, and Mark Purdon, "Comparative Politics of Sub-Federal Cap-and-Trade: Implementing the Western Climate Initiative," *Global Environmental Politics* 15, no. 3 (2015): 49–73, doi:10.1162/GLEP_a_00311; Amy

Williams, "New Mexico's Land Grant and Severance Tax Permanent Funds: Renewable Wealth from Non-Renewable Resources," *Natural Resources Journal* 48 (Summer 2008): 719–743.

52. Craig, "Six US States Leave the Western Climate Initiative," para. 12; also see Klinsky, "Bottom-Up Policy Lessons Emerging from the Western Climate Initiative's Development Challenges."

53. "Christie's Carbon Awakening," *Wall Street Journal*, June 3, 2011, http:// www .wsj.com/articles/SB10001424052702303657404576357620250781498.

54. Barry G. Rabe, "Building on Sub-Federal Climate Strategies: The Challenges of Regionalism," in *Climate Change Policy in North America: Designing Integration in a Regional System*, ed. Neil Craik, Isabel Studer, and Debora VanNijnatten (Toronto: University of Toronto Press, 2013), 89–90.

55. Leah C. Stokes, "Electoral Backlash Against Climate Policy," *American Journal of Political Science* 60, no. 4 (October 2016): 958–974; Rowlands, "The Development of Renewable Electricity Policy in the Province of Ontario"; David Houle, *Obstacles to Carbon Pricing in Canadian Provinces* (Ottawa: Sustainable Prosperity, 2014), 32 and 42, http://www.sustainableprosperity.ca/sites/default/files/SSRN-id2598985_0 .pdf; also see David Houle, *Carbon Pricing in Canada: Bounded Provincial Autonomy and Climate Policy Innovation* (Toronto: University of Toronto Press, forthcoming).

56. Roger Wilkins, *Possible Design for a National Greenhouse Gas Emissions Trading System* (Canberra: National Emissions Trading Taskforce, 2006).

57. Erick Lachapelle and Jean-Philippe Gauvin, "Against the Odds: The Politics of Carbon Pricing in Australia" (presentation, 2012 Annual Meeting of the Canadian Political Science Association, Edmonton, Alberta, June 13–15, 2012).

58. Kate Crowley, "Pricing Carbon: The Politics of Climate Policy in Australia," *WIREs Climate Change* 4 (2013): 603–613, doi:10.1002/wcc/239.

59. As *The Economist* noted, "Bitter rows over carbon pricing have cost two prime ministers and an opposition leader their jobs." See more in "Axed: The Prime Minister Follows through on an Election Promise," *The Economist*, July 19, 2014, http:// www.economist.com/news/asia/21607865-prime-minister-follows-through-election -promise-axed.

60. Kate Crowley, "Up and Down with Climate Politics 2013–2016: The Repeal of Carbon Pricing in Australia," *WIREs Climate Change* 8 (May/June 2017): 1–13, doi:10.11002/wcc.458.

61. Geoff Bertram and Simon Terry, *The Carbon Challenge: New Zealand's Emissions Trading Scheme* (Wellington: Bridget Williams Books, 2010).

62. Nigel Haigh, *EU Environmental Policy: Its Journey to Centre Stage* (Abingdon: Routledge, 2015).

63. A. Denny Ellerman, Barbara K. Buchner, and Carlo Carraro, eds., *Allocation in the European Emissions Trading System: Rights, Rents and Fairness* (New York: Cambridge University Press, 2007).

64. Joseph Kruger and William A. Pizer, "The EU Emissions Trading Directive: Opportunities and Potential Pitfalls," Resources for the Future Discussion Paper 04-24,Washington, DC, 2014; Jørgen Wettestad and Torbjørg Jevnaker, *Rescuing EU Emissions Trading: The Climate Policy Flagship* (London: Palgrave Macmillan, 2016) 1–2.

65. In 2014, Charlemagne columnist Tom Nuttall noted that "the emissions-trading scheme, which covers 12,000 industrial polluters and half of Europe's total carbon emissions, is at the heart of the EU's plans—and it is a farce. The market is massively oversupplied with permits...meaning there is little incentive to ditch dirty fuels. Europe is actually burning more coal than ever." Tom Nuttall, "The Environmental Union: On Climate Change, if Little Else, Europe Still Aspires to Global Leadership," *The Economist*, November 1, 2014, http://www.economist.com/news/europe/21629387-climate-change-if-little-else-europe-still-aspires-global-leadership-environmental.

66. In 2013, Nordic utility company CEO Oeystein Loeseth noted, "The emissions trading system has sadly become marginalized, and we are concerned that it has lost its ability to prompt low-carbon investments. Against this backdrop, the EU needs to recalibrate." Matthew Carr, "Harvard Don Tells EU Kill Grants to Save Carbon: Energy Markets," *Bloomberg*, April 17, 2013, http://www.bloomberg.com/news/articles/2013-04-17/harvard-don-tells-eu-kill-grants-to-save-carbon-energy-markets.

67. "Breathing Difficulties," *The Economist*, March 3, 2012, http://www.economist.com/node/21548962.

68. In 2013, Jeff Swartz of the International Emissions Trading Association, a pro cap-and-trade lobbying organization based in Washington, DC, said that the ETS "may well become an example of what not to do." He also made clear that he and his organization support emissions trading. See "ETS, RIP?," *The Economist*, April 20, 2013, http://www.economist.com/news/finance-and-economics/21576388-failure-reform-europes-carbon-market-will-reverberate-round-world-ets.

69. In 2014, Gabrielle Williamson, a German environmental attorney and columnist for the Environmental Law Institute, noted that "the vaunted Emissions Trading System does not perform as well as expected at its launch." Gabrielle Williamson, "Still a Chance for Recovery?," *The Environmental Forum* 30, no. 4 (2014): 20.

70. Harro Van Asselt, "Emissions Trading: The Enthusiastic Adoption of an 'Alien' Instrument?," in *Climate Policy in the European Union: Confronting the Dilemmas of Mitigation and Adaptation*, ed. Andrew Jordan, Dave Huitema, Harro Van Asselt, Tim Rayner, and Frans Berkhout (Cambridge: Cambridge University Press, 2010), 139.

71. Lowry, "Disentangling Energy Policy from Environmental Policy," 1195–1211.

72. Elinor Ostrom, *A Polycentric Approach for Coping with Climate Change* (Washington, DC: World Bank, 2009); Elinor Ostrom, *Governing the Commons: The Evolution of Institutions for Collective Action* (Cambridge: Cambridge University Press, 1990); Craik, Studer, and VanNijnatten, *Climate Change Policy in North America.*

73. Paul E. Peterson, Barry G. Rabe, and Kenneth K. Wong, *When Federalism Works* (Washington, DC: Brookings Institution Press, 1986), 160–179.

74. Peterson, Rabe, and Wong, *When Federalism Works.*

75. Nigel Haigh, *EU Environmental Policy: Its Journey to Centre Stage* (London: Routledge, 2016).

76. Van Asselt, "Emissions Trading," 131; Erick Lachapelle, "Energy Security and Climate Policy in the OECD: The Political Economy of Carbon-Energy Taxation" (PhD diss., University of Toronto, 2011), 76, https://tspace.library.utoronto.ca /bitstream/1807/29780/1/Lachapelle_Erick_201106 _PhD_thesis.pdf.

77. Van Asselt, "Emissions Trading," 132.

78. US Government Accountability Office (GAO), *Lessons Learned from the European Union's Emissions Trading Scheme and the Kyoto Protocol's Clean Development Mechanism* (Washington, DC: GAO, November 2008), http://www.gao.gov/assets /290/283397.pdf.

79. Nicolas Koch, Sabine Fuss, Godfrey Grosjean, and Ottmar Edenhofer, "Causes of the EU ETS Price Drop: Recession, CDM, Renewable Policies, or a Bit of Everything? New Evidence," *Energy Policy* 73 (2014): 676–685, doi:10.1016/j.enpol.2014.06.024.

80. Simone Borghesi and Massimiliano Montini, "The Allocation of Carbon Emission Permits: Theoretical Aspects and Practical Problems in the EU ETS" (working paper, Financialisation, Economy, Society and Sustainable Development, January 2015), http://fessud.eu/wp-content/uploads/2015/01/The-allocation-of-carbon-emission -permits-theoretical-aspects-and-practical-problems-in-the-EU-ETS_working-paper -75-.pdf.

81. Jessica Green, "Don't Link Carbon Markets," *Nature* 543 (March 2017): 485–486; Daniel Matisoff, "Making Cap-and-Trade Work: Lessons from the European Union Experience," *Environment* (January–February 2010).

82. One EUA is equivalent to one ton of traded carbon dioxide under the ETS. See Kyle O'Meara, "A Review of the European Union Emissions Trading System," unpublished paper on reserve at the Center for Local, State, and Urban Policy at the Ford School of Public Policy, University of Michigan, May 2015, 13.

83. Inger Weibust, *Green Leviathan: The Case for a Federal Role in Environmental Policy* (Abingdon: Routledge, 2009). For an excellent discussion of the challenges facing the European Union as a "fledgling federation," see Jenna Bednar, *The Robust Federation: Principles of Design* (Cambridge: Cambridge University Press, 2009), 137–139.

84. Decentralization pressures are considerably greater on such issues as climate and energy as opposed to air and water quality, as "the EU has less certain jurisdiction" in the former areas. Douglas Macdonald, "Allocating Greenhouse Gas Emission Reductions amongst Sectors and Jurisdictions in Federated Systems: the European Union, Germany and Canada," in *Multilevel Environmental Governance: Managing Water and Climate Change in Europe and North America*, ed. Inger Weibust and James Meadowcroft (Cheltenham, UK: Edward Elgar, 2014), 190; Cass, *The Failures of American and European Climate Policy* (Albany: State University of New York, 2006), 194–200.

85. Vivian E. Thomson, *Sophisticated Interdependence in Climate Policy: Federalism in the United States, Brazil, and Germany* (London: Anthem Press, 2014), 57.

86. John W. Miller, "Europe Emissions Markets to Reopen Gradually," *Wall Street Journal*, February 2, 2011, http://www.wsj.com/articles/SB1000142405274870412 4504576118261149778674; "Green Fleeces, Red Faces: A Theft of Carbon Credits Embarrasses an Entire Market," *The Economist*, February 3, 2011, http://www.economist .com/node/18063834.

87. Jos Sijm, Karsten Neuhoff, and Yihsu Chen, "CO_2 Cost Pass-Through and Windfall Profits in the Power Sector," *Climate Policy* 6, no. 1 (2006): 49–72, doi:10.1080/1 4693062.2006.9685588.

88. Rob Elsworth, Bryony Worthington, and Damien Morris, *Help or Hindrance? Offsetting in the EU ETS* (London: Sandbag Climate Campaign, 2012), https://sandbag .org.uk/site_media/pdfs/reports/Help_or_Hindrance_Offsetting_2012_3.pdf.

89. Germa Bel and Stephen Joseph, "Emission Abatement: Untangling the Impacts of the EU ETS and the Economic Crisis," *Energy Economics* 49 (2015): 531–539, doi:10.1016/j.eneco.2015.03.014; Tim Laing, Misato Sato, Michael Grubb, and Claudia Comberti, *Assessing the Effectiveness of the EU Emissions Trading System* (Leeds and London: Center for Climate Change Economics and Policy, 2013), http://www .lse.ac.uk/GranthamInstitute/wp-content/uploads/2014/02/WP106-effectiveness-eu -emissions-trading-system.pdf.

90. Williamson, "Still a Chance for Recovery?"; Borghesi and Montini, "The Allocation of Carbon Emission Permits."

91. Wettestad and Jevnaker, *Rescuing EU Emissions Trading*, 103.

92. Steinar Andresen et al., "The Paris Agreement: Consequences for the EU and Carbon Markets?," *Politics and Governance* 4, no. 3 (2016): 188–196.

93. Ralph Klein, "Letter to the Prime Minister, September 2003," commentary on the web page of the Government of Alberta, 2003. In author's possession.

94. Ian Urquhart, *Making It Work: Kyoto, Trade, and Politics* (Edmonton, AB: Parkland Institute, 2002), 66, http://s3-us-west-2.amazonaws.com/parkland-research-pdfs /makingitwork.pdf.

95. Jennifer Smith, *Federalism* (Vancouver: University of British Columbia Press, 2004).

96. Reeves, "Ulysses Goes to Washington," 19. Political scientists have examined this concept, although much of this work has focused on American social welfare policy. See Jacob B. Hacker, "Privatizing Risk Without Privatizing the Welfare State: The Hidden Politics of Social Policy Retrenchment in the United States," *American Political Science Review* 98, no. 2 (2004): 243–260; Suzanne Mettler, "The Policyscape and the Challenges of Contemporary Politics to Policy Maintenance," *Perspective on Politics* 14, no. 2 (2016): 369–390. For consideration of this concept in the context of Canadian energy policy, see Angela V. Carter, Gail S. Fraser, and Anna Zalik, "Environmental Policy Convergence in Canada's Fossil Fuel Provinces? Regulatory Streamlining, Impediments, and Drift," *Canadian Public Policy* (March 2017): 61–76, doi:10.31.38/cpp.2016-041.

97. Barry G. Rabe, "Shale Play Politics: The Intergovernmental Odyssey of American Shale Governance," *Environmental Science & Technology* 48, no. 15 (2014): 8371–8375, doi:10.1021/es4051132.; Jonathan M. Fisk, *The Fracking Debate: The Intergovernmental Politics of the Oil and Gas Renaissance* (Boca Raton, FL: CRC Press, 2017); Carter, Fraser, and Zalik, "Environmental Policy Convergence in Canada's Fossil Fuel Provinces?"

98. Ann E. Carlson and Robert W. Fri, "Designing a Durable Energy Policy," *Daedalus* 142, no. 1 (2013): 123, doi:10.1162/DAED_a_00189.

99. Government of Alberta, *Albertans and Climate Change: A Strategy for Managing Environmental and Economic Risks* (Edmonton: Government of Alberta, 2002), https://extranet.gov.ab.ca/env/infocentre/info/library/5895.pdf.

100. Alexandre Kossoy et al., *State and Trends of Carbon Pricing 2014* (Washington, DC: World Bank, 2014), 58–59, http://documents.worldbank.org/curated/en/505431468148506727/pdf/882840AR0REPLA00EPI2102680Box385232.pdf.

101. Boyd, "Learning to Address Climate Change," 161.

102. A detailed analysis of the program concluded, "Clearly these credits do not represent emissions reductions attributable to the SGER. It is not plausible that investors or project developers would have committed to projects on the basis of a future revenue stream (from credit sales) that depended on government regulations that had not yet been drafted and whose implementation could have been delayed many years." See Matthew Bramley, Marc Huot, Simon Dyer, and Matt Horne, *Responsible Action? An Assessment of Alberta's Greenhouse Gas Policies* (Drayton Valley, AB: Pembina Institute, 2011), 12, https://www.pembina.org/reports/responsible-action.pdf.

103. Canada's Ecofiscal Commission, *The Way Forward: A Practical Approach to Reducing Canada's Greenhouse Gas Emissions* (Montreal: Canada's Ecofiscal Commission,

2015), 35, http://ecofiscal. ca/wp-content/uploads/2015/04/Ecofiscal-Commission
-Report-The-Way-Forward-April-2015.pdf.

104. Christa Marshall, "Alberta Cancels Major 'Clean' Coal Project Amid Low Gas
Prices," *E&E News*, February 26, 2013, http://www.eenews.net/climatewire/stories
/1059976887; Boyd, "Learning to Address Climate Change," 167.

105. Bramley et al., *Responsible Action?*, 14. Some place this level below 5 percent,
such as Canada's Ecofiscal Commission, *The Way Forward*, 35.

106. Branko Bošković and Andrew Leach, *Leave It in the Ground? Oil Sands Extraction
in the Carbon Bubble* (Edmonton: University of Alberta, 2014), http://www.uwinnipeg
.ca/economics/docs/leach-oil-sands.pdf.

107. Canada's Ecofiscal Commission, *The Way Forward*, 22.

108. Deepak Rajagopal, *Firm Behavior and Emissions under Emission Intensity Regulation: Evidence from Alberta's Specified Gas Emitters Regulation* (Los Angeles: UCLA
Institute of the Environmental and Sustainability, 2014), http://escholarship.org/uc
/item/5t40p9ht.

109. David McLaughlin, "Red Flags for Green Targets: The New and Same Climate
for Canadian Climate Policy," keynote address, Climate Choices Canada Conference, Waterloo, ON, February 18–20, 2016.

110. Alison Redford, "Keystone Is Responsible Oil Sands Development," *USA
Today*, February 25, 2013, http://www.usatoday.com/story/opinion/2013/02/25
/keystone-pipeline-alberta-column/1943029/.

Chapter 4

1. Barry G. Rabe, "The Durability of Carbon Cap-and-Trade Policy," *Governances* 29,
no. 1 (2016): 103–199; Suzanne Mettler, "The Policyscape and the Challenges of
Contemporary Politics to Policy Maintenance," *Perspectives on Politics* 14, no. 2 (2016):
369–390, doi:10.1017/S1537592716000074.

2. Jenny Sumner, Lori Bird, and Hillary Smith, *Carbon Taxes: A Review of Experience
and Policy Design Considerations* (Golden, CO: National Renewable Energy Laboratory,
2009), http://www.nrel.gov/docs/fy10osti/47312.pdf.

3. Francis Sejersted, *The Age of Social Democracy: Norway and Sweden in the
20th Century* (Princeton, NJ: Princeton University Press, 2011), 333–342; Erick Lachapelle, "Energy Security and Climate Policy in the OECD: The Political Economy of
Carbon-Energy Taxation" (PhD diss., University of Toronto, 2011), 76.

4. Henrik Jacobsen Kleven, "How Can Scandinavians Tax So Much?," *Journal of
Economic Perspectives* 28, no. 4 (Fall 2014): 77–98. On the divergent paths between
European and American gasoline taxes, as well as an estimate of their impact on

vehicle sector emissions, see Pietro S. Nivola, *The Long and Winding Road: Automotive Fuel Economy and American Politics* (Washington, DC: Brookings Institution, February 2009), https://www.brookings.edu/wp-content/uploads/2016/06/0225_cafe_nivola.pdf.

5. Erick Lachapelle, "Following the Doctor's Orders? Theory and Practice of Carbon Pricing in the OECD" (presentation, Annual Convention of the International Studies Association, New Orleans, February 17–20, 2010).

6. Lars Zetterberg, "Sweden," in *Allocation in the European Emissions Trading Scheme*, ed. A. Denny Ellerman, Barbara K. Buchner, and Carlo Carraro (New York: Cambridge University Press, 2007), 133–134.

7. William G. Gale, Samuel Brown, and Fernando Saltiel, "Carbon Taxes as Part of the Fiscal Solution," in *Implementing a US Carbon Tax: Challenges and Debates*, ed. Ian Perry, Adele Morris, and Robertson C. Williams III (London: Routledge, 2015), 1–17.

8. Sumner, Bird, and Smith, *Carbon Taxes*, 8–13; David G. Duff and Andrew J. Green, "Policies to Promote the Generation of Electricity from Renewable Sources," in *A Globally Integrated Climate Policy for Canada*, ed. Steven Bernstein, Jutta Brunnee, David G. Duff, and Andrew J. Green (Toronto: University of Toronto Press, 2008), 235–236.

9. Matt Horne, Ekaterina Petropavlova, and P. J. Parrington, *British Columbia's Carbon Tax: Exploring Perspectives and Seeking Common Ground* (Drayton Valley, AB: Pembina Institute, 2012), 9, https://www.pembina.org/reports/carbon-tax-interviews.pdf; Monica Prasad, "Taxation as a Regulatory Tool: Lessons from Environmental Taxes in Europe," in *Government and Markets: Toward a New Theory on Regulation*, ed. Edward J. Balleisen and David A. Moss (New York: Cambridge University Press, 2009), 363–390. For an overview of these taxes and a broader set of European environmental taxes, see Paul Ekins, "European Environmental Taxes and Charges: Recent Experience, Issues, and Trends," *Ecological Economics* 31 (1999): 39–62.

10. Partnership for Market Readiness, *Carbon Tax Guide: A Handbook for Policy Makers. Appendix: Carbon Tax Case Studies* (Washington, DC: World Bank, 2017), 87.

11. Odd Godal and Bjart Holtsmark, "Greenhouse Gas Taxation and the Distribution of Costs and Benefits: The Case of Norway," *Energy Policy* 29, no. 8 (2001): 653–662, doi:10.1016/S0301-4215(00)00158-0; Sjur Kasa, "Policy Networks as Barriers to Green Tax Reform: The Case of CO_2-Taxes in Norway," *Environmental Politics* 9, no. 4 (2007): 104–122, doi:10.1080/096440100084 14553.

12. Anne Therese Gullberg and Tora Skodvin, "Cost Effectiveness and Target Group Influence in Norwegian Climate Policy," *Scandinavian Political Studies* 34, no. 2 (2011): 125, doi: 10.1111/j.1467-9477.2011.00266.x.

13. Loren R. Cass, *The Failures of American and European Climate Policy* (Albany: State University of New York Press, 2006), chap. 6; on the relatively light treatment of coal versus other fossil fuels in many EU carbon taxes, see Lachapelle, "Following the Doctor's Orders?," 15–16.

14. On the British Columbia experience between 1997 and 2002 with the Greenhouse Gas Emissions Reduction Trading Pilot (GERT), see David Houle, *Obstacles to Carbon Pricing in Canadian Provinces* (Ottawa: Sustainable Prosperity, 2014), 153–157.

15. Michael Howlett and Keith Brownsey, "British Columbia: Politics in a Post-Staples Political Economy," in *The Provincial State in Canada: Politics in the Provinces and Territories*, ed. Keith Brownsey and Michael Howlett (Vancouver: University of British Columbia Press, 2001), 309–334.

16. Philip Resnick, *The Politics of Resentment: British Columbia Regionalism and Canadian Unity* (Vancouver: University of British Columbia Press, 2000).

17. As quoted in Resnick, *The Politics of Resentment*, 28.

18. Daniel Dufour, "The Canadian Lumber Industry: Recent Trends," *Statistics Canada*, last modified November 12, 2009, http://www.statcan.gc.ca/pub/11-621-m/11-621 -m2007055-eng.htm.

19. National Energy Board of Canada, "Marketable Natural Gas Production in Canada," accessed August 1, 2016, https://www.neb-one.gc.ca/nrg/sttstc/ntrlgs/stt /mrktblntrlgsprdctn2016.xls.

20. As Alex Boston of the David Suzuki Foundation noted, "BC has decided its oil and gas industry is growing—and it wants to protect this." Boston, in discussion with author, June 11, 2004. Jim Prentice with Jean-Sebastian Rioux, *Triple Crown: Winning Canada's Energy Future* (Toronto: HarperCollins, 2017), 24, 267–270.

21. Government of British Columbia, *Energy for Our Future: A Plan for BC* (Vancouver, BC: Government of British Columbia, 2002), 13, http://www.bcenergyblog .com/uploads/file/2002%20B.C.%20Energy%20Plan.pdf.

22. Barry G. Rabe, *Statehouse and Greenhouse: The Emerging Politics of American Climate Change Policy* (Washington, DC: Brookings Institution Press, 2004); Michael Mintrom and Phillipa Norman, "Policy Entrepreneurship and Policy Change," *Policy Studies Journal* 37, no. 4 (2009): 649–667, doi:10.1111/j.1541-0072.2009.00329.x.

23. Iona Campagnolo, "Speech from the Throne at the Opening of the Third Session, Thirty-Eighth Parliament of the Province of British Columbia," Legislative Assembly of British Columbia, Victoria, February 13, 2007, https://www.leg.bc.ca /content/legacy/web/38th3rd/Throne_Speech_2007.pdf.

24. Kathryn Harrison, "A Tale of Two Taxes: The Fate of Environmental Tax Reform in Canada," *Review of Policy Research* 29, no. 3 (2012): 383–407; Brendan Boyd,

"Learning to Address Climate Change: Collaboration, Policy Transfer, and Choosing Policy Instruments in Canadian Provinces" (PhD diss., University of Victoria, 2015), 115–116.

25. British Columbia Ministry of Water, Land, and Air Protection, *Indicators of Climate Change for British Columbia 2002* (Vancouver, BC: Ministry of Water, Land, and Air Protection, 2002), 40–42, http://www.rcbc.ca/files/u3/indcc.pdf.

26. Michal Carlson, Nicholas Ukrainetz, and Vicky Berger, "Lodgepole Pine, Western White Pine (Interior), Ponderosa Pine, Broadleaves (Interior)," *British Columbia Ministry of Forestry, Lands, and Natural Resource Operations,* last modified June 2009, https://www.for.gov.bc.ca/hre/forgen/interior/pine.htm; Michael Levi, *The Power Surge: Energy, Opportunity, and the Battle for America's Future* (New York: Oxford University Press, 2013), 83–84.

27. The premier has "phenomenal reading habits, far more than any other premier I have ever seen," explained Steven Anderson, executive director of the British Columbia Climate Action Secretariat in 2008. Anderson and other accounts confirm that Campbell sought considerable reading material for his 2007 Christmas vacation and returned having devoured it. See Steven Anderson (speech, Conference on Carbon Pricing and Environmental Federalism, Kingston, ON, October 17–18, 2008).

28. Taylor later described the carbon tax experience as the kind of "political challenge, intellectual challenge, communications challenge," that rarely comes along in public life. Quoted in Clean Energy Canada, *How to Adopt a Winning Carbon Price* (Vancouver, BC: Clean Energy Canada, 2015), 25, http://cleanenergycanada.org/wp-content/uploads/2015/02/Clean-Energy-Canada-How-to-Adopt-a-Winning-Carbon-Price-2015.pdf.

29. Boyd, "Learning to Address Climate Change," 118–120, 127–128, 132, 177–178.

30. Upon witnessing the air pollution in Beijing, China, Campbell recalled, "You saw the impact of millions of individual actions on the environment around you. I don't know if you have ever been in the middle of a hazardous air day, it is visible manifestation of man's impact on the environment." Quoted in Justine Hunter, "How Beijing Set Off a Premier's Smoke Alarm," *The Globe and Mail*, February 23, 2008, http://www.theglobeandmail.com/news/national/how-beijing-set-off-a-premiers-smoke-alarm/article1051845/.

31. Campbell routinely invoked intergenerational responsibility in his public comments during the period leading up to carbon tax adoption. In a 2007 address to local government officials, he noted, "The test of every generation is whether or not it will give or take away from the generations that follow. I can tell you this—this government, this province, will not turn its back on tomorrow's children." Gordon Campbell, "Address to Union of B.C. Municipalities Annual Convention," Vancouver, September–October 2007.

32. Boyd, "Learning to Address Climate Change," 115–116.

33. Warren G. Brazier, "British Columbia—Becoming a Renewable Energy Power-house," *Slaw*, June 23, 2009, http://www.slaw.ca/2009/06/23/british-columbia-be coming-a-renewable-energy-powerhouse/. Campbell also strongly emphasized in the campaign that the tax would offer long-term benefits for the provincial economy and prepare it for a leading role in a global transition toward cleaner energy. "We are going to be the alternative energy powerhouse in North America. We are going to be the example." Doug Ward and Rob Shaw, "Premier Says Policies Will Help B.C. Recover from Recession," *Vancouver Sun*, April 23, 2009, http://www.pressreader .com/canada/the-vancouver-sun/20090423/282707633002367.

34. Numerous examples in other policy areas, ranging from medical care to over-sight of financial institutions. As James Madison noted in *Federalist* no. 62, laws are of little public benefit if they are "so voluminous that they cannot be read, or so incoherent that they cannot be understood; if they be repealed or revised before they are promulgated, or undergo such incessant change that no man who knows what the law is to-day can guess what it will be tomorrow." Quoted in Robert A. Katzmann, *Judging Statutes* (Oxford: Oxford University Press, 2014), 12.

35. *Carbon Tax Act*, S.B.C. 2008, c. 40, p. 5, d. 2, http://www.bclaws.ca/Recon/document /ID/freeside/00_08040_01.

36. Ibid.

37. Shi-Lung Hsu, *The Case for a Carbon Tax* (Washington, DC: Island Press, 2011), 16.

38. "Motor Fuel Tax and Carbon Tax for Businesses That Manufacture, Import, or Sell Fuel," *Province of British Columbia*, accessed April 7, 2016, http://www2.gov.bc .ca/gov/content/taxes/sales-taxes/motor-fuel-carbon-tax/business.

39. Hsu, *The Case for a Carbon Tax*, 16.

40. Canada's Ecofiscal Commission, *The Way Forward: A Practical Approach to Reduc-ing Canada's Greenhouse Gas Emissions* (Montreal: Canada's Ecofiscal Commission, 2015), 37, http://ecofiscal. ca/wp-content/uploads/2015/04/Ecofiscal-Commission -Report-The-Way-Forward-April-2015.pdf.

41. Barry G. Rabe and Christopher P. Borick, "Carbon Taxation and Policy Labeling: Experience from American States and Canadian Provinces," *Review of Policy Research* 29, no. 3 (2012): 358–382, doi:10.1111/j.1541-1338.2012.00564.x.

42. British Columbia Ministry of Finance, *Budget and Fiscal Plan 2008/09–2010/11* (Victoria, BC: Ministry of Finance, 2008), http://www.bcbudget.gov.bc.ca/2008 /bfp/2008_Budget_Fiscal_Plan.pdf; David G. Duff, "Carbon Taxation in British Colum-bia," *Vermont Journal of Environmental Law* 10, no. 1 (Fall 2008): 87–107, http://vjel .vermontlaw.edu/files/2013/06/Carbon_Taxation_in_British_Columbia.pdf.

43. Brendan Burke and Margaret Ferguson, "Going Alone or Moving Together: Canadian and American Middle Tier Strategies on Climate Change," *Publius: The Journal of Federalism* 40, no. 3 (May 2010): 453, doi:10.1093/publius/pjq012.

44. Barry G. Rabe, "Governing the Climate from Sacramento," in *Unlocking the Power of Networks: Keys to High-Performance Government*, ed. Stephen Goldsmith and Donald F. Kettl (Washington, DC: Brookings Institution Press, 2009).

45. Houle, *Obstacles to Carbon Pricing*, 27.

46. On the uses of this reporting, see Brian C. Murray and Nicholas Rivers, "British Columbia's Revenue-Neutral Carbon Tax: A Review of the Latest 'Grand Experiment' in Environmental Policy" (Working Paper NI WP 15-04, Duke Nicholas Institute of Environmental Policy Solutions, Sustainable Prosperity, and the University of Ottawa Institute of the Environment, 2015), 17, https://nicholasinstitute.duke.edu /sites/default/files/publications/ni_wp_15-04_full.pdf.

47. Economists Stewart Elgie and Stephanie Cairns have noted "the ease of establishment" in the British Columbia carbon tax case. Elgie and Cairns, "Shifting to a Low-Carbon Economy: It Starts with a Price on Emissions," *Policy Options*, December 1, 2009, http://policyoptions.irpp.org/ magazines/the-2010-olympics/shifting-t o-a-low-carbon-economy-it-starts-with-a-price-on-emissions/.

48. Rabe and Borick, "Carbon Taxation and Policy Labeling," 358–382.

49. Carole Taylor, quoted in Clean Energy Canada, *How to Adopt a Winning Carbon Price*, 14. Also see discussion in British Columbia Ministry of Finance, *Budget and Fiscal Plan 2008/09–2010/11*, cited in David Duff, "Carbon Taxation in British Columbia."

50. Horne, Petropavlova, and Parrington, *British Columbia's Carbon Tax*, 1.

51. Quoted in Clean Energy Canada, *How to Adopt a Winning Carbon Price*, 25.

52. Jonathan Fowlie and Fiona Anderson, "B.C. Introduces Carbon Tax," *Vancouver Sun*, February 22, 2008.

53. Quoted in British Columbia Ministry of Finance, *Budget and Fiscal Plan 2008/09–2010/11*, 2.

54. Quoted in Clean Energy Canada, *How to Adopt a Winning Carbon Price*, 18.

55. Fowlie and Anderson, "B.C. Introduces Carbon Tax."

56. Stewart Elgie and Jessica McClay, "Policy Commentary/Commentaire: BC's Carbon Tax Shift Is Working Well after Four Years," *Canadian Public Policy* 39, no. 2 (July 2013): 1–10, http://www.utpjournals.press/doi/abs/10.3138/CPP.39.Supplement2.S1.

57. Quoted from an anonymous source in Clean Energy Canada, *How to Adopt a Winning Carbon Price*, 16. As *Grist* columnist David Roberts observed, "Linking the

carbon tax to tax cuts has proven politically effective in practice. Now that it is in place, abandoning the carbon tax would effectively mean a huge tax hike elsewhere to cover the revenue shortfall. B.C.'s corporate taxes are now below the international average, which gives politicians and businesses something to brag about and something with which to attract more people and businesses. They don't want to lose that." David Roberts, "What We Can Learn from British Columbia's Carbon Tax?," *Grist*, February 23, 2015, http://grist.org/climate-energy/what-we-can-learn -from-british-columbias-carbon-tax/; Kathryn Harrison, "The Political Economy of British Columbia's Carbon Tax," OECD Environment Working Paper No. 63, 2013, doi:10.1787/ 5k3z04gkkhkg-en; Alexandre Kossoy et al., *State and Trends of Carbon Pricing 2014* (Washington, DC: World Bank, 2014), 87, https://openknowledge .worldbank.org/handle/10986/18415.

58. Doug Ward and Rob Shaw, "Premier Says Policies Will Help B.C. Recover from Recession," *Vancouver Sun*, April 22, 2009, http://www.pressreader.com/canada/the -vancouver-sun/20090423/282707633002367.

59. Ibid.

60. "Carbonated Vote in B.C. Election," *Toronto Star*, May 14, 2009, https://www .thestar.com/opinion/2009/05/14/carbonated_vote_in_bc_election.html.

61. Hsu, *The Case for a Carbon Tax*, 187.

62. "Carbonated Vote in B.C. Election," *Toronto Star*.

63. Rob Shaw, "Horgan's Platform in NDP Leadership Bid Includes Expanding Carbon Tax," *Times Colonist*, February 16, 2011, http://www.timescolonist.com /horgan-s-platform-in-ndp-leadership-bid-includes-expanding-carbon-tax-1.22726.

64. Doug Ward, "Candidates Take a Swing at 'Out-of-Touch' Axe-the-Tax Carbon Concept," *Vancouver Sun*, April 2, 2011.

65. As one postelection editorial observed, "Here is a right-leaning politician who had the foresight to implement the continent's first carbon tax, and the courage to campaign for it even when under attack—from, of all people, the erstwhile environmentalists in the NDP." See "Carbonated Vote in B.C. Election."

66. Rabe and Borick, "Carbon Taxation and Policy Labeling," 364.

67. For a direct comparison of the different impacts of the British Columbia and Alberta carbon pricing strategies, see Canada's Ecofiscal Commission, *The Way Forward*, 22.

68. For a useful overview of these studies, see Murray and Rivers, "British Columbia's Revenue-Neutral Carbon Tax," 7–9.

69. Elgie and McClay, "Policy Commentary/Commentaire: BC's Carbon Tax Shift Is Working Well," 3–4.

70. Robert P. Murphy, Patrick J. Michaels, and Paul C. Knappenberger, "The Case against a U.S. Carbon Tax," CATO Institute Policy Analysis Number 801, October 17, 2016.

71. Barry G. Rabe and Christopher P. Borick, "Carbon Taxation and Policy Labeling," 370–371.

72. Nicholas Rivers and Brandon Schaufele, "Salience of Carbon Taxes in the Gasoline Market," *Social Sciences Research Network Paper* (2014): 1–33, doi:10.2139/ ssrn.2131468; Canada's Ecofiscal Commission, *The Way Forward*, 22.

73. Zahra Gholami, "Case Study on the Effectiveness of Carbon Pricing Estimating the Impact of Carbon Tax on Natural Gas Demand in British Columbia," (master's thesis, University of British Columbia, 2014), https://open.library.ubc.ca/cIRcle /collections/ubctheses/24/items/1.0166938.

74. Gilbert E. Metcalf, "A Conceptual Framework for Measuring the Effectiveness of Green Fiscal Reforms" (presentation, Green Growth Knowledge Platform Conference, Verona, Italy, January 2015), http://www.greengrowthknowledge.org/sites /default/files/Metcalf_A_Conceptual_Framework_for_Measuring_the_Effective ness_of_Green_Fiscal.pdf.

75. Murray and Rivers, "British Columbia's Revenue-Neutral Carbon Tax," 10–12.

76. The Pembina Institute, *The B.C. Carbon Tax: Backgrounder* (Drayton Valley, AB: Pembina Institute, 2014), 2, https://www.pembina.org/reports/lessons-bc-carbon -tax-112014.pdf.

77. Marisa Beck, Nicholas Rivers, Randall Wigle, and Hidemichi Yonezawa, "Carbon Taxes and Revenue Recycling: Impacts on Households in British Columbia," *Resource and Energy Economics* 41 (2015): 40–69, doi:10.1016/j.reseneeco.2015.04.005; Hsu, *The Case for a Carbon Tax*, 137; Murray and Rivers, "British Columbia's Revenue-Neutral Carbon Tax," 13–14; The Pembina Institute, *The B.C. Carbon Tax*, 4.

78. The Environics Institute for Survey Research and the David Suzuki Foundation, "Focus Canada 2015: Canadian Public Opinion about Climate Change," 2015, 6, http://www.environicsinstitute.org/uploads/institute-projects/environicsinstitute -dsf%20focus%20canada%202015%20-%20climate%20change%20survey%20-%20 final%20report%20-%20english.pdf.

79. Matt Horne, *Measuring the Appetite for Climate Action in B.C.* (Drayton Valley, AB: Pembina Institute, June 30, 2011), http://www.pembina.org/reports/measuring-the -appepite-for-climate-action-in-bc.pdf.

80. Erick Lachapelle, "Climate Change Opinions in the United States and Canada" (presentation, Woodrow Wilson Center, Washington, DC, October 13, 2015).

81. "Climate Policy in Canada: The Land of Green and Money," *The Economist*, August 4, 2013, http://www.economist.com/blogs/americasview/2013/08

/climate-policy-canada. In a separate account, the magazine noted that British Columbia had demonstrated "that a carbon tax can achieve multiple benefits at minimal cost." See "We Have a Winner: British Columbia's Carbon Tax Woos Sceptics," *The Economist*, July 21, 2011, http://www.economist.com/node/18989175.

82. Mark Hume, "B.C. Carbon Tax an Effective Model for National Climate Change Approach: Report," *The Globe and Mail*, December 10, 2014, http://www.theglobean dmail.com/news/british-columbia/bcs-carbon-tax-effective-in-reducing-greenhouse -gas-emissions-report/article22017313/. As political scientist Kathryn Harrison has noted, the British Columbia carbon tax has been "celebrated internationally." See Harrison, "International Carbon Trade and Domestic Climate Politics," *Global Environmental Politics* 15, no. 3 (2015): 39.

83. Quoted in Pembina Institute, *The B.C. Carbon Tax*, 1.

84. Angus Reid Institute, "BC NDP Remains Ahead, As Campbell Drops to Single Digits," 2010, accessed April 9, 2016, http://angusreidglobal.com/wp-content /uploads/2010/10/2010.10.16_Politics_BC.pdf.

85. Murray and Rivers, "British Columbia's Revenue-Neutral Carbon Tax," 7.

86. See Metcalf, "A Conceptual Framework."

87. Kossoy et al., *State and Trends of Carbon Pricing*, 79, 86.

88. Jake Haselswerdt, "The Lifespan of a Tax Break: Comparing the Durability of Tax Expenditures and Spending Programs," *American Politics Research* 42, no. 5 (2014): 731–759, doi:10.1177/ 1532673X13516992.

89. Mineral rights are far more likely to be held by governments in Canada and around the world than in the United States. Royalties in Canada and internationally thus tend to reflect governmental revenue derived from a tax or fee placed on mineral extraction. In the United States, mineral rights are more likely to be held privately, particularly if extraction occurs on privately owned lands, hence leading to a tax commonly known as a form of severance. However, governments often collect royalties on minerals extracted from public lands and private owners often receive so-called royalty payments once minerals are removed. For a detailed overview of these systems in the United States, Canada, and other nations, see George Anderson ed., *Oil and Gas in Federal Systems* (New York: Oxford University Press, 2012).

90. Flaring involves igniting methane at its point of release, whereby it is transformed into carbon dioxide. Venting involves direct release of methane into the atmosphere. In either event, failure to capture methane during drilling entails the permanent loss of a nonrenewable natural resource into the atmosphere, without its use for energy and exempt from any taxation or royalties to compensate for this loss of a valuable mineral.

91. Lachapelle, "Energy Security and Climate Policy in the OECD," 107.

92. Ibid., 108.

93. David Houle, Erick Lachapelle, and Mark Purdon, "Comparative Politics of Sub-Federal Cap-and-Trade: Implementing the Western Climate Initiative," *Global Environmental Politics* 15, no. 3 (2015): 59 and 65, doi:10.1162/GLEP_a_00311; Kossoy et al., *State and Trends of Carbon Pricing 2014*, 79.

94. Eleanor Stephenson and Karena Shaw, "A Dilemma of Abundance: Governance Challenges of Reconciling Shale Gas Development and Climate Change Mitigation," *Sustainability* 5, no. 5 (2013): 2219, doi:10.3390/su5052210; National Energy Board, *Canada's Energy Future: Energy Supply and Demand Projections to 2035* (Ottawa, ON: National Energy Board, 2011), https://www.neb-one.gc.ca/ nrg/ntgrtd/ftr /archive/2011/nrgsppldmndprjctn2035-eng.pdf.

95. Gordon Jaremko, "British Columbia's Shale Gas Resources Rising," *Natural Gas Intelligence's Shale Daily*, January 16, 2014, http://www.naturalgasintel.com/articles/97087 -british-columbias-shale-gas-resources-rising.

96. Ibid.

97. Michael Lerner, "Opportunity, Risk, and Public Acceptability: The Question of Shale Gas Exploitation in Quebec," *Issues in Energy and Environmental Policy*, no. 16 (2014): 1–29, http://closup.umich.edu/files/ieep-2014-shale-exploitation-quebec.pdf.

98. Henry Gass, "Proposed LNG Exports Spark Controversy in British Columbia," *E&E News*, October 7, 2013, http://www.eenews.net/stories/1059988405.

99. David Yerger, "The Shale Gas Revolution: Its Current and Potential Impacts on Ontario's Economic Relationship with the USA and Western Canada," paper, MANECCS Annual Conference, Niagara Falls, ON, September 25–27, 2014, 25.

100. Ibid.

101. B.C. Natural Gas Workforce Strategy Committee, "B.C. Natural Gas Workforce Strategy and Action Plan," July 2013, http://bclnginfo.com/images/uploads/docu ments/BC%20Natural%20Gas%20Workforce%20Strategy%20and%20Action%20 Plan%20July%202013.pdf.

102. Ibid.; Pamela King, "How Do You Recruit 75K New Workers? British Columbia Sets Up a Plan," *E&E News*, July 26, 2013, http://www.eenews.net/energywire /stories/1059985115.

103. Chester Dawson and Ben Lefebrve, "U.S. and Canada Vie for Big Gas Projects," *Wall Street Journal*, August 5, 2013, http://www.wsj.com/articles/SB10001424127887 324260204578585883862305950.

104. Brent Jang and Justine Hunter, "Petronas Plays Hardball with B.C. over Pacific NorthWest LNG," *The Globe and Mail*, September 25, 2014, http://www

.theglobeandmail.com/report-on-business/industry-news/energy-and-resources/petr
onas-plays-hardball-with-bc-over-pacific-northwest-lng/article20798686/.

105. Nathan Vanderklippe, "Climate Takes Back Seat as Fledgling B.C. LNG Industry
Courts China," *The Globe and Mail*, November 24, 2013, http://www.theglobeand
mail.com/report-on-business/industry-news/energy-and-resources/climate-takes-back
-seat-as-fledgling-bc-lng-industry-courts-china/article15579405/.

106. Barry G. Rabe and Rachel Hampton, "Taxing Fracking: The Politics of State Severance Taxes in the Shale Era," *Review of Policy Research* 32, no. 4 (2015): 389–412,
doi:10.1111/ropr.12127.

107. Marc Lee, "BC Is Giving Away Its Natural Gas," *Policy Note*, November 21,
2012, http://www.policynote.ca/bc-is-giving-away-its-natural-gas/.

108. Pawel Mirski and Len Coad, *Managing Expectations: Assessing the Potential of BC's
Liquid Natural Gas Industry* (Calgary, AB: Canada West Foundation, 2013), http://
cwf.ca/research/publications/managing-expectations-assessing-the-potential-of
-bcs-liquid-natural-gas-industry/; Tim Boersma, Charles K. Ebinger, and Heather L.
Greenley, *Natural Gas Issue Brief #4: An Assessment of U.S. Natural Gas Exports* (Washington, DC: Brookings Institution, 2015), https://www.brookings.edu/wp-content
/uploads/2016/06/lng_markets.pdf.

109. Policy briefing with James Mack, British Columbia Climate Action Secretariat,
February 13, 2013.

110. Quoted in Mike Hager, "B.C. Liberals Set to Announce Five-Year Carbon Tax
Freeze," *Vancouver Sun*, April 3, 2013, http://www.vancouversun.com/technology
/Liberals+announce+five+year+carbon+freeze/8186348/story.html.

111. Dirk Meissner, "Three Years On, Only B.C. Has a Carbon Tax," *The Globe and
Mail*, June 30, 2011, http://www.theglobeandmail.com/news/british-columbia/three
-years-on-only-bc-has-a-carbon-tax/article585153/.

112. For fuller discussion of these emerging cases, see Partnership for Market Readiness and World Bank Group, *Carbon Tax Guide: A Handbook for Policy Makers* (Washington, DC: World Bank, 2017). For more information on the American state carbon
tax proposals, see table 6.4. On Mexico, see Metcalf, "A Conceptual Framework,"
21–26. On New Zealand, see Kerri Metz and Nina Tannenbaum, "The Status of
New Zealand's Emissions Trading Scheme" (Working Paper No. 1, Center for Local,
State, and Urban Policy at the Gerald R. Ford School of Public Policy, University of
Michigan, 2015), http://closup.umich.edu/files/closup-swp-1-metz-tannenbaum-new
-zealand-emissions-trading-scheme.pdf. These cases are discussed in greater detail in
chapter 8.

113. Robert Noel de Tilly, "The Cap-and-Trade Program of the Western Climate
Initiative" (presentation, ITU Symposium on ICTs, the Environment, and Climate

Change, Montreal, May 29, 2012); Houle, *Obstacles to Carbon Pricing in Canadian Provinces*.

114. Rabe and Borick, "Carbon Taxation and Policy Labeling," 372–373.

115. Sanya Carley, "The Era of State Policy Innovation: A Review of Policy Instruments," *Review of Policy Research* 28, no. 3 (2011): 265–294, doi:10.1111/j.1541-1338 .2011.00495.x.

116. Frank Convery, Louise Dunne, and Deirdre Joyce, "Ireland's Carbon Tax in the Context of the Fiscal Crisis," *Cyprus Economic Policy Review* 8, no. 2 (2014): 135–143, https://www.ucy.ac.cy/erc/documents/Convey_et_al_135-143.pdf.

117. Institute for European Environmental Policy, *Evaluation of Environmental Tax Reforms: International Experiences* (Brussels: IEEP, 2013), 25, http://www.ieep.eu /assets/1283/ETR_study_by_IEEP_for_the_Swiss_Government_-_Final_report_-_21 _June_2013.pdf.

118. Elisabeth Rosenthal, "Carbon Taxes Make Ireland Even Greener," *New York Times*, December 27, 2012, http://www.nytimes.com/2012/12/28/science/earth/in -ireland-carbon-taxes-pay-off.html.

119. Convery, Dunne, and Joyce, "Ireland's Carbon Tax," 131–137.

120. Ibid.

Chapter 5

1. Erick Lachapelle, "Assessing Public Support for Cap-and-Trade Systems," *Policy Options* 36, no. 8 (December 2015), http://policyoptions.irpp.org/magazines/december -2015/lappui-du-public-aumarche-du-carbone/. Also see Erick Lachapelle, Christopher Borick, and Barry G. Rabe, "Public Opinion on Climate Change and Support for Various Policy Instruments in Canada and the U.S.: Findings from a Comparative 2013 Poll," *Issues in Energy and Environmental Policy*, no. 11 (June 2014): 1–21, http://closup.umich.edu/files/ieep-nsee-2013-fall-canada-us.pdf.

2. David M. Konisky and Neal D. Woods, "Environmental Policy, Federalism, and the Obama Presidency," *Publius: The Journal of Federalism* 46, no. 3 (Summer 2016): 366–391.

3. Eric M. Patashnik, "The Clean Air Act's Use of Market Mechanisms," in *The Durability of the Clean Air Act*, ed. Ann Carlson and Dallas Burtraw (New York: Cambridge University Press, 2018).

4. The extensive literature on the performance of cap-and-trade for sulfur dioxide emissions is generally quite positive in environmental quality and economic impact assessment. For a valuable summary, see Patashnik, "The Clean Air Act's Use of Market Mechanisms." There has been some analysis in more longitudinal research

that asks whether the flexible trading systems produced high concentrations of emissions in certain local contexts, in many respects consistent with concerns that environmental justice groups have raised about the distributional impacts of carbon cap-and-trade. See H. Ron Chan, B. Andrew Chupp, Maureen L. Cropper, and Nicholas Z. Muller, "The Market for Sulfur Dioxide Allowances: What Have We Learned from the Grand Policy Experiment?" (Working Paper No. 21583, National Bureau of Economic Research, 2016), doi:10.3386/w21383.

5. Leigh Raymond, "Reclaiming the Atmospheric Commons" (presentation, Midwest Political Science Association Annual Conference, Chicago, March 31–April 1, 2011). For the definitive account of this auctioning process and its potential longer-term ramifications, see Leigh Raymond, *Reclaiming the Atmospheric Commons: The Regional Greenhouse Gas Initiative and a New Model of Emissions Trading* (Cambridge, MA: MIT Press, 2016).

6. Daniel J. Elazar, *American Federalism: A View from the States*, 3rd ed. (New York: Harper and Row, 1984).

7. Ann O'M. Bowman, "Horizontal Federalism: Exploring Interstate Interactions," *Journal of Public Administration Research and Theory* 14, no. 4 (October 2004): 540, doi:10.1093/jopart/muh035.

8. Joseph F. Zimmerman, *Interstate Competition: Compacts and Administrative Agreements,* 2nd ed. (Albany: State University of New York Press, 2012).

9. Jørgen K. Knudsen, "Integration of Environmental Concerns in a Trans-Atlantic Perspective: The Case of Renewable Electricity," *Review of Policy Research* 27, no. 2 (March 2010): 140, doi:10.1111/ j.1541-1338.2009.00434.x.

10. Christopher James (Connecticut Department of Environmental Protection), interview with the author, May 2, 2006.

11. Barry G. Rabe, "Leveraged Federalism and the Clean Air Act: The Case of Vehicle Emissions Control," in *The Future of U.S. Energy Policy: Lessons from the Clean Air Act*, ed. Ann E. Carlson and Dallas Burtraw (New York: Cambridge University Press, 2018).

12.The OTC consists of all RGGI states along with New Jersey, Pennsylvania, and Virginia. The core RGGI group overlaps closely with the core OTC group engaged in the trading system. See Gary C. Bryner, *Blue Skies, Green Politics: The Clean Air Act of 1990 and Its Implementation* (Washington, DC: CQ Press, 1995).

13. Andrew Aulisi, Alexander E. Farrell, Jonathan Pershing, Stacy VanDeveer, *Greenhouse Gas Emissions in the U.S. States: Observations and Lessons from the OTC NOx Budget Program* (Washington, DC: World Resources Institute, 2005), http://pdf.wri .org/nox_ghg.pdf; A. Denny Ellerman, Paul L. Joskow, and David Harrison, Jr., *Emissions Trading in the U.S.: Experience, Lessons, and Considerations for Greenhouse Gases* (Arlington, VA: Pew Center on Global Climate Change, 2003), 29–31, http://web .mit.edu/globalchange/www/PewCtr_MIT_Rpt_Ellerman.pdf.

14. Chris Nelson (Connecticut Department of Environmental Protection), interview with the author, May 1, 2006.

15. Quoted in Barry G. Rabe, *Statehouse and Greenhouse: The Emerging Politics of American Climate Change Policy* (Washington, DC: Brookings Institution Press, 2004), 77.

16. Cat Lazaroff, "New Hampshire Passes Nation's First CO_2 Cap," *ENS Newswire.com*, April 22, 2002, http://www.ens-newswire.com/ens/apr2002/2002-04-22-06.html.

17. Rabe, *Statehouse and Greenhouse*, 78.

18. Bruce R. Huber, "How Did RGGI Do It? Political Economy and Emissions Auctions," *Ecological Law Quarterly* 40, no. 59 (2013): 100–101, http://scholarship.law .nd.edu/law_faculty_scholarship/473/; Leigh Raymond, "States Leading the Way to a New Paradigm for Climate Policy" (presentation, Midwest Political Science Association Annual Conference, Chicago, April 3–6, 2014.) Also see Roger Karapin, *Political Opportunities for Climate Policy: California, New York, and the Federal Government* (New York: Cambridge University Press, 2016), chap. 8.

19. Raymond, *Reclaiming the Atmospheric Commons*; Susan Tierney, untitled lecture, University of Michigan, February 22, 2006.

20. George E. Pataki and Thomas J. Vilsack, *Confronting Climate Change: A Strategy for U.S. Foreign Policy* (New York: Council on Foreign Relations, 2008), http://i.cfr .org/content/publications/attachments/Climate_ChangeTF.pdf. Pataki ultimately ran, albeit unsuccessfully, for the Republican presidential nomination in 2016; Vilsack went on to serve as secretary of agriculture under President Barack Obama.

21. Gina McCarthy (remarks, Regional Greenhouse Gas Initiative Stakeholder Group Meeting, Hartford, Connecticut, May 2, 2006).

22. Regional Greenhouse Gas Initiative, "Memorandum of Understanding," December 20, 2005, http://www.rggi.org/docs/mou_12_20_05.pdf.

23. Jonathan L. Ramseur, *The Regional Greenhouse Gas Initiative: Lessons Learned and Issues for Congress* (Washington, DC: Congressional Research Service, 2016), 19, https://www.fas.org/sgp/crs/misc/R41836.pdf. If the RGGI states were combined with California, the only other state operating a cap-and-trade program, they would rank seventh nationally in total emissions, behind Germany and ahead of South Korea.

24. Regional Greenhouse Gas Initiative, "Memorandum of Understanding."

25. Ibid., 4.

26. Maria Gallucci, "GOP Bill to Remove New Hampshire from Carbon Trading Pact Moves Forward," *InsideClimate News*, February 21, 2011, https://insideclimatenews.org /news/20110221/gop-bill-remove-new-hampshire-carbon-trading-pact-moves-forward.

27. Quoted in Brian J. Cook, "Arenas of Power in Climate Change Policymaking," *Policy Studies Journal* 38, no. 3 (2010): 478, doi:10.1111/j.1541-0072.2010.00370.x.

28. Raymond, *Reclaiming the Atmospheric Commons*, 109.

29. Barry G. Rabe, "The Aversion to Direct Cost Imposition: Selecting Climate Policy Tools in the United States," *Governance* 23, no.4 (2010): 598, doi:10.1111/j.1468-0491.2010.01499.x.

30. As political scientist Brian Cook noted, at the time, incoming Governor Patrick "had the independent legal authority and the political power gained through a strong electoral victory and veto-proof party control of the state legislature to overcome the resistance of the concentrated cost bearers," See Cook, "Arenas of Power in Climate Change Policymaking," 480.

31. Ramseur, *The Regional Greenhouse Gas Initiative*, 9.

32. See Raymond, *Reclaiming the Atmospheric Commons*.

33. Barry G. Rabe, "Regionalism and Global Climate Change Policy: Revisiting Multistate Collaboration as an Intergovernmental Management Tool," in *Intergovernmental Management for the 21st Century*, ed. Timothy J. Conlan and Paul L. Posner (Washington, DC: Brookings Institution Press, 2008), 198.

34. Rabe, "The Aversion to Direct Cost Imposition," 598.

35. Karl Widerquist and Michael W. Howard, eds., *Alaska's Permanent Fund Dividend: Examining Its Suitability as a Model* (New York: Palgrave, 2012).

36. Portions of this section previously were published in Barry G. Rabe, "The Durability of Carbon Cap-and-Trade Policy," *Governance* 29, no. 1 (2016): 103–199, doi:10.1111/gove.12151.

37. Ramseur, *The Regional Greenhouse Gas Initiative*, 9.

38. Cook, "Arenas of Power in Climate Change Policymaking."

39. Regional Greenhouse Gas Initiative Inc., "Investment of RGGI Proceeds through 2013," April 2015, https://www.rggi.org/docs/ProceedsReport/Investment-RGGI-Proceeds-Through-2013.pdf.

40. Ibid., 8.

41. Quoted in Rabe, "The Durability of Carbon Cap-and-Trade Policy," 117.

42. Regional Greenhouse Gas Initiative Inc., "RGGI Report: Investments General Savings, Reduce Pollution (news release, September 26, 2016). Paper copy on file with author.

43. Regional Greenhouse Gas Initiative Inc., "RGGI: The Investment of RGGI Proceeds through 2014," September 2016, https://www.rggi.org/docs/ProceedsReport/RGGI_Proceeds_Report_2014.pdf.

44. Sarah B. Mills, Barry G. Rabe, and Christopher Borick, "Cap-and-Trade Support Linked to Revenue Use," *Issues in Energy and Environmental Policy*, no. 23 (2015): 12, http://closup.umich.edu/files/ieep-nsee-2015-cap-and-trade.pdf.

45. Jean Chemnick, "RGGI Tightens Industrial Emissions Cap," *E&E News*, February 7, 2013, http://www.eenews.net/greenwire/stories/1059975997.

46. Quoted in Doug Obey, "Clean Energy Firms Seek to Strengthen Northeast Climate Program," *Inside EPA Clean Energy Report*, July 25, 2011. Paper copy on file with author.

47. Doug Obey, "Draft RGGI Analysis Sees Little Power Price Impact from Stricter GHG Cap," *Inside EPA*, January 14, 2013. Paper copy on file with author.

48. Delaware's chief environmental official and RGGI Vice-Chair Collin O'Mara noted that "our first auction under the new cap demonstrates how market-based programs cost-effectively reduce carbon pollution while driving investments in a clean energy economy." Quoted in "CO_2 Allowances Sold at $4.00 at 23rd RGGI Auction," Regional Greenhouse Gas Initiative Inc. (news release, March 7, 2014), http://www.rggi.org/docs/Auctions/23/PR030714_Auction23.pdf.

49. Dawn Reeves, "Higher RGGI Auction Prices Boost Confidence in Plan to Tighten GHG Cap," *Inside EPA*, April 11, 2013, http://insideepa.com/daily-news /higher-rggi-auction-prices-boost-confidence-plan-tighten-ghg-cap. University of Virginia economist Bill Shobe added after this initial auction that "the market has spoken" and that this first test provided an "indication that there is some expectation that this market is going to be healthy." Shobe also observed that the lower cap was needed to enable RGGI "to be taken seriously," noting that if states were able to sustain this cap, "this will really be a huge leap in RGGI's credibility." Quoted in ibid.

50. Ramseur, *The Regional Greenhouse Gas Initiative*, 15.

51. Colin Sullivan, "Northeast 'Off to a Running Start' in Advance of Obama Emissions Plan," *E&E News*, June 3, 2014, http://www.eenews.net/energywire/stories /1060000600.

52. Ann McLane Kuster and Niki Tsongas, letter to Gina McCarthy, January 31, 2014, https://kuster.house.gov/sites/kuster.house.gov/files/wysiwyg_uploaded/Kuster TsongasEPALetter.pdf.

53. Regional Greenhouse Gas Initiative Inc., "RGGI States' Comments on Proposed Carbon Pollution Emission Guidelines for Existing Stationary Sources: Electric Utility Generating Units, 79 FR 34830," November 2014, 8, http://www.rggi.org/docs /PressReleases/PR110714_CPP_Joint_Comments.pdf.

54. Kristi E. Swartz, "A Lot of Benefit Seen on Regional Approach to EPA Climate Rule," *E&E News*, April 1, 2015, http://www.eenews.net/energywire/stories/1060016098.

55. Regional Greenhouse Gas Initiative Inc., "RGGI States Comments Support EPA Proposed Clean Power Plan" (news release, November 7, 2014), http://www.dec.ny .gov/docs/administration_pdf/rggicommentpr1114.pdf.

56. Peter Shattuck and Jordan Stutt, *The Regional Greenhouse Gas Initiative: A Model Program for the Power Sector* (Boston: Acadia Center, 2015), http://acadiacenter .org/wp-content/uploads/2015/07/RGGI-Emissions-Trends-Report_Final.pdf; Peter Shattuck, *The Regional Greenhouse Gas Initiative: Performance To-Date and the Path Ahead* (Boston: Acadia Center, 2014), http://acadiacenter.org/wp-content /uploads/2014/05/AcadiaCenter_RGGI_Report_140523_Final3.pdf; Ramseur, *The Regional Greenhouse Gas Initiative.* For detailed electricity-sector emissions on a state-by-state basis over a longer time period, see US Energy Information Administration, "Energy-Related Carbon Dioxide Emissions at the State Level, 2000–2014," 2017), http://www.eia.gov/environment/emissions/state/analysis/pdf/stateanalysis.pdf.

57. Brian C. Murray and Peter T. Maniloff, "Why Have Greenhouse Emissions in RGGI States Declined? An Econometric Attribution to Economic, Energy Market, and Policy Factors," *Energy Economics* 51 (2015): 581, doi:10.1016/j.eneco.2015.07.013.

58. Christa Marshall, "Regional Carbon Cap Gets Second Look as 'Template' for National Plan," *New York Times*, July 14, 2010, http://www.nytimes.com/cwire /2010/07/14/14climatewire-regional-carbon-cap-gets-second-look-as-temp-89444. html?pagewanted=all; Environment Northeast (ENE), "RGGI Emission Trends and the Second Allowance Auction," December 2008, http://www.lawandenvironment .com/uploads/file/ENE_2nd_RGGI_Emissions_Report_v2.pdf; "Environmentalists, Industry Clash on Tighter Cap Allowances for RGGI," *CarbonControlNews*, December 8, 2010. Paper copies on file with author. See also Pamela F. Faggert of Dominion Energy, letter to Jonathan Schrag, executive director of the Regional Greenhouse Gas Initiative Inc., November 30, 2010, https://www.rggi.org/docs/Dominion _Energy_NE_Nov_2010.pdf; Michael E. Van Brunt of Covanta Energy, letter to the Regional Greenhouse Gas Initiative Inc., November 30, 2010, https://www.rggi.org /docs/Covanta_Nov_2010.pdf; William L. Fang of Edison Electric Institute, letter to Jonathan Schrag, executive director of the Regional Greenhouse Gas Initiative Inc., Nov. 30, 2010, https://www.rggi.org/docs/Edison_Electric_Institute_Nov_2010.pdf; Ann Ingerson of the Wilderness Society, letter to Regional Greenhouse Gas Initiative Participating States, November 30, 2010, https://www.rggi.org/docs/The_Wilderness _Society_Nov_2010.pdf.

59. Doug Obey, "Coal Plant's Retirement despite Upgrades Illustrates Sector's Hurdles," *Inside EPA*, October 16, 2013. Paper copy on file with author.

60. Ramseur, *The Regional Greenhouse Gas Initiative*, 5–6.

61. Regional Greenhouse Gas Initiative Inc., "Report on Emission Reduction Efforts of the States Participating in the Regional Greenhouse Gas Initiative and Recommendations for Guidelines under Section 111(d) of the Clean Air Act," December 2013,

https://www.rggi.org/docs/RGGI_States_111d_Letter_Comments.pdf. According to this fifteen-page report, the "reduction in the emission intensity of electricity generation in the RGGI states is due in part to the ramping up of renewable energy standards that provide for steep increases in the percentage of renewable energy sold in each state" (4).

62. Kirsten H. Engel, "Regional Coordination in Mitigating Climate Change, *New York University Environmental Law Journal* 14, no. 1 (2005): 54–83; Barry G. Rabe, "Building on Sub-Federal Climate Strategies: The Challenges of Regionalism," in *Climate Change Policy in North America: Designing Integration in a Regional System*, ed. Neil Craik, Isabel Studer, and Debora VanNijnatten (Toronto: University of Toronto Press, 2013), 85–86.

63. Regional Greenhouse Gas Initiative Inc., "Potential Emissions Leakage and the Regional Greenhouse Gas Initiative: Evaluating Market Dynamics, Monitoring Options, and Possible Mitigation Mechanisms," March 2007, https://www.rggi.org/docs/il_report_final_3_14_07.pdf; Dawn Reeves, "New Efforts to Address GHG 'Leakage' Highlights Wide Gap among States," *Inside EPA*, May 8, 2013. Paper copies on file with author.

64. Ramseur, *The Regional Greenhouse Gas Initiative*, 19.

65. Ibid., 17.

66. American Council for an Energy Efficient Economy (ACEEE), *The State Energy Efficiency Scorecard* (Washington, DC: ACEEE, 2015), http://aceee.org/state-policy/scorecard.

67. For complementary analyses of this development, see Shattuck, *The Regional Greenhouse Gas Initiative: Performance To-Date and the Path Ahead*, 9–10; Shattuck and Stutt, *The Regional Greenhouse Gas Initiative: A Model Program for the Power Sector*, 9–10. For a detailed summary of energy efficiency expenditures within states and various regional groupings that include electricity transmission, see Paul J. Hibbard, Andrea M. Okie, Susan F. Tierney, and Pavel G. Darling, *The Economic Impacts of the Regional Greenhouse Gas Initiative on Nine Northeast and Mid-Atlantic States* (Boston: Analysis Group, 2015), http://www.analysisgroup.com/uploadedfiles/content/insights/publishing/analysis_group_rggi_report_july_2015.pdf.

68. Shattuck and Stutt, *The Regional Greenhouse Gas Initiative: A Model Program for the Power Sector*, 9–10.

69. Ibid.

70. Hibbard et al., *The Economic Impacts of the Regional Greenhouse Gas Initiative*, 39–40.

71. Jordan Stutt and Peter Shattuck, *Regional Greenhouse Gas Initiative Status Report* (Boston: Acadia Center, 2016), http://acadiacenter.org/document/measuring-rggi-success.

72. Shattuck and Stutt, *The Regional Greenhouse Gas Initiative: A Model Program for the Power Sector*, 4.

Chapter 6

1. Anne C. Mulkern and Debra Kahn, "Calif. Chamber Sues to Stop Cap and Trade, Calling It an Illegal 'Tax,'" *E&E News*, November 14, 2012, http://www.eenews.net /stories/1059972479.

2. Barry G. Rabe, *Statehouse and Greenhouse: The Emerging Politics of American Climate Change Policy* (Washington, DC: Brookings Institution Press, 2004), 141–144.

3. David Vogel, *California Greenin': How the Golden State Became an Environmental Leader* (Princeton, NJ: Princeton University Press, 2018).

4. Barry G. Rabe, "Leveraged Federalism and the Clean Air Act: The Case of Vehicle Emissions Control," in *The Future of U.S. Energy Policy: Lessons from the Clean Air Act*, ed. Ann E. Carlson and Dallas Burtraw (Cambridge: Cambridge University Press, 2018).

5. Portions of this section are derived from Barry G. Rabe, "The Durability of Carbon Cap-and-Trade Policy," *Governance* 29, no. 1 (2016): 103–199, doi:10.1111/ gove.12151.

6. Brown served two previous terms as governor of California, from 1975 to 1983.

7. Curt Barry, "Brown Skirts Debate on Post-2020 GHG Goals but Plans New 2030 Programs," *Inside EPA*, January 5, 2015. Paper copy on file with author. Governor Brown stated: "Recently, both the secretary-general of the United Nations and the president of the World Bank made clear that properly pricing carbon is a key strategy. California's cap-and-trade system fashioned under AB 32 is doing just that and showing how the market itself can generate the innovations we need."

8. Diana Forster and Daniel A. Smith, "Environmental Policies on the Ballot," in *Changing Climate Politics*, ed. Yael Wolinsky-Nahmias (Washington, DC: Sage/CQ, 2015), 171–196.

9. Barry G. Rabe, "Governing the Climate from Sacramento," in *Unlocking the Power of Networks: Keys to High-Performance Governments*, ed. Stephen Goldsmith and Donald F. Kettl (Washington, DC: Brookings Institution Press, 2009), 34–61.

10. Debra Kahn, "Calif's Cap-and-Trade Overseer Steers Ambitious Program through Rough Seas," *E&E News*, November 14, 2012, http://www.eenews.net/sto ries/1059972480; Chris Megerian, "Mary Nichols Has 'Rock Star' Influence as Top Air Quality Regulator," *Los Angeles Times*, December 27, 2014, http://www.latimes .com/local/politics/la-me-pol-adv-mary-nichols-20141228-story.html.

11. "California Will Delay Cap and Trade, Easing Angst over Program Operation," *Clean Energy Report*, June 30, 2011.

12. Rabe, "The Durability of Carbon Cap-and-Trade Policy," 112.

13. Curt Barry, "California Poised to Launch CCS Program, including GHG Quantification Method," *Inside EPA*, February 4, 2016; Curt Barry, "California Plan to End CCS Project Spurs Debate over Climate Impacts," *Inside EPA*, February 12, 2016. Paper copies on file with author.

14. Jean-Thomas Bernard and Jean-Yves Duclos, "Quebec's Green Future: The Lowest-Cost Route to Greenhouse Gas Reductions," C. D. Howe Institute Backgrounder No. 118, October 2009, https://www.cdhowe.org/sites/default/files/attachments /research_papers/mixed//backgrounder_118_English.pdf; Marcel Boyer, *Higher Electricity Prices Can Unleash the Value of Quebec's Energy Potential* (Montreal: Montreal Economic Institute, 2007), http://www.iedm.org/files/avril2007_en.pdf.

15. For an extensive analysis of the evolution of carbon pricing in Quebec, see David Houle, *Carbon Pricing in Canada: Bounded Provincial Autonomy and Climate Policy Innovation* (Toronto: University of Toronto Press, forthcoming).

16. Michael Lerner, "Opportunity, Risk, and Public Acceptability: The Question of Shale Gas Exploitation in Quebec," *Issues in Energy and Environmental Policy*, no. 16 (2014): 1–29, http://closup.umich.edu/files/ieep-2014-shale-exploitation-quebec.pdf.

17. "Quebec Adopts Cap-and-Trade Regulation," *Western Climate Initiative*, December 16, 2011, http://www.westernclimateinitiative.org/news-and-updates/139-quebec -adopts-cap-and-trade-regulation?format=pdf. Arcand also declared that "Quebec is one of the leaders in the fight against climate change, and that is something to be proud of" (para. 6).

18. Debra Kahn, "Calif. Proves That Its Cap-and-Trade Works, with One Hiccup," *E&E News*, November 5, 2015, http://www.eenews.net/climatewire/stories/10600 27520.

19. Katherine Hsia-Kiung and Erica Morehouse, *Carbon Market California: A Comprehensive Analysis of the Golden State's Cap-and-Trade Program* (Washington, DC: Environmental Defense Fund, 2015), 7, http://www.edf.org/sites/default/files/content /carbon-market-california-year_two.pdf.

20. Ibid., 6–7.

21. Debra Kahn, "Calif. Carbon Offsets Face Slowdown in Market Development," *E&E News*, October 14, 2015, http://www.eenews.net/climatewire/stories/1060026292; Curt Barry, "Finding Fraud, California Invalidates GHG Offset Credits but Limits Scope," *Inside EPA*, October 9, 2014. Paper copy on file with author.

22. Hsia-Kiung and Morehouse, *Carbon Market California,* 25–26.

23. "Total Electricity System Power," *California Energy Commission*, last modified July 11, 2016, http://www.energy.ca.gov/almanac/electricity_data/total_system _power.html.

24. Danny Cullenward, "The Limits of Administrative Law as Regulatory Oversight in Linked Carbon Markets," *UCLA Journal of Environmental Law and Policy* 33, no. 1 (2015): 12, http://escholarship.org/uc/item/3tz3n5zf; Danny Cullenward, "How California's Carbon Market Actually Works," *Bulletin of the Atomic Scientists* 79, no. 5 (September 2014): 35–44, http://thebulletin.org/2014/september/how-califo rnias-carbon-market-actually-works7589.

25. Cullenward, "The Limits of Administrative Law," 36.

26. Debra Kahn, "Leaders Mull Direction, Significance of State's Energy and Climate Policies," *E&E News*, April 22, 2013, http://www.eenews.net/climatewire/stories /1059979844.

27. Leigh Raymond, *Reclaiming the Atmospheric Commons: The Regional Greenhouse Gas Initiative and a New Model of Emissions Trading* (Cambridge, MA: MIT Press, 2016), 135–136.

28. Portions of this section are drawn from Rabe, "The Durability of Carbon Cap-and-Trade."

29. Vauhini Vara and Cassandra Sweet, "California Auctions Emission Permits," *Wall Street Journal*, November 14, 2012, http://www.wsj.com/articles/SB100014241 27887324595904578119254205657698.

30. Various statutes in effect for fiscal year 2016 designated that funding should be allocated to the following categories: "(1) 25 percent for the state's high-speed rail project, (2) 20 percent for affordable housing and sustainable communities grants (with at least half of this amount for affordable housing), (3) 10 percent for intercity rail capital projects, and (4) 5 percent for low carbon transit operations. The remaining 40 percent is available for annual appropriation by the Legislature." Mac Taylor, *The 2016–2017 Budget: Resources and Environmental Protection* (Sacramento, CA: Legislative Analyst's Office, 2016), 8–9, http://www.lao.ca.gov/reports/2016/3354 /resources-analysis-021616.pdf.

31. Anne C. Mulkern, "Regulators Get to the Tough Part of Cap and Trade—How to Spend the Money Effectively," *E&E News*, April 26, 2013, http://www.eenews.net /climatewire/ stories/1059980194.

32. Debra Kahn, "Former White House Adviser Rails against Governor's Budget Proposal," *E&E News*, May 20, 2013, http://www.eenews.net/climatewire/stories /1059981446.

33. Benjamin K. Sovacool and Michael H. Dworkin, *Global Energy Justice: Problems, Principles, and Practices* (New York: Cambridge University Press, 2014); Christopher H. Foreman, Jr., "Book Review: Questions of Fairness," *Issues in Science and Technology* 32, no. 2 (Winter 2016): 87–88, http://issues.org/32-2/book-review -questions-of-fairness/; Michael J. Sandel, *What Money Can't Buy: The Moral Limits of Markets* (New York: Farrar, Straus and Giroux, 2012), 72–79.

34. Curt Barry, "Scant Data on GHG Spending Hampers California Lawmakers' New Budget," *Inside EPA*, March 7, 2016. Paper copy on file with author.

35. Taylor, *The 2016–2017 Budget*, 14–15, 19.

36. Legislative Analyst's Office, "Administration's Cap-and-Trade Report Provides New Information, Raises Issues for Consideration," April 20, 2016.

37. "Big Reserves, Big Reservations," *The Economist*, February 14, 2013, http://www.economist.com/news/united-states/21571899-california-tries-decide-if-it-wants-join-shale-revolution-big-reserves-big; "California Official Downplays Fracking Threats, but Promises Robust Rules," *Clean Energy Report*, June 12, 2012. Paper copies on file with author.

38. During a 2016 bus tour of California drilling sites, actor Mark Ruffalo said, "If change does not start in California, it won't happen anywhere. The fossil fuel industry has worked to prevent a much needed paradigm shift in our energy and environmental policy. We seek to end oil and gas development in California and more rapidly toward 100 percent renewable energy." Quoted in Anne C. Mulkern, "Mark Ruffalo, Other Actors Push to Stop Calif. Oil Drilling," *E&E News*, March 7, 2016, http://www.eenews.net/energywire/stories/1060033529.

39. Bridget DiCosmo, "Environmentalists Eye California as Key Battleground for Drilling Rules," *Inside EPA*, March 22, 2013, http://insideepa.com/daily-news/environmentalists-eye-california-key-battleground-drilling-rules. Brown was engulfed in controversy in 2015 when it was revealed that he sought a state assessment of the oil drilling potential on the ranch that he owns and received a fifty-one-page report. There was no evidence that he intended to pursue extraction, although numerous additional California land owners began to seek state assessments of their own land, perhaps responding to advertising by a consumer protection non-profit organization that encouraged Californians to "Ask for Your Free Jerry Brown Oil Map."

40. Barry G. Rabe, "Shale Play Politics: The Intergovernmental Odyssey of American Shale Governance," *Environmental Science & Technology* 48, no. 15 (2014): 8371–8375, doi:10.1021/ es4051132.

41. Curt Barry, "California Lauds EPA Oil and Gas Methane Plan but Further Delays State Rule," *Inside EPA*, September 3, 2015.

42. Joby Warrick, "California Gas Leak Was the Worst Man-Made Greenhouse-Gas Disaster in U.S. History, Study Says," *Washington Post*, February 25, 2016, http://wapo.st/1Q51TVQ.

43. Richard Nemec, "California Governor Reiterates Fracking Support," *Natural Gas Intelligence's Shale Daily*, December 3, 2015, http://www.naturalgasintel.com/articles/104548-california-governor-reiterates-fracking-support.

44. Cassarah Brown, *State Revenues and the Natural Gas Boom: An Assessment of State Oil and Gas Production Taxes* (Denver: National Conference of State Legislatures, 2013), http://www.ncsl.org/documents/energy/pdf_version_final.pdf.

45. Rachel L. Hampton and Barry G. Rabe, "Leaving Money on the Table: Pennsylvania Exceptionalism in Resisting Energy Severance Taxes," *Commonwealth* 17, no. 1 (2017): 5–32, http://dx.doi.org/10.15367/com.v19i1.131.

46. "Big Reserves, Big Reservations," *The Economist*; Anne C. Mulkern, "New Battle Strategies Emerge in Fight over Oil Severance Tax," *Energy Wire*, April 24, 2014. Paper copies on file with author.

47. Barry G. Rabe and Rachel Hampton, "Taxing Fracking: The Politics of State Severance Taxes in the Shale Era," *Review of Policy Research* 32, no. 4 (2015): 400; Hampton and Rabe, "Leaving Money on the Table."

Chapter 7

1. Jonathan L. Ramseur, "U.S. Carbon Dioxide Emission Trends and the Role of the Clean Power Plan," Congressional Research Service, April 11, 2016.

2. Barack Obama, "Remarks by the President in Announcing the Clean Power Plan" (speech, the White House, Washington, DC, August 3, 2015), https://www.whitehouse .gov/the-press-office/2015/08/03/remarks-president-announcing-clean-power-plan.

3. "Numbers: EIA Says CO_2 from Energy on a Decline," *Inside EPA*, May 9, 2016, http:// www.insideepaclimate.com/climate-beat/numbers-eia-says-co2-energy-decline; Perry Lindstrom, "U.S. Energy-Related Carbon Dioxide Emissions in 2015 Are 12% below Their 2005 Levels," *Today in Energy*, May 9, 2016, https://www.eia.gov/todayinenergy /detail.cfm?id=26152.

4. "Numbers: EIA Says CO_2 from Energy on a Decline"; Lindstrom, "U.S. Energy-Related Carbon Dioxide Emissions"; "Numbers: EIA Finds CO_2 from Electricity at Lowest Level since 1993," *Inside EPA*, May 13, 2016, http://www.insideepaclimate .com/climate-beat/numbers-eia-finds-co2-electricity-lowest-level-1993.

5. For early efforts to interpret the various factors contributing to this decline in emissions, see Kuishuang Feng, Steven J. Davis, Laixiang Sun, and Klaus Hubacek, "Drivers of the U.S. CO_2 Emissions 1997–2013," *Nature Communications* 6 (2015): 1–8, doi:10.1038/ncomms8714; Jonathan L. Ramseur, *U.S. Greenhouse Gas Emissions: Recent Trends and Factors* (Washington, DC: Congressional Research Service, 2014), https:// www.fas.org/sgp/crs/misc/R43795.pdf; Hal T. Nelson, David von Hippel, Tom Peterson, and Roman Garagulagian, "The Great Recession or Progressive Energy Policies? Explaining the Decline in US Greenhouse Gas Emissions Forecasts," *Journal of Environmental Planning and Management* 59, no. 3 (2016): 480–500, doi:10.1080/096405 68.2015.1017042.

6. "The Deepest Cuts," *The Economist*, September 20, 2014, http://www.economist .com/news/briefing/21618680-our-guide-actions-have-done-most-slow-global-warming-deepest-cuts. This article reflects analysis conducted by Climate Action Tracker, a group of scientists who examine emissions policies and impacts.

7. See, for example, Paul Roberts, *The End of Oil: On the Edge of a Perilous New World* (Boston: Houghton Mifflin, 2005).

8. Barry G. Rabe, *Statehouse and Greenhouse: The Emerging Politics of American Climate Change Policy* (Washington, DC: Brookings Institution Press, 2004), chap. 1; Michael Mintrom and Phillipa Norman, "Policy Entrepreneurs and Policy Change," *Policy Studies Journal* 37, no. 4 (2009): 649–667, doi:10.1111/j.1541-0072.2009.00329.x; Rachel M. Krause, "Symbolic or Substantive Policy? Measuring the Extent of Local Commitment to Climate Protection," *Environmental Planning C: Government and Policy* 29, no. 1 (2011): 46–62, doi:10.1068/c09185.

9. Barry G. Rabe and Christopher P. Borick, "The Decline of Public Support for State Climate Change Policies: 2008–2013," *Issues in Energy and Environmental Policy*, no. 7 (2014): 1–10, http://closup.umich.edu/files/ieep-nsee-2013-fall-state-policy-options.pdf.

10. For an earlier framing of this question, see Jenny Sumner, Lori Bird, and Hillary Smith, *Carbon Taxes: A Review of Experience and Policy Design Considerations* (Golden, CO: National Renewable Energy Laboratory, 2009), iv, http://www.nrel.gov/docs /fy10osti/47312.pdf.

11. Leigh Raymond, *Reclaiming the Atmospheric Commons: The Regional Greenhouse Gas Initiative and a New Model of Emissions Trading* (Cambridge, MA: MIT Press, 2016).

12. Brian J. Cook, "Arenas of Power in Climate Change Policymaking," *Policy Studies Journal* 38, no. 3 (2010): 465–486, doi:10.1111/j.1541-0072.2010.00370.x; Eric M. Patashnik, *Reforms at Risk: What Happens after Major Policy Changes Are Enacted* (Princeton, NJ: Princeton University Press, 2008); Suzanne Mettler, "The Policyscape and the Challenges of Contemporary Politics to Policy Maintenance," *Perspectives on Politics* 14, no. 2 (2016): 369–390, doi:10.1017/S1537592710004068.

13. Christopher R. Berry, Barry C. Burden, and William G. Howell, "After Enactment: The Lives and Deaths of Federal Programs," *American Journal of Political Science* 54, no. 1 (2010): 1–17, doi:10.1111/j.1540-5907.2009.00414.x.

14. Leif Wenar, *Blood Oil: Tyrants, Violence, and the Rules That Run the World* (New York: Oxford University Press, 2016).

15. Barry G. Rabe and Rachel L. Hampton, "Trusting in the Future: The Re-emergence of State Trust Funds in the Shale Era," *Energy Research & Social Science* (2016): 1–11, doi:10.1016/j.erss.2016.06. 011; Devashree Saha and Mark Muro, *Permanent Trust Funds: Funding Economic Change with Fracking Revenues* (Washington, DC: Brookings Institution, 2016), https://www.brookings.edu/wp-content/uploads/2016/07 /Permanent-Trust-Funds-Saha-Muro-418-1.pdf.

16. Rabe and Hampton, "Trusting in the Future."

17. Widerquist and Howard eds., *Alaska's Permanent Fund Dividend.*

18. Barry G. Rabe and Rachel Hampton, "Taxing Fracking: The Politics of State Severance Taxes in the Shale Era," *Review of Policy Research* 32, no. 4 (2015): 389–412, doi:10.1111/ropr.12127.

19. Rachel L. Hampton and Barry G. Rabe, "Leaving Money on the Table: Pennsylvania Exceptionalism in Resisting Energy Severance Taxes," *Commonwealth* 17, no. 1 (2017): 4–32.

20. Aaditya Mattoo and Arvind Subramanian, *Greenprint: A New Approach to Cooperation on Climate Change* (Washington, DC: Brookings Institution Press, 2013); David Garman and Samuel Thernstrom, "Breaking the Silos," *The Environmental Forum* 31, no. 3 (2014): 34–38, https://www.eli. org/the-environmental-forum/breaking-silos; Richard K. Lester and David M. Hart, *Unlocking Energy Innovation: How America Can Build a Low-Cost, Low-Carbon Energy System* (Cambridge, MA: MIT Press, 2012); Bruce Babbitt, "Preparing for Rising Water along U.S. Coastlines," in *Climate Change and Land Policies,* ed. Gregory K. Ingram and Yu-Hung Hong (Cambridge: Lincoln Institute of Land Policy, 2011), chap. 2.

21. Donald F. Kettl, *Escaping Jurassic Government: How to Recover America's Lost Commitment to Competence* (Washington, DC: Brookings Institution Press, 2016).

22. Donald F. Kettl, "Private-Market Misfires and Misconceptions," *Governing,* February 2016, http://www. governing.com/columns/potomac-chronicle/gov-free-market-failures-government.html.

23. Sarah B. Mills, Barry G. Rabe, and Christopher Borick, "Cap-and-Trade Support Linked to Revenue Use," *Issues in Energy and Environmental Policy,* no. 23 (2015): 12, http://closup.umich.edu/files/ieep-nsee-2015-cap-and-trade.pdf; Rabe and Borick, "Decline of Public Support."

24. Vivian E. Thomson, *Sophisticated Interdependence in Climate Policy: Federalism in the United States, Brazil, and Germany* (London: Anthem Press, 2014).

25. Jenna Bednar, *The Robust Federation: Principles of Design* (Cambridge: Cambridge University Press, 2009), 1.

26. Ibid., 16.

Chapter 8

1. Mai Farid et al. *After Paris: Fiscal, Macroeconomic and Financial Implications of Climate Change* (Washington, DC: International Monetary Fund, 2016), 5, https://www.imf.org/external/pubs/ft/sdn/2016/sdn1601.pdf.

2. Jean Chemnick, "IMF Call for Pricing Carbon in Wake of Global Climate Deal," *E&E News*, January 13, 2016, http://www.eenews.net/climatewire/stories/1060030516.

3. Quoted in Matt McGrath, "Pressure Grows for Price on Carbon Ahead of UN Signing," *BBC News*, April 21, 2016, para. 7 under "Cap, Trade or Tax," http://www.bbc .com/news/science-environment-36098318; "Push for Carbon Price Growing with Paris Agreement," *E&E News*, April 25, 2016, http://www.eenews.net/climatewire /stories/ 1060036140.

4. Robert Inglis would be honored in 2014 with a John F. Kennedy Profile in Courage Award for having proposed a revenue-neutral carbon tax that contributed to the end of his career in electoral politics in the previous decade.

5. Ian W. H. Parry and Roberton C. Williams, III, *Is a Carbon Tax the Only Good Climate Policy? Options to Cut CO₂ Emissions* (Washington, DC: Resources for the Future, 2010), http://www.rff.org/files/sharepoint/WorkImages/Download/RFF-Resources-176_Car bonTax.pdf.

6. David Amdur, Barry G. Rabe, and Christopher P. Borick, "Public Views on a Carbon Tax Depend on the Proposed Use of Revenue," *Issues in Energy and Environmental Policy*, no. 13 (2014): 1, 8, http://closup.umich.edu/files/ieep-nsee-2014-spring-carbon-tax .pdf; Stephen Ansolabehere and David Konisky, *Cheap and Clean: How Americans Think about Energy in the Age of Global Warming* (Cambridge, MA: MIT Press, 2014), chap. 8.

7. Emily Holden, Hannah Hess, and Evan Lehmann, "The Carbon Tax That Clinton Decided Not to Use: $42," *E&E News*, October 21, 2016.

8. Dawn Reeves, "Whitehouse Slated to Offer Carbon Tax Bill That Could Replace EPA Rules," *Inside EPA*, October 28, 2014, http://insideepa.com/daily-news/white house-slated-offer-carbon-tax-bill-could-replace-epa-rules.

9. A08372, New York State Assembly 2015–2016 Session, http://assembly.state.ny .us/leg/?default_fld=&bn=A08372&term=2015&Summary=Y& Memo=Y&Text=Y; Doug Obey, "Joining Other State Efforts, New York Bill Adds Heft to Carbon Tax Push," *Inside EPA*, September 4, 2015. Paper copies on file with author.

10. A08372, New York State Assembly.

11. Climate Leadership Council, *The Conservative Case for Carbon Dividends* (Washington, DC: Climate Leadership Council, 2017), https://www.clcouncil.org/wp-content /uploads/2017/02/TheConservativeCaseforCarbonDividends.pdf.

12. Alan Thein Durning, Rachel Gussett, and Yoram Bauman, *Tax Shift: How to Help the Economy, Improve the Environment, and Get the Tax Man off Our Backs* (Seattle: Sightline Institute, 1998), http://www.sightline.org/research_item/tax/.

13. Quoted in "States: Activists in Washington May Force Legislature to Consider Carbon Tax," *Inside EPA*, January 6, 2016, http://www.insideepaclimate.com /climate-beat/states-activists-washington-may-force-legislature-consider-carbon-tax.

14. The Chilean tax focuses on the electricity sector and major sectors, beginning at a rate equivalent to US$5 per ton in 2018. See Kate Galbraith, "Climate Change Concerns Push Chile to Forefront of Carbon Tax Movement," *New York Times*, October 29, 2014, http://www.nytimes.com/2014/10/30/business/international /climate-change-concerns-push-chile-to-forefront-of-carbon-tax-movement.html. The Mexican tax was set at a rate equivalent to US$3.50 per ton in 2014, although it entirely exempts natural gas and allows for purchase of offset credits as an alternative compliance mechanism. For a comparative review of these recent carbon tax initiatives, see Partnership for Market Readiness and World Bank Group, *Carbon Tax Guide: A Handbook for Policy Makers* (Washington, DC: World Bank, 2017).

15. For example, in 2013 then-premier Alison Redford made a heavily publicized trip to Washington, DC, to seek support for Keystone construction and to defend Alberta energy and climate policies. The visit included meetings with members of Congress and a public talk at the Brookings Institution that was disrupted by protesters. See Christa Marshall, "Alberta's Premier Says Focus on Greenhouse Gas Regulations Is Premature," *E&E News*, April 13, 2013, http://www.eenews.net/cli matewire/stories/ 1059979187.

16. Laurie E. Adkin, ed., *First World Petro-Politics: The Political Ecology and Governance of Alberta* (Toronto: University of Toronto Press, 2016); Gary Mason, "Notley's Fiscal Straightjacket Gets a Bit Tighter," *The Globe and Mail*, August 28, 2015, http:// www.theglobeandmail.com/opinion/notleys-fiscal-straitjacket-gets-a-bit-tighter /article26135186/.

17. Chester Dawson, "Oil-Rich Alberta Moves Ahead with Energy Royalty Review," *Wall Street Journal*, August 28, 2015, http://www.wsj.com/articles/oil-rich-alberta-mov es-ahead-with-energy-royalty-review-1440789261.

18. Benjamin Hulac, "In Oil-Rich Alberta, Premier Addresses Climate, Economic Concerns," *E&E News*, September 26, 2015, http://www.eenews.net/climatewire /stories/1060025301.

19. Barry G. Rabe, "Can Congress Govern the Climate?," in *Greenhouse Governance: Addressing Climate Change in America*, ed. Barry G. Rabe (Washington, DC: Brookings Institution Press, 2010), chap. 11.

20. Gary C. Bryner, *Blue Skies, Green Politics: The Clean Air Act of 1990 and Its Implementation* (Washington, DC: CQ Press, 1995); Richard E. Cohen, *Washington at Work: Back Rooms and Clean Air*, 2nd ed. (Boston: Allyn and Bacon, 1995).

21. Massachusetts v. U.S. Environmental Protection Agency, 549 U.S. 497 (2007).

22. Brendan Boyd, "Working Together on Climate Change: Policy Transfer and Convergence in Four Canadian Provinces," *Publius* 47, no. 4 (October 2017): 546–571.

23. Jonathan L. Ramseur and James E. McCarthy, *EPA's Clean Power Plan: Highlights of the Final Rule* (Washington, DC: Congressional Research Service, 2016), https://www.fas.org/sgp/crs/misc/R44145.pdf.

24. Quoted in Lee Logan, "EPA Strengthens Final ESPS and Sees Coal Generation Taking a Bigger Hit," *Inside EPA*, August 2, 2015, http://insideepa.com/daily-news/epa-strengthens-final-esps-and-sees-coal-generation-taking-bigger-hit.

25. See, for example, Franz T. Litz and Jennifer Macedonia, *Choosing a Policy Pathway for State 111(d) Plans to Meet State Objectives* (Washington, DC: Bipartisan Policy Center and Great Plains Institute, 2015), http://bipartisanpolicy.org/wp-content/uploads/2015/04/BPC-111d-Report.pdf.

26. "RGGI States Recommend That EPA Support Flexible Market-Based Carbon Pollution Programs," *Regional Greenhouse Gas Initiative*, December 2, 2013, https://www.rggi.org/docs/PressReleases/PR120213_EPAComments_Final.pdf; RGGI State Agency Heads, letter to Regina McCarthy, December 2, 2013, *Regional Greenhouse Gas Initiative*, https://www.rggi.org/docs/RGGI_States_111d_Letter_ Comments.pdf.

27. Quoted in Colin Sullivan, "Northeast 'Off to a Running Start' in Advance of Obama Emissions Plan," *E&E News*, June 3, 2014, http://www.eenews.net/energywire/stories/1060000600.

28. Adrian Morrow, Jane Taber, and Sean Silcoff, "Ontario Plans Cap-and-Trade on Greenhouse Gas Emissions," *The Globe and Mail*, April 2, 2015, http://www.theglobeandmail.com/news/politics/ontario-plans-cap-and-trade-on-greenhouse-gas-emissions/article23786538/.

29. James Fitz-Morris, "Justin Trudeau, Premiers Seek to Unify Canada's Message on Climate Change," *CBC News*, November 23, 2015, para. 7 under "Many Options," http://www.cbc.ca/m/touch/politics/story/1.3330284.

30. On the origins and early implementation of this policy, see Ian H. Rowlands, "The Development of Renewable Electricity Policy in the Province of Ontario: The Influence of Ideas and Timing," *Review of Policy Research* 24, no. 3 (2007): 185–207. doi:10.1111/j.1541-1338.2007.00277.x.

31. The Ontario government claimed in 2015 that "ending coal-fired power is the single largest greenhouse gas reduction initiative in North America, equivalent to taking seven million cars off the road." Ministry of Environment and Climate Change, Government of Ontario, "Ontario Releases Climate Change Strategy Discussion Paper" (news release, February 12, 2015). Also see Brendan Boyd, "Learning to Address Climate Change: Collaboration, Policy Transfer, and Choosing Policy Instruments in Canadian Provinces" (PhD diss., University of Victoria, 2015), 109; Melissa Harris, Marisa Beck, and Ivetta Gerasimchuk, *The End of Coal: Ontario's Coal Phase-Out* (Winnipeg, MB: International Institute for Sustainable Development,

2015), www.iisd.org/sites/default/files/publications/end-of-coal-ontario-coal-phase
-out.pdf.

32. Barry G. Rabe and Rachel Hampton, "Taxing Fracking: The Politics of State Severance Taxes in the Shale Era," *Review of Policy Research* 32, no. 4 (2015): 389–412, doi:10.1111/ropr.12127.

33. Kathryn Harrison, "International Carbon Trade and Domestic Climate Politics," *Global Environmental Politics* 15, no. 3 (2015): 27–47.

34. Barry G. Rabe and Rachel L. Hampton, "Trusting in the Future: The Re-emergence of State Trust Funds in the Shale Era," *Energy Research & Social Science* (2016): 1–11, doi:10.1016/j.erss.2016.06. 011. On the broader issue of trust funds in the United States, see Eric M. Patashnik, *Putting Trust in the U.S. Budget: Federal Trust Funds and the Politics of Commitment* (New York: Cambridge University Press, 2000).

35. Leif Wenar, *Blood Oil: Tyrants, Violence, and the Rules that Run the World* (New York: Oxford University Press, 2016); Michael L. Ross, *The Oil Curse: How Petroleum Wealth Shapes the Development of Nations* (Princeton, NJ: Princeton University Press, 2012); Francis Sejerstad, *The Age of Social Democracy: Norway and Sweden in the Twentieth Century* (Princeton, NJ: Princeton University Press, 2011).

36. Wenar, *Blood Oil*; Ross, *The Oil Curse*; Sejerstad, *Age of Social Democracy*.

37. Rabe and Hampton, "Taxing Fracking," 405–406.

38. Rabe and Hampton, "Trusting in the Future," 9.

39. Elwyn B. Robinson, *History of North Dakota*, rev. ed. (Lincoln, NE: University of Nebraska Press, 1996).

40. A separate 5 percent Oil Gross Production Tax was adopted in 1953, and a 6.5 percent Oil Extraction Tax was adopted by ballot proposition in 1980 to produce a combined rate. This rate was reduced to 10 percent in 2015 along with elimination of triggers that allowed for deeper reductions during steep price declines. See Ryan Rauschenberger, *2014 State and Local Taxes: An Overview and Comparative Guide* (Bismarck, ND: Office of State Tax Commissioner, 2014), accessed May 14, 2015, https://issuu.com/ndtax/docs/state_and_local_taxes_guide_flip.

41. Barry G. Rabe, "Contested Federalism," in *Environmental Governance Reconsidered: Challenges, Choices, and Opportunities*, ed. Robert F. Durant, Daniel J. Fiorino, and Rosemary O'Leary (Cambridge, MA: MIT Press, 2016), 144–146.

42. Arthur A. Link, "Political Constraint and North Dakota's Coal Severance Tax," *National Tax Association* 31, no. 3 (September 1978): 263–268. Link was a two-term Democratic Governor of North Dakota between 1973 and 1981 and is widely viewed as the driving force behind this policy.

43. Rabe and Hampton, "Taxing Fracking," 405–407.

44. Ibid., 403–404.

45. Richard Nemec, "North Dakota Not Going Easy on Flaring Any Longer, Governor Says," *Natural Gas Intelligence's Shale Daily*, May 27, 2014, http://www.naturalgasintel .com/articles/98495-north-dakota-not-going-easy-on-flaring-any-longer-governor-says.

46. Chester Dawson, "North Dakota's Latest Fracking Problem," *Wall Street Journal*, June 30, 2014, http://www.wsj.com/articles/north-dakotas-latest-fracking-problem -1404170442.

47. A. J. Turner et al., "A Large Increase in U.S. Methane Emissions over the Past Decade Inferred from Satellite Data and Surface Observations," *Geophysical Research Letters* 43, no. 5 (2016): 2218–2224, doi:10.1002/2016GL067987; Daniel Zavala-Araiza et al., "Reconciling Divergent Estimates of Oil and Gas Methane Emission," *Proceedings of the National Academy of Sciences of the United States of America* 112, no. 51 (2015): 15597–15602, doi:10.1073/pnas.1522126112; Sean Wright and Carlos Villacis, *Risking Risk: Improving Methane Disclosure in the Oil and Gas Industry* (New York: Environmental Defense Fund, 2016), http://business.edf.org/files/2016/01/rising_risk_full_report .pdf; Anthony J. Marchese et al., "Methane Emissions from United States Natural Gas Gathering and Processing," *Environmental Science and Technology* 49, no. 17 (2015): 10718–10727, doi:10. 1021/acs.est.5b02275.

48. The greenhouse gas emissions from this leak were comparable to annual emissions from nearly 600,000 cars or 160 coal plants over a twenty-year period. See Joby Warrick, "Calif. Methane Leak Is Called Historic," *Washington Post*, February 26, 2016; Fred Krupp, "Fixing the Methane Leaks That Deflate Natural-Gas Gains," *Wall Street Journal*, February 3, 2016.

49. Global Gas Flaring Reduction Partnership, *Guidance on Upstream Flaring and Venting: Policy and Regulation* (Washington, DC: World Bank, 2009); Prentice with Rioux, *Triple Crown*, 112 and 205–206.

50. Mary Kang et al., "Identification and Characterization of High Methane-Emitting Abandoned Oil and Gas Wells," *Proceedings of the National Academy of Sciences* 113, no. 48 (2016): 13636–13641, doi:10.1073/pnas.16059.3113.

51. John Fialka, "Methane Leaks Declining Even as Natural Gas Production Grows," *E&E News*, October 6, 2016.

52. Nick Smith, "More Restrictions on Flaring Introduced," *Bismarck Tribune*, February 6, 2015, http://bismarcktribune.com/bakken/more-restrictions-on-flaring-introduced /article_ 5c1377b0-d183-56d0-b72d-0bbf3428ed33.html; Chester Dawson, "Dispute Flares over Burned-Off Natural Gas," *Wall Street Journal*, August 3, 2014, http://www .wsj.com/articles/ dispute-flares-over-burned-off-natural-gas-1407108281.

53. In the case of coal mining, see Nidhi Thakar and Michael Madowitz, *Federal Coal Leasing in the Powder River Basin: A Bad Deal for Taxpayers* (Washington, DC: Center

for American Progress, 2014), https://cdn.americanprogress.org/wp-content/uploads/2014/07/ThakarPowderRiver-brief.pdf.

54. Thomas S. Burack and A. Stanley Meiburg, "Collaborative Federalism," *Environmental Forum* 33, no. 3 (2016): 23–27, https://eli.org/the-environmental-forum/collaborative-federalism.

55. Jonathan M. Fisk, *The Fracking Debate: The Intergovernmental Politics of the Oil and Gas Renaissance* (Boca Raton, FL: CRC Press, 2017), chap. 4.

56. Jack Calder, "Administration of a US Carbon Tax," in *Implementing a US Carbon Tax: Challenges and Debates*, ed. Ian Perry, Adele Morris, and Robertson C. Williams III (London: Routledge, 2015), 53–55; Gilbert E. Metcalf and David E. Weisbach, "The Design of a Carbon Tax," *Harvard Environmental Law Review* 3 (2009): 499–556.

57. "Scrap Them," *The Economist*, June 14, 2014, https://www.economist.com/news/leaders/21604170-there-are-moves-around-world-get-rid-energy-subsidies-heres-best-way-going; David Coady, Ian Parry, Louis Sears, and Baoping Shang, "IMF Working Paper: How Large Are Global Energy Subsidies?," May 2015, https://www.imf.org/en/News/Articles/2015/09/28/04/53/sonew070215a; International Energy Agency, "World Energy Outlook 2011 Factsheet: How Will Global Energy Markets Evolve to 2035?," 2011, http://www.worldenergyoutlook.org/media/weowebsite/factsheets/factsheets.pdf.

58. Elizabeth Bast et al., *G20 Subsidies to Oil, Gas, and Coal Production* (Washington, DC: Overseas Development Institute, 2015); Geof Koss, "U.S. Is 'Laggard' in Fossil Fuel Subsidy Reform—Study," *E&E News Greenwire*, November 12, 2015, https://www.eenews.net/greenwire/2015/11/12/stories/1060027888.

59. Gilbert Metcalf, *The Impact of Removing Tax Preferences for U.S. Oil and Gas Production* (New York: Council on Foreign Relations, August 2016); Joseph E. Aldy, "Money for Nothing: The Case for Eliminating U.S. Fossil Fuel Subsidies," *Resources* (2015): 33–37, http://www.rff.org/research/publications/money-nothing-case-eliminating-us-fossil-fuel-subsidies.

60. Merrill Matthews, "Mineral Rights Can Make You Rich," *Wall Street Journal*, July 9, 2017.

61. US Government Accountability Office, *Coal Leasing: BLM Could Enhance Appraisal Process, More Explicitly Consider Coal Exports, and Provide More Public Information*, December 2013, https://www.gao/assets/660/659801.pdf; Office of Inspector General, *Coal Management Program, U.S. Department of Interior*, 2013, https://www.doioig.gov/sites/doioig.gov/files/CR-EV-BLM-0001-2012Public.pdf; Nidhi Thakar and Michael Madowitz, *Federal Coal Leasing in the Powder River Basin: A Bad Deal for Taxpayers* (Washington, DC: Center for American Progress, 2014), https://cdn.americanprogress.org/wp-content/uploads/2014/07/ThakarPowderRiver-brief.pdf.

62. Barry G. Rabe, *Statehouse and Greenhouse: The Emerging Politics of American Climate Change Policy* (Washington, DC: Brookings Institution Press, 2004), chap. 1–2; Barry G. Rabe and Christopher P. Borick, "Carbon Taxation and Policy Labeling: Experience from American States and Canadian Provinces," *Review of Policy Research* 29, no. 3 (2012): 358–382, doi:10.1111/j.1541-1338.2012.00564.x.

63. Kate Galbraith and Asher Price, *The Great Texas Wind Rush: How George Bush, Ann Richards, and a Bunch of Tinkerers Helped the Oil and Gas State Win the Race to Wind Power* (Austin: University of Texas Press, 2013); Texas Office of the Governor Economic Development Division, *The Texas Renewable Energy Industry* (Austin: Texas Office of the Governor, 2014), http://gov.texas.gov/files/ecodev/Renewable_Energy.pdf.

64. Rabe, *Statehouse and Greenhouse*, chap. 2.

65. Jim Malewitz, "$7 Billion CREZ Project Nears Finish, Aiding Wind Power," *Texas Tribune*, October 14, 2013, https://www.texastribune.org/2013/10/14/7-billion-crez-project-nears-finish-aiding-wind-po/.

66. Adam Fremeth and Alfred A. Marcus, "The Role of Governance Systems and Rules in Wind Energy Development: Evidence from Minnesota and Texas," *Business and Politics* 18, no. 3 (2016): 337–365.

67. Vivian E. Thomson, *Sophisticated Interdependence in Climate Policy: Federalism in the United States, Brazil, and Germany* (London: Anthem Press, 2014), 14–15; Robert Fares, "Texas Sets New All-Time Wind Energy Record," *Scientific American*, January 14, 2016, http://blogs. scientificamerican.com/plugged-in/texas-sets-new-all-time-wind-energy-record/.

68. American Wind Energy Association, *U.S. Wind Industry Annual Market Report, Year Ending 2015* (Washington, DC: AWEA, 2016), http://www.awea.org/amr2015.

69. Malewitz, "$7 billion CREZ Project Nears Finish, Aiding Wind Power."

70. Rabe and Borick, "Carbon Taxation and Policy Labeling."

71. Ruth Greenspan Bell, "Silver Buckshot: Alternative Pathways towards Greenhouse Gas Mitigation" (presentation, Woodrow Wilson Center for International Scholars, Washington, DC, June 24, 2014), https://www.wilsoncenter.org/event/silver-buckshot-alternative-pathways-towards-greenhouse-gas-mitigation.

72. Michael J. Sandel, *What Money Can't Buy: The Moral Limits of Markets* (New York: Farrar, Straus and Giroux, 2012), chap. 2; Wenar, *Blood Oil*. For a valuable contribution on the normative framing of carbon pricing from a political science perspective, see Leigh Raymond, *Reclaiming Our Atmospheric Commons: The Regional Greenhouse Gas Initiative and a New Model of Emissions Trading* (Cambridge, MA: MIT Press, 2016).

73. Pope Francis, *Laudato Si': On Care for Our Common Home* (Huntington, IN: Our Sunday Visitor, 2016).

74. Ibid., 112.

75. Ibid., 120–121.

76. Ibid., 110–111.

77. Ibid., 112–113.

78. Sarah B. Mills, Barry G. Rabe, and Christopher Borick, "Acceptance of Global Warming Rising for Americans of All Religious Beliefs," *Issues in Energy and Environmental Policy*, no. 26 (2015): 1–10, http://closup.umich.edu/files/ieep-nsee-2015-fall-religion.pdf; Nan Li et al., "Cross-Pressuring Conservative Catholics? Effects of Pope Francis' Encyclical on the U.S. Public Opinion on Climate Change," *Climatic Change* 139, issue 3–4 (2016): 367–380; Asheley R. Landrum et al., "Processing the Papal Encyclical through Perceptual Filters," *Cognition* (September 2017): 1–12.

79. Pope Francis, *Laudato Si'*, 126.

80. Coral Davenport, "Championing Environment, Francis Takes Aim at Global Capitalism," *New York Times*, June 18, 2015, http://www.nytimes.com/2015/06/19/world/europe/pope-targets-carbon-credits-economists-favored-path-to-change.html.

81. Robert N. Stavins, "Are the Pope's Critiques of Markets on Point or Somewhat Misguided?," *The Environmental Forum* 33, no. 1 (2016): 15, http://www.eli.org/sites/default/files/docs/tef/tef33-1.pdf.

82. William D. Nordhaus, "The Pope and the Market," *New York Review of Books* 62, no. 15 (October 8, 2015), http://www.nybooks.com/articles/2015/10/08/pope-and-market/.

83. For a particularly thorough account of Francis and the evolution of his thinking on theology and public affairs, see Austen Iverleigh, *The Great Reformer: Francis and the Making of a Radical Pope* (New York: Henry Holt, 2014).

84. Paul Sherman, "Vatican's Position on Carbon Offset Systems" (unpublished paper, University of Michigan, May 13, 2016).

85. Daniel Stone, "How Green Was the 'Green Pope'?," *National Geographic News*, February 28, 2013, http://news.nationalgeographic.com/news/2013/02/130228-environmental-pope-green-efficiency-vatican-city/; Tomek Rolski, "Vatican Hung(a)ry for Carbon Offset," *ABC News*, September 18, 2007, http://abcnews.go.com/International/story?id=3620636.

86. Doug Struck, "Buying Carbon Offsets May Ease Eco-Guilt but Not Global Warming," *Christian Science Monitor*, April 20, 2010, http://www.csmonitor.com/Environment/2010/0420/Buying-carbon-offsets-may-ease-eco-guilt-but-not-global-warming.

Bibliography

A08372. New York State Assembly 2015–2016 Session. http://assembly.state.ny.us /leg/?default fld=&bn=A08372&term=2015&Summary=Y& Memo=Y&Text=Y.

Adkin, Laurie E., ed. *First World Petro-Politics: The Political Ecology and Governance of Alberta*. Toronto: University of Toronto Press, 2016.

Aldy, Joseph E. "Money for Nothing: The Case for Eliminating U.S. Fossil Fuel Subsidies." *Resources* (2015): 33–37. http://www.rff.org/research/publications/money-nothing-case-eliminating-us-fossil-fuel-subsidies.

Alexander, Serena E. *From Planning to Action: An Evaluation of State Level Climate Action Plans*. PhD diss., Cleveland State University, College of Urban Affairs, 2016.

Amdur, David, Barry G. Rabe, and Christopher P. Borick. "Public Views on a Carbon Tax Depend on the Proposed Use of Revenue." *Issues in Energy and Environmental Policy*, no. 13 (2014): 1–8. http://closup.umich.edu/files/ieep-nsee-2014-spring-carbon-tax.pdf.

American Council for an Energy Efficient Economy (ACEEE). *The State Energy Efficiency Scorecard*. Washington, DC: ACEEE, 2015. http://aceee.org/state-policy/scorecard.

American Wind Energy Association (AWEA). *U.S. Wind Industry Annual Market Report, Year Ending 2015*. Washington, DC: AWEA, 2016. http://www.awea.org/amr2015.

Anderson, George, ed. *Oil and Gas in Federal Systems*. New York: Oxford University Press, 2012.

Anderson, Steven. Speech given at the Conference on Carbon Pricing and Environmental Federalism, Kingston, ON, October 17–18, 2008.

Andresen, Steiner, Jon Birgen Skjærseth, Torbjørg Jevnaker, and Jørgen Wettestad, "The Paris Agreement: Consequences for the EU and Carbon Markets?" *Politics and Governance* 4, no. 3 (2016): 188–196.

Angus Reid Institute. "BC NDP Remains Ahead, As Campbell Drops to Single Digits," 2010. Accessed April 9, 2016. http://angusreidglobal.com/wp-content/uploads /2010/10/2010.10.16_Politics_BC.pdf.

Ansolabehere, Stephen, and David Konisky. *Cheap and Clean: How Americans Think about Energy in the Age of Global Warming*. Cambridge, MA: MIT Press, 2014.

Aulisi, Andrew, Alexander E. Farrell, Jonathan Pershing, and Stacy VanDeveer. *Greenhouse Gas Emissions in the U.S. States: Observations and Lessons from the OTC NOx Budget Program*. Washington, DC: World Resources Institute, 2005. http://pdf.wri.org/nox_ghg.pdf.

Babbitt, Bruce. "Preparing for Rising Water along U.S. Coastlines." In *Climate Change and Land Policies*, edited by Gregory K. Ingram and Yu-Hung Hong, chap. 2. Cambridge: Lincoln Institute of Land Policy, 2011.

Bahl, Roy and Musharraf Cyan. "Tax Assignment: Does the Practice Match the Theory?" *Environment and Planning C: Government and Policy* 29, no. 2 (2011): 264–280. doi:10.1068/c1045r.

Barry, Curt. "Brown Skirts Debate on Post-2020 GHG Goals but Plans New 2030 Programs." *Inside EPA*, January 5, 2015.

Barry, Curt. "California Lauds EPA Oil and Gas Methane Plan but Further Delays State Rule." *Inside EPA*, September 3, 2015.

Barry, Curt. "California Plan to End CCS Project Spurs Debate over Climate Impacts." *Inside EPA*, February 12, 2016.

Barry, Curt. "California Poised to Launch CCS Program, including GHG Quantification Method." *Inside EPA*, February 4, 2016.

Barry, Curt. "Finding Fraud, California Invalidates GHG Offset Credits but Limits Scope." *Inside EPA*, October 9, 2014.

Barry, Curt. "Scant Data on GHG Spending Hampers California Lawmakers' New Budget." *Inside EPA*, March 7, 2016.

Bast, Elizabeth, et al. *G20 Subsidies to Oil, Gas, and Coal Production*. Washington, DC: Overseas Development Institute, 2015.

Baumgartner, Frank R., and Bryan D. Jones. *Agendas and Instability in American Politics*. Chicago: University of Chicago Press, 1993.

B.C. Natural Gas Workforce Strategy Committee. *B.C. Natural Gas Workforce Strategy and Action Plan*. British Columbia: B.C. Natural Gas Workforce Strategy Committee, 2013. http://bclnginfo.com/images/uploads/documents/BC%20Natural%20Gas%20Workforce%20Strategy%20and%20Action%20Plan%20July%202013.pdf.

Beck, Marisa, Nicholas Rivers, Randall Wigle, and Hidemichi Yonezawa. "Carbon Taxes and Revenue Recycling: Impacts on Households in British Columbia." *Resource and Energy Economics* 41 (2015): 40–69. doi:10.1016/j.reseneeco.2015.04.005.

Bednar, Jenna. *The Robust Federation: Principles of Design.* Cambridge: Cambridge University Press, 2009.

Bel, Germa, and Stephen Joseph. "Emission Abatement: Untangling the Impacts of the EU ETS and the Economic Crisis." *Energy Economics* 49 (2015): 531–539. doi:10.1016/j.eneco.2015.03.014.

Bell, Ruth Greenspan. "Silver Buckshot: Alternative Pathways towards Greenhouse Gas Mitigation." Presentation at the Woodrow Wilson Center for International Scholars, Washington, DC, June 24, 2014. https://www.wilsoncenter.org/event/silver -buckshot-alternative-pathways-towards-greenhouse-gas-mitigation.

Bernard, Jean-Thomas, and Jean-Yves Duclos. "Quebec's Green Future: The Lowest-Cost Route to Greenhouse Gas Reductions." *Backgrounder* No. 118, C. D. Howe Institute, Toronto, October 2009. https://www.cdhowe.org/sites/default/files/attachments /research_papers/mixed//backgrounder_118_English.pdf.

Berry, Christopher R., Barry C. Burden, and William G. Howell. "After Enactment: The Lives and Deaths of Federal Programs." *American Journal of Political Science* 54, no. 1 (2010): 1–17. doi:10.1111/j.1540-5907.2009.00414.x.

Bertram, Geoff, and Simon Terry. *The Carbon Challenge: New Zealand's Emissions Trading Scheme.* Wellington: Bridget Williams Books, 2010.

Birnbaum, Jeffrey H., and Alan S. Murray. *Showdown at Gucci Gulch.* New York: Vintage, 1988.

Boersma, Tim, Charles K. Ebinger, and Heather L. Greenley. *Natural Gas Issue Brief #4: An Assessment of U.S. Natural Gas Exports.* Washington, DC: Brookings Institution, 2015. https://www.brookings.edu/wp-content/uploads/2016/06/lng_markets.pdf.

Borghesi, Simone, and Massimiliano Montini. "The Allocation of Carbon Emission Permits: Theoretical Aspects and Practical Problems in the EU ETS." Financialisation, Economy, Society, and Sustainable Development Working Paper, January 2015. http://fessud.eu/wp-content/uploads/2015/01/The-allocation-of-carbon-emission -permits-theoretical-aspects-and-practical-problems-in-the-EU-ETS_working-paper -75-.pdf.

Borick, Christopher P., Barry G. Rabe, and Sarah B. Mills. "Acceptance of Global Warming among Americans Reaches Highest Level since 2008." *Issues in Energy and Environmental Policy*, no. 25 (2015): 1–8. http://closup.umich.edu/files/ieep-nsee -2015-fall-climate-belief.pdf.

Bošković, Branko, and Andrew Leach. *Leave It in the Ground? Oil Sands Extraction in the Carbon Bubble.* Edmonton: University of Alberta, 2014. http://www.uwinnipeg .ca/economics/docs/leach-oil-sands.pdf.

Bosso, Christopher J. *Pesticides and Politics: The Life Cycle of a Public Issue.* Pittsburgh: University of Pittsburgh Press, 1987.

Bowman, Ann O'M. "Horizontal Federalism: Exploring Interstate Interactions." *Journal of Public Administration Research and Theory* 14, no. 4 (October 2004): 540. doi:10.1093/jopart/muh035.

Boyd, Brendan. "Learning to Address Climate Change: Collaboration, Policy Transfer, and Choosing Policy Instruments in Canadian Provinces." PhD diss., University of Victoria, 2015.

Boyd, Brendan. "Working Together on Climate Change: Policy Transfer and Convergence in Four Canadian Provinces." *Publius* 47, no. 4 (October 2017): 546–571. https://academic.oup.com/publius/article/3798730/Working-Together-on-Climate -Change-Policy-Transfer?.

Boyer, Marcel. *Higher Electricity Prices Can Unleash the Value of Quebec's Energy Potential.* Montreal: Montreal Economic Institute, 2007. http://www.iedm.org/files /avril2007_en.pdf.

Bramley, Matthew, Marc Huot, Simon Dyer, and Matt Horne. *Responsible Action? An Assessment of Alberta's Greenhouse Gas Policies.* Drayton Valley, AB: Pembina Institute, 2011. https://www.pembina.org/reports/responsible-action.pdf.

Bramley, Matthew, P. J. Partington, and Dave Sawyer. *Linking National Cap-and-Trade Systems in North America.* Drayton Valley, AB: Pembina Institute; Winnipeg: International Institute for Sustainable Development, 2009. https://www.iisd.org /sites/default/files/publications/linking_nat_cap_north_america.pdf.

Brazier, Warren G. "British Columbia—Becoming a Renewable Energy Powerhouse." *Slaw*, June 23, 2009. http://www.slaw.ca/2009/06/23/british-columbia-becoming-a-re newable-energy-powerhouse/.

British Columbia Ministry of Finance. *Budget and Fiscal Plan 2008/09–2010/11.* Victoria, BC: Ministry of Finance, 2008. http://www.bcbudget.gov.bc.ca/2008/bfp/2008 _Budget_Fiscal_Plan.pdf.

British Columbia Ministry of Water, Land, and Air Protection. *Indicators of Climate Change for British Columbia 2002.* Vancouver, BC: Ministry of Water, Land, and Air Protection, 2002. http://www.rcbc.ca/files/u3/indcc.pdf.

Broder, David, and Haynes Johnson. *The System: The American Way of Politics at the Breaking Point.* Boston: Little, Brown, 1996.

Broder, John M. "House Bill for a Carbon Tax to Cut Emissions Faced a Steep Climb." *New York Times*, March 6, 2009. http://www.nytimes.com/2009/03/07/us /politics/07carbon.html.

Brown, Cassarah. *State Revenues and the Natural Gas Boom: An Assessment of State Oil and Gas Production Taxes.* Denver: National Conference of State Legislatures, 2013. http://www.ncsl.org/documents/energy/pdf_ version_final.pdf.

Bryner, Gary C. *Blue Skies, Green Politics: The Clean Air Act of 1990 and Its Implementation*. Washington, DC: CQ Press, 1995.

Burack, Thomas S., and A. Stanley Meiburg. "Collaborative Federalism." *Environmental Forum* 33, no. 3 (2016): 23–27. https://eli.org/the-environmental-forum /collaborative-federalism.

Burke, Brendan, and Margaret Ferguson. "Going Alone or Moving Together: Canadian and American Middle Tier Strategies on Climate Change." *Publius* 40, no. 3 (May 2010): 453. doi:10.1093/publius/pjq012.

Burtraw, Dallas. "The Institutional Blind Spot in Environmental Economics." *Daedalus* 142, no. 1 (Winter 2013): 113. doi:10.2139/ssrn.2145576.

Bushnell, James, Carla Peterman, and Catherine Wolfram. "California's Greenhouse Gas Policies: Local Solutions to a Global Problem." University of California Energy Institute, Center for the Study of Energy Markets, April 2007. faculty.haas.berkeley .edu/wolfram/papers/local_global_040207_wtables.pdf.

Cairney, Paul, Donley T. Studlar, and Hadii M. Mamudu. *Global Tobacco Policy: Power, Policy, Governance, and Transfer*. London: Palgrave Macmillan, 2012.

Calder, Jack. "Administration of a U.S. Carbon Tax." In *Implementing a U.S. Carbon Tax: Challenges and Debates*, edited by Ian Perry, Adele Morris, and Robertson C. Williams III, 53–55. New York: Routledge, 2015.

California Energy Commission. "Total Electricity System Power." July 11, 2016. http://www.energy.ca.gov/almanac/electricity_data/total_system_power.html.

"California Official Downplays Fracking Threats, but Promises Robust Rules." *Clean Energy Report*, June 12, 2012. In author's possession.

"California Will Delay Cap and Trade, Easing Angst over Program Operation." *Clean Energy Report*, June 30, 2011. In author's possession.

Campagnolo, Iona. "Speech from the Throne at the Opening of the Third Session, Thirty-Eighth Parliament of the Province of British Columbia." Legislative Assembly of British Columbia, Victoria, February 13, 2007. https://www.leg.bc.ca/content /legacy/web/38th3rd/Throne_Speech_2007.pdf.

Campbell, Gordon. "Address to Union of B.C. Municipalities Annual Convention." Vancouver, September–October 2007.

Canada's Ecofiscal Commission. *The Way Forward: A Practical Approach to Reducing Canada's Greenhouse Gas Emissions*. Montreal: Canada's Ecofiscal Commission, 2015. http://ecofiscal.ca/wp-content/uploads/2015/04/Ecofiscal-Commission-Report-The -Way-Forward-April-2015.pdf.

CarbonControlNews. "Court's Order Fails to End Uncertainty over Fate of New Mexico's GHG Rule." January 27, 2011, file 240. In author's possession.

CarbonControlNews. "Environmentalists, Industry Clash on Tighter Cap Allowances for RGGI." December 8, 2010. In author's possession.

Carbon Tax Act. S.B.C. 2008, c. 40, p. 5, d. 2. http://www.bclaws.ca/Recon/document /ID/ freeside/00_08040_01.

Carley, Sanya. "The Era of State Policy Innovation: A Review of Policy Instruments." *Review of Policy Research* 28, no. 3 (2011): 265–294. doi:10.1111/j.1541-1338.2011.00495.x.

Carlson, Ann E. "Iterative Federalism and Climate Change." *Northwestern University Law Review* 103, no. 3 (2009): 1097–1160.

Carlson, Ann E., and Dallas Burtraw, eds. *The Future of U.S. Energy Policy: Lessons from the Clean Air Act.* New York: Cambridge University Press, 2018.

Carlson, Ann E., and Robert W. Fri. "Designing a Durable Energy Policy." *Daedalus* 142, no. 1 (2013): 123. doi:10.1162/DAED_a_00189.

Carlson, Michael, Nicholas Ukrainetz, and Vicky Berger. "Lodgepole Pine, Western White Pine (Interior), Ponderosa Pine, Broadleaves (Interior)." *British Columbia Ministry of Forestry, Lands, and Natural Resource Operations.* https://www.for.gov.bc.ca/hre /forgen/interior/pine.htm.

Carr, Matthew. "Harvard Don Tells EU Kill Grants to Save Carbon: Energy Markets." *Bloomberg,* April 17, 2013. http://www.bloomberg.com/news/articles/2013-04-17/ha rvard-don-tells-eu-kill-grants-to-save-carbon-energy-markets.

Carter, Angela V., Gail S. Fraser, and Anna Zalik. "Environmental Policy Convergence in Canada's Fossil Fuel Provinces? Regulatory Streamlining, Impediments, and Drift." *Canadian Public Policy,* March 2017, 61–76. doi:10.31.38/cpp.2016-041.

Cass, Loren R. *The Failures of American and European Climate Policy.* Albany: State University of New York Press, 2006.

CBC News (Manitoba: CBC). "Doer Teams Up with Gubernator over Climate Change." September 27, 2006. http://www.cbc.ca/news/canada/manitoba/doer-teams-up-with -gubernator-over-climate-change-1.627954.

Centers for Disease Control and Prevention (CDC). *Best Practices for Comprehensive Tobacco Control Programs–2007.* Atlanta: US Department of Health and Human Services, Public Health Service, CDC, National Center for Chronic Disease Prevention and Health Promotion, Office on Smoking and Health, 2007.

Chan, H. Ron, B. Andrew Chupp, Maureen L. Cropper, and Nicholas Z. Muller. "The Market for Sulfur Dioxide Allowances: What Have We Learned from the Grand Policy Experiment?" Working Paper No. 21583, National Bureau of Economic Research, 2016. doi:10.3386/w21383.

Chemnick, Jean. "IMF Call for Pricing Carbon in Wake of Global Climate Deal." *E&E News,* January 13, 2016. http://www.eenews.net/climatewire/stories/1060030516.

Chemnick, Jean. "RGGI Tightens Industrial Emissions Cap." *E&E News*, February 7, 2013. http://www.eenews.net/greenwire/stories/1059975997.

Chicago Climate Exchange Inc. and the Province of Manitoba. *Letter of Understanding*, February 3, 2004. http://digitalcollection.gov.mb.ca/awweb/pdfopener?smd=1&did =11744&md=1.

Choloupka, Frank, Kurt Straif, and Maria E. Leon. "Effectiveness of Tax Price Policies in Tobacco Control." *Tobacco Control* 20, no. 3 (2011): 235–238. doi:10.1136/ tc.2010.039982.

Clean Energy Canada. *How to Adopt a Winning Carbon Price*. Vancouver, BC: Clean Energy Canada, 2015. http://cleanenergycanada.org/wp-content/uploads/2015/02 /Clean-Energy-Canada-How-to-Adopt-a-Winning-Carbon-Price-2015.pdf.

Climate Leadership Council. *The Conservative Case for Carbon Dividends*. Washington, DC: Climate Leadership Council, 2017. https://www.clcouncil.org/wp-content /uploads/2017/02/TheConservativeCaseforCarbonDividends.pdf.

Coad, Len. *Greenhouse Gas Mitigation in Canada*. Ottawa: Conference Board of Canada, 2011.

Coady, David, Ian Parry, Louis Sears, and Baoping Shang. "IMF Working Paper: How Large Are Global Energy Subsidies?" May 2015. https://www.imf.org/en/News /Articles/2015/09/28/04/53/sonew070215a.

Coase, Ronald H. "The Problem of Social Cost." *Journal of Law and Economics* 3 (1960): 1–44. http://www2.econ.iastate.edu/classes/tsc220/hallam/Coase.pdf.

Cohen, Richard E. *Washington at Work: Back Rooms and Clean Air*. 2nd ed. Boston: Allyn and Bacon, 1995.

Conlan, Timothy J., Paul L. Posner, and David R. Beam. *Pathways of Power: The Dynamics of National Policymaking*. Washington, DC: Georgetown University Press, 2014.

Conlan, Timothy J., Margaret T. Wrightson, and David R. Beam. *Taxing Choices: The Politics of Tax Reform*. Washington, DC: Congressional Quarterly, 1990.

Convery, Frank, Louise Dunne, and Deirdre Joyce. "Ireland's Carbon Tax in the Context of the Fiscal Crisis." *Cyprus Economic Policy Review* 8, no. 2 (2014): 135–143. https://www.ucy.ac.cy/erc/documents/Convey_et_al_135-143.pdf.

Cook, Brian J. "Arenas of Power in Climate Change Policymaking." *Policy Studies Journal* 38, no. 3 (2010): 465–486. doi:10.1111/j.1541-0072.2010.00370.x.

Craig, Geoffrey. "Six U.S. States Leave the Western Climate Initiative." *Platts*, November 18, 2011. http://www.platts.com/latest-news/electric-power/washington /six-us-states-leave-the-western-climate-initiative-6695863.

Craik, Neil, Isabel Studer, and Debora VanNijnatten, eds. *Climate Change Policy in North America: Designing Integration in a Regional System.* Toronto: University of Toronto Press, 2013.

Crocker, Thomas. "The Structuring of Atmospheric Pollution Control Systems." In *The Economics of Air Pollution,* edited by Harold Wolozin, 61–86. New York: W. W. Norton, 1966.

Crowley, Kate. "Pricing Carbon: The Politics of Climate Policy in Australia." *WIREs Climate Change* 4 (2013): 603–613. doi:10.1002/wcc/239.

Crowley, Kate. "Up and Down with Climate Politics 2013–2016: The Repeal of Carbon Pricing in Australia." *WIREs Climate Change* 8 (May/June 2017): 1–13. doi:10.11002/wcc.458.

Cullenward, Danny. "How California's Carbon Market Actually Works." *Bulletin of the Atomic Scientists* 79, no. 5 (September 2014): 35–44. http://thebulletin.org/2014 /september/how-californias-carbon-market-actually-works7589.

Cullenward, Danny. "The Limits of Administrative Law as Regulatory Oversight in Linked Carbon Markets." *UCLA Journal of Environmental Law and Policy* 33, no. 1 (2015): 12. http://escholarship.org/uc/item/3tz3n5zf.

Dales, John H. *Pollution, Property, and Prices: An Essay in Policy-Making and Economics.* Toronto: University of Toronto Press, 1968.

Davenport, Coral. "Championing Environment, Francis Takes Aim at Global Capitalism." *New York Times,* June 18, 2015. http://www.nytimes.com/2015/06/19/world /europe/pope-targets-carbon-credits-economists-favored-path-to-change.html.

Dawson, Chester. "Dispute Flares over Burned-Off Natural Gas." *Wall Street Journal.* August 3, 2014. http://www.wsj.com/articles/dispute-flares-over-burned-off-natural -gas-1407108281.

Dawson, Chester. "North Dakota's Latest Fracking Problem." *Wall Street Journal,* June 30, 2014. http://www.wsj.com/articles/north-dakotas-latest-fracking-problem -1404170442.

Dawson, Chester. "Oil-Rich Alberta Moves Ahead with Energy Royalty Review." *Wall Street Journal,* August 28, 2015. http://www.wsj.com/articles/oil-rich-alberta -moves-ahead-with-energy-royalty-review-1440789261.

Dawson, Chester, and Ben Lefebrve. "U.S. and Canada Vie for Big Gas Projects." *Wall Street Journal,* August 5, 2013. http://www.wsj.com/articles/SB10001424127887 324260204578585883862305950.

Derthick, Martha. *Policymaking for Social Security.* Washington, DC: Brookings Institution Press, 1979.

Desmaris, Bruce A., Jeffrey J. Harden, and Frederick J. Boehnke. "Persistent Policy Pathways: Inferring Diffusion Networks in the American States." *American Political Science Review* 109, no. 2 (2015): 392–406. http://myweb.uiowa.edu/fboehmke /shambaugh2014/papers/desmarais_etal_2014.pdf.

DiCosmo, Bridget. "Environmentalists Eye California as Key Battleground for Drilling Rules." *Inside EPA*, March 22, 2013. http://insideepa.com/daily-news/environ mentalists-eye-california-key-battleground-drilling-rules.

Dion, Stéphane. "Carbon Taxes: Can a Good Policy Become Good Politics?" In *Tax Is Not a Four-Letter Word: A Different Take on Taxes in Canada*, edited by Alex Himelfarb and Jordan Himelfarb. Waterloo, ON: Wilfrid Laurier University Press, 2013.

Dobesova, Katerina, Jay Apt, and Lester B. Lave. "Are Renewables Portfolio Standards Cost-Effective Emission Abatement Policy?" *Environmental Science & Technology* 39, no. 22 (2005): 8578–8583. doi:10.1021/es048024j.

Duff, David G. "Carbon Taxation in British Columbia." *Vermont Journal of Environmental Law* 10, no. 1 (Fall 2008): 87–107. http://vjel.vermontlaw.edu/files/2013/06 /Carbon_Taxation_in_British_Columbia.pdf.

Duff, David G., and Andrew J. Green. "Policies to Promote the Generation of Electricity from Renewable Sources." In *A Globally Integrated Climate Policy for Canada*, edited by Steven Bernstein, Jutta Brunnee, David G. Duff, and Andrew J. Green, 235–236. Toronto: University of Toronto Press, 2008.

Dufour, Daniel. "The Canadian Lumber Industry: Recent Trends." *Statistics Canada*, 2009. http://www.statcan.gc.ca/pub/11-621-m/11-621-m2007055-eng.htm.

Durning, Alan Thein, Rachel Gussett, and Yoram Bauman. *Tax Shift: How to Help the Economy, Improve the Environment, and Get the Tax Man Off Our Backs*. Seattle: Sightline Institute, 1998. http://www.sightline.org/research_item/tax/.

The Economist. "Axed: The Prime Minister Follows through on an Election Promise." July 19, 2014. http://www.economist.com/news/asia/21607865-prime-minister-follo ws-through-election-promise-axed.

The Economist. "Big Reserves, Big Reservations." February 14, 2013. http://www .economist.com/news/united-states/21571899-california-tries-decide-if-it-wants-join -shale-revolution-big-reserves-big.

The Economist. "Breathing Difficulties." March 3, 2012. http://www.economist.com /node/2154 8962.

The Economist. "Climate Policy in Canada: The Land of Green and Money." August 4, 2013. http://www.economist.com/blogs/americasview/2013/08/climate -policy-canada.

The Economist. "The Deepest Cuts." September 20, 2014. http://www.economist.com /news/briefing/21618680-our-guide-actions-have-done-most-slow-global-warming -deepest-cuts.

The Economist. "ETS, RIP?" April 20, 2013. http://www.economist.com/news/finance -and-economics/21576388-failure-reform-europes-carbon-market-will-reverberate-ro und-world-ets.

The Economist. "Green Fleeces, Red Faces: A Theft of Carbon Credits Embarrasses an Entire Market." February 3, 2011. http://www.economist.com/node/18063834.

The Economist. "Scrap Them." June 14, 2014. https://www.economist.com/news /leaders/21604170-there-are-moves-around-world-get-rid-energy-subsidies-heres -best-way-going.

The Economist. "We Have a Winner: British Columbia's Carbon Tax Woos Sceptics." July 21, 2011. http://www.economist.com/node/18989175.

E&E News. "Push for Carbon Price Growing with Paris Agreement." April 25, 2016. http://www.eenews.net/climatewire/stories/1060036140.

Ekins, Paul. "European Environmental Taxes and Charges: Recent Experience, Issues, and Trends." *Ecological Economics* 31 (1999): 39–62.

Elazar, Daniel J. *American Federalism: A View from the States.* 3rd ed. New York: Harper and Row, 1984.

Elgie, Stewart, and Stephanie Cairns. "Shifting to a Low-Carbon Economy: It Starts with a Price on Emissions." *Policy Options,* December 1, 2009. http://policyoptions.irpp .org/ magazines/the-2010-olympics/shifting-to-a-low-carbon-economy-it-starts-wit h-a-price-on-emissions/.

Elgie, Stewart, and Jessica McClay. "Policy Commentary/Commentaire: BC's Carbon Tax Shift Is Working Well after Four Years." *Canadian Public Policy* 39, no. 2 (July 2013): 1–10. http://www.utpjournals.press/doi/abs/10.3138/CPP.39.Supplement2.S1.

Ellerman, A. Denny, Barbara K. Buchner, and Carlo Carraro, eds. *Allocation in the European Emissions Trading System: Rights, Rents and Fairness.* New York: Cambridge University Press, 2007.

Ellerman, A. Denny, Paul L. Joskow, and David Harrison, Jr. *Emissions Trading in the U.S.: Experience, Lessons, and Considerations for Greenhouse Gases.* Arlington, VA: Pew Center on Global Climate Change, 2003. http://web.mit.edu/globalchange/www /PewCtr_MIT_Rpt_Ellerman.pdf.

Elsworth, Rob, Bryony Worthington, and Damien Morris. *Help or Hindrance? Offsetting in the EU ETS.* London: Sandbag Climate Campaign, 2012. https://sandbag.org .uk/site_media/pdfs/reports/Help_or_Hindrance_Offsetting_2012_3.pdf.

Engel, Kirsten H. "Regional Coordination in Mitigating Climate Change." *New York University Environmental Law Journal* 14, no. 1 (2005): 54–83.

Environics Institute for Survey Research and the David Suzuki Foundation. "Focus Canada 2015: Canadian Public Opinion about Climate Change." 2015. http://www .environicsinstitute.org/uploads/institute-projects/environicsinstitute-dsf%20 focus%20canada%202015%20-%20climate%20change%20survey%20-%20final%20 report%20-%20english.pdf.

Environment and Energy Publishing. "Economist Says Carbon Tax Is Tough but Crucial Climate Solution." *E&E News*, February 13, 2014. http://www.eenews.net /climatewire/stories/1059994518.

Environment Northeast (ENE). "RGGI Emission Trends and the Second Allowance Auction," December 2008. http://www.lawandenvironment.com/uploads/file /ENE_2nd_RGGI_Emissions_Report_v2.pdf.

Erlandson, Dawn. "The BTU Tax Experience: What Happened and Why It Happened." *Pace Environmental Law Review* 12, no. 1 (Fall 1994): 173–184. http:// digitalcommons.pace.edu /cgi/viewcontent.cgi?article=1528&context=pelr.

EUP News Staff. "McMillin Proposes Withdrawal from Regional Cap and Trade Agreement." *EUP News*, May 6, 2010. http://eupnews.com/mcmillin-proposes-withdrawal -from-regional-cap-and-trade-agreement-editors-note-do-it.

Ezekiel, Ronald, and Ivan Gold. "Greenhouse Gas Cap and Trade Legislative Developments in the United States and in the Western Climate Initiative." *Climate Perspectives* (2009). http://www.fasken.com/files/Publication/fd4d089d -770a-486c-b183-b4bf303e5a8d/Presentation/PublicationAttachment/e1c8a815 -6124-41c6-9173-c0a93bbb6ee1/WCI%20Bulletin%20-%20May%202009.English .pdf.

Faggert, Pamela F., Dominion Energy. Letter to Jonathan Schrag, Executive Director of the Regional Greenhouse Gas Initiative Inc., November 30, 2010. https://www .rggi.org/docs/Dominion_Energy_NE_Nov_2010.pdf.

Fang, William L., Edison Electric Institute. Letter to Jonathan Schrag, Executive Director of the Regional Greenhouse Gas Initiative Inc., November 30, 2010. https:// www.rggi.org/docs/Edison_Electric_Institute_Nov_2010.pdf.

Fares, Robert. "Texas Sets New All-Time Wind Energy Record." *Scientific American*, January 14, 2016. http://blogs. scientificamerican.com/plugged-in/texas-sets-new-all -time-wind-energy-record/.

Farid, Mai, et al. *After Paris: Fiscal, Macroeconomic, and Financial Implications of Climate Change.* Washington, DC: International Monetary Fund, 2016. https://www .imf.org/external/pubs/ft/sdn/2016/sdn1601.pdf.

Feng, Kuishuang, Steven J. Davis, Laixiang Sun, and Klaus Hubacek. "Drivers of the US CO_2 Emissions 1997–2013." *Nature Communications* 6 (2015): 1–8. doi:10.1038/ncomms8714.

Fialka, John. "Methane Leaks Declining Even as Natural Gas Production Grows." *E&E News*, October 6, 2016.

Fischer, Carolyn, and Richard C. Newell. "Environmental and Technology Policies for Climate Mitigation." *Journal of Environmental Economics and Management* 55 (2008): 142–162. doi:10.1016/j.jeem.2007.11.001.

Fisk, Jonathan M. *The Fracking Debate: The Intergovernmental Politics of the Oil and Gas Renaissance.* Boca Raton, FL: CRC Press, 2017.

Fitz-Morris, James. "Justin Trudeau, Premiers Seek to Unify Canada's Message on Climate Change." *CBC News*, November 23, 2015. http://www.cbc.ca/m/touch/politics/story/1.3330284.

Foreman, Jr., Christopher H. "Book Review: Questions of Fairness." *Issues in Science and Technology* 32, no. 2 (Winter 2016): 87–88. http://issues.org/32-2/book-review-questions-of-fairness/.

Forster, Diana, and Daniel A. Smith. "Environmental Policies on the Ballot." In *Changing Climate Politics*, edited by Yael Wolinsky-Nahmias, 171–196. Washington, DC: Sage/CQ, 2015.

Fowlie, Jonathan, and Fiona Anderson. "B.C. Introduces Carbon Tax." *Vancouver Sun*, February 22, 2008.

Fremeth, Adam, and Alfred A. Marcus. "The Role of Governance Systems and Rules in Wind Energy Development: Evidence from Minnesota and Texas." *Business and Politics* 18, no. 3 (2016): 337–365.

Galbraith, Kate. "Climate Change Concerns Push Chile to Forefront of Carbon Tax Movement." *New York Times*, October 29, 2014. http://www.nytimes.com/2014/10/30/business/international/climate-change-concerns-push-chile-to-forefront-of-carbon-tax-movement.html.

Galbraith, Kate, and Asher Price. *The Great Texas Wind Rush: How George Bush, Ann Richards, and a Bunch of Tinkerers Helped the Oil and Gas State Win the Race to Wind Power.* Austin: University of Texas Press, 2013.

Gale, William G., Samuel Brown, and Fernando Saltiel. "Carbon Taxes as Part of the Fiscal Solution." In *Implementing a U.S. Carbon Tax: Challenges and Debates*, edited by Ian Perry, Adele Morris, and Robertson C. Williams III, 1–17. London: Routledge, 2015.

Gallucci, Maria. "GOP Bill to Remove New Hampshire from Carbon Trading Pact Moves Forward." *InsideClimate News*, February 21, 2011. https://insideclimatenews.org/news/20110221/gop-bill-remove-new-hampshire-carbon-trading-pact-moves-forward.

Garman, David, and Samuel Thernstrom. "Breaking the Silos." *The Environmental Forum* 31, no. 3 (2014): 34–38. https://www.eli. org/the-environmental-forum /breaking-silos.

Gass, Henry. "Proposed LNG Exports Spark Controversy in British Columbia." *E&E News*, October 7, 2013. http://www.eenews.net/stories/1059988405.

Gayer, Ted. Remarks at Brookings Institution Conference on Energy and Climate Change 2010: Back to the Future, Washington, DC, May 18, 2010.

Gholami, Zahra. "Case Study on the Effectiveness of Carbon Pricing Estimating the Impact of Carbon Tax on Natural Gas Demand in British Columbia." Master's thesis, University of British Columbia, 2014. https://open.library.ubc.ca/cIRcle/collections /ubctheses/24/items/1.0166938.

Global Gas Flaring Reduction Partnership. *Guidance on Upstream Flaring and Venting: Policy and Regulation.* Washington, DC: World Bank, 2009.

Godal, Odd, and Bjart Holtsmark. "Greenhouse Gas Taxation and the Distribution of Costs and Benefits: The Case of Norway." *Energy Policy* 29, no. 8 (2001): 653–662. doi:10.1016/S0301-4215(00)00158-0.

Gore, Al. *Earth in the Balance: Ecology and the Human Spirit.* Boston: Houghton Mifflin, 1992.

Government of Alberta. *Albertans and Climate Change: A Strategy for Managing Environmental and Economic Risks.* Edmonton: Government of Alberta, 2002. https://extranet .gov.ab.ca/env/infocentre/info/library/5895.pdf.

Government of British Columbia. *Energy for Our Future: A Plan for BC.* Vancouver, BC: Government of British Columbia, 2002. http://www.bcenergyblog.com/uploads /file/2002%20B.C.%20Energy%20Plan.pdf.

Graetz, Michael J. *The End of Energy: The Unmaking of America's Environment, Security, and Independence.* Cambridge, MA: MIT Press, 2011.

Grant, Don, Kelly Bergstrand, and Katrina Running. "Effectiveness of US State Policies in Reducing CO_2 Emissions from Power Plants." *Nature Climate Change* 4 (2014): 977–982. doi:10.1038/nclimate2385.

Gray, Jane. "Manitoba: Towards a Climate Friendly Economy." Presentation at Conference of the Reducers, Toronto, May 3–4, 2003.

Green, Jessica. "Don't Link Carbon Markets." *Nature* 543 (March 2017): 485–486.

Greenstone, Michael, Cass Sunstein, and Sam Ori. *The Next Generation of Transportation Policy.* Washington, DC: Brookings Institution, 2017. https://www.brookings .edu/wp-content/uploads/2017/03/es_20170327_next_generation_transportation _policy_pp.pdf.

Gullberg, Anne Therese, and Tora Skodvin. "Cost Effectiveness and Target Group Influence in Norwegian Climate Policy." *Scandinavian Political Studies* 34, no. 2 (2011): 125. doi:10.1111/j.1467-9477.2011.00266.x.

Hacker, Jacob B. "Privatizing Risk without Privatizing the Welfare State: The Hidden Politics of Social Policy Retrenchment in the United States." *American Political Science Review* 98, no. 2 (2004): 243–260.

Hager, Mike. "B.C. Liberals Set to Announce Five-Year Carbon Tax Freeze." *Vancouver Sun*, April 3, 2013. http://www.vancouversun.com/technology/Liberals+announce +five+year+carbon+freeze/8186348/story.html.

Haigh, Nigel. *EU Environmental Policy: Its Journey to Centre Stage.* Abingdon: Routledge, 2015.

Hampton, Rachel L., and Barry G. Rabe. "Leaving Money on the Table: Pennsylvania Exceptionalism in Resisting Energy Severance Taxes." *Commonwealth* 17, no. 1 (2017): 5–32. http://dx.doi.org/10.15367/com.v19i1.131.

Harris, Melissa, Marisa Beck, and Ivetta Gerasimchuk. *The End of Coal: Ontario's Coal Phase-Out.* Winnipeg: International Institute for Sustainable Development, 2015. www.iisd.org/sites/default/files/publications/end-of-coal-ontario-coal-phase-out.pdf.

Harrison, Kathryn. "International Carbon Trade and Domestic Climate Politics." *Global Environmental Politics* 15, no. 3 (2015): 27–47.

Harrison, Kathryn. "The Political Economy of British Columbia's Carbon Tax." OECD Environment Working Paper No. 63, 2013. doi:10.1787/ 5k3z04gkkhkg-en.

Harrison, Kathryn. "A Tale of Two Taxes: The Fate of Environmental Tax Reform in Canada." *Review of Policy Research* 29, no. 3 (2012): 383–407. doi:10.1111/j.1541 -1338.2012.0056 5.x.

Haselswerdt, Jake. "The Lifespan of a Tax Break: Comparing the Durability of Tax Expenditures and Spending Programs." *American Politics Research* 42, no. 5 (2014): 731–759. doi:10.1177/ 1532673X13516992.

Hellerstein, Walter. "Political Perspectives on State and Local Taxation of Natural Resources." *Georgia Law Review* 19, no. 1 (Fall 1984): 31–69. http://digitalcommons .law.uga.edu/cgi/viewcontent.cgi?article=1127&context=fac_artchop.

Hibbard, Paul J., Andrea M. Okie, Susan F. Tierney, and Pavel G. Darling. *The Economic Impacts of the Regional Greenhouse Gas Initiative on Nine Northeast and Mid-Atlantic States.* Boston: Analysis Group, 2015. http://www.analysisgroup.com/uploadedfiles /content/insights/publishing/analysis_group_rggi_report_july_2015.pdf.

Hoffmann, Matthew J. *Climate Governance at the Crossroads: Experimenting with a Global Response after Kyoto.* New York: Oxford University Press, 2011.

Holden, Emily, Hannah Hess, and Evan Lehmann. "The Carbon Tax That Clinton Decided Not to Use: $42." *E&E News*, October 21, 2016.

Horne, Matt. *Measuring the Appetite for Climate Action in B.C.* Drayton Valley, AB: Pembina Institute, June 30, 2011. http://www.pembina.org/reports/measuring-the -appepite-for-climate-action-in-bc.pdf.

Horne, Matt, Ekaterina Petropavlova, and P. J. Parrington. *British Columbia's Carbon Tax: Exploring Perspectives and Seeking Common Ground.* Drayton Valley, AB: Pembina Institute, 2012. https://www.pembina.org/reports/carbon-tax-interviews.pdf.

Houle, David. *Carbon Pricing in Canada: Bounded Provincial Autonomy and Climate Policy Innovation.* Toronto: University of Toronto Press, forthcoming.

Houle, David. *Obstacles to Carbon Pricing in Canadian Provinces.* Ottawa: Sustainable Prosperity, 2014. http://www.sustainableprosperity.ca/sites/default/files/SSRN-id2598985 _0.pdf.

Houle, David, Erick Lachapelle, and Mark Purdon. "Comparative Politics of Sub-Federal Cap-and-Trade: Implementing the Western Climate Initiative." *Global Environmental Politics* 15, no. 3 (2015): 49–73. doi:10.1162/GLEP_a_00311.

Howard, Peter and Derek Sylvan. *Expert Consensus on the Economics of Climate Change.* New York: Institute for Public Integrity, 2015. http://policyintegrity.org /files/publications/ExpertConsensus Report.pdf.

Howlett, Michael, and Keith Brownsey. "British Columbia: Politics in a Post-Staples Political Economy." In *The Provincial State in Canada: Politics in the Provinces and Territories*, edited by Keith Brownsey and Michael Howlett, 309–334. Vancouver: University of British Columbia Press, 2001.

Hsia-Kiung, Katherine, and Erica Morehouse. *Carbon Market California: A Comprehensive Analysis of the Golden State's Cap-and-Trade Program.* Washington, DC: Environmental Defense Fund, 2015. http://www.edf.org/sites/default/files/content /carbon-market-california-year_two.pdf.

Hsu, Shi-Ling. *The Case for a Carbon Tax.* Washington, DC: Island Press, 2011.

Huber, Bruce R. "How Did RGGI Do It? Political Economy and Emissions Auctions." *Ecological Law Quarterly* 40, no. 59 (2013): 100–101. http://scholarship.law.nd.edu /law_faculty_scholarship/473/.

Hulac, Benjamin. "In Oil-Rich Alberta, Premier Addresses Climate, Economic Concerns." *E&E News*, September 26, 2015. http://www.eenews.net/climatewire/stories /1060025301.

Hulac, Benjamin. "Yale to Impose Carbon Tax on Itself, Led by the Man Who Helped Invent It." *E&E News*, April 22, 2015. http://www.eenews.net/stories/1060017204.

Hume, Mark. "B.C. Carbon Tax an Effective Model for National Climate Change Approach: Report." *The Globe and Mail*, December 10, 2014. http://www.theglobean dmail.com/news/british-columbia/bcs-carbon-tax-effective-in-reducing-greenhouse -gas-emissions-report/article22017313/.

Hunter, Justine. "How Beijing Set Off a Premier's Smoke Alarm." *The Globe and Mail*, February 23, 2008. http://www.theglobeandmail.com/news/national/how-beijing-set -off-a-premiers-smoke-alarm/article1051845/.

Hylton v. United States, 3 US 171 (1796).

Ingerson, Ann, The Wilderness Society. Letter to Regional Greenhouse Gas Initiative Participating States, November 30, 2010. https://www.rggi.org/docs/The_Wilderness _Society_Nov_2010.pdf.

Inside EPA. "Numbers: EIA Finds CO_2 from Electricity at Lowest Level since 1993." May 13, 2016. http://www.insideepaclimate.com/climate-beat/numbers-eia-finds-co 2-electricity-lowest-level-1993.

Inside EPA. "Numbers: EIA Says CO_2 from Energy on a Decline." May 9, 2016. http:// www.insideepaclimate.com/climate-beat/numbers-eia-says-co2-energy-decline.

Inside EPA. "States: Activists in Washington May Force Legislature to Consider Carbon Tax." January 6, 2016. http://www.insideepaclimate.com/climate-beat/states -activists-washington-may-force-legislature-consider-carbon-tax.

Institute for European Environmental Policy. *Evaluation of Environmental Tax Reforms: International Experiences*. Brussels: IEEP, 2013. http://www.ieep.eu/assets/1283/ETR _study_by_IEEP_for_the_Swiss_Government_-_Final_report_-_21_June_2013.pdf.

International Agency for Research on Cancer. *Effectiveness of Tax and Price Policies in Tobacco Control*, vol. 13. Lyon, France: World Health Organization, 2009.

International Energy Agency. "World Energy Outlook 2011 Factsheet: How Will Global Energy Markets Evolve to 2035?" 2011. http://www.worldenergyoutlook.org /media/weowebsite/factsheets/factsheets.pdf.

International Institute for Sustainable Development (IISD) Task Force on Emissions Trading and the Manitoba Economy. *Realizing Opportunities: Emissions Trading in Manitoba*. Winnipeg: IISD, 2004. http://www.iisd.org/sites/default/files/publications /climate_realizing_opportunities.pdf.

Iverleigh, Austen. *The Great Reformer: Francis and the Making of a Radical Pope*. New York: Henry Holt, 2014.

Izzo, Phil. "Is It Time for a New Tax on Energy?" *Wall Street Journal*, February 9, 2007, http://www.wsj.com/articles/SB117086898234001121.

Jang, Brent, and Justine Hunter. "Petronas Plays Hardball with B.C. over Pacific NorthWest LNG." *The Globe and Mail*, September 25, 2014. http://www.the

globeandmail.com/report-on-business/industry-news/energy-and-resources/petronas
-plays-hardball-with-bc-over-pacific-northwest-lng/article20798686/.

Jaremko, Gordon. "British Columbia's Shale Gas Resources Rising." *Natural Gas Intelligence's Shale Daily*, January 16, 2014. http://www.naturalgasintel.com/articles/9708
7-british-columbias-shale-gas-resources-rising.

Kahn, Debra. "Calif. Carbon Offsets Face Slowdown in Market Development." *E&E News*, October 14, 2015. http://www.eenews.net/climatewire/stories/1060026292.

Kahn, Debra. "Calif. Proves That Its Cap-and-Trade Works, with One Hiccup." *E&E News*, November 5, 2015. http://www.eenews.net/climatewire/stories/1060027520.

Kahn, Debra. "Calif's Cap-and-Trade Overseer Steers Ambitious Program through Rough Seas." *E&E News*, November 14, 2012. http://www.eenews.net/stories/1059972480.

Kahn, Debra. "Former White House Adviser Rails against Governor's Budget Proposal." *E&E News*, May 20, 2013. http://www.eenews.net/climatewire/stories/1059981446.

Kahn, Debra. "Leaders Mull Direction, Significance of State's Energy and Climate Policies." *E&E News*, April 22, 2013. http://www.eenews.net/climatewire/stories
/1059979844.

Kahneman, Daniel. *Thinking, Fast and Slow*. New York: Farrar, Straus and Giroux, 2011.

Kang, Mary, et al. "Identification and Characterization of High Methane-Emitting Abandoned Oil and Gas Wells." *Proceedings of the National Academy of Sciences* 113, no. 48 (2016): 13636–13641. doi:10.1073/pnas.16059.3113.

Karapin, Roger. *Political Opportunities for Climate Policy: California, New York, and the Federal Government*. New York: Cambridge University Press, 2016.

Karch, Andrew. *Democratic Laboratories: Policy Diffusion among the American States*. Ann Arbor: University of Michigan Press, 2007.

Kasa, Sjur. "Policy Networks as Barriers to Green Tax Reform: The Case of CO_2-Taxes in Norway." *Environmental Politics* 9, no. 4 (2007): 104–122. doi:10.1080/096440100084
14553.

Katzmann, Robert A. *Judging Statutes*. Oxford: Oxford University Press, 2014.

Keohane, Robert O., and David G. Victor. "The Regime Complex for Climate Change." *Perspectives on Politics* 9, no. 1 (March 2011): 17. doi:10.1017/S1537592710004068.

Kettl, Donald F. *Escaping Jurassic Government: How to Recover America's Lost Commitment to Competence*. Washington, DC: Brookings Institution Press, 2016.

Kettl, Donald F. "Private-Market Misfires and Misconceptions." *Governing*, February 2016. http://www. governing.com/columns/potomac-chronicle/gov-free-market-failures
-government.html.

King, Pamela. "How Do You Recruit 75K New Workers? British Columbia Sets Up a Plan." *E&E News*, July 26, 2013, http://www.eenews.net/energywire/stories/1059985115.

Kingdon, John W. *Agendas, Alternatives, and Public Policies*. 2nd ed. New York: Longman, 2003.

Klein, Ralph. "Letter to the Prime Minister, September 2003." Commentary on the web page of the Government of Alberta, 2003 (no longer available online). Accessed March 22, 2012.

Kleven, Henrik Jacobsen. "How Can Scandinavians Tax So Much?" *Journal of Economic Perspectives* 28, no. 4 (Fall 2014): 77–98.

Klinsky, Sonja. "Bottom-Up Policy Lessons Emerging from the Western Climate Initiative's Development Challenges." *Climate Policy* 13, no. 2 (2013): 143–169. doi:10.1080/14693062.2012.712457.

Knudsen, Jørgen K. "Integration of Environmental Concerns in a Trans-Atlantic Perspective: The Case of Renewable Electricity." *Review of Policy Research* 27, no. 2 (March 2010): 140. doi:10.1111/ j.1541-1338.2009.00434.x.

Koch, Nicolas, Sabine Fuss, Godfrey Grosjean, and Ottmar Edenhofer. "Causes of the EU ETS Price Drop: Recession, CDM, Renewable Policies, or a Bit of Everything? New Evidence." *Energy Policy* 73 (2014): 676–685. doi:10.1016/j.enpol.2014.06.024.

Konisky, David M., and Neal D. Woods. "Environmental Policy, Federalism, and the Obama Presidency." *Publius* 46, no. 3 (Summer 2016): 366–391.

Koss, Geof. "U.S. Is 'Laggard' in Fossil Fuel Subsidy Reform—Study." *E&E News Greenwire*, November 12, 2015. https://www.eenews.net/greenwire/2015/11/12/stories/1060027888.

Kossoy, Alexandre, et al. *State and Trends of Carbon Pricing 2014*. Washington, DC: World Bank, 2014. http://documents.worldbank.org/curated/en/505431468148506727/pdf/882840AR0REPLA00EPI2102680Box385232.pdf.

Krause, Rachel M. "Symbolic or Substantive Policy? Measuring the Extent of Local Commitment to Climate Protection." *Environment and Planning C: Government and Policy* 29 (2011): 46–62.

Kruger, Joseph, and William A. Pizer. "The EU Emissions Trading Directive: Opportunities and Potential Pitfalls." Resources for the Future Discussion Paper 04-24, Washington, DC, 2014.

Krupp, Fred. "Fixing the Methane Leaks That Deflate Natural-Gas Gains." *Wall Street Journal*. February 3, 2016.

Kuster, Ann McLane, and Niki Tsongas. Letter to Gina McCarthy. January 31, 2014, https://kuster.house.gov/sites/kuster.house.gov/files/wysiwyg_uploaded/Kuster TsongasEPALetter.pdf.

Kyoto and Beyond: A Plan of Action to Meet and Exceed Manitoba's Kyoto Targets. Winnipeg: Manitoba Conservation Climate Change Branch, 2002.

Lachapelle, Erick. "Assessing Public Support for Cap-and-Trade Systems." *Policy Options* 36, no. 8 (December 2015). http://policyoptions.irpp.org/magazines /december-2015/lappui-du-public-aumarche-du-carbone/.

Lachapelle, Erick. "Climate Change Opinions in the United States and Canada." Presentation at Woodrow Wilson Center, Washington, DC, October 13, 2015.

Lachapelle, Erick. "Energy Security and Climate Policy in the OECD: The Political Economy of Carbon-Energy Taxation." PhD diss., University of Toronto, 2011. https://tspace.library.utoronto.ca/bitstream/1807/29780/1/Lachapelle_Erick_201106 _PhD_thesis.pdf.

Lachapelle, Erick. "Following the Doctor's Orders? Theory and Practice of Carbon Pricing in the OECD." Presentation at the Annual Convention of the International Studies Association, New Orleans, February 17–20, 2010.

Lachapelle, Erick, Christopher Borick, and Barry G. Rabe. "Public Attitudes toward Climate Science and Climate Policy in Federal Systems: Canada and the United States Compared." *Review of Policy Research* 29, no. 3 (2012): 334–357. Doi:10.1111 /j.1541-1338.2012.004563.x.

Lachapelle, Erick, Christopher Borick, and Barry G. Rabe. "Public Opinion on Climate Change and Support for Various Policy Instruments in Canada and the U.S.: Findings from a Comparative 2013 Poll." *Issues in Energy and Environmental Policy*, no. 11 (2014): 1–21. http://closup.umich.edu /files/ieep-nsee-2013-fall -canada-us.pdf.

Lachapelle, Erick, and Jean-Philippe Gauvin. "Against the Odds: The Politics of Carbon Pricing in Australia." Presentation at the 2012 Annual Meeting of the Canadian Political Science Association, Edmonton, AB, June 13–15, 2012.

Laing, Tim, Misato Sato, Michael Grubb, and Claudia Comberti. *Assessing the Effectiveness of the EU Emissions Trading System.* Leeds and London: Center for Climate Change Economics and Policy, 2013. http://www.lse.ac.uk/GranthamInstitute/wp -content/uploads/2014/02/WP106-effectiveness-eu-emissions-trading-system.pdf.

Landrum, Asheley R., et al. "Processing the Papal Encyclical through Perceptual Filters." *Cognition* (September 2017): 1–12.

Layzer, Judith. "Cold Front: How the Recession Stalled Obama's Clean-Energy Agenda." In *Reaching for a New Deal: Ambitious Governance, Economic Meltdown, and Polarized Politics in Obama's First Two Years,* edited by Theda Skocpol and Lawrence R. Jacobs, 321–385. New York: Russell Sage Foundation, 2011.

Layzer, Judith. *Open for Business: Conservatives' Opposition to Environmental Regulation.* Cambridge, MA: MIT Press, 2012.

Lazaroff, Cat. "New Hampshire Passes Nation's First CO_2 Cap." *ENS Newswire.com*, April 22, 2002. http://www.ens-newswire.com/ens/apr2002/2002-04-22-06.html.

Lee, Marc. "BC Is Giving Away Its Natural Gas." *Policy Note*, November 21, 2012. http://www.policynote.ca/bc-is-giving-away-its-natural-gas/.

Legislative Analyst's Office. "Administration's Cap-and-Trade Report Provides New Information, Raises Issues for Consideration," April 20, 2016.

Lerner, Michael. "Opportunity, Risk, and Public Acceptability: The Question of Shale Gas Exploitation in Quebec." *Issues in Energy and Environmental Policy*, no. 16 (2014): 1–29. http://closup.umich.edu/files/ieep-2014-shale-exploitation-quebec .pdf.

Lester, Richard K., and David M. Hart. *Unlocking Energy Innovation: How America Can Build a Low-Cost, Low-Carbon Energy System*. Cambridge, MA: MIT Press, 2012.

Levi, Michael. *The Power Surge: Energy, Opportunity, and the Battle for America's Future*. New York: Oxford University Press, 2013.

Levin, Kelly, et al. "Overcoming the Tragedy of Super-Wicked Problems: Constraining Our Future Selves to Ameliorate Global Climate Change." *Policy Sciences* 45, no. 2 (2012): 123–152. doi:10.1007/s11077-012-9151-0.

Li, Nan, et al. "Cross-Pressuring Conservative Catholics? Effects of Pope Francis' Encyclical on the U.S. Public Opinion on Climate Change." *Climatic Change* 139, no. 3–4 (2016): 367–380.

Lindstrom, Perry. "U.S. Energy-Related Carbon Dioxide Emissions in 2015 Are 12% below Their 2005 Levels." *Today in Energy*, May 9, 2016. https://www.eia.gov /todayinenergy/detail.cfm?id=26152.

Link, Arthur A. "Political Constraint and North Dakota's Coal Severance Tax." *National Tax Association* 31, no. 3 (September 1978): 263–268.

Litz, Franz T., and Jennifer Macedonia. *Choosing a Policy Pathway for State 111(d) Plans to Meet State Objectives*. Washington, DC: Bipartisan Policy Center and Great Plains Institute, 2015. http://bipartisanpolicy.org/wp-content/uploads/2015/04/BPC-111d -Report.pdf.

Logan, Lee. "EPA Strengthens Final ESPS and Sees Coal Generation Taking a Bigger Hit." *Inside EPA*, August 2, 2015. http://insideepa.com/daily-news/epa-strengthens-fi nal-esps-and-sees-coal-generation-taking-bigger-hit.

Logan, Lee. "Time Horizon Crucial as Parties Respond to Novel Minnesota CO_2 Cost Plan." *Inside EPA/Climate*, May 3, 2016. http:// insideepaclimate.com/daily-news /time-horizon-crucial-parties-respond-novel-minnesota-co2-cost-plan.

Lowry, William. "Disentangling Energy Policy from Environmental Policy." *Social Science Quarterly* 89, no. 5 (2008): 1195–1211. doi:10.1111/j.1540-6237.2008.00565.x.

Macdonald, Douglas. "Allocating Greenhouse Gas Emission Reductions Amongst Sectors and Jurisdictions in Federated Systems: The European Union, Germany and Canada." In *Multilevel Environmental Governance: Managing Water and Climate Change in Europe and North America,* edited by Inger Weibust and James Meadowcroft, 190. Cheltenham, U.K.: Edward Elgar, 2014.

Mack, James. Policy briefing at British Columbia Climate Action Secretariat, February 13, 2013.

Malewitz, Jim. "$7 Billion CREZ Project Nears Finish, Aiding Wind Power." *Texas Tribune*, October 14, 2013. https://www.texastribune.org/2013/10/14/7-billion-crez -project-nears-finish-aiding-wind-po/.

Malone, Ruth E., ed. "The Tobacco Endgame." Special issue, *Tobacco Control* 22, no. 1 (2013).

Mankiw, Gregory. "Smart Taxes: An Open Invitation to Join the Pigou Club." Paper presented at the Annual Meeting of the Eastern Economic Association, March 8, 2008.

Marchese, Anthony J., et al. "Methane Emissions from United States Natural Gas Gathering and Processing." *Environmental Science and Technology* 49, no. 17 (2015): 10718–10727. doi:10. 1021/acs.est.5b02275.

Marshall, Christa. "Alberta Cancels Major 'Clean' Coal Project amid Low Gas Prices." *E&E News*, February 26, 2013. http://www.eenews.net/climatewire/stories /1059976887.

Marshall, Christa. "Alberta's Premier Says Focus on Greenhouse Gas Regulations Is Premature." *E&E News*, April 13, 2013. http://www.eenews.net/climatewire/stories / 1059979187.

Marshall, Christa. "Regional Carbon Cap Gets Second Look as 'Template' for National Plan." *New York Times*, July 14, 2010. http://www.nytimes.com/cwire/2010 /07/14/14climatewire-regional-carbon-cap-gets-second-look-as-temp-89444 .html?pagewanted=all.

Mason, Gary. "Notley's Fiscal Straightjacket Gets a Bit Tighter." *The Globe and Mail*, August 28, 2015. http://www.theglobeandmail.com/opinion/notleys-fiscal-straitjack et-gets-a-bit-tighter/article26135186/.

Massachusetts v. US Environmental Protection Agency, 549 US 497 (2007).

Matisoff, Daniel. "Making Cap-and-Trade Work: Lessons from the European Union Experience." *Environment* (January–February 2010).

Matthews, Merrill. "Mineral Rights Can Make You Rich." *Wall Street Journal*, July 9, 2017.

Mattoo, Aaditya, and Arvind Subramanian. *Greenprint: A New Approach to Cooperation on Climate Change*. Washington, DC: Brookings Institution Press, 2013.

McCarthy, Gina. Remarks at the Regional Greenhouse Gas Initiative Stakeholder Group Meeting, Hartford, CT, May 2, 2006.

McGrath, Matt. "Pressure Grows for Price on Carbon Ahead of UN Signing." *BBC News*, April 21, 2016. http://www.bbc.com/news/science-environment-36098318.

McLaughlin, David. "Red Flags for Green Targets: The New and Same Climate for Canadian Climate Policy." Keynote address at Climate Choices Canada Conference, Waterloo, ON, February 18–20, 2016.

Meadowcroft, James. Remarks at Canada Climate Choices Conference, Wilfrid Laurier University, Waterloo, ON, February 18–20, 2016.

Meckling, Jonas. *Carbon Coalitions: Business, Climate Politics, and the Rise of Emissions Trading*. Cambridge, MA: MIT Press, 2011.

Megerian, Chris. "Mary Nichols Has 'Rock Star' Influence as Top Air Quality Regulator." *Los Angeles Times*, December 27, 2014. http://www.latimes.com/local/politics/la-me-pol-adv-mary-nichols-20141228-story.html.

Meier, Kenneth J., and Michael J. Licari. "The Effect of Cigarette Taxes on Cigarette Consumption, 1955 through 1994." *American Journal of Public Health* 87, no. 7 (1997): 1126–1130. doi:10.2105/AJPH.87.7.1126.

Meissner, Dirk. "Three Years On, Only B.C. Has a Carbon Tax." *The Globe and Mail*, June 30, 2011. http://www.theglobeandmail.com/news/british-columbia/three-years-on-only-bc-has-a-carbon-tax/article585153/.

Metcalf, Gilbert. *The Impact of Removing Tax Preferences for U.S. Oil and Gas Production*. New York: Council on Foreign Relations, 2016.

Metcalf, Gilbert E. "A Conceptual Framework for Measuring the Effectiveness of Green Fiscal Reforms." Presentation at the Green Growth Knowledge Platform Conference, Verona, Italy, January 2015. http://www.greengrowthknowledge.org/sites/default/files/Metcalf_A_Conceptual_Framework_for_Measuring_the_Effectiveness_of_Green_Fiscal.pdf.

Metcalf, Gilbert E., and David E. Weisbach. "The Design of a Carbon Tax." *Harvard Environmental Law Review* 3 (2009): 499–556.

Mettler, Suzanne. "The Policyscape and the Challenges of Contemporary Politics to Policy Maintenance." *Perspectives on Politics* 14, no. 2 (2016): 369–390. doi:10.1017/S1537592716000074.

Metz, Kerri, and Nina Tannenbaum. "The Status of New Zealand's Emissions Trading Scheme." Working Paper No. 1, Center for Local, State, and Urban Policy at the

Gerald R. Ford School of Public Policy, University of Michigan, 2015. http://closup.umich.edu/files/closup-swp-1-metz-tannenbaum-new-zealand-emissions-trading-scheme.pdf.

Midwestern Energy Security and Climate Stewardship Summit, Midwestern Governors' Association. *Midwestern Greenhouse Gas Accord*. Milwaukee, WI, November 15, 2007. In author's possession.

Mildenberger, Matto. "Fiddling while the World Burns: The Double Representation of Carbon Polluters in Comparative Climate Policymaking." PhD diss., Yale University, 2015.

Miller, John W. "Europe Emissions Markets to Reopen Gradually." *Wall Street Journal*, February 2, 2011. http://www.wsj.com/articles/SB10001424052748704124504576118261149778674.

Mills, Sarah B., Barry G. Rabe, and Christopher Borick. "Acceptance of Global Warming Rising for Americans of All Religious Beliefs." *Issues in Energy and Environmental Policy*, no. 26 (2015): 1–10. http://closup.umich.edu/files/ieep-nsee-2015-fall-religion.pdf.

Mills, Sarah B., Barry G. Rabe, and Christopher Borick. "Cap-and-Trade Support Linked to Revenue Use." *Issues in Energy and Environmental Policy*, no. 23 (2015): 12. http://closup.umich.edu/files/ieep-nsee-2015-cap-and-trade.pdf.

Ministry of Environment and Climate Change, Government of Ontario. "Ontario Releases Climate Change Strategy Discussion Paper." News release, February 12, 2015.

Mintrom, Michael, and Phillipa Norman. "Policy Entrepreneurs and Policy Change." *Policy Studies Journal* 37, no. 4 (2009): 649–667. doi:10.1111/j.1541-0072.2009.00329.x.

Mirski, Pawel, and Len Coad. *Managing Expectations: Assessing the Potential of BC's Liquid Natural Gas Industry*. Calgary, AB: Canada West Foundation, 2013. http://cwf.ca/research/publications/managing-expectations-assessing-the-potential-of-bcs-liquid-natural-gas-industry/.

Mohl, Raymond A. "Ike and the Interstates: Creeping toward Comprehensive Planning." *Journal of Planning History* 2, no. 3 (2003): 244. doi:10.1177/1538513203256244.

Morrow, Adrian, Jane Taber, and Sean Silcoff. "Ontario Plans Cap-and-Trade on Greenhouse Gas Emissions." *The Globe and Mail*, April 2, 2015. http://www.theglobeandmail.com/news/politics/ontario-plans-cap-and-trade-on-greenhouse-gas-emissions/article23786538/.

Mulkern, Anne C. "Mark Ruffalo, Other Actors Push to Stop Calif. Oil Drilling." *E&E News*, March 7, 2016. http://www.eenews.net/energywire/stories/1060033529.

Mulkern, Anne C. "New Battle Strategies Emerge in Fight over Oil Severance Tax." *Energy Wire*, April 24, 2014.

Mulkern, Anne C. "Regulators Get to the Tough Part of Cap and Trade—How to Spend the Money Effectively." *E&E News*, April 26, 2013. http://www.eenews.net /climatewire/ stories/1059980194.

Mulkern, Anne C., and Debra Kahn. "Calif. Chamber Sues to Stop Cap and Trade, Calling It an Illegal 'Tax.'" *E&E News*, November 14, 2012. http://www.eenews.net /stories/1059972479.

Murphy, Robert P., Patrick J. Michaels, and Paul C. Knappenberger. "The Case against a U.S. Carbon Tax." CATO Institute Policy Analysis Number 801, October 17, 2016.

Murray, Brian C., and Peter T. Maniloff. "Why Have Greenhouse Emissions in RGGI States Declined? An Econometric Attribution to Economic, Energy Market, and Policy Factors." *Energy Economics* 51 (2015): 581. doi:10.1016/j.eneco.2015.07.013.

Murray, Brian C., and Nicholas Rivers. "British Columbia's Revenue-Neutral Carbon Tax: A Review of the Latest 'Grand Experiment' in Environmental Policy." Working Paper NI WP 15-04, Duke Nicholas Institute of Environmental Policy Solutions, Sustainable Prosperity, and the University of Ottawa Institute of the Environment, 2015. https://nicholasinstitute.duke.edu/sites/default/files/publications/ni_wp_15 -04_full.pdf.

National Energy Board. *Canada's Energy Future: Energy Supply and Demand Projections to 2035*. Ottawa, ON: National Energy Board, 2011. https://www.neb-one.gc.ca/nrg /ntgrtd/ftr/archive/2011/nrgsppldmndprjctn2035-eng.pdf.

National Energy Board of Canada. "Marketable Natural Gas Production in Canada," 2016. https://www.neb-one.gc.ca/nrg/sttstc/ntrlgs/stt/mrktblntrlgsprdctn 2016.xls.

Nelson, Hal T., David von Hippel, Tom Peterson, and Roman Garagulagian. "The Great Recession or Progressive Energy Policies? Explaining the Decline in US Green-house Gas Emissions Forecasts." *Journal of Environmental Planning and Management* 59, no. 3 (2016): 480–500. doi:10.1080/09640568.2015.1017042.

Nemec, Richard. "California Governor Reiterates Fracking Support." *Natural Gas Intelligence's Shale Daily*, December 3, 2015. http://www.naturalgasintel.com/arti cles/104548-california-governor-reiterates-fracking-support.

Nemec, Richard. "North Dakota Not Going Easy on Flaring Any Longer, Governor Says." *Natural Gas Intelligence's Shale Daily*, May 27, 2014. http://www.naturalgasintel.com /articles/98495-north-dakota-not-going-easy-on-flaring-any-longer-governor-says.

Nivola, Pietro S. *The Long and Winding Road: Automotive Fuel Economy and Ameri-can Politics*. Washington, DC: Brookings Institution, February 2009. https://www .brookings.edu/wp-content/uploads/2016/06/0225_cafe_nivola.pdf.

Noel de Tilly, Robert. "The Cap-and-Trade Program of the Western Climate Initiative." Presentation at the ITU Symposium on ICTs, the Environment, and Climate Change, Montreal, May 29, 2012.

Nordhaus, William. *A Question of Balance: Weighing the Options on Global Warming Policies*. New Haven, CT: Yale University Press, 2008.

Nordhaus, William D. *The Climate Casino: Risk, Uncertainty, and Economics for a Warming World*. New Haven, CT: Yale University Press, 2013.

Nordhaus, William D. "Expert Opinion on Climatic Change." *American Scientist* 82, no. 1 (1994): 45–51.

Nordhaus, William D. "The Pope and the Market." *The New York Review of Books* 62, no. 15 (October 8, 2015). http://www.nybooks.com/articles/2015/10/08/pope -and-market/.

Nordhaus, William, interview by Richard Harris. "All Things Considered," *National Public Radio*. February 11, 2014.

Novak, Viveca. "Pawlenty's Political Climate Change," *FactCheck.org*, January 20, 2011. http://www.factcheck.org/2011/01/pawlentys-political-climate-change/.

Nuttall, Tom. "The Environmental Union: On Climate Change, if Little Else, Europe Still Aspires to Global Leadership." *The Economist*, November 1, 2014. http://www .economist.com/news/europe/21629387-climate-change-if-little-else-europe-still-asp ires-global-leadership-environmental.

Office of the Governor, State of Illinois. "Governor Blagojevich Signs Midwestern Regional Greenhouse Gas Reduction Accord." News release, November 15, 2007. http://www3.illinois.gov/PressReleases/ShowPressRelease.cfm?SubjectID=1&Rec Num=6424.

O'Meara, Kyle. "A Review of the European Union Emissions Trading System." Unpublished paper on reserve at the Center for Local, State, and Urban Policy at the Ford School of Public Policy, University of Michigan, May 2015.

Obama, Barack. "Remarks by the President in Announcing the Clean Power Plan." The White House, Washington, DC, August 3, 2015. https://www.whitehouse.gov/the -press-office/2015/08/03/remarks-president-announcing-clean-power-plan.

Oberlander, Jonathan. *The Political Life of Medicare*. Chicago: University of Chicago Press, 2003.

Obey, Doug. "Clean Energy Firms Seek to Strengthen Northeast Climate Program." *Inside EPA Clean Energy Report*, July 25, 2011. In author's possession.

Obey, Doug. "Coal Plant's Retirement despite Upgrades Illustrates Sector's Hurdles." *Inside EPA*, October 16, 2013.

Obey, Doug. "Draft RGGI Analysis Sees Little Power Price Impact from Stricter GHG Cap." *Inside EPA*, January 14, 2013.

Obey, Doug. "Joining Other State Efforts, New York Bill Adds Heft to Carbon Tax Push." *Inside EPA*, September 4, 2015.

Ochs, Alexander. *Overcoming the Lethargy: Climate Change, Energy Security, and the Case for a Third Industrial Revolution.* Washington, DC: American Institute for Contemporary German Studies, 2008.

Office of Inspector General. *Coal Management Program, U.S. Department of Interior.* June 2013. https://www.doioig.gov/sites/doioig.gov/files/CR-EV-BLM-0001-2012 Public.pdf.

Orszag, Peter. "Issues in Climate Change." Lecture at 2007 Congressional Budget Office Director's Conference on Climate Change. Washington, DC, November 16, 2007.

Ostrom, Elinor. *Governing the Commons: The Evolution of Institutions for Collective Action.* Cambridge: Cambridge University Press, 1990.

Ostrom, Elinor. *A Polycentric Approach for Coping with Climate Change.* Washington, DC: World Bank, 2009.

Pacheco, Julianna. "Trends: Public Opinion on Smoking and Anti-Smoking Policies." *Public Opinion Quarterly* 75, no. 3 (2011): 576–592. doi:10.1093/poq/nfr031.

Pal, Leslie A., and R. Kent Weaver, eds. *The Government Taketh Away: The Politics of Pain in the United States and Canada.* Washington, DC: Georgetown University Press, 2003.

Parry, Ian W. H., and Roberton C. Williams, III. *Is a Carbon Tax the Only Good Climate Policy? Options to Cut CO_2 Emissions.* Washington, DC: Resources for the Future, 2010. http://www.rff.org/files/sharepoint/WorkImages/Download/RFF -Resources-176_CarbonTax.pdf.

Partnership for Market Readiness and World Bank Group. *Carbon Tax Guide: A Handbook for Policy Makers.* Washington, DC: World Bank, 2017.

Pataki, George E., and Thomas J. Vilsack. *Confronting Climate Change: A Strategy for U.S. Foreign Policy.* New York: Council on Foreign Relations, 2008. http://i.cfr.org /content/publications/attachments/Climate_ChangeTF.pdf.

Patashnik, Eric M. "The Clean Air Act's Use of Market Mechanisms." In *The Future of U.S. Energy Policy: Lessons from the Clean Air Act,* edited by Ann E. Carlson and Dallas Burtraw. New York: Cambridge University Press, 2018.

Patashnik, Eric M. *Putting Trust in the U.S. Budget: Federal Trust Funds and the Politics of Commitment.* New York: Cambridge University Press, 2000.

Patashnik, Eric M. *Reforms at Risk: What Happens after Major Policy Changes Are Enacted.* Princeton, NJ: Princeton University Press, 2008.

Patashnik, Eric M. "Why Some Reforms Last and Others Collapse: The Tax Reform Act of 1986 Versus Airline Deregulation." In *Living Legislation: Durability, Change, and the Politics of American Lawmaking*, edited by Jeffery A. Jenkins and Eric M. Patashnik, 146–174. Chicago: University of Chicago Press, 2012.

Paulman, Ken. "Midwest Cap and Trade: Not Dead, Just Sleeping." *Midwest Energy News*, March 4, 2011. http://midwestenergynews.com/2011/03/04/midwest-cap-and-trade-is-it-dead-or-no.

Pembina Institute, The. *The B.C. Carbon Tax: Backgrounder*. Drayton Valley, AB: Pembina Institute, 2014. https://www.pembina.org/reports/lessons-bc-carbon-tax-112014.pdf.

Pendergrass, John. "Arizona Pulls Out of Climate Initiative." *The Environmental Forum* 27, no. 2 (Spring 2010): 12.

Perry, Ian, Adele Morris, and Robertson C. Williams III, eds. *Implementing a U.S. Carbon Tax: Challenges and Debates*. London: Routledge, 2015.

Peterson, Paul E., Barry G. Rabe, and Kenneth K. Wong. *When Federalism Works*. Washington, DC: Brookings Institution Press, 1986.

Petroski, Henry. *The Road Taken: The History and Future of America's Infrastructure*. New York: Bloomsbury, 2016.

Pigou, Arthur Cecil. *The Economics of Welfare*. London: Macmillan, 1920.

Pless, Jacquelyn. "Oil and Gas Severance Taxes: States Work to Alleviate Fiscal Pressures amid the Natural Gas Boom." *National Conference of State Legislatures*, updated February 2012. http://www.ncsl.org/research/energy/oil-and-gas-severance-taxes.aspx.

Pooley, Eric. *The Climate War: True Believers, Power Brokers, and the Fight to Save the Earth*. New York: Hyperion, 2010.

Pope Francis. *Laudato Si': On Care for Our Common Home*. Huntington, IN: Our Sunday Visitor, 2016.

Posner, Paul L. "The Politics of Vertical Diffusion: The States and Climate Change." In *Greenhouse Governance: Addressing Climate Change in America*, edited by Barry G. Rabe, 73–100. Washington, DC: Brookings Institution Press, 2010.

Powers, Carol. "State Taxation of Energy Resources: Affirmation of *Commonwealth Edison Company v. Montana*." *Boston College Environmental Law Review* 10, no. 2 (1982): 503–564. http://lawdigitalcommons.bc.edu/ealr/vol10/iss2/5.

Prasad, Monica. "Taxation as a Regulatory Tool: Lessons from Environmental Taxes in Europe." In *Government and Markets: Toward a New Theory on Regulation*, edited by Edward J. Balleisen and David A. Moss, 363–390. New York: Cambridge University Press, 2009.

Prentice, Jim, with Jean-Sebastian Rioux. *Triple Crown: Winning Canada's Energy Future*. Toronto: HarperCollins, 2017.

Preston, Samuel, Andrew Stokes, Neil H. Mehta, and Bochen Cao. "Projecting the Effect of Changes in Smoking and Obesity on Future Life Expectancy in the United States." *Demography* 15, no. 1 (2014): 27–49. doi:10.1007/S13524-013-0246-9.

Province of British Columbia. "Motor Fuel Tax and Carbon Tax for Businesses That Manufacture, Import, or Sell Fuel." Accessed April 7, 2016. http://www2.gov.bc.ca /gov/content/taxes/sales-taxes/motor-fuel-carbon-tax/business.

Rabe, Barry G. "The Aversion to Direct Cost Imposition: Selecting Climate Policy Tools in the United States." *Governance* 23, no.4 (2010): 583–608. doi:10.1111 /j.1468-0491.2010.01499.x.

Rabe, Barry G. "Beyond Kyoto: Climate Change in Multilevel Governance Systems." *Governance* 20, no. 3 (2007): 423–444. doi:10.1111/j.1468-0491.2007.00365.x.

Rabe, Barry G. "Building on Sub-Federal Climate Strategies: The Challenges of Regionalism." In *Climate Change Policy in North America: Designing Integration in a Regional System*, edited by Neil Craik, Isabel Studer, and Debora VanNijnatten, 89–90. Toronto: University of Toronto Press, 2013.

Rabe, Barry G. "Can Congress Govern the Climate?" In *Greenhouse Governance: Addressing Climate Change in America*, edited by Barry G. Rabe, 260–285. Washington, DC: Brookings Institution Press, 2010.

Rabe, Barry G. "Contested Federalism." In *Environmental Governance Reconsidered: Challenges, Choices, and Opportunities*, edited by Robert F. Durant, Daniel J. Fiorino, and Rosemary O'Leary, 133–164. Cambridge, MA: MIT Press, 2016.

Rabe, Barry G. "The Durability of Carbon Cap-and-Trade Policy." *Governance* 29, no. 1 (2016): 103–199. doi:10.1111/gove.12151.

Rabe, Barry G. "Governing the Climate from Sacramento." In *Unlocking the Power of Networks: Keys to High-Performance Government*, edited by Stephen Goldsmith and Donald F. Kettl, 34–61. Washington, DC: Brookings Institution Press, 2009.

Rabe, Barry G. "Leveraged Federalism and the Clean Air Act: The Case of Vehicle Emissions Control." In *The Future of U.S. Energy Policy: The Case of the Clean Air Act*, edited by Ann E. Carlson and Dallas Burtraw. Cambridge: Cambridge University Press, forthcoming.

Rabe, Barry G. "Racing to the Top, the Bottom, or the Middle of the Pack? The Evolving State Government Role in Environmental Protection." Chap. 2 in *Environmental Policy: New Directions for the Twenty-First Century*, 10th ed., edited by Norman J. Vig and Michael E. Kraft. Washington, DC: Sage, 2018.

Rabe, Barry G. "Regionalism and Global Climate Change Policy: Revisiting Multistate Collaboration as an Intergovernmental Management Tool." In *Intergovernmental Management for the 21st Century*, edited by Timothy J. Conlan and Paul L. Posner, 198. Washington, DC: Brookings Institution Press, 2008.

Rabe, Barry G. "Shale Play Politics: The Intergovernmental Odyssey of American Shale Governance." *Environmental Science & Technology* 48, no. 15 (2014): 8371–8375. doi:10.1021/ es4051132.

Rabe, Barry G. *Statehouse and Greenhouse: The Emerging Politics of American Climate Change Policy*. Washington, DC: Brookings Institution Press, 2004.

Rabe, Barry G. "States on Steroids: The Intergovernmental Odyssey of American Climate Policy." *Review of Policy Research* 25, no. 2 (2008): 105–128. doi:10.1111/j.1541-1338.2007.00314.x.

Rabe, Barry G., and Christopher P. Borick. "Carbon Taxation and Policy Labeling: Experience from American States and Canadian Provinces." *Review of Policy Research* 29, no. 3 (2012): 358–382. doi:10.1111/j.1541-1338.2012.00564.x.

Rabe, Barry G., and Christopher P. Borick. "The Decline of Public Support for State Climate Change Policies: 2008–2013." *Issues in Energy and Environmental Policy*, no. 7 (2014): 1–10. http://closup.umich.edu/files/ieep-nsee-2013-fall-state-policy-options.pdf.

Rabe, Barry G., and Rachel Hampton. "Taxing Fracking: The Politics of State Severance Taxes in the Shale Era." *Review of Policy Research* 32, no. 4 (2015): 389–412. doi:10.1111/ropr.12127.

Rabe, Barry G., and Rachel L. Hampton. "Trusting in the Future: The Re-emergence of State Trust Funds in the Shale Era." *Energy Research & Social Science* (2016): 1–11. doi:10.1016/j.erss.2016.06. 011.

Rajagopal, Deepak. *Firm Behavior and Emissions under Emission Intensity Regulation: Evidence from Alberta's Specified Gas Emitters Regulation*. Los Angeles: UCLA Institute of the Environmental and Sustainability, 2014. http://escholarship.org/uc/item/5t40p9ht.

Ramseur, Jonathan L. *The Regional Greenhouse Gas Initiative: Lessons Learned and Issues for Congress*. Washington, DC: Congressional Research Service, 2016. https://www.fas.org/sgp/crs/misc/R41836.pdf.

Ramseur, Jonathan L. "U.S. Carbon Dioxide Emission Trends and the Role of the Clean Power Plan." Congressional Research Service, April 11, 2016.

Ramseur, Jonathan L. *U.S. Greenhouse Gas Emissions: Recent Trends and Factors*. Washington, DC: Congressional Research Service, 2014. https://www.fas.org/sgp/crs/misc/R43795.pdf.

Ramseur, Jonathan L., and James E. McCarthy. *EPA's Clean Power Plan: Highlights of the Final Rule*. Washington, DC: Congressional Research Service, 2016. https://www .fas.org/sgp/crs/misc/R44145.pdf.

Rauschenberger, Ryan. *2014 State and Local Taxes: An Overview and Comparative Guide*. Bismarck, ND: Office of State Tax Commissioner, 2014. https://issuu.com /ndtax/docs/.

Raymond, Leigh. "Reclaiming the Atmospheric Commons." Presentation at the Midwest Political Science Association Annual Conference, Chicago, March 31–April 1, 2011.

Raymond, Leigh. *Reclaiming the Atmospheric Commons: The Regional Greenhouse Gas Initiative and a New Model of Emissions Trading*. Cambridge, MA: MIT Press, 2016.

Raymond, Lee. "States Leading the Way to a New Paradigm for Climate Policy." Presentation at the Midwest Political Science Association Annual Conference, Chicago, April 3–6, 2014.

Redford, Alison. "Keystone Is Responsible Oil Sands Development." *USA Today*, February 25, 2013. http://www.usatoday.com/story/opinion/2013/02/25/keystone-pipe line-alberta-column/1943029/.

Reeves, Dawn. "Higher RGGI Auction Prices Boost Confidence in Plan to Tighten GHG Cap." *Inside EPA*, April 11, 2013. http://insideepa.com/daily-news/higher-rggi -auction-prices-boost-confidence-plan-tighten-ghg-cap.

Reeves, Dawn. "New Efforts to Address GHG 'Leakage' Highlights Wide Gap among States." *Inside EPA*, May 8, 2013.

Reeves, Dawn. "Whitehouse Slated to Offer Carbon Tax Bill That Could Replace EPA Rules." *Inside EPA*, October 28, 2014. http://insideepa.com/daily-news/white house-slated-offer-carbon-tax-bill-could-replace-epa-rules.

Reeves, Richard V. *Ulysses Goes to Washington: Political Myopia and Policy Commitment Devices*. Washington, DC: Brookings Institution, 2015. https://www.brookings.edu /wp-content/uploads/2016/06/Ulysses.pdf.

Regional Greenhouse Gas Initiative. "CO_2 Allowances Sold at \$4.00 at 23rd RGGI Auction." News release, March 7, 2014. http://www.rggi.org/docs/Auctions/23 /PR030714_Auction23.pdf.

Regional Greenhouse Gas Initiative. "Investment of RGGI Proceeds through 2013." April 2015. https://www.rggi.org/docs/ProceedsReport/Investment-RGGI-Proceeds -Through-2013.pdf.

Regional Greenhouse Gas Initiative. "Memorandum of Understanding." December 20, 2005, http://www.rggi.org/docs/mou_12_20_05.pdf.

Regional Greenhouse Gas Initiative. "Potential Emissions Leakage and the Regional Greenhouse Gas Initiative: Evaluating Market Dynamics, Monitoring Options, and

Possible Mitigation Mechanisms." March 2007. https://www.rggi.org/docs/il_report _final_3_14_07.pdf.

Regional Greenhouse Gas Initiative. "Report on Emission Reduction Efforts of the States Participating in the Regional Greenhouse Gas Initiative and Recommendations for Guidelines under Section 111(d) of the Clean Air Act." December 2013. https://www.rggi.org/docs/RGGI_States_111d_Letter_Comments.pdf.

Regional Greenhouse Gas Initiative. "RGGI Report: Investments General Savings, Reduce Pollution." News release, September 26, 2016.

Regional Greenhouse Gas Initiative. "RGGI States' Comments on Proposed Carbon Pollution Emission Guidelines for Existing Stationary Sources: Electric Utility Generating Units, 79 FR 34830." November 2014. http://www.rggi.org/docs/PressReleases /PR110714_CPP_Joint_Comments.pdf.

Regional Greenhouse Gas Initiative. "RGGI States Comments Support EPA Proposed Clean Power Plan." News release, November 7, 2014. http://www.dec.ny.gov/docs /administration_pdf/rggicommentpr1114.pdf.

Regional Greenhouse Gas Initiative. "RGGI States Recommend That EPA Support Flexible Market-Based Carbon Pollution Programs." News release, December 2, 2013. https://www.rggi.org/docs/PressReleases/PR120213_EPAComments_Final .pdf.

Regional Greenhouse Gas Initiative. "RGGI: The Investment of RGGI Proceeds through 2014." September 2016. https://www.rggi.org/docs/ProceedsReport/RGGI _Proceeds_Report_2014.pdf.

Resnick, Philip. *The Politics of Resentment: British Columbia Regionalism and Canadian Unity*. Vancouver: University of British Columbia Press, 2000.

RGGI State Agency Heads. Letter to Regina McCarthy, December 2, 2013. Regional Greenhouse Gas Initiative, https://www.rggi.org/docs/RGGI_States_111d_Letter _Comments.pdf.

Rivers, Nicholas, and Brandon Schaufele. "Salience of Carbon Taxes in the Gasoline Market." *Social Sciences Research Network Paper* (2014): 1–33. doi:10.2139/ ssrn.2131468.

Roberts, David. "What We Can Learn from British Columbia's Carbon Tax?" *Grist*, February 23, 2015. http://grist.org/climate-energy/what-we-can-learn-from-british -columbias-carbon-tax/.

Roberts, Paul. *The End of Oil: On the Edge of a Perilous New World*. Boston: Houghton Mifflin, 2005.

Robinson, Elwyn B. *History of North Dakota*, rev. ed. Lincoln: University of Nebraska Press, 1996.

Rolski, Tomek. "Vatican Hung(a)ry for Carbon Offset." *ABC News*, September 18, 2007. http://abcnews.go.com/International/story?id=3620636.

Rosenthal, Elisabeth. "Carbon Taxes Make Ireland Even Greener." *New York Times*, December 27, 2012. http://www.nytimes.com/2012/12/28/science/earth/in-ireland -carbon-taxes-pay-off.html.

Ross, Michael L. *The Oil Curse: How Petroleum Wealth Shapes the Development of Nations*. Princeton, NJ: Princeton University Press, 2012.

Rowlands, Ian H. "The Development of Renewable Electricity Policy in the Province of Ontario: The Influence of Ideas and Timing." *Review of Policy Research* 24, no. 3 (2007): 185–207. doi:10.1111/j.1541-1338.2007.00277.x.

Saha, Devashree, and Mark Muro. *Permanent Trust Funds: Funding Economic Change with Fracking Revenues*. Washington, DC: Brookings Institution, 2016. https://www .brookings.edu/wp-content/uploads/2016/07/Permanent-Trust-Funds-Saha-Muro-418 -1.pdf.

Sandel, Michael J. *What Money Can't Buy: The Moral Limits of Markets*. New York: Farrar, Straus and Giroux, 2012.

Sejersted, Francis. *The Age of Social Democracy: Norway and Sweden in the Twentieth Century*. Princeton, NJ: Princeton University Press, 2011.

Sekar, Samantha, and Brent Sohngen. *The Effects of Renewable Portfolio Standards on Carbon Intensity in the United States*. Washington, DC: Resources for the Future, 2014. http://www.rff.org/files/sharepoint/WorkImages/Download/RFF-DP-14-10.pdf.

Sharp, Elaine B. "The Dynamics of Issue Expansion: Cases from Disability Rights and Fetal Research Controversy." *Journal of Politics* 56, no. 4 (1994): 919–939. doi:10.2307/2132067.

Shattuck, Peter. *The Regional Greenhouse Gas Initiative: Performance To-Date and the Path Ahead*. Boston: Acadia Center, 2014. http://acadiacenter.org/wp-content /uploads/2014/05/AcadiaCenter_RGGI_Report_140523_Final3.pdf.

Shattuck, Peter, and Jordan Stutt. *The Regional Greenhouse Gas Initiative: A Model Program for the Power Sector*. Boston: Acadia Center, 2015. http://acadiacenter.org /wp-content/uploads/2015/07/RGGI-Emissions-Trends-Report_Final.pdf.

Shaw, Rob. "Horgan's Platform in NDP Leadership Bid Includes Expanding Carbon Tax." *Times Colonist*, February 16, 2011. http://www.timescolonist.com/horgan-s-pla tform-in-ndp-leadership-bid-includes-expanding-carbon-tax-1.22726.

Sherman, Paul. "Vatican's Position on Carbon Offset Systems." Unpublished paper, University of Michigan, May 13, 2016.

Shipan, Charles R., and Craig Volden. "Bottom-Up Federalism: The Diffusion of Anti-smoking Policies from U.S. Cities to States." *American Journal of Political Science* 50, no. 4

(2006): 825–843. https://www.unc.edu/~fbaum/teaching/articles/AJPS-2006-smoking .pdf.

Sijm, Jos, Karsten Neuhoff, and Yihsu Chen. "CO_2 Cost Pass-through and Windfall Profits in the Power Sector." *Climate Policy* 6, no. 1 (2006): 49–72. doi:10.1080/1469 3062.2006.9685588.

Skocpol, Theda. *Boomerang: Health Care Reform and the Turn against Government.* New York: W. W. Norton, 1997.

Skocpol, Theda. "Naming the Problem: What It Will Take to Counter Extremism and Engage Americans in the Fight against Global Warming?" Paper for the Symposium on the Politics of America's Fight Against Global Warming, Harvard University, February 14, 2013. http://www.scholarsstrategynetwork.org/sites/default/files /skocpol_captrade_report_january_2013_0.pdf.

Smith, Adam. *An Inquiry into the Nature and Causes of the Wealth of Nations.* London: Metheun, 1904.

Smith, Jennifer. *Federalism.* Vancouver: University of British Columbia Press, 2004.

Smith, Nick. "More Restrictions on Flaring Introduced." *Bismarck Tribune*, February 6, 2015. http://bismarcktribune.com/bakken/more-restrictions-on-flaring-introduced /article_ 5c1377b0-d183-56d0-b72d-0bbf3428ed33.html.

Sovacool, Benjamin K., and Michael H. Dworkin. *Global Energy Justice: Problems, Principles, and Practices.* New York: Cambridge University Press, 2014.

Stavins, Robert N. "Are the Pope's Critiques of Markets on Point or Somewhat Misguided?" *The Environmental Forum* 33, no. 1 (2016), 15. http://www.eli.org/sites /default/files/docs/tef/tef33-1.pdf.

Stephenson, Eleanor, and Karena Shaw. "A Dilemma of Abundance: Governance Challenges of Reconciling Shale Gas Development and Climate Change Mitigation." *Sustainability* 5, no. 5 (2013): 2219. doi:10.3390/su5052210.

Stokes, Leah C. "Electoral Backlash Against Climate Policy." *American Journal of Political Science* 60, no. 4 (October 2016): 958–974.

Stokes, Leah C. "Power Politics: Energy Policy Change in the U.S. States." PhD diss., Massachusetts Institute of Technology, 2015.

Stokes, Leah C., and Christopher Warshaw. "Renewable Energy Policy Design and Framing Influence Public Support in the United States." *Nature Energy* 2, no. 17107 (June 2017), doi:10.1038/nenergy.2017.107.

Stone, Daniel. "How Green Was the 'Green Pope'?" *National Geographic News*, February 28, 2013. http://news.nationalgeographic.com/news/2013/02/130228-environm ental-pope-green-efficiency-vatican-city/.

Struck, Doug. "Buying Carbon Offsets May Ease Eco-Guilt but Not Global Warming." *Christian Science Monitor*, April 20, 2010. http://www.csmonitor.com/Environ ment/2010/0420/Buying-carbon-offsets-may-ease-eco-guilt-but-not-global-warming.

Stutt, Jordan, and Peter Shattuck. *Regional Greenhouse Gas Initiative Status Report.* Boston: Acadia Center, 2016. http://acadiacenter.org/document/measuring-rggi -success.

Sullivan, Colin. "Northeast 'Off to a Running Start' in Advance of Obama Emissions Plan." *E&E News*, June 3, 2014. http://www.eenews.net/energywire/stories /1060000600.

Sullivan, Martin A. *Gas Tax Politics, Part 1.* Falls Church, VA: The Tax Analysts, 2008. http://www.taxhistory.org/thp/readings.nsf/ArtWeb/5DDB79194769C2BF852574D 5003C28D5?OpenDocument.

Sumner, Jenny, Lori Bird, and Hillary Smith. *Carbon Taxes: A Review of Experience and Policy Design Considerations.* Golden, CO: National Renewable Energy Laboratory, 2009. http://www.nrel.gov/docs/fy10osti/47312.pdf.

Swartz, Kristi E. "'A Lot of Benefit' Seen on Regional Approach to EPA Climate Rule." *E&E News*, April 1, 2015. http://www.eenews.net/energywire/stories/1060016098.

Tang, Zhenghong, et al. "Moving from Agenda to Action: Evaluating Local Climate Change Action Plans." *Journal of Environmental Planning and Management* 53, no. 1 (January 2010): 41–62.

Taylor, Mac. *The 2016–2017 Budget: Resources and Environmental Protection.* Sacramento, CA: Legislative Analyst's Office, 2016. http://www.lao.ca.gov/reports/2016 /3354/resources-analysis-021616.pdf.

Texas Office of the Governor Economic Development Division. *The Texas Renewable Energy Industry.* Austin: Texas Office of the Governor, 2014. http://gov.texas.gov /files/ecodev/Renewable_Energy.pdf.

Thakar, Nidhi, and Michael Madowitz. *Federal Coal Leasing in the Powder River Basin: A Bad Deal for Taxpayers.* Washington, DC: Center for American Progress, 2014. https://cdn.americanprogress.org/wp-content/uploads/2014/07/ThakarPowderRiver -brief.pdf.

Thomson, George, et al. "Ending Appreciable Tobacco Use in a Nation: Using a Sinking Lid on Supply." *Tobacco Control* 19, no. 5 (2010): 431–435. doi:10.1136/tc.2010.036681.

Thomson, Vivian E. *Sophisticated Interdependence in Climate Policy: Federalism in the United States, Brazil, and Germany.* London: Anthem Press, 2014.

Three-Regions Offsets Working Group, Regional Greenhouse Gas Initiative, Midwestern Greenhouse Gas Reduction Accord, and Western Climate Initiative. "Ensuring Offset Quality: Design and Implementation Criteria for a High-Quality

Offset Program," May 2010. http://www.westernclimateinitiative.org/component /remository/general/Ensuring-Offset-Quality-Design-and-Implementation-Criteria -for-a-High-Quality-Offset-Program/.

Tierney, Susan. Lecture at University of Michigan, February 22, 2006.

Tomich, Jeffrey. "Minn. PUC Aligns Carbon Cost with Clean Power Plan." *E&E News,* July 1, 2016. http://www.eenews.net/stories/1060039705.

Tomich, Jeffrey. "Minn. Weighs Adopting Federal 'Social Cost of Carbon.'" *E&E News,* June 17, 2014. http://www.eenews.net/energywire/stories/1060001399.

Tompkins-Stange, Megan E. *Policy Patrons.* Cambridge, MA: Harvard University Press, 2017.

Toronto Star. "Carbonated Vote in B.C. Election." May 14, 2009. https://www.thestar .com/opinion/2009/05/14/carbonated_vote_in_bc_election.html.

Turner, A.J., et al. "A Large Increase in U.S. Methane Emissions over the Past Decade Inferred from Satellite Data and Surface Observations." *Geophysical Research Letters* 43, no. 5 (2016): 2218–2224. doi:10.1002/2016GL067987.

Urquhart, Ian. *Making It Work: Kyoto, Trade, and Politics.* Edmonton, AB: Parkland Institute, 2002. http://s3-us-west-2.amazonaws.com/parkland-research-pdfs/making itwork.pdf.

US Climate Action Partnership (USCAP). *Blueprint for Leadership: Consensus Recommendations for U.S. Climate Protection Legislation.* Washington, DC: USCAP, 2009. http://www.c2es.org/docUploads/USCAP-legislative-blueprint.pdf.

US Energy Information Administration. "Energy-Related Carbon Dioxide Emissions at the State Level, 2000–2014," January 2017. http://www.eia.gov/environment /emissions/state/analysis/pdf/stateanalysis.pdf.

US Energy Information Administration. "Natural Gas Withdrawals and Production Annual-Million Cubic Feet." April 2017. https://www.eia.gov/dnav/ng/NG_PRUD _SUM_A_EPG0_VGV_MMCF_A.htm.

US Government Accountability Office (GAO). *Coal Leasing: BLM Could Enhance Appraisal Process, More Explicitly Consider Coal Exports, and Provide More Public Information.* December 2013. https://www.gao.gov/assets/660/659801.pdf.

US Government Accountability Office (GAO). *Expert Opinion on the Economics of Policy Options to Address Climate Change.* Washington, DC: GAO, 2008. http://www .gao.gov/assets/280/275448.pdf.

US Government Accountability Office (GAO). *Lessons Learned from the European Union's Emissions Trading Scheme and the Kyoto Protocol's Clean Development Mechanism.* Washington, DC: GAO, November 2008. http://www.gao.gov/assets/290/283397.pdf.

US Government Interagency Working Group on Social Cost of Carbon. *Technical Support Document: Technical Update of the Social Cost of Carbon for Regulatory Impact Analysis under Executive Order 12866.* Washington, DC: US Government, 2013.

Van Asselt, Harro. "Emissions Trading: The Enthusiastic Adoption of an 'Alien' Instrument?" In *Climate Change Policy in the European Union: Confronting the Dilemmas of Mitigation and Adaptation,* edited by Andrew Jordan, Dave Huitema, Harro Van Asselt, Tim Rayner, and Frans Berkhout, 125–144. Cambridge: Cambridge University Press, 2010.

Van Brunt, Michael E., Covanta Energy. Letter to the Regional Greenhouse Gas Initiative Inc., November 30, 2010. https://www.rggi.org/docs/Covanta_Nov_2010 .pdf.

Van der Heijden, Jeroen. "Selecting Cases and Inferential Types in Comparative Public Policy Research." In *Comparative Policy Studies: Conceptual and Methodological Challenges,* edited by Isabelle Engeli and Christine Rothmayr Allison, 35–56. London: Palgrave, 2014.

Vanderklippe, Nathan. "Climate Takes Back Seat as Fledgling B.C. LNG Industry Courts China." *The Globe and Mail,* November 24, 2013. http://www.theglobeand mail.com/report-on-business/industry-news/energy-and-resources/climate-takes-bac k-seat-as-fledgling-bc-lng-industry-courts-china/article15579405/.

Van Meijgaard, Jeroen, and Jonathan E. Fielding. "Estimating Benefits of Past, Current, and Future Reductions in Smoking Rates Using a Comprehensive Model with Competing Causes of Death." *Preventing Chronic Disease* 9 (2012): 110295. doi:http://dx.doi.org/10.5888/pcd9.110295.

Vara, Vauhini, and Cassandra Sweet. "California Auctions Emission Permits." *Wall Street Journal,* November 14, 2012. http://www.wsj.com/articles/SB10001424127887 324595904578119254205657698.

Victor, David. *The Collapse of the Kyoto Protocol and the Struggle to Slow Global Warming.* Princeton, NJ: Princeton University Press, 2001.

Vock, Daniel C. "States, Not Just Feds, Struggle to Keep Gas Tax Revenue Flowing." *Governing,* May 18, 2015. http://www.governing.com/topics/transportation -infrastructure/gov-gas-tax-revenue-states-inflation.html.

Vogel, David. *California Greenin': How the Golden State Became an Environmental Leader.* Princeton, NJ: Princeton University Press, 2018.

Wall Street Journal. "Christie's Carbon Awakening." June 3, 2011. http://www.wsj .com/articles/SB10001424052702303657404576357620250781498.

Ward, Doug. "Candidates Take a Swing at 'Out-of-Touch' Axe-the-Tax Carbon Concept." *Vancouver Sun,* April 2, 2011.

Ward, Doug, and Rob Shaw. "Premier Says Policies Will Help B.C. Recover from Recession." *Vancouver Sun*, April 23, 2009. http://www.pressreader.com/canada/the-vancouver-sun/20090423/282707633002367.

Warner, Kenneth E. "Effects of the Antismoking Campaign: An Update." *American Journal of Public Health* 79, no. 2 (1989): 144–152. doi:10.2105/AJPH.79.2.144.

Warrick, Joby. "Calif. Methane Leak Is Called Historic." *Washington Post* February 26, 2016.

Warrick, Joby. "California Gas Leak Was the Worst Man-Made Greenhouse-Gas Disaster in U.S. History, Study Says." *Washington Post*, February 25, 2016. http://wapo.st/1Q51TVQ.

Weibust, Inger. *Green Leviathan: The Case for a Federal Role in Environmental Policy.* Abingdon: Routledge, 2009.

Wenar, Leif. *Blood Oil: Tyrants, Violence, and the Rules That Run the World.* New York: Oxford University Press, 2016.

Western Climate Initiative. "Quebec Adopts Cap-and-Trade Regulation." December 16, 2011. http://www.westernclimateinitiative.org/news-and-updates/139-quebec-adopts-cap-and-trade-regulation?format=pdf.

Wettestad, Jørgen, and Torbjørg Jevnaker. *Rescuing EU Emissions Trading: The Climate Policy Flagship.* London: Palgrave Macmillan, 2016.

Widerquist, Karl, and Michael W. Howard, eds. *Alaska's Permanent Fund Dividend: Examining Its Suitability as a Model.* New York: Palgrave, 2012.

Wilkins, Roger. *Possible Design for a National Greenhouse Gas Emissions Trading System.* Canberra: National Emissions Trading Taskforce, 2006.

Williams, Amy. "New Mexico's Land Grant and Severance Tax Permanent Funds: Renewable Wealth from Non-Renewable Resources." *Natural Resources Journal* 48 (Summer 2008): 719–743.

Williamson, Gabrielle. "Still a Chance for Recovery?" *The Environmental Forum* 30, no. 4 (2014): 20.

Wilson, Nick, et al. "Potential Advantages and Disadvantages of an Endgame Strategy: A 'Sinking Lid' on Tobacco Supply." *Tobacco Control* 22, no. 1 (2013): 118–121. doi:10.1136/tobaccocontrol-2012-050791.

Wingett Sanchez, Yvonne. "Gov. Jan Brewer Chides Reporter over Question." *The Arizona Republic*, December 6, 2012. http://archive.azcentral.com/news/politics/articles/20121206gov-jan-brewer-chides-reporter-over-question.html.

Witte, John F. *The Politics and Development of the Federal Income Tax.* Madison: University of Wisconsin Press, 1985.

Witte, John F. "The Tax Reform Act of 1986: A New Era in Tax Policy?" *American Political Quarterly* 19 (1991): 438–457.

Wright, Sean, and Carlos Villacis. *Risking Risk: Improving Methane Disclosure in the Oil and Gas Industry*. New York: Environmental Defense Fund, 2016. http://business.edf .org/files/2016/01/rising_risk_full_report.pdf.

Yerger, David. "The Shale Gas Revolution: Its Current and Potential Impacts on Ontario's Economic Relationship with the USA and Western Canada." Paper at MANECCS Annual Conference, Niagara Falls, ON, September 25–27, 2014.

Zavala-Araiza, Daniel, et al. "Reconciling Divergent Estimates of Oil and Gas Methane Emission." *Proceedings of the National Academy of Sciences of the United States of America* 112, no. 51 (2015): 15597–15602. doi:10.1073/pnas.1522126112.

Zetterberg, Lars. "Sweden." In *Allocation in the European Emissions Trading Scheme*, edited by A. Denny Ellerman, Barbara K. Buchner, and Carlo Carrera, chap. 6. New York: Cambridge University Press, 2007.

Zimmerman, Joseph F. *Interstate Competition: Compacts and Administrative Agreements*. 2nd ed. Albany: State University of New York Press, 2012.

Index

American and Comparative Environmental Policy
Sheldon Kamieniecki and Michael E. Kraft, series editors

Russell J. Dalton, Paula Garb, Nicholas P. Lovrich, John C. Pierce, and John M. Whiteley, *Critical Masses: Citizens, Nuclear Weapons Production, and Environmental Destruction in the United States and Russia*

Daniel A. Mazmanian and Michael E. Kraft, editors, *Toward Sustainable Communities: Transition and Transformations in Environmental Policy*

Elizabeth R. DeSombre, *Domestic Sources of International Environmental Policy: Industry, Environmentalists, and U.S. Power*

Kate O'Neill, *Waste Trading among Rich Nations: Building a New Theory of Environmental Regulation*

Joachim Blatter and Helen Ingram, editors, *Reflections on Water: New Approaches to Transboundary Conflicts and Cooperation*

Paul F. Steinberg, *Environmental Leadership in Developing Countries: Transnational Relations and Biodiversity Policy in Costa Rica and Bolivia*

Uday Desai, editor, *Environmental Politics and Policy in Industrialized Countries*

Kent Portney, *Taking Sustainable Cities Seriously: Economic Development, the Environment, and Quality of Life in American Cities*

Edward P. Weber, *Bringing Society Back In: Grassroots Ecosystem Management, Accountability, and Sustainable Communities*

Norman J. Vig and Michael G. Faure, editors, *Green Giants? Environmental Policies of the United States and the European Union*

Robert F. Durant, Daniel J. Fiorino, and Rosemary O'Leary, editors, *Environmental Governance Reconsidered: Challenges, Choices, and Opportunities*

Paul A. Sabatier, Will Focht, Mark Lubell, Zev Trachtenberg, Arnold Vedlitz, and Marty Matlock, editors, *Swimming Upstream: Collaborative Approaches to Watershed Management*

Sally K. Fairfax, Lauren Gwin, Mary Ann King, Leigh S. Raymond, and Laura Watt, *Buying Nature: The Limits of Land Acquisition as a Conservation Strategy, 1780–2004*

Steven Cohen, Sheldon Kamieniecki, and Matthew A. Cahn, *Strategic Planning in Environmental Regulation: A Policy Approach That Works*

Michael E. Kraft and Sheldon Kamieniecki, editors, *Business and Environmental Policy: Corporate Interests in the American Political System*

Joseph F. C. DiMento and Pamela Doughman, editors, *Climate Change: What It Means for Us, Our Children, and Our Grandchildren*

Christopher McGrory Klyza and David J. Sousa, *American Environmental Policy, 1990–2006: Beyond Gridlock*

John M. Whiteley, Helen Ingram, and Richard Perry, editors, *Water, Place, and Equity*

Judith A. Layzer, *Natural Experiments: Ecosystem-Based Management and the Environment*

Daniel A. Mazmanian and Michael E. Kraft, editors, *Toward Sustainable Communities: Transition and Transformations in Environmental Policy*, 2nd edition

Henrik Selin and Stacy D. VanDeveer, editors, *Changing Climates in North American Politics: Institutions, Policymaking, and Multilevel Governance*